For the last decade, Neil _____ leading investigative business writers. He is currently a ____ writer at *The Australian Financial Review*.

In 2004, Chenoweth won the Gold Walkley for helping uncover a money trail from a payout on the Offset Alpine Printing fire to secret Swiss bank accounts held by Rene Rivkin, Trevor Kennedy and Graham Richardson. He won a second Walkley in 2006 for his book *Packer's Lunch* and a third in 2008 for his reporting on the Opes Prime scandal.

MURDOCH'S PIRATES

Before the phone hacking, there was Rupert's pay-TV skullduggery

Neil Chenoweth

ALLEN&UNWIN
SYDNEY•MELBOURNE•AUCKLAND•LONDON

First published in Australia in 2012
This paperback edition published in 2013

Allen & Unwin
Sydney, Melbourne, Auckland, London

83 Alexander Street
Crows Nest NSW 2065
Australia
Phone: (61 2) 8425 0100
Fax: (61 2) 9906 2218
Email: info@allenandunwin.com
Web: www.allenandunwin.com

Cataloguing-in-Publication details are available from the
National Library of Australia
www.trove.nla.gov.au

ISBN 978 1 74331 741 9

Typeset in 12.5/15pt Granjon by Midland Typesetters, Australia
Printed and bound in Australia by Griffin Press

10 9 8 7 6 5 4 3 2 1

Contents

HORATIO: . . . He never gave commandment for their death. But since, so jump upon this bloody question, you from the Polack wars, and you from England, are here arrived, give order that these bodies high on a stage be placed to the view; and let me speak to the yet unknowing world how these things came about: so shall you hear of carnal, bloody and unnatural acts, of accidental judgements, casual slaughters, of deaths put on by cunning and forced cause, and, in this upshot, purposes mistook fallen on the inventors' heads: all this can I truly deliver.

Tom Stoppard, *Rosencrantz and Guildenstern Are Dead*

It's not terrorism, it's not suicide bombing, it's not weapons of mass destruction. It's just pay television.

Jan Saggiori, 2010

List of Organisations and Characters

Conditional access systems

Irdeto	Mindport, South Africa–Netherlands
Nagra	Kudelski Corporation, Switzerland
NDS	News Corporation, Israel–United Kingdom
SECA	Canal+ Technologies, France

News Corporation subsidiaries and associates

BSkyB	British Sky Broadcasting, 39 per cent owned by News, NDS encryption
Foxtel	Australian pay TV business, 25 per cent owned by News, NDS and Irdeto encrpytion
Star TV	Asian pay TV News subsidiary, NDS encryption
Stream SpA	Italian pay TV arm later merged with Telepiu to form Sky Italia, initially Irdeto encryption, later NDS

News Corporation pay TV rivals

Astro	Malaysian satellite broadcaster, SECA encryption
Austar	Australian regional satellite broadcaster, Irdeto encryption
Canal+	French pay TV group with operations throughout Europe, SECA encryption
DirecTV	US satellite broadcaster, NDS encryption
EchoStar	US satellite broadcaster (now Dish Network), Nagra encryption
OnDigital	UK terrestrial broadcaster, renamed ITV Digital, SECA encryption
Optus Vision	Australian cable business, Irdeto encryption
Premiere	German pay TV business, Irdeto encryption
Sogecable	Spanish pay TV business, SECA encryption
Telepiu	Canal+ subsidiary in Italy, SECA encryption

News Corporation

Chase Carey	Currently News Corp Chief Operating Officer, NDS director, was News executive overseeing NDS in late 1990s
David DeVoe	News Chief Financial Officer, NDS director
Genie Gavenchak	Senior News lawyer reporting to Siskind
James Murdoch	NDS director, had oversight of online gamer Kesmai

Lachlan Murdoch	NDS director, had oversight of HarperCollins
Arthur Siskind	News legal counsel, part of Office of Chairman, NDS director

NDS

Ray Adams	UK chief NDS Operational Security, former commander Metropolitan Police, head of SO11 intelligence unit
Michael Clinger	CEO of NDS 1990–92
Avigail Gutman	NDS Operational Security, Israel and Asia
Reuven Hasak	Former deputy head of Shin Beit, head of NDS Operational Security
Bruce Hundertmark	News International director who set up NDS in 1988
John Norris	US chief NDS Operational Security, former US Army intelligence
Abe Peled	CEO of NDS since July 1995
Yossi Tsuria	Chief Technology Officer for NDS Israel

NDS rivals

François Carayol	Head of Canal+ Technologies
Charlie Ergen	Head of EchoStar, Dish Network
J.J. Gee	Head of security for EchoStar from 2001, former FBI agent
Alan Guggenheim	Head of Nagra US and NagraStar
Gilles Kaehlin	Canal+ security chief, former French intelligence officer, Renseignements Généraux
Roger Kinsbourg	Head of Eurotica Rendez-Vous channel

Andre Kudelski	Head of Kudelski Corporation
Pierre Lescure	Head of Canal+
Larry Rissler	Head of security for DirecTV, former FBI agent

European hackers

Rolf Deubel (Madmax)	German hacker
Plamen Donev (Pluto)	Bulgarian hacker, ex-military
Boris Floricic (Tron)	German hacker
Lee Gibling	Founder of Thoic.com (The House of Ill Compute)
Oliver Kömmerling (Alex, Cyberdine)	German master hacker hired by NDS
Markus Kuhn (Castor)	Founder of TVcrypt List, now lecturer, University of Cambridge
Vesselin Nedeltchev (Vesco)	Bulgarian hacker, ex-military
Jan Saggiori (Hannibal)	Swiss hacker
Chris Tarnovsky (Mike George, biggun, Von)	US serviceman in Germany, NDS agent in US

Canadian pirates

Dave Dawson	
Ron Ereiser	
Allen Menard	Operator of DR7.com website, Edmonton, Canada
Marty Mullen	

Preface

This story starts a long way back.

Before the telephone hacking furore exploded in Britain. Before News Corporation had to pay out $650 million over some unpleasantness about business practices at its News America Marketing business. It was in March 2002, the same month that Surrey schoolgirl Milly Dowler went missing and her telephone messages were hacked by *News of the World*, that Rupert Murdoch's empire faced its first global scandal.

The story of that scandal made spectacular headlines around the world . . . if only briefly. Allegations about pay TV piracy tabled in a court case in California went to the heart of corporate governance and accountability at News Corporation's highest levels. The case raised extraordinary claims against a major media company, which is perhaps why they would be so readily dismissed. The wave of damages claims that rolled out in its wake made this case exponentially larger than any of the scandals that would follow. But just weeks after the first claim was made, it was settled. Nondisclosure orders went into place, evidence files were sealed. The case disappeared from public gaze.

The timing was horribly inconvenient for me. When news of the Californian court case broke I was wrestling with a book project that had taken on a life of its own, which was frankly a little unnerving. I was writing a business biography of Rupert Murdoch, but the narrative kept being hijacked by the bizarre goings on in one small part of his empire. I had discovered a technology arm of News Corporation called NDS Group, based in Israel and Britain, which was the most outlandish company I had ever come across. NDS's history had expanded from a brief cameo to fill several chapters. I was ready to sign off on the manuscript when the Californian court case exploded everything I had previously known about NDS. I did what I could to cover the new developments in a postscript to the book. But I knew I had merely scratched the surface of this strange substratum of the Murdoch empire.

Five years later the story came back to me, as I learned that rather than ending back in 2002, the saga had continued to bubble along below the radar. A number of hackers, lawyers and senior media executives told me different parts of a remarkable story— one that many of them had at first struggled to accept.

And here was the problem. The story was everything a journalist could hope for. Five of the biggest pay TV companies in the world had each filed legal actions claiming that a News Corporation subsidiary had conducted a dirty tricks campaign to sabotage their products. Said to be the work of a specialist unit within NDS called Operational Security, its operatives were former spies, senior policemen and US Army Intelligence and Secret Service officers, along with a network of pirates and hackers. Taken together, the claims painted a picture of a global policy of industrial espionage by a major wing of Rupert Murdoch's empire.

It was too sensational to be credible. The suggestion that one of the world's biggest media companies would be dabbling in something like this was beyond bizarre. How would you begin to prove something like this? The allegations had been raised in 2002 and dropped. NDS executive chairman Abe Peled could rightly say that none of the actions against NDS had succeeded. But had all five of the pay TV broadcasters that sued NDS been motivated by a malicious attempt to cripple a superior competitor, as Peled claimed? Who was in the right here? What was going on? Any investigation required extensive substantiation—and not from a single source.

The first step was to look at the lengthy legal pleadings against NDS by French media group Canal+ in 2002 and US statellite broadcaster DirecTV in 2000 and 2002. US broadcaster EchoStar's 2008 trial brought key players in the saga into the public gaze with thousands more pages of exhibits and filings as well as a 3000-page transcript in which some of the key NDS executives and engineers appeared in the witness box for the first time.

The documents and transcripts had to be analysed in direct inter-views with many of the people in the story. Surprisingly, my book *Rupert Murdoch* opened doors for me. In California, hacker Chris Tarnovsky told me an NDS staffer had asked for his autograph after reading it. My friend François Pilet at *Le Matin Dimanche* in Geneva spotted the book in an online photograph of German hacker Oliver Kömmerling's boat in Monaco—reading my earnest work had propelled one of Oliver's friends into deep slumber.

My interviews opened new leads and provided other document troves, including the hard drives of former Scotland Yard commander Ray Adams and also Lee Gibling, who ran NDS's pirate website The House of Ill Compute. That meant going back to primary sources, and much more travel, to Europe repeatedly, and to North America. It took more than four years before I was in a position to tell the story.

And then it needed to be reported, under robust conditions. In late 2011, I became a consultant to the BBC's *Panorama* program for an exposé on how NDS had helped to cripple a rival pay TV company to Murdoch's BSkyB in Britain. The program went to air in March 2012, followed seventeen hours later by the release of a major part of Ray Adams' emails by the *Australian Financial Review*.

The story attracted worldwide attention—the *Panorama* website alone had 500,000 hits in the first two days. It also triggered a spirited response from NDS, from News Corporation newspapers and from Rupert Murdoch himself, via his Twitter account. 'Enemies many different agendas, but worst old toffs and right wingers who still want last century's status quo with their monopolies,' he tweeted. And again, 'Seems every competitor and enemy piling on with lies and libels. So bad, easy to hit back hard, which preparing.' And finally in a reference to my employer Fairfax Media, the publisher of the *Financial Review*, 'Proof you can't trust anything in Australian Fairfax papers, unless you are just another crazy.'

The response Murdoch had foreshadowed soon took shape. In the next six weeks his Australian newspapers published 33 articles attacking my *Financial Review* stories. Meanwhile Abe Peled took out full-page advertisements to carry an open letter to *Panorama*, claiming that emails had been manipulated and mischaracterised, and that the program painted a picture of NDS which was 'incorrect, misleading and deeply damaging'. In a second open letter to the *Financial Review,* Peled claimed that my articles 'accusing NDS of promoting and facilitating piracy are based on gross mischaracterisations of the evidence'. The articles consistently misrepresented NDS's fight against piracy and its efforts to protect the investments of its clients and the content they carried, he said. Peled robustly denied any actions by NDS to promote piracy in Australia, and was particularly severe on Swiss hacker Jan Saggiori, vehemently denying any suggestion that NDS had fabricated a US court case against him.

In an article Peled wrote for a Murdoch newspaper he said legal claims against NDS had been 'tested to destruction'. He repeatedly claimed (inaccurately) that NDS had not been given details of allegations before publication. Certainly, talking to NDS is no straightforward procedure. Along the way I had repeatedly tried to seek information and responses from NDS executives or spokesmen. On a 2010 trip to Britain I was told to put any urgent queries to the Hong Kong office. In August 2011, I asked a detailed series of questions about an Italian criminal trial where prosecutors claimed that a senior anti-piracy official was actually fostering piracy 'in the express interests of NDS'. An NDS spokeswoman emailed me a two-sentence response that began, 'We are surprised by the tone of your questions . . .' In fact NDS was one of the victims of piracy, she maintained.

By March 2012 the NDS responses had increased to two paragraphs: 'NDS were vindicated by a jury and pronounced the sole prevailing party in the [2008] trial you refer to. I appreciate that you have been to extensive lengths to review the documentation from the trial, but the verdict stands that NDS were not found guilty of any accusations of piracy—nor has the company ever been found to have participated in unlawful activity, whether in relation to the EchoStar case or otherwise, and any insinuation it has done so is inaccurate.'

Two days later NDS sent me a copy of the letter it had sent to UK newspapers to inform them that the *Panorama* program, which would go to air ten days later, focused on issues that had been 'conclusively disproven', and to warn that 'NDS will take all necessary action to hold responsible anyone who chooses to repeat these baseless and damaging allegations'. Later, NDS sent me copies of Peled's open letters but made no further reply to my series of long queries.

News Corporation's head office had taken over directing NDS responses. In June 2012, a spokesman wrote me a charming letter thanking me for my questions, but noting that as he was 'transitioning into a new role' he was 'looping in' a senior colleague. 'Going forward, she will best be able to address your concerns or determine who at News Corporation can better assist you. Have a good weekend.'

When a week passed with no response, I wrote directly to the senior colleague, adding some more queries to the original list. The response was prompt: 'Neil, what is your question, exactly?' There was nothing further. Former Scotland Yard commander Ray Adams was less inhibited. He sent me an email with the subject line, 'IDIOT!' and roundly denied any suggestion he had framed Jan Saggiori.

But this account was never about the stilted releases that constitute corporate communications. The heart of this story was a group of young men who took up hacking for the fun, for adventure, for comradeship . . . and found themselves wandering into a dark part of the forest. It's about what happens when an international corporation hires its own spy force, and the way that that changes a corporate culture. And whatever you believe NDS did or didn't do, it's about how that culture collided with these young men's lives, and what it left them. There would be a few winners, but many losers. The question one must inevitably ask in talking to them today is—how did it come to this?

Prelude

Toronto, 24 October 1997

Toronto is a mean town when you're looking for a bolthole. The operation was blown, and the agent was running. No ordered retreat, this was panicked flight, strung out on adrenaline. Far beyond the threshold of fear and desperation, it is a state when the quarry knows his pursuers are close and all he wants in life is a place to go to ground.

Any halfway serious intelligence operation has an emergency plan. It's Spy Stuff 101—in the world of John le Carré, a little in-house tradecraft. This means fallback options, safe houses, collateral assets to call on and a whole range of contingencies, long before you get round to explaining the really neat pension scheme. But it was well past any of that. Alex couldn't go back to the hotel, the telephone call had made that clear. It was the first place the police would look for him after the Stop and Detain alert went out to the airports.

The order was to arrest him on probable cause. There were $25,000 in money orders and some expensive computer equipment in his hotel room, but Alex had to walk away. This too was a measure of his distressing situation, for he wasn't the sort of man to walk away from money easily. But now he was heading across the US border to find yet another anonymous hotel room in one of the towns that stretched along the shore of Lake Ontario, all the time feeling his panic building inside. He cursed himself for using a credit card that might be traced, and fled his new lodging to find himself back on the street. The Ontario shore in late October had the chill of late fall; a towering blond German, he was trying to look inconspicuous. He managed to find another hotel, cheap and nondescript, but he was jumpy as a cat, ready to take flight again if any police car cruised past. By morning he was in his fourth hotel. It seemed only a matter of time before his luck ran out.

In London, his controller was trying to work out where the operation had gone wrong. Ray Adams had made the travel arrangements himself. In a previous life he had been a commander at Scotland Yard, running its intelligence division, SO11. Now he ran a network of seventeen agents in Europe for Rupert Murdoch. He knew how to do this stuff. He had put Alex on a business-class ticket on Lufthansa flight LH 474 out of Frankfurt at 5 p.m., 21 October, to arrive in Toronto at 7.20 that same Tuesday evening. The return flight was a week later.

The complicating factor here was that Alex wasn't travelling alone. He was travelling with a business contact known as 'Jellyfish', who only knew Alex in his undercover role. Adams had booked a ticket for Alex's wife as well. In part, it was because Adams didn't see any real danger. It would be a little vacation for her, a treat. Agents sometimes needed something unexpected like that; their family needed to feel the love. It was just a chance to kick back, really. Think of it as a bit like *Date Night*, on Uncle Rupert's dime.

At an operational level (he didn't tell Alex this, let alone his wife) it was a nice domestic touch, to disarm the suspicions of the people Alex would be meeting. How could they think he was a spy when he brought his wife along with him? What kind of man puts his partner in danger? It was a gesture that had 'Trust Me' written all over it. And the meetings with the Canadian pirates had gone well. Then hours later they had ratted on him. Did it without a second thought.

'Sure I did it,' the pirate who fingered Alex tells me a decade later when I run him down. 'What's to think about? He was going to help the opposition. Of course I took him out.'

So now there were three of them—Alex, the missus and Jellyfish—on the run together, hotel hopping. Alex had wiped the hard drive of his laptop repeatedly during the night. It would take a very, very good forensic technician to retrieve anything from it, which was not completely out of the question. It had come to this: a hacker on the payroll of NDS, the arm of News Corporation that provided security for its pay TV operations, was on the run from the police in two countries. The best prospect, now that he had crossed the Canadian border, was for him to hide in the vastness of the United States, then fly out through an airport with low security. If he was caught, the repercussions for NDS, for News Corporation and for Rupert Murdoch, in the glare of publicity, were potentially disastrous. The first question would be how News Corporation came to be involved in what looked like criminal piracy directed against NDS's biggest client, DirecTV.

Senior employees of one of the biggest and most powerful media organisations in the world would spend days figuring out how to hide their man from the FBI and the Royal Canadian Mounted Police, long enough to slip him out of North America. Adams ordered Alex to disassemble his laptop into two parts, with each part posted by two different courier companies to two different addresses in Germany. But Alex still had to walk through those airport gates.

'Alex had absolutely nothing with him,' Adams later told his superior. 'I even disobeyed your advice that he could walk through with his laptop. He did not even have a credit card with him. There would have been absolutely no legitimate grounds for detaining him for a second. Had anyone done so, there was a lawyer ready to get him out of trouble.'

Alex arrived home safe, and that was the end of it. Everyone walked away clean . . . except that there were enduring problems. The questions were: What part of News Corporation should have been alerted as to what was going on? What part of a modern media business involves hiding people from the police and working out the best way to smuggle them out of the country, betraying the confidence of the customers whom they were paid to protect? And how was it that none of these players were ever called to account?

The most troubling thing was that this was just the beginning, the first desperate adventure. The drama that followed would trigger four separate major court actions against NDS, in which almost every major satellite broadcaster in the world sued the News Corp arm for billions of dollars in damages from industrial espionage. And yet, in the end, NDS proved staggeringly profitable for Rupert Murdoch's empire.

The stakes were very high and the casualties would not just be on the balance sheet. Twelve months later, Alex's friend in Germany would be dead, and Alex himself would be considering hiring bodyguards.

Adelaide, October 1997

A little disclosure here. To write about News Corporation means spending a lot of time talking to lawyers. When I was writing *Virtual Murdoch* in 2001, I received legal threats from half a dozen law firms around the world. It was educational in highlighting the different national legal styles.

Australian lawyers, in my experience, have not distinguished themselves with a tremendous sense of humour—at times they can be a little snippy. American lawyers don't bother with small threats. They have it down to a routine: they press the button and launch an intercontinental ballistic missile, perhaps in their spare moments between their coffee break and the next client meeting. When I wrote in 1999 to Squadron Ellenoff & Sheinfeld, seeking information from the New York firm that had represented News Corporation since the 1970s, their reply came from Ira Lee Sorkin. These days Ira is better known for his sterling work over the last two decades as Bernie Madoff's lawyer. Ira duly dropped a thermonuclear device on my head, but I could tell he had more important things to do—his response was so impersonal I think it lost something along the way. But when it comes to causing pain and discomfort—in short when you want a lawyer to club your target somewhere soft and vulnerable with a large pointy stick— it's hard to go past the British. It's that old-world charm.

Law firms, though, are just the sideshow. For decades the man who was News Corp's front line of defence, as chief legal counsel (now Rupert Murdoch's personal advisor), was Arthur Siskind. Arthur and I have never really hit it off. It's October 1997, the month that Alex has his little imbroglio in Toronto, when I speak to him face to face for the first time. I'm on the opposite side of the world from Toronto, in South Australia, and Arthur is about to throw me out of the News Corp annual meeting. Actually, it's the morning tea for shareholders after the meeting. And he's being pretty polite about it, which really shows he's a model of restraint.

The annual meeting just finished has been a showcase for what the global media empire is doing: from the newspapers and fledgling pay TV operation Foxtel in Australia to Star TV, the satellite broadcaster that covered all of India and Asia from its base in Hong Kong, and BSkyB in Britain, along with the *Sun*, *News of the World* and the *Times* and *Sunday Times*. Then there are the big bets that Murdoch has recently made on cable channels in the US: Fox Sports and a maverick operation called Fox News, which Roger Ailes launched just a year before at a cost of $1 billion. Will it really work? As well, there are the Fox television network and stations, together with Twentieth Century Fox. My head is still full of the finale, a breathtaking trailer played at the end of the meeting for a film that James Cameron has directed, which is due to launch in two months time, called *Titanic*.

Annual meetings are a nightmare for Rupert Murdoch's minders. Back in the United States he can handle any number of public outings without making a ripple, but in Australia he has a gift for unhappy headlines. He has just told shareholders what a bad idea the current push for tighter privacy laws was. Really, who needs them, when newspapers are so good at self-policing?

'Privacy laws are for the protection of the people who are already privileged and not for the ordinary man or woman,' he tells reporters at the press conference after the meeting. After the recent death of Prince Diana, he continues, 'I think you'll see a great deal more restraint by all the newspapers in Britain and I think you will see a stronger and better policed code of ethics.' That restraint will mean paying less money for paparazzi photographs.

'Princess Diana, whom we all had great respect for, generally worked with photographers to her satisfaction . . . I think newspapers paid far too much for them and there'll be a major cost saving if we can bring this thing through.'

Before now, no one has thought to turn Diana's death into a budget line item. Murdoch also offers a small rebuke to questions from the *Sydney Morning Herald* as 'part of the consistent and nagging denigration of News Corporation that goes on in your newspaper day after day, orchestrated by "Friends of Another Organisation" . . . but I won't go any further than that'. That was the support group for the Australian public broadcaster, Friends of the ABC, that Murdoch is being arch about. It's important when you're kicking your rivals to keep a light touch.

During the refreshments offered to attendees after this is when I bounce up to mend a few bridges with News Corp's chief legal officer. Ever since the 1980s Arthur Siskind has been Rupert

Murdoch's go-to guy, when he needs someone to stomp up and down with hobnailed boots. His critics call him pugnacious: 'He is, in a term, a tough son of a bitch—he knows what he wants and he won't back down until he gets it,' a US lawyer, Randy Mastro of Gibson, Dunn & Crutcher, told the *American Lawyer* in 1993. At some point Arthur and I have got off on the wrong foot. Maybe it's the American–Australian cultural thing. Maybe it's that awkwardness many lawyers have around journalists—the need to treat them like something particularly sticky and unpleasant that has attached itself to their shoe. But I think it was probably one particular article that did it. The year before this, I had described him as an unindicted co-conspirator in a New York fraud case. In hindsight I can see why he'd be a little unhappy.

In late 1996 I wrote to Siskind about an old case from when he was head of corporate at Squadron Ellenoff Plesent & Sheinfeld. In the 1980s his biggest client after News was a defence contractor called Wedtech Corporation. It was back in the days when Rudy Giuliani was the aggressive US Attorney for New York, before he ran for mayor. Wedtech collapsed in the late 1980s after senior executives and congressmen were convicted of fraud, bribery, extortion and racketeering. In one of those trials, Giuliani's senior Assistant US Attorney, Howard Wilson, described Siskind as an unindicted co-conspirator in what Wilson said was a sham stock transfer to win defence contracts. But Siskind told me that it was just a legal strategy to allow the prosecutor to table an allegedly incriminating memo that Wedtech management had sent him. Siskind certainly did not know after reading the memo that they were trying to defraud the US government: 'I don't believe that the US Attorney's office ever seriously considered laying any charge against me.'

A year after this, in Adelaide, I can see all this coming back to Siskind as I introduce myself. 'I was having drinks with Rudy Giuliani that day your letter came in asking about that,' Arthur tells me. 'We had a little laugh together, that anyone would be bringing that old story up.' It is soon after this exchange that Arthur begins to make pointed comments about whether I am entitled to be in the shareholders' enclosure, hitting the tea and scones. It is always a risk letting a journalist loose on a food tray—I've made quite a dint in it.

The reason I had been contacting Siskind the year before was to ask about a tax investigation the Israeli government was conducting into a technology company that News Corp owned in Jerusalem called News Datacom, which I understood had something to do with smartcards. We exchanged some correspondence over several months and had a few telephone conversations. On the second occasion Siskind faxed me that he would speak to me, but only under protest, because the queries put to him were 'indicative of your propensity to mix and match facts and untruths to benefit a sensational story . . . the facts make very little difference to you'.

It seemed promising that he remembered me, but perhaps that's a glass-half-full kind of reading. News Corporation has a broad church in its many corporate manifestations, and yet News Datacom was like nothing I had ever come across before. Siskind attributed all of News Datacom's tax problems to a former executive called Michael Clinger, whom News Corp was suing for fraud. I discovered Clinger had an arrest warrant for securities fraud outstanding against him in New York. Curiously, the arrest warrant had been issued while he was the chief executive of News Datacom. He had continued to run this little arm of News Corporation for a year, even though he was an international fugitive.

A London *Financial Times* journalist, Will Lewis, had been leading the international coverage of the Israeli tax investigation of News Datacom, despite some trenchant responses from Siskind, who was supervising News Corp's action against Clinger. Siskind was convinced that Clinger was the main source for Lewis's stories—so much so that Siskind told me he could quote dates and times when Clinger and Lewis had talked. Siskind's responses to some of the questions Lewis fired off to him had become personal. It seemed so marked that I asked Siskind in an email how it was that he knew so much about Will Lewis's family; for example, his wife's job prospects. Had he put Lewis under surveillance? He told me that any information he had about Lewis's personal life came from News Corp's surveillance of Clinger.

'Our instructions to our agents are to act within the law at all times,' Siskind said.

Several months later, in March 1997, serious allegations arose in a London court case that private investigators hired by News Datacom had been bugging Michael Clinger's telephone calls. Israeli police had raided News Datacom's offices and in the safe of the current chief executive of News Datacom they had found tapes of phone calls Clinger had made to his Jerusalem and London lawyers. When I asked Siskind for a comment on all this, he was done talking with me and passed my query to his offsider, Genie Gavenchak. She roundly denied any wiretapping had taken place. She said News Corp believed that no tapes had been found in the News Datacom safe and, if they had been found, it was because Michael Clinger had put them there.

This all ended neatly enough. Ultimately, News Datacom settled the Israeli tax claim for $3 million. The High Court in London awarded the company $47 million damages against Clinger. News Datacom renamed itself NDS. Will Lewis's story came to an end with the court case and he ended up as editor of the London *Telegraph*. Later still, he joined News International and became deputy chief executive under Rebekah Brooks, with no more word about phone tapping. And the good ship NDS sailed on.

In fact the NDS story was just beginning. Working out what happened next at NDS, though, would prove a long, frustrating trail. The first part would be understanding the people and events that led up to Alex's close call in Toronto in 1997. The single feature that would link most of the players in this saga is a history of extreme violence. That's the nature of the secret world. The question that would recur for me time and again was: Who dropped the ball? In other words, who was overseeing the dramas that played out at NDS? And who at some point should have told the NDS black-hat operations that what they were doing was a really bad idea? NDS was always tight with the Office of the Chairman at News Corporation. NDS execs reported to Rupert Murdoch's closest people. Arthur Siskind and News Corp's chief financial officer David DeVoe sat on the NDS board, as did James and Lachlan Murdoch and Chase Carey, who was by then co-COO of News Corp (although not all of them were on the board at the time of the events described in this book).

In October 1997 I knew nothing of the adventure in Toronto. In hindsight it's tempting to link it in the same time frame as the annual meeting in Adelaide, when I was getting thrown out of the morning tea, as some sort of indication that senior management's attention was focused elsewhere. But that doesn't really work because the annual meeting was in early October, a fortnight before Alex's great escape. On 24 October 1997 the record shows that Rupert Murdoch was in Beijing for a meeting in the Great Hall of the People with Ding Guangen, the head of the Chinese government's Central Propaganda Department.

Actually that was later in the day. Earlier in the morning, around the time that Alex was desperately working his way through the seedier hotels along the edge of Lake Ontario, Murdoch had taken time off for a little sightseeing and to buy some ties in Xiushui Market, or Silk Street. He had dispensed for the morning with the services of local exec Bruce Dover. Instead he was accompanied by a vivacious young Chinese executive from Star TV, acting as his interpreter for the first time, Wendi Deng.

PART 1

The Hunters

These bloody days have broken my heart.

Sir Thomas Wyatt, 1536

Hebron, 6 June 1980

Dawn was still creeping across the sky when the initial explosion came. Minutes earlier, the faint glimmer of light brushing the horizon had produced that critical moment when imams can first discern the difference between a white hair and a black hair, which is the signal for the calls to prayer to echo across the mosques of Israel's West Bank.

There had been no warning. At 6.15 a.m. one of the first traders to arrive at the Hebron market triggered a booby trapped hand grenade that in turn set off an explosive charge that tore through the traders and others passing by. The casualty toll was seven, none fatal. The bomb had been designed to injure, to maim, to disfigure, not to kill.

Ninety minutes later, a second bomb exploded when the mayor of Ramallah, Karim Khalaf, turned the key in the ignition of his car. He lost his right leg. At 8.30, some 30 kilometres north, another explosion tore off the front of the car of the mayor of Nablus, Bassam Shakaa, seconds after he turned on the ignition. After six hours of surgery, doctors amputated both his legs. Another mayor, Ibrahim Tawil of El-Bira, had rushed to see Khalaf at the hospital in a friend's car. Tawil's mercy dash saved him from a similar fate. Instead, a bomb disposal expert from the Israeli Police took the force of the bomb meant for Tawil as he gingerly opened the mayor's garage door. He lost his sight.

Across Israel a shadowy group of conspirators waited for reports of more explosions, but nothing followed. Two of the bomb teams despatched to plant their deadly charges the night before had missed their targets.

It was enough. By nine that morning it was clear that Israel had a new terror group. It was the first series of attacks by the Jewish Underground, targeting Arab leaders. It barely made a mention on the news wires.

Sydney, November 1980

God was in his heaven, all was well with the world, and Rupert Murdoch was doing two of the things he loves best. First off, he was acquiring another couple of television stations. He wasn't really buying the stations—he had done that two years before by buying half an airline. He was now beating off the tiresome nitpickers at the Australian Broadcasting Tribunal who had been trying ever since his purchase to prise his fingers off them. He had been diverted briefly by his first attempt to buy Australia's biggest newspaper chain, the Herald and Weekly Times Group. He hadn't succeeded this time round, but he'd made a neat profit before making his tactical retreat, and Ansett Airlines' television stations were worth every penny—as long as he held on to them like a limpet.

Australian television stations were supposed to be owned only by Australian citizens and these ABT people had the impertinence to question his current status and future intentions. Murdoch explained to them, hand over heart, how he was regrettably forced to spend a great deal of time overseas running his overseas newspapers—the *News of the World* and the *Sun* in London, the

New York Post in America, you might have heard of them. And something small and a little grubby in San Antonio. But in his heart of hearts he always considered that his chief residence was here in Australia, here on the farm at Cavan, on the rich alluvial plain near Canberra.

It was a noble thought, well expressed, and yet the ABT was not entirely convinced, contrasting these admirable patriotic sentiments with his tax returns, which stated he lived in New York. They even mentioned something about his green card, which requires you to state your place of residence as somewhere *American*. You can see right there the tension of being Keith Rupert Murdoch, global media baron in the making. He's never going to be quite where you want him—you say tomato, I say US tax residency status.

Really, though, this was just light relief. He would hold on to his television stations in the end, but the real action was in London, where he had picked up the faint signals of a newspaper owner in distress. This was the second thing that Murdoch really loved— acquiring newspapers. Getting hold of Times Newspapers could get interesting.

Pointe-à-Pitre, 30 December 1980

Alan Guggenheim had always been a fidget. It was bred deep into his marrow, the need to be tactile, to pick up and handle *les trucs*, 'the gadgets', to fiddle with the controls, to make them function just a little better. There was a perfect way everything could work and it was only a question of working out what it was. Why wouldn't anyone want to do that? He was just . . . a gadget guy. So it was natural, as he accelerated away from his home, that his first thought was to turn on the car radio to get a little news.

It was the silly season after Christmas with little world news. In Britain, Rupert Murdoch was on the final approach in his quest to buy the *Times* and the *Sunday Times*. He had set up a supervisory board, which he promised would give their world-acclaimed staff complete editorial independence but, the way some journalists were describing it, the process felt like watching pirates clambering on board over the gunwales. As Alan stirred restlessly in his seat, this wasn't exactly the lead story on the radio in Guadeloupe, that tiny island outpost of metropolitan France nestling in the Antilles and close to the West Indies.

That morning, on the quiet back road from his house in Guadeloupe, Guggenheim's fidget would save his life. But it was about the only thing he had going for him. Everything else he was doing wrong, beginning with being on the road in the first place at seven o'clock in the morning. It's Counterterrorism Basics. When you've received a credible death threat, the first thing you do is vary your movements, vary the times you go to work, change the routes you take, make sure your killers never know where you'll be. The security consultants teach you other things, like dropping your keys on the ground to give you an excuse to look under the car for bombs. Taking the back rooms in hotels to avoid the car bomb blast from the front. But chiefly they tell you the most important element is unpredictability: security through obscurity.

For Alan, that morning, this wasn't an option. He lived on an estate on the edge of Pointe-à-Pitre, a housing cluster with a couple of local side roads but only one way out to the main highway. He and his wife Suzanne were to be part of the official send-off party of local dignitaries at the airport to farewell the president of the republic, Valéry Giscard d'Estaing, after his Christmas in the Caribbean. They had to be there, at that time, travelling on the only road out. Alan and Suzanne were toast.

The French state at this time was sending an elaborate message. In August the military arm of the local independence movement, the Groupe de Libération Armée de la Guadeloupe (GLA), had delivered an ultimatum: all French settlers must be out of the country by 31 December or they would die. But that is not the way one addresses the Fifth Republic. In November the Élysée Palace had announced coolly that life would go on as usual, that in fact Giscard d'Estaing was intending to spend Christmas at Guadeloupe to demonstrate that it was as much a part of France as ever.

The first direct threat against Alan had come during a board meeting of the employers' association, the Conseil Régional du Patronat de la Guadeloupe, which he ran as executive director. His secretary interrupted the meeting to deliver letters that had been addressed to each of the directors by the GLA, which repeated the 31 December deadline. Each letter had been personalised, with several lines detailing the movements of a family member of each director—a child or marriage partner—outlining how the GLA could reach them at such and such a place, at such and such a time. Two leading business figures had already been wounded in shootings in the street, and in September a soldier died when a bomb he was defusing at the airport exploded, part of a wave of bombings targeted at French businesses.

Alan was on the GLA hit list because for two years he had been working to bring local working conditions—notably wages, unemployment and superannuation benefits—in line with France. This would result in a huge improvement for working people; but it was a delicate negotiating process between employers, trade unions and the French government, and it meant he had to travel to Paris every few weeks. If Alan succeeded, the changes would make it much harder for the communist GLA to convince Guadeloupe's population to seek independence—and embrace third-world poverty. This made Alan a particular target, as well as Suzanne, who was chancellor of the university, which was a hotbed of the independence movement.

Prefect Guy Maillard had done what he could. Alan and Suzanne had received basic anti-terrorism training. Police patrols came past their house three times a night—'Always at the same time, because they are gendarmes,' Alan noted. Sometimes a police car would drive ahead of Alan's grey Renault R30 to check for ambush sites as he drove to work. Yet, even though there had been an attack on the television station on Christmas Eve and a bomb had wounded a tourist at the airport on 28 December, there had been no dreadful catastrophe. And now, with the president in town, these precautions had to be put on hold.

The prefect had been apologetic when he called Alan about dropping the police patrols: 'By the way we don't have enough manpower for security with the president's visit, we need to lighten up your protection. There's just not enough military and police. You understand we have to put the president first.' Alan said sure.

Two days later, as Alan and Suzanne pulled out of their driveway, the whole unnerving process of the president's visit was almost over. It was just on seven o'clock, the heat of the day already beginning to build. Alan had the windows up and the air conditioning on. He was running late and he switched on the car radio to check for news as he accelerated around the curve in the long run out to the highway.

The news bulletin was reporting the president's imminent arrival at the airport to catch his plane as Alan approached the first cross-street in the development, 200 metres from his home. He noticed a department of social security car stopped in the street on his right. As he approached, the car turned out in front of him. Then it stopped. Alan braked, but his mind was on the broadcast as he reached forward to fiddle with the radio, struggling to hear what was being said about the president.

There was an explosion of noise, and he felt a blow high up in his chest and a feeling of warmth. Glass fragments from the side window shattered across him. Suzanne looked across at her husband as he slumped, then looked beyond him at the roadside. She saw a hole had been cut in the hedge of the vacant house on the corner. Behind the hedge, just six metres away, was a figure with a rifle. With a shock she realised the assassin was a woman, and her face wore an expression of the most intense hatred Suzanne had ever seen. Three decades later, when I spoke to her, the memory of that face remained etched in her memory. She would replay forever those frenzied moments as her husband struggled to save their lives.

The Cuban-trained hit team had been in position at the deserted house for several days. They had cut a window in the hedge and then covered it over with a sign. That morning, as the grey Renault approached, all they had to do was take away the covering and expose the gap. The shooter was in position waiting for the team in the car on the side street to halt the Guggenheims in the kill zone. The set-up was perfect because both Suzanne and Alan would be in the car on the way to the airport for Giscard d'Estaing's official farewell. The plan was Alan would be killed and Suzanne kidnapped—the chancellor of the university would be a prize hostage, a coup that would completely overshadow the French president's visit.

Life often turns on very simple happenstances. Alan had been fiddling with the radio, leaning forward to raise the volume to hear the update on d'Estaing's arrival at the airport. The shooter compensated, tracked forward slightly in her sights, and fired. But that tiny movement put the edge of the car's wing mirror into the line of fire. The shooter was using a .22 Magnum with expanding ammunition. It's a weapon favoured by assassins and spy agencies around the world—accurate, relatively quiet, while the hollow-point rounds do massive damage.

The bullet punched straight through the corner of the wing mirror, then through the glass of the side window. But the round had already begun to break up before it hit Alan. He received a spray of bullet fragments across his face and shoulders. The still disintegrating main round hit him on his collar, just missing major arteries and nerve bundles in the neck, before ploughing into his chest, carrying portions of his shirt and collar button that helped seal the wound.

None of this had sunk in for Alan as he realised dully that he had been shot, that the killers were just metres away, that he and Suzanne were still in danger. Besides holding a degree in mathematics and a masters in civil engineering, he was a major in the army reserve, and a graduate of the French Command and General Staff Reserve College. He had served in a reconnaissance unit and been trained to drive the French Army's nimble EBR armoured cars, designed to get up close to the enemy and then to get out again. This was something he had trained for.

He put his car into reverse and accelerated hard away from the ambush site, along the bumpy road, back around the bend and into his driveway. As he drove he was conscious that he was unarmed, but he had his 9-millimetre army issue weapon back at his home. By this time there was a lot of blood. He stumbled out of the car, lurched into the house, ignored the 9 millimetre and reached instead for a hunting rifle. Back outside, he fired two shots in the air.

The pain was beginning to be overpowering. Through a fog he asked Suzanne to call the emergency number. But there were no gendarmes to send to him—they were all on duty at the airport. The ambulance refused to go into a fire zone. Instead it was the fire brigade that came down the road, klaxon blaring, and firemen who scooped him up, put him in their fire truck and whisked him to hospital.

Paris, 1981

The French have a helpful phrase, *tête à claque*—a 'head for hitting'. You see some people, you know you just want to slap them. Mitterrand's Paris offered few certainties for a young *flic* on the make, but his 26 years had taught Gilles Kaehlin two things. The first was the rock-solid assurance that, sooner or later, almost anyone who spent time with him would be irritated. The second was that he really didn't care. So what if they hated him. He did what had to be done. On his more fanciful days he saw himself as Don Quixote, the idealist challenging the windmills with no thought for the personal cost. His colleagues called him *le loup blanc*—'The White Wolf'. They also called him Darth Vader, the Hyena, KKK, Mad Dog, the Terminator and other little badges of affection.

Kaehlin had been born in Nice, which left him with the accent problem. Well-bred Parisians are too polite to mention it directly, but the entire south of the country is populated by people who speak like their bottom lip is recovering from anaesthetic. They call the Nice accent 'lilting', by which they mean it sounds like the speaker is gargling last century's mouthwash. Gilles grew up in the gritty northern suburbs of Nice, the part of town that doesn't boast a lot of waterfront views. His father worked himself up to be maître d' at the Negresco hotel on the Promenade des Anglais. His grandparents ran a dance hall in the north of Nice. His politics were hard left, including an early link up with the Communist Youth, but throughout his life his politics would seem more of a marriage of convenience than an ideological commitment. He finished his baccalaureate at nineteen and then did his national service.

In 1976, aged 21, he joined the police—not to change the world, but because he was afraid of being unemployed. He quickly caught the eye of the legendary head of the Direction Centrale des Renseignements Généraux, France's domestic intelligence service, often simply referred to as RG. It was his first big break. By 1980 he was an inspector, with long hair, jeans and sneakers, in the elite anti-terrorism team hunting Action Directe, which was in the process of becoming France's most lethal terror group. He was part of the team that pulled a sting operation that caught Action Directe's founders, Jean-Marc Rouillan and Nathalie Ménigon, in a dramatic confrontation near Avenue Foch in Paris on 13 September 1980. Everyone on that squad was a hero.

It didn't last. By early 1981 Kaehlin had talked himself into trouble. His superiors complained of his friendships with left-wing journalists on the daily newspaper, *Libération*, and the satirical weekly, *Canard Enchaîné*. He had also managed to mouth off at his bosses a few too many times. He was transferred to an archive facility on the outskirts of Paris, his career in tatters, when a piece of outrageous fortune befell him.

On 10 May 1981 François Mitterrand defeated Giscard d'Estaing to become the twenty-first president of the republic. The Socialists came to power with a deep and abiding mistrust of the right-wing French security forces. The question was: Whom could they trust? And here, Kaehlin's friends at *Libération* and *Canard Enchaîné* could vouch for a certain young RG inspector. In late July, Kaehlin was transferred to the Élysée Palace to work directly under Mitterrand's long-time security advisor, François de Grossouvre.

A fortnight later Mitterrand signed an order that abolished the Cour de sûreté de l'État, the Court of State Security, and passed a general amnesty for a wide range of acts of political offences, freeing 6300 prisoners. The Socialists took the view that with their ascent to power the need for armed revolution was over. What need was there for further political dissent? The job of reaching an agreement with the dozens of political groups thus affected went to Grossouvre and his tough new assistant.

'I was asked to negotiate with the militants, one by one,' Kaehlin said later. 'We offered them money so they could rebuild their lives overseas.' Those released included the leaders of Action Directe, Jean-Marc Rouillan and Nathalie Ménigon. Kaehlin dealt closely with them in the negotiations that followed. In hindsight this turned out to be a mistake.

London, 22 October 1981

It was a corporate event that passed entirely without remark. On 9 September 1980, the day that Kaehlin was busy with the team catching Action Directe, London law firm Herbert Smith & Co registered a shelf company, Precis Eight Limited, at Companies House. Three months later, Precis Eight changed its name to Satellite Television Limited. Ten months later, on 22 October 1981, Satellite Television was re-incorporated as a public company.

Former Thames Television executive Brian Hayes had raised £4.1 million in loans and capital to launch Europe's first satellite broadcaster. The C-band transmissions could be pulled in only if you had a 3-metre satellite dish to pick up the signal. The dishes cost more than £15,000 to install, and fewer than 50 people in Britain had one. But Hayes believed this was the way of the future. Satellite Television began broadcasting on 26 April 1982. But public response was a little underwhelming. In a year Hayes would be out of money and looking for a media company that could see the big picture.

Hayes wasn't the only media exec looking at the skies. The C-band dishes were slightly more popular in the United States, where they were used in isolated areas like the Rocky Mountains, which cable companies did not service. One night when he was playing poker, Charlie Ergen, a financial analyst for snack-food group Frito-Lay Inc., had decided satellite was the way of the future. In 1980, he packed up his family and headed to Denver, Colorado, with three partners to start a business selling the big satellite dishes.

Like Hayes, Ergen found that the flood of customers he had expected for his satellite dishes did not eventuate. But he hung in there. As the price of dishes went down through the 1980s, he began manufacturing them. He called his company Ecosphere, but he would later change that to EchoStar Communications on the way to building a $20 billion satellite broadcasting company.

It would be a long road to reach that point and Ergen would find himself in colourful company. Back in 1980 he had never been to France, had never heard of Alan Guggenheim and certainly never of Gilles Kaehlin. But that would change.

Guadeloupe, 17 February 1982

Alan was looking forward to getting back to Guadeloupe again and seeing his old friends. His convalescence after the shooting fourteen months before had been a rushed affair. Within weeks he was in Paris, meeting with French intelligence groups and becoming part of a major push against the Cuban-backed terrorist movement in the Antilles. He had wandered on to the edges of the secret world, a reluctant participant. But he had little choice than to join. And results were quick.

By March 1981 came the first arrests of suspected GLA militants—a house painter and a sales clerk at Air France, later an education ministry employee. They were flown to Paris to be tried by the Court of State Security, but here the operation came unstuck. When the new Mitterrand government abolished the Court of State Security on 4 August, the three GLA suspects were among the 6300 prisoners released.

With them back on the street, the GLA threats continued. Alan and Suzanne had had enough. As conservatives, they had been dismayed by the rise of the Socialists. Now the release of the men who they believed had tried to kill them was too much—they made the momentous decision to leave Guadeloupe and France behind them and set out on a new life in the United States. Alan had done a little work in Guadeloupe for a pay TV system his father owned; he liked this field and believed there were more opportunities in America.

At the end of 1981 Alan and Suzanne and their young family moved to California. Alan had an aunt there who, after a colourful career, had ended up in real estate. Before they moved Alan asked her to use the little nest egg he and Suzanne had built up to find them a place to live. They arrived to find their money had been spent on a broken-down shack that had been owned by his aunt's ex-husband. Welcome to capitalism.

Alan still had matters in Guadeloupe that he needed to finalise as he flew in for a last visit in February 1982. But when he arrived, the airport was in lockdown after an old friend of Alan's, Max Martin, was shot dead. Alan flew back to California and didn't come back.

In France, the deals that Grossouvre and Kaehlin had made with the militant groups in 1981 were coming apart, most spectacularly in the case of Action Directe. Somehow Rouillan and Ménigon had learned how the French intelligence agency had caught them in September 1980. The RG had trapped them with the help of an undercover informant, a Lebanese artist called Gabriel Chahine. The first confirmation that Action Directe was back in business came with two shotgun blasts directly into Chahine's chest when he opened the door of his shop on a Saturday evening in Paris on 13 March 1982.

The RG didn't like it, but for the moment Kaehlin's position at the Élysée was untouchable. He had just begun his new job escorting Mitterrand's illegitimate daughter, Mazarine, to and from school.

'Twice a week, we would go by car to the Rue de Bièvre [Mitterrand's home], then branch off to the Quai Branly where he [Mitterrand] spent the night with Anne Pingeot. In the morning we arrived early to get Mazarine to school,' he testified later. It was Kaehlin who came up with the codename the security services would use for Mitterrand for the next decade—'Tonton' ('Uncle'). When *Minute* magazine threatened to publish photos of Mazarine with Mitterrand, Grossouvre bought them off with a suitcase full of money, while Kaehlin provided security. The pictures never reappeared—another job well done—but that would not keep Kaehlin out of trouble.

London, 1982

Harold Evans wasn't really working out for Rupert Murdoch. There had been a honeymoon period, as always with new editors, after Murdoch moved Evans from the *Sunday Times* to edit the *Times*. Invariably, all editors believe they have succeeded in doing what every other editor has failed to do—to change Murdoch. And Murdoch will indulge them for a while. But Evans was never going to be Murdoch's kind of guy. Rupert liked his newspapers a little more robust.

Evans was asked to resign in March 1982. While he resisted for a time, Evans knew that, for all the promises Murdoch had made when he bought the *Times* in 1981—to cede power to an editorial board to safeguard the paper's independence—none of this made any real difference when he wanted to dump an editor. So Evans was gone, just in time to miss the Falklands War and watch the *Sun* covering itself with glory with its happy little headlines . . . 'STICK IT UP YOUR JUNTA!', 'GOTCHA' and 'DARE TO CALL IT TREASON' (for those in Britain who showed a reluctance to get with the program).

In the middle of the Falklands War Israel had a minor brush with Syria; then in June Israel invaded Lebanon, pushing up to encircle Beirut. There was never any doubt which side Murdoch's papers would support. For many years people have tried to claim that Rupert Murdoch is Jewish. Quite why this should be important has never been clear. But while he has always been one of Israel's staunchest supporters, his ancestral roots are Scottish Presbyterian, Australian Methodist, Anglican and a little Irish Catholic. The links with Israel are personal, and go back to the 1960s. In the early 1980s Murdoch had developed a close relationship with Defence Minister Ariel Sharon. In the 1990s it would be Binyamin Netanyahu.

Ramat HaSharon, outside Tel Aviv, 1982

Yossi's friends were scandalised. He was a man marked for great things, with a spiritual maturity that had won him the respect of men well his senior. But what to make of his choice of a wife?

Anat Shalev represented the very worst of Israeli culture. That is, if you measured such things from a religious perspective. She had grown up in a secular home, the eldest of four children. Her grandmother was a pioneering feminist. Her mother, a fringe artist and gallery curator, had been raised in an assimilated family that did not even celebrate Passover. Anat's father, Aner, was a soldier–artist. A brigadier-general he would be tapped to head Yad Vashem, the Holocaust memorial—a gruelling task that was a measure of his humanity and basic decency. But he wasn't a religious man.

All of this made Anat completely unsuitable for Yosef 'Yossi' Tsuria, in the eyes of his friends. She was 21, and an attractive, intense young woman with compelling brown eyes, struggling with a secular culture she described as feather light. She had been working as an army tour guide when they met. He had been an officer in the Golani Brigade. Yossi had grown up among the ultra-orthodox, the Haredi, and specifically within the ranks of the religious Zionists led by Rabbi Zvi Yehuda Kook. While most Haredi had no time for the secular state of Israel or its armed struggle, Kook's followers saw the establishment of Israel and settlements on the West Bank as part of the process of ushering in the age of the Messiah and the redemption of the people of Israel.

The 1973 Yom Kippur War had spurred the rise of such religious nationalism, including the formation of Gush Emunim, a movement that pioneered a string of new settlements on the West Bank. Yossi's father had been a leading light of the settler movement and Yossi's teenage years had been dominated by the hard struggle of life in the settlements. It was a life lived under constant threat of attack, which inevitably fostered a hardline approach to dealing with the Arab population of the West Bank.

Remarkably, from this background Yossi had grown up to become a gentle man, full of humour, vitality and wisdom, a deeply spiritual figure whose life was profoundly imbued with the study of the Torah. He was also a mathematics genius. A side effect of endless study of the Kabbalah had given him a love for numbers and secret symbols. He could talk at length about the significance and meaning that resided in the shape of a number. Bar-Ilan University in Tel Aviv, with its religious Zionist culture, was the natural choice for his science degree in pure maths.

Anat's family also struggled to make sense of the romance; to her mother, Naomi, her daughter's choice of taking on the life of the ultra-Orthodox woman seemed inconceivable. Yet, under the circumstances, the wedding was a triumph of diplomacy. On the bride's side were her mother's friends from the alternative art scene, who already looked askance at her father's army friends. Among the guests was also Reuven Hasak, an old friend of her father's who was now deputy head of Shin Beit, Israel's fearsome internal security service. There might have been a little coolness between Hasak and Yossi, but perhaps that was just imagination. It was natural for Hasak to be protective. He had known Anat since she was a child.

But there was an undercurrent at the wedding of which Anat Shalev's family was completely unaware. For Gush Emunim, which now loudly advocated the forcible expulsion of all Arabs from the Occupied Terriories, had a dark side—and it had claimed Yossi Tsuria—Anat's gentle, wise Yossi. He attended meetings at a house in Samaria every Thursday night, but these were not just for religious discussions. The Jewish Underground, as it was later called, was an extended group of friends and acquaintances, all of them settlers on the West Bank. They had known each other for years; they met at weddings and other social events.

In June 1980 their shared concerns about Palestinians had coalesced into a plan to set bombs in the cars of the Arab mayors. There would be other operations—bombs on Arab buses, attacks on mosques, and a grenade and machine-gun attack on a Muslim seminary. But the central mission for this Messianic group was to target the Dome of the Rock, one of Islam's most revered shrines, which stands on the Temple Mount in Jerusalem.

Demolishing the shrine was a prerequisite for restoring a Jewish temple on this site—two earlier Jewish temples here had been destroyed in past millennia. Their plan, finalised after extensive reconnaissance, was to produce a controlled collapse of the dome with hundreds of kilograms of explosives packed in specially constructed containers.

By early 1982 the explosives had been prepared and a route into the precinct planned. The unarmed Arab guards at the site presented a small problem—they would have to be killed. This would require special weapons, and Yossi became involved in their procurement.

By March 1982 the plotters had all the weapons and explosives they needed, and were awaiting final approval. But at this point the leaders of the underground fell into disagreement. In the end, they could not get rabbinical approval to bomb the dome, and the consequences were too uncertain. In April the attack was called off, at least for the time being. The explosives and weapons remained in place, but other operations now had priority.

London, 1983

These were the dog years for Rupert Murdoch. As the proprietor of the *Times* and the *Sunday Times*, he had finally won a modicum of respectability in Britain. But then in April 1983 the decision to publish the fraudulent 'Hitler Diaries' brought him down again. The historian Hugh Trevor-Roper, recently ennobled by Prime Minister Margaret Thatcher as Baron Dacre of Glanton, was a director of the *Times* and a renowned Hitler scholar; he had originally authenticated the diaries, but then expressed last-minute doubts. It was Murdoch's decision to push ahead with publishing them, which proved a commercial success for the paper, but at a great cost to its reputation.

Meanwhile, in the United States, Murdoch had been kicking tyres in his search for a big play. Mostly these became greenmail plays—buying into a company like Warner Bros but then, after realising its takeover defences were too formidable, taking a fee to walk away. The month after the Hitler Diaries fiasco, with nothing else working out, Murdoch quietly took over Brian Hayes' Satellite Television operation, which had lost £2.5 million in its first year. News International proceeded to pump £9.6 million into Satellite Television in the following year. In January 1984 News changed its name to Sky Channel. The programming improved, but after fifteen months it had lost another £5.8 million.

Murdoch remained as fascinated with Israel as ever. With international criticism mounting over the Israeli invasion of Lebanon, Murdoch and several of his newspaper editors took up an offer from Ariel Sharon, then Israel's defence minister, for a bird's-eye view of Israeli fortifications on the Golan Heights from an Israeli helicopter gunship. Sharon stepped down as defence minister shortly afterwards, but Murdoch knew who his friends were.

Gaza Strip, 12 April 1984

When the first confused reports came in late afternoon, Shin Beit's Reuven Hasak realised it was going to be a bad day, but he was still a little hopeful. In Hasak's world, a bad day meant a security incident, when someone threatened the lives of some of the four million Israelis in his care. A very bad day was when some of those Israelis died in a flurry of shots or explosions.

In the era before the suicide bomber, early morning was the danger time for lethal terrorist attacks. So this call, late in the day, suggested something else. There would be live hostages and a good chance to rescue at least some of them. But that wouldn't be the biggest problem.

The first reports were disjointed. Bus 300 was the Egged company's service from Tel Aviv down the coast to Ashkelon; it had been hijacked a quarter of an hour into the trip by an unidentified group of Palestinians. The bus was now barrelling south down the coastal highway through the Gaza Strip as fast as its ageing motor could push it. Border police were in pursuit. Nothing was known about the hijackers except that there were at least four of them, and that they were stupid. Really, *really* stupid. The evidence of that had come with their first act after commandeering the bus. They had stopped to let off a woman passenger who was pregnant. The woman was an off-duty Israeli soldier, who immediately flagged down a car and sounded the alert. The chase was on and the hijackers' plan to drive to Egypt was history.

Afterwards, hardly anyone remembered them at all. There was a fat kid—there's always a fat kid—two other teenagers and a tougher 21-year old. It was a spur-of-the-moment piece of idiocy. Their plan came to no more than this: they were in Tel Aviv, they were bored, and they suddenly figured out a 'guaranteed' ticket to success, power and worldwide fame. They would hijack a bus, drive down to the Egyptian border, and force the Israeli government to release hundreds of Palestinian prisoners before they escaped to live in Tripoli.

Their criminal genius had not extended to bringing along any guns. Their weapons complement came to a few knives and a hand grenade, and they were now being pursued by one of the most formidable military machines in the world. Later they would pretend that they had a petrol bomb. While all that was not enough to be any help, it could still get people killed.

Actually they got further than you would expect. The bus crashed through two separate police checkpoints, each time weathering a storm of gunfire, and it was still barrelling along at 110 kilometres an hour, the Palestinian driver with a knife to his throat. The security forces pursuing finally lost their patience 15 kilometres south of Gaza City, and shot out the tyres. Another few kilometres on and the bus finally ground to a halt in an olive grove at Deir el-Balah, its windows shot out and one of the 41 passengers bleeding from serious gunshot wounds.

In the confusion the bus driver scrambled out and ran to the cordon of soldiers and border police surrounding the crashed bus. He was beaten soundly, under the mistaken belief he was one of the terrorists. The Arab hijackers claimed to be members of the Popular Front for the Liberation of Palestine, headed by George Habash, and they demanded the release of 500 PLO prisoners in Israeli jails. The Israeli negotiator told them he would get back to them.

The hijack then settled into a siege, producing a minor hiatus that allowed the security forces surrounding the bus to work out their turf issue—who was in charge? The border police had had first contact with the runaway bus and had finally brought it to a stop. From here on the army would take over. Brigadier General Yitzhak Mordechai was the ranking officer. He was a decorated war hero, winning the Medal of Valour for leading a paratroop battalion across the Suez Canal during the 1973 Yom Kippur War. The army might be in charge for now but, once the siege was over, the scene would become the responsibility of the senior Shin Beit agent on hand—Ehud Yatom, who at 36 was standing in as Head of Operations at Shin Beit, the domestic version of Mossad, though its brief also runs to securing embassies, airlines and Israeli government missions around the world.

For the deputy director of Shin Beit, Reuven Hasak, this was looking like a lose–lose proposition. As head of the agency's anti-terror operations, he would be blamed for not knowing the hijack would take place—though how anyone could predict this shambles of an operation was a mystery. If fingers were pointed at Shin Beit, then Hasak's boss, Avraham Shalom, would sheet the blame home to his deputy. Meanwhile Shalom was on the phone constantly to his man at the scene, Ehud Yatom, who was one of his favourites. If, by some miracle, this mess had a happy ending there would be no surprise about who would claim credit.

Avraham Shalom and Reuven Hasak detested each other. It didn't help that Shalom knew that Hasak wanted his job. Hasak had been recruited to Shin Beit in 1964 and had risen swiftly through the ranks. He had the bearing and steady gaze of the Good Soldier that reassured politicians, set him out from the crowd and earmarked him for promotion. He spoke Hebrew, Russian and English, in that order. After the army, he had done a masters degree and worked briefly as a lecturer. But in 1979, when Shalom was closing in on the top job, Hasak had walked away from the agency. He took what was to be a three-year sabbatical in 1979 and became the chief administrator running the Jerusalem municipality. His security skills, however, were too important to waste.

In 1981 the prime minister, Menachem Begin, personally persuaded Hasak to return to Shin Beit as deputy director under Shalom. Begin promised that in two years Shalom would be shuffled off and Hasak would have the top spot. But when Begin retired from politics in August 1983, after the disastrous invasion of Lebanon the year before, he left Yitzhak Shamir to succeed him as prime minister and the promise to Hasak was forgotten. At 46 years of age, all Hasak could hope for was to outlast Shalom, and to survive the internal sniping.

The talks with the hijackers of Bus 300 continued desultorily through the night. The Israelis were stalling. At one point a handful of passengers managed to escape through the back window. At dawn, an elite military unit led by Brigadier General Mordechai stormed the bus from all sides. The well-organised attack took just 30 seconds. Even so, by the time the shooting stopped, a young woman had been killed and seven other passengers wounded, all of them caught in the army crossfire. Two of the terrorists had also been killed inside the bus.

As the two remaining hijackers were taken off the bus, camera flashes went off from the media cordon. A Shin Beit agent beside one of the hijackers gestured angrily at one of the photographers and marched over to insist he give up the film. The photographer reluctantly agreed, but managed to palm the real film. He gave the Shin Beit agent a dummy.

When the photographer developed the film he had smuggled out, it carried a high-quality picture of one of the hijackers in handcuffs, walking from the bus unassisted and clearly unhurt. Another photographer had a picture of the second hijacker, also in good health. Both captives were led away for interrogation.

In the minutes that followed, the two hijackers were savagely beaten. The father of one of them, who was shown his son's body several days later, claimed that one of his eyes had been gouged out and was hanging from the socket. The prisoners were injured, bleeding and could not stand—like 'two sacks of potatoes', Shin Beit's man, Ehud Yatom, told the Hebrew daily *Yediot Aharonot* twelve years later.

'We put them in our van, and then I received instructions from Avraham Shalom to kill them, so I killed them,' Yatom recalled. He used a rock. 'I crushed their skulls. Believe me, there was no need for too much of an effort.' Yatom would later deny he had made these admissions but *Yediot Aharonot* stood by its account.

This would remain a dark secret. The Israeli Defence Forces reported at the time that the surviving hijackers had been badly wounded and died en route to hospital. The Israeli censor blocked publication of the press photographs, but the story circulated anyway. The photographs were published in Europe and, later, on page one of the Israeli daily newspaper, *Hadashot*. The army continued to insist that the last two hijackers had died from wounds they received when the bus was stormed. Perhaps the pictures taken had been of passengers who had been freed, an army spokesman suggested. But the stories would not go away. On 23 April, two weeks after the bus siege, the *New York Times* ran an article filed by their Jerusalem correspondent, David K. Shipler, called 'Death of a Hijacker: Stirrings in Israel'.

Two events would turn world opinion around completely, both of them orchestrated by Reuven Hasak. Five days after the *New York Times* report, the Israeli government announced a three-man commission, to be headed by Major General Meir Zorea, would investigate the deaths. There was no mistaking that this mess was Shin Beit's problem. More specifically, it was Avraham Shalom's problem. But Shalom was too experienced and too wily an operator to let this dismay him. He turned to his ambitious deputy, Reuven Hasak.

Of course they would have to lie about it, but successful lies take a lot of organisation. Each night Shalom and Hasak met with Yossi Ginosar, a senior Shin Beit officer who had been appointed to the Zorea Commission; they worked out how to cover up the killings, planned tactics and decided what the witnesses called to the inquiry had to say. The inquiry needed a fall guy. So they would have one—Brigadier General Mordechai would be painted as the killer. Yatom would lead a chain of Shin Beit witnesses who claimed they had seen Mordechai bludgeon both terrorists to death with his pistol. Shalom and Hasak would produce a trail of fabricated evidence and perjured testimony from agent after agent that would leave Mordechai squarely in the frame.

This was nothing new. Much later, the Landau Commission would conclude that perjured evidence and the torture of suspects was a regular part of Shin Beit procedure at the time. As Shalom's' deputy, much of the legwork in arranging all this would fall to Hasak. His job was to get his boss off the hook. Yet Hasak didn't like it: pursuing terrorists was one thing, but now he had to blacken the name of an Israeli general and war hero—a former paratrooper, dammit—to save the man whose job he should have from the results of his own dirty deeds. This stuck in Hasak's craw.

This was not Hasak's only crisis of conscience. As chance would have it, on 27 April, four days after the *New York Times* article and the day before the Zorea Commission was announced,

Hasak led a series of raids that rounded up twenty members of the Jewish Underground. They had planted bombs with timers set to detonate that morning on four buses that would be packed with Palestinians. The group had been responsible for many other atrocities.

How did Shin Beit learn about the bomb plot? The most widely accepted account is that Hasak had had an informer in the group. That was the Shin Beit pattern. Their motto is 'The Hidden Defender', their tradecraft is about setting up spy networks, getting a group of their people into the enemy camp, and then controlling or influencing it. Now, just when Shin Beit was under pressure for being anti-Arab, it was able to roll up this Jewish Underground network in a fortuitous piece of timing.

The Shin Beit arrest teams spread out silently across the West Bank and the Golan Heights on 27 April. One team also headed for the Tel Aviv feeder town of Ramat HaSharon. Their quarry was a 25-year-old student with a wife and young baby daughter—Yossi Tsuria, whose wedding Hasak had attended. At the same time as he was organising a conspiracy to produce perjured evidence in the Bus 300 inquiry to frame a Brigadier General for murder, Hasak was arresting his friend's son-in-law, propelling his friend's family into a world of pain. How to resolve this? He needed to see Yossi Tsuria, to explain what he had to do. For now, the heat was off Israel—the combination of the inquiry into the Bus 300 killings and the crackdown on Jewish terrorism convinced the *New York Times* that Israel was taking allegations of mistreatment of Arabs seriously.

When the Zorea Commission exhumed the bodies of the two hijackers, a new autopsy found both men had died from blows to the back of their heads, which had fractured their skulls. But the bodies showed evidence of other extensive trauma before death. By 24 May Zorea had made his findings. The public section of his report found that the two hijackers had been murdered by persons unknown. Behind the scenes, based on the evidence concocted by the Shin Beit witnesses, the fingers were pointing at Brigadier General Mordechai as the murderer. Zorea's findings prompted the creation of a new investigative commission, headed by state attorney Yona Blattman, to recommend whether to file criminal charges. The new investigation would take fourteen months.

In the Jewish Underground case, prosecutors had cut deals with three of the suspects. In return for a guilty plea and testimony against the others, the charges they faced were substantially down-graded. One of the three was Yossi Tsuria. The plea deal removed any claim that he had been involved in bombing Arab buses or Arab mayors. He said he renounced violence and pleaded guilty to being part of a conspiracy to blow up the Dome of the Rock site.

As part of the deal, Tsuria admitted to knowing about the plot to bomb the shrine. He also pleaded guilty to possession of weapons and aggravated fraud—in the impersonation of a military officer to obtain silencers for Uzi machine guns from army stores, as well as the special ammunition that need to be used with the silencer. He was sentenced to three years in an open prison—he would use the time to do a Master of Science at the Weizmann Institute of Science at Rehovot, south of Tel Aviv, during the day, and come back to the prison at night. He would be eligible for parole in two years.

Meanwhile Yona Blattman's new commission reopened the Bus 300 Affair, and the false evidence that Shalom and Hasak orchestrated about the death of the hijackers was more of the same. Blattman's report, when it was completed in August 1985, concluded there was suspicion of unseemly behaviour by Mordechai, five Shin Beit agents and three border policemen. The two Palestinians had been lynched, and it was Mordechai himself who had finished them off with the butt of his pistol. Mordechai was referred to a military disciplinary court, which exonerated him. A Shin Beit tribunal cleared its five agents as well. That just left the three border policemen on the hook but, after Mordechai and the Shin Beit people walked, the attorney-general withdrew the complaints against the policemen as well. It was all an implausibly happy ending. Then two months later Reuven Hasak changed the game. It was too much. Or he had just got tired of waiting.

On 14 October 1985 Hasak walked into Avraham Shalom's office and told his chief to resign. Hasak was flanked by Rafi Malka, the agency's head of operations, and Peleg Radai, the head of counterespionage and subversion. They had experienced much soul-searching over recent months. The affair had been put to bed without cost to Shin Beit's standing—they had done what had to be done. Shalom was in the clear, but now he needed to go.

Of course, Shalom didn't see it that way. He stared his three subordinates down and told them to go away. He saw it as an attempted coup, led by an ambitious deputy who wanted his job. The rebuff left Hasak hanging, while Shalom left for a five-week overseas vacation. On 29 October, with his boss out of the country, Hasak went to the prime minister, Shimon Peres.

'Reuven Hasak told me that he had some doubts about what happened in the bus affair,' Peres said later. 'He told me that there were some misdeeds in the bus affair and after it. The conversation was very short.'

In Hasak's version, the shame had just become too great. That shame did not appear to have been triggered by concerns over the murder of the two Palestinians. Nor apparently by his daily involvement and participation over more than a year in an elaborate conspiracy to commit perjury, to mislead the courts and corrupt the justice process. Nor from his role in restructuring Shin Beit, the national security service in which the Landau Commission had found perjury and fabricated evidence had become endemic. What seems unforgivable was that they had framed an innocent army officer to protect Shalom. Mordechai was a former paratrooper, just like Hasak and Malfa. How did Hasak feel after coming clean with his confession?

'He told me he'd felt as though he'd had a potato stuck in his throat, and now it had come out,' scriptwriter Motti Lerner said later, after he wrote a mini-series about the Bus 300 Affair.

Peres sat on what Hasak had told him for a week. He consulted Yitzhak Shamir, who had been prime minister when the bus was stormed. Peres concluded he had no reason to doubt Shalom's account of what had happened, but the dispute had become too big for both men to stay with Shin Beit. Peres suggested Hasak resign. Hasak left with Rafi Malka and Peleg Radai, and then Peres took no more action. The agency had lost its top echelon of management. At 47, Hasak's spying career was over.

Ultimately, it all came out in a series of leaks to journalists. The attorney-general was sacked for wanting to follow the matter up; Shalom was forced to resign, but said he had been authorised to kill the two hijackers by the prime minister, Shamir—who denied this, but said he wanted no more prying into the affair. Shalom and ten Shin Beit officers were given pardons for perjury. Ehud Yatom, the Shin Beit agent who would later tell a journalist he had crushed the Palestinians' skulls, was promoted into Rafi Malka's old job, as head of operations. Brigadier General Mordechai was exonerated and later became defence minister. No politicians were injured in the making of this story.

The members of the Jewish Underground were given light sentences, which were later discounted further. Yossi Tsuria was pardoned by President Chaim Herzog in November 1985, days after Hasak had made his approach to the prime minister. Tsuria had served nineteen months for terrorism in a day prison, but had renounced violence. Meanwhile, in his studies at the Weizmann Institute, he had developed a new expertise in cryptography.

Hasak, Malfa and Radai were left to remake their lives. With a few false starts they ended up doing what old spies all over the world do when times get hard—they started their own security business, which they called Shafran Limited. Together they had three lifetimes of experience running one of the world's most frightening and effective security agencies. They had the credentials to open almost any doors. They knew almost everything that was to be known about setting up networks of informers, running agents, vetting security, protecting assets or producing disinformation.

Meanwhile, in Britain a peculiar set of events was shaping the future of the man who would later become one of Hasak's deputies. He was a rising star at Scotland Yard called Ray Adams, and his career was about to hit a road hump.

Kent, 26 January 1985

In the cold light of a January morning Brian Boyce surveyed the wreckage of a failed operation. Hours before, his team had been on the brink of a stunning breakthrough. Fourteen months of careful work had come down to this moment of opportunity, when the final pieces of the puzzle had clicked into place and the target was tantalisingly close. It was the stuff policemen dream about, the sort of coup that makes careers. Then in five horrible minutes it had become a disaster zone.

The case had been marked from the start by violence. On 26 November 1983, six masked men broke into the Brinks-MAT warehouse near Heathrow Airport, overpowered the guards and doused them with petrol before lighting a match and threatening to set them on fire if they did not open the vault. The robbers had escaped with 2.67 tonnes of gold worth more than £26 million. It had taken police only ten days to arrest the two leaders of the gang, Micky McAvoy and Brian Robinson, but the gold disappeared without trace.

The first clue to its whereabouts came when the British treasury alerted Scotland Yard to large cash movements through a bank branch in Bristol that traced back to a precious metals trader in Kent called Kenneth Noye. By late January 1985 a Flying Squad operation under Acting Detective Chief Superintendent Brian Boyce was ready to move against the group.

Boyce had search warrants for fifteen addresses in London, Kent and Bristol ready to be issued. But the key was Noye and another man, Brian Reader. Boyce had to link the two men to each other and to the gold before the suspects realised they were under surveillance. That seemed simple enough when Reader visited Noye at his home, Hollywood Cottage, a mock Tudor mansion on eleven acres at West Kingsdown, Kent, on the evening of 26 January 1985. The grounds included a series of concrete bunkers dating from the Second World War that could hide almost anything. If only the police could be sure of finding the gold.

The surveillance operation was directed that night from Scotland Yard by Detective Chief Inspector Tony Brightwell. At 6.15 p.m. he ordered a two-man surveillance team into the grounds to see what Noye and Reader were doing. John Fordham and Neil Murphy were dressed in army camouflage clothing over diving wetsuits, together with a double layer of balaclavas, as they climbed over the wall of Hollywood Cottage and made their way through the trees beside the driveway. Light snow had fallen and it was bitterly cold as the two men settled in a position near the corner of the house. It was then that the dogs scented them.

When the two Rottweilers came barrelling out of the dark towards the two men, the covert operation descended into chaos. The two dogs were jumping at the men hidden in the shrubbery and barking.

'Dogs—hostile!' Murphy radioed, and ran for the fence. But Fordham stayed where he was, baled up by the dogs—until Kenneth Noye rushed out of the house and in a frenzied melee stabbed him eleven times.

The scene had acquired the slow-motion quality of catastrophe—the police car tearing up the driveway, the two officers inside leaping out as Noye threatened them with a shotgun: 'Fuck off or I will do you as well.' Even from the front gate Murphy heard him shout, 'I'll blow your head off.' There were three dogs now threatening the two police as they walked over to where Fordham was breathing shallowly. He whispered, 'He's done me, he's stabbed me.'

'You do understand that a police officer is dying,' they told Noye.

'He shouldn't have been on my property,' Noye said. 'I hope he fucking dies.'

Events became a blur. The ambulance arrived too late for Fordham. Even from London it was clear the night had turned into a total disaster. Aside from losing a popular officer, the investigation had collapsed. The search team found eleven gold bars wrapped in an old cloth buried in a gutter beside a garage wall at Hollywood Cottage, but the gold had already been melted down, retaining none of the distinctive marking that would link it to the Brinks-MAT robbery. The prospects of ever locating the remaining gold had become nil. This was total failure.

Kenny Noye showed no sign of panic about facing a murder charge. He had already called for photographs to be taken of his face—he was sporting a black eye and a cut on his nose and eyebrow, which he said was from the desperate struggle he had had to defend himself after a man in a balaclava jumped out of the bushes and attacked him. Noye wasn't a violent man—he wanted to make that very clear. He wasn't a killer—that was the real point—anyone who knew him well would attest to that. They should talk to Chief Superintendent Ray Adams at New Scotland Yard. He would tell them Noye was no killer. They should definitely talk to Ray.

This was playing the big card. Adams was New Scotland Yard's rising star. At 42, able and ambitious, he was already one of the most decorated policemen in Britain. Adams had had a brilliant career in SO11, the Met's criminal intelligence division, and was on track for higher things. He had made his name as a detective in the early 1970s in south London. That time had defined his character and operating style, alternately playing the charmer and the hard man. It had put him on speaking terms with many of London's major criminals. He had shown a flair for cultivating informants, which is what had drawn him towards SO11.

Noye had been one of Adams' informants since 1977, when he had been arrested by the Metropolitan Police for holding stolen property. Something told Adams that Noye would be useful and he had cultivated the relationship. Here was a man who was always ready to do a deal. In return for information Adams had done what he could from time to time to help Noye out after brushes with the law. Police officers walk a fine line between running their informants (which is necessary), socialising with them (which can be useful) and becoming their associates. The question is always: Who is running whom? Adams had his share of critics at the Met, but he also had strong supporters in the senior ranks.

DCI Brightwell had driven down to Dartford police station, where Noye was being held, to conduct one of the first interviews. When Brightwell walked into the interview room Noye immediately stood up and walked towards him, holding out his arm. He gripped Brightwell's hand in a curious manner, his thumb resting between Brightwell's second and third knuckle. Brightwell recognised it immediately as a Freemason handshake—a Tubalcain, the pass grip of a master Mason.

'I formed the opinion that here was a man that was showing out to me from . . . in hope that I was a fellow Mason, that would help him,' Brightwell said later.

The Freemason thing was a sore point. From the 1970s a succession of scandals had dogged the Met over the link between some Masonic lodges and corrupt associations with criminals, promotions for colleagues and lenient treatment of offenders who were fellow Masons. Months earlier the commissioner, Kenneth Newman, had published a new handbook for policing that underlined the impossible position faced by police officers who were Freemasons: 'A Freemason's oath holds inevitably the implication that loyalty to fellow Freemasons may supersede any other loyalty.' Despite this, a new Masonic lodge had been set up specifically for Freemasons at the Met. In the prevailing political climate, Noye's move to identify himself as a Freemason immediately suggested to Brightwell that he was seeking preferential treatment. It also raised the question whether this was the first time he had called on his Freemason links when he was in trouble.

Noye had a reputation for being close to a number of policemen.

'Extreme wealth, extreme visible wealth,' was Brightwell's perception. Superintendent Nick Biddiss, who would investigate Noye a decade later in connection with a road rage case, had a similar view of him: 'He has a reputation whereby, because of his wealth, he can influence and corrupt police officers.'

Noye had joined the Hammersmith Freemasons Lodge in West London in 1977. The lodge had a large number of police members and Noye's admission was reportedly proposed and seconded by policemen. By the mid 1980s he had risen to be master of the lodge. For the most part, Noye had clammed up after his suggestion the Met officers should talk to Adams. Then Noye asked to see the head of the investigation, Brian Boyce. He had something important to say. Boyce showed up several hours later with a DCI. But Noye wanted to speak with Boyce alone.

Brian Boyce had been to see Fordham's widow and three children. He wasn't a stranger to violence. He had been a soldier in Cyprus chasing EOKA terrorists before he joined the Met. But the meeting affected him deeply. He had given the assurance that policemen always give to grieving relatives—they would bring those responsible to justice. Now, walking into the interview room in Kent, Boyce had to find a way of making that promise count.

Brightwell had already briefed Boyce on his interrogation and told him about Noye's claim that Chief Superintendent Adams would vouch for him. How was Boyce going to play it? What could be extracted from this debacle? What did he have to lose? Boyce walked directly up to Noye, nodded his head in recognition and gripped Noye's hand firmly with the familiar clasp of a Masonic handshake.

Los Angeles and London, 1985

For Rupert Murdoch, it was showtime. Thirty-two years after he had taken control of News Corporation, he used that company to make a spectacular bet. During a one-week period he agreed to buy half of a Hollywood movie studio, Twentieth Century Fox, for $250 million and then set up a deal, which would be announced weeks later, to buy John Kluge's Metromedia chain of television stations for $1.55 billion. Within six months he had bought the other half of Twentieth Century Fox as well, as a base to launch the Fox television network. In order to qualify to own an American television network, he would take out American citizenship on 16 September. The structure had its share of smoke and mirrors: while he was telling the Federal Communications Commission that he personally owned and controlled the Fox television stations, he was telling the US Securities and Exchange Commission that it was News Corporation, the Australian company, that had economic control of the stations.

Murdoch has never believed in small gambles. At the same time as he was loading News Corporation with astronomical debt, he was making preparations to move News International newspapers from Fleet Street in London to a new plant he was building at Wapping. This high-risk move would mean bypassing the printers from the Society of Graphical and Allied Trades, who currently produced his newspapers, and hiring instead members of the electricians' union. The move would cut £100 million a year from his costs, but it would trigger a year of violent picket lines outside the new site when it opened in January 1986.

London, October 1985

Brian Boyce was furious. Neil Murphy was livid. In the same month that Reuven Hasak was having his confrontation with Prime Minister Peres, Kenneth Noye's trial concluded. After twelve and a half hours of deliberations the jury found Noye not guilty of murdering Murphy's partner, John Fordham. In the end only Noye knew what had passed between himself and Fordham that night. He said it was self-defence—he had panicked at the sight of the masked man in the shadows, struggled with him and found himself fighting for his life.

Noye's freedom, though, was shortlived. He was sentenced to fourteen years prison for laundering the Brinks-MAT gold. He served only eight years but then, two years after he was released, he killed again, stabbing Stephen Cameron during a road-rage fight at an interchange near Swanley, Kent, in front of Cameron's seventeen-year-old girlfriend.

Brian Boyce, however, wasn't finished with the Noye case. There was the private conversation he had had with Noye at Dartford police station. It had come up at the trial. Back in the interview room the accused had looked keenly at Boyce; Noye's face had been a mixture of relief and caution after the detective chief superintendent's Masonic handshake. Boyce knew a lot of Freemasons in the Met—knew them to be good conscientious policemen. But what did Noye expect from a fellow Mason? To begin with, Noye circled around for a bit, always smooth. He wasn't a violent man. Yes, he had panicked and acted out of character. He was shattered at the outcome—he could feel for Fordham's widow and his children; he wanted to set up some sort of trust or foundation for them. And what about Acting Detective

Chief Superintendent Boyce then—had he ever thought of his retirement? Noye was affability itself: 'I can put a million quid into any bank account you want anywhere in the world, it's completely untraceable. It's yours if you make sure I don't go to prison.' Boyce told him he was wasting his time and walked out.

The exchange came out in the murder trial—Noye said it was Boyce who had asked him for a bribe. Boyce spent a lot of time thinking about it after Noye was acquitted. He had a burning resentment that Noye had killed a policeman and got away with it. In his view the man was filth, as was anyone who worked with him. If nothing else, it showed a serious lack of judgement on the part of any policeman who associated with him. Was Detective Chief Superintendent Ray Adams a Freemason, Boyce wondered. Had he taken money from Noye in the past?

Except that it was no longer DCS Adams. By early 1987 it was Commander Ray Adams, head of SO11, the man in charge of the Met's entire criminal intelligence division. At 44 he was the second youngest commander appointed in the history of the Met. To put the newly appointed SO11 chief under investigation would be an extraordinary step because, while Noye's actions raised questions about Adams' judgement, there was no evidence of corruption. And broader concerns were being raised at this time about corruption at the Met.

On 10 March 1987, Daniel Morgan, a former policeman turned private investigator, was found dead beside his BMW in the car park of the Golden Lion pub in south London. He had been battered to death with an axe. In a statement later submitted to the police, an unidentified witness said that, a week before he died, Daniel Morgan had said he was taking a story to a newspaper exposing police corruption. The following month the Met's anti-corruption squad, CIB2, opened an unrelated investigation of Ray Adams when, in early 1987, a petty criminal who had been picked up by police made sensational claims to the Police

Complaints Authority that Adams and others had taken bribes and had improper relations with criminal informants, including Kenny Noye.

The investigation began disastrously. CIB2 targeted the Masonic links between Adams and Noye by interrogating a member of the team that had worked on the Brinks-MAT case. DC Alan Holmes, a burly, no-nonsense ex-footballer, was known to be the head of Lodge No. 7114, the Manor of Bensham. He was also known to be close to Adams. In the course of an all-day grilling, Holmes apparently was told that CIB2 had a tape recording of Holmes talking about corrupt acts by fellow officers. There was no evidence that Holmes himself had been corrupt, it was later reported, but his indiscreet comments were said to have incriminated fellow Freemasons.

As it was subsequently reported in the press, Holmes came home deeply distressed, believing that he had betrayed a former friend. He felt it placed him in an impossible position. Several days later he shot himself in the back garden of his home in Shirley, Surrey.

His death became a public scandal. Whatever suspicions might have been held about Holmes when he was alive, the line for public consumption was now clear: Holmes had died without a shadow on his name. The new commissioner made a public statement that Holmes had never been under suspicion; it was Ray Adams who was under investigation. This revelation compromised the CIB2 investigation, and even more so when the *News of the World* claimed there had never been any tape and that the allegations put to Holmes were merely a bluff. This also put Adams in a hard place. How does the head of criminal intelligence operate when he himself is under suspicion?

The investigation ground on for years and in the meantime Adams was transferred to the Met's Inspectorate. On 22 January 1990 the Police Complaints Authority called it a day. The final report of its investigation into the corruption allegations involving Ray Adams and Kenny Noye ran to more than 44 volumes of documents, but ultimately the Director of Public Prosecutions announced there was no evidence to support charges against Mr Adams or any of the other officers under investigation. No disciplinary action was taken. Adams said with considerable feeling that he always knew it would come to nothing: 'There is no complaint from me despite the pain such an inquiry inflicts on a person. But I always knew what the outcome would be—I wouldn't have been trusted with the very sensitive jobs I have been otherwise.'

So Adams was cleared, but the investigation had taken its toll. In hindsight his relationship with Noye seemed poor judgement. He was no longer the bright young Met commander on the way up. Adams had the political skills to manage the next step up the pole, but his moment had passed.

In the fallout from John Fordham's death at Hollywood Cottage, that dark night five years before, Ray Adams had been the chief casualty. He would never make it to commissioner. But the Metropolitan Police was not the only organisation that would value his skill set.

Saint Martin, June 1986

Gilles Kaehlin's star began to fade as his patron, Françis de Grossouvre, was squeezed out of power. In 1983 a new Élysée anti-terrorism unit was established. The new unit's brief was to protect the president, though in reality much of their work would involve tapping the phones of almost anyone who could remotely be a threat to Mitterand—or, more to the point, who might be a critic.

Kaehlin by now was savagely out of favour. He was speedily removed from his duties with Mitterrand's daughter. Inevitably, a wire tap was placed on his home phone in Paris. By 1994 he had been exiled to the Caribbean to run the police post at the airport and the little fishing port of Saint Martin. This didn't turn out so well. In two years he managed to enrage the local civil service, its business leaders, the drug cartels that operated out of the island, and the general populace. In June 1986 a police operation led by Kaehlin triggered a riot and the enraged crowd proceeded to burn his house down. They threw his car into the harbour and put the police under siege. When Paris mounted an emergency repatriation to get Kaehlin off the island, the crowd threw rocks at the plane's windscreen. He was that sort of policeman.

London, November 1988

By the end of 1988, Alan Guggenheim had lived in America for almost seven years. He found it suited him. He had taken out American citizenship and built up a prosperous business consultancy. He would shortly be headhunted by the Republican Party to stand for the California state legislature—though he would lose the primary. In Israel, Reuven Hasak was taking a hand in politics as well, acting as campaign manager for Teddy Kollek's re-election campaign as mayor of Jerusalem. Yossi Tsuria had a new job with a technology company. Ray Adams was waiting on the result of the ongoing police investigation of his links with underworld figures—it would be another year before he was exonerated. Kaehlin was back in Paris, given another dead-end job. What trouble could he possibly make investigating financial crime?

The five men were following very different career trajectories. Only Guggenheim and Tsuria knew anything about technology. The sole thing that linked them, the single feature that they shared, was that their past histories had brought them close to violence and terror—albeit reluctantly in Alan Guggenheim's case, and professionally in the cases of Adams, Hasak and Kaehlin. That would remain the only thing that ever linked them, if not for a telephone call that Rupert Murdoch made on 9 November 1988. From that point, the circle began closing.

It was the kind of call that is uncomfortable for anyone in Murdoch's empire, the call that Rupert makes when he is in a spot of bother and he is reaching out to ask for a little help. Actually help is far too kind a word. It's Rupert Murdoch's 'Beam me up Scotty' call: Get me out of this mess—now.

Murdoch was calling Bruce Hundertmark, a former Australian diplomat turned entrepreneur, whom he had been using as his technology consultant since early 1987. Or rather, one of his technology consultants. Murdoch called Hundertmark at 5 p.m. on 9 November to ask him to come to a meeting at News International's Wapping site at 10.30 the next morning. A technical group from Thomson Consumer Electronics, the renowned innovative powerhouse based in Paris, was coming over to make a presentation.

Five months earlier, on 8 June 1988, Murdoch had stunned British media with the announcement that News would launch a new free-to-air satellite broadcaster called Sky Television, based on the old Sky Channel operation he had taken over back in 1983 and which broadcast across Europe.

Satellite broadcasting requires a satellite in stationary orbit overhead. But satellites need room in space to avoid interfering with each other. What this means is that there are a limited number of orbital slots allocated between countries. In December 1986 the British government had awarded the British orbital slot, along with a fifteen-year satellite broadcasting licence, to British Satellite Broadcasting (a venture set up by Granada Television, Pearson, Virgin and Anglia Television). The BSB technology would be state-of-the-art, but it took until early 1990 to build the new system from scratch, to launch two satellites to carry the signal, and to design and build receivers for the high-power digital signal. Murdoch jumped the gun by promising to use old PAL technology and leasing transponders on a new Astra satellite in the Luxembourg orbital slot, so as to get his new operation up and running within eight months. Sky Television would be a new-age version of the old pirate radio ships that had once challenged the cosy British radio establishment; this was just the sort of audacious play Murdoch loved.

But five months after his announcement Murdoch hit a snag. In his mind Sky was always going to be a free-to-air broadcast. The problem was that while Sky's target audience was in Britain, the satellite signal could be picked up right across Europe by anyone with the appropriate satellite dish and receiver box. The movie and television industries make their money out of selling rights in as many territorial markets as they can. Having material available for free on Sky would reduce their potential income from selling the same films and programming elsewhere in Europe. Although Sky would be theoretically selling British rights to its programs, in effect it would be selling trans-European rights.

In the first week of November, BSB took out a full-page ad in *Variety* magazine. With a skull and crossbones flag, it was headed, 'Dear Hollywood, Don't let Rupert feed your product to the pirates.' In the United States, whenever a pay TV system had been comprehensively pirated—allowing viewers to access these channels by purchasing cheap access cards off the pirates—it was estimated the pirates could earn three times as much as the pay TV company that broadcast the signal. In turn this meant that Hollywood studios earned much less from their films because what they charged pay TV was proportional to their paid subscriber numbers. So they were naturally reluctant to lease their product to someone who had insecure systems—let alone to someone who was providing a free-to-air broadcast across an entire continent.

Suddenly Murdoch was facing a full-blown crisis: clearly he was unable to buy quality programming for his channels unless he turned Sky into a pay TV service. In order to do that, he needed some way to encrypt Sky's signal. But the PAL technology he was using was so old and outdated that no one had ever bothered to devise an encryption system for it.

Much was riding on the emergency meeting Murdoch had called with the Thomson Consumer Electronics' technical team for 10 November. What he needed first of all was to find a way to scramble the Sky television picture. Murdoch has made his fortune from shrewd bets on technology but, outside of knowing every detail of how a printing press works, he has little interest in technical subjects. In fact Rupert Murdoch doesn't get technology at any level. In his heart of hearts lurks a cast-iron Luddite. But he is better at adapting to change, at seeing opportunity and transforming that opportunity into advantage, than almost anyone on the planet. Part of his genius is a willingness to be wooed by new people, by new ideas. But how had it got to the point where he actually had to try and *understand* this stuff? He was in for some trying moments as he bent his mind to what the Thomson people were saying.

The solution Thomson proposed went like this. Under the PAL system, the picture is made up of 625 lines. What Thomson suggested was to cut each of those lines into two pieces, but to make the cut at a different point along each line. There were 256 places along each line where such a cut could be made, but the choice of where would be relatively random. Once the line had been cut, the two bits would be switched around (they called it 'rotating the line'). One way of understanding how this would work is by using some lines of text:

> as a cloud I wandered lonely
> and hills, that floats on high o'er vales
> once I saw a crowd, When all at
> golden daffodils; A host, of

Natty, isn't it?

I'm all for wandering lonely, but this fixation with all things flowery is unhealthy. As a very young journalist I once took this same sort of approach when subediting the astrology column. My thinking was that it surely wasn't possible to make the text any more obtuse and meaningless than the way that our astro-star voyager had written it. I thought that randomly chopping the lines up changed it for the better. My editor, ever the traditionalist, thought otherwise and relieved me of astrology duties immediately, which proved satisfactory to all parties.

Of course if you are a dyed-in-the-wool Wordsworth fancier, you would want to unscramble these lines. In that case you would need to have a little instruction set after each stanza that would tell you where each line needed to be switched around. It would tell you that the first line should start with the fourth word, so that it read: 'I wandered lonely as a cloud.' The second line must start with the third word; the third line the sixth word; and so on. If you feed in the instruction set, the poem would be back just as it was.

It's a little more complicated with a television picture, but it's the same principle. Each PAL picture frame has 625 lines to mix up, and there are 25 frames per second, which means you end up with a completely chaotic picture. And the key to unscrambling it is that, embedded in the videostreaming there are instruction sets explaining how to unscramble each line. But this is where the system that the Thomson executives outlined to Rupert Murdoch fell down.

Yes, it was a wonderfully scrambled picture, but the thing about pay TV is that you need some way to distinguish between the people who are paying customers and the rest of the great unwashed. As it was, anyone who could detect the instruction set in the scrambled signal could unscramble it, so the instruction set needed to be encrypted. That one flaw would make the whole system insecure, Hundertmark explained to his boss. But there was good news because a little company in Israel that Hundertmark had set up for Rupert nine months earlier had developed a better way of doing it. It was called News Datacom, and it could provide that missing part of the security system by using a smartcard.

'Don't talk to me about fucking smartcards,' Murdoch said. 'You're interested in the technology—I'm only interested in the result. There *must* be satisfactory pay TV systems existing already in the world without you introducing your News Datacom.'

He had a point. No one at News was the least bit interested in the little technology start-up Hundertmark had talked Murdoch into bankrolling nine months before. The whole premise of Sky was to use off-the-shelf technology as a way to launch it a year before BSB could begin transmitting. But in the days that followed it became clear that there was no quick fix for Sky anywhere in the world. Hundertmark kept promising to get a combined News Datacom and Thomson Consumer Electronics system up and running in six months, which was really one of those crazy brave kinds of commitments. In the end Murdoch had little choice but to sign up for it. He committed the huge gamble on Sky, the future of his whole empire, on the belief that Hundertmark and News Datacom could come through with the goods with this wacky scheme.

Now here's the thing about keeping secrets. It's easier to make them than to unmake them. In 1977 three professors at the Massachusetts Institute of Technology—Ronald Rivest, Adi Shamir and Leonard Adleman—changed the way most codes work. Their system is an algorithm called RSA, after their initials, and it has two parts. There is a key to encode a message (which is called the public key), and a separate key (called the private key) that decodes the message. So if someone wants to send a secret message to you, you can give them your public key. Actually you can give your key to anyone—the fraud squad, the tax man, your least favourite Telly Tubby, that guy at work who wants your job, whoever. They can use your public key to encrypt a message to you, but that's all that they can do. Once the message is encrypted with your public key, the only person who can decode it is you, using your private key.

It's one of those inside-out things that makes it so delicious. You can be in as public a space as you like, and yet your secret is safe. But it took a little while to work out just how revolutionary this was. It's perfect for two computers who want to talk to each other. And it's ideal for banking, which is where Hundertmark saw the most opportunity.

In 1987 Hundertmark was interested in encryption. Murdoch had given him a roving brief to look out for ideas worth putting some money into, and Hundertmark remembered that he had met Adi Shamir, one of the original three who developed RSA, several years before. Shamir had returned to Israel to work at the Weizmann Institute of Science. Hundertmark approached Shamir and proposed that News Corporation set up a company together with the Weizmann Institute's commercial arm, the Yeda Research and Development Company, to exploit Shamir's discoveries.

Shamir had no commercial experience and little practical interest—at the first meeting to discuss the commercial possibilities Shamir delivered a formal three-hour lecture on encryption, public-key techniques and identification procedures based on the Fiat-Shamir algorithm, which he had developed with another Israeli mathematician, Dr Amos Fiat. It really wasn't very promising. But, after surviving a series of tortuous negotiations, by February 1998 Hundertmark had hammered out a corporate structure that saw News Corporation investing $3.6 million for a 60 per cent stake in the new venture, News Data Security Products Limited. For tax reasons it was incorporated as an offshore British company in Hong Kong. It had an Israeli subsidiary, News Datacom Research.

Everything had to be set up from scratch. In the course of the wheeling and dealing, an American-Israeli entrepreneur called Michael Clinger had attached himself to the venture. He had experience in taking high-tech ventures public, having successfully launched an IPO in the United States for a company selling surgical lasers. At a breakfast meeting in August 1987 at the King David Hotel in Jerusalem, Hundertmark was introduced to Leo Krieger, an accountant he engaged as financial officer. Krieger, it turned out, was an old friend of Clinger's.

On 15 December 1987 Hundertmark and Clinger were in Tel Aviv with Shamir and Itzhak Kohlberg, the head of Yeda Research and Development, to interview applicants for positions in the new company. Two management teams were applying. One group was ex-military personnel, while the other was headed by Dr Dov Rubin, a businessman with experience in other technology start-ups. It was Rubin's group that was selected. Rubin was a devout man, as were a surprising number of the management group. In the years that followed the level of religious observance at News Datacom would be unusual enough to prompt comments in the Israeli media.

It was never quite clear why Rupert Murdoch had agreed to set up a data encryption operation in the first place. Part of the appeal seemed to be that he liked the idea of doing something in Israel. Certainly no one else at News Corporation showed the slightest interest.

Undaunted, Hundertmark and Clinger were looking for potential users for News Datacom technology. The strongest interest came from an Iraqi businessman working for the Libyan government, a Dr Ihsan Barbouti, who was intrigued by the encryption technology and anxious to provide finance and take an equity stake in the business. Barbouti would in time become better known to Western intelligence agencies as the architect of Libyan president Moammar Gadhafi's chemical weapons plant in Rabta, diligently crisscrossing Europe and North America buying up ingredients for weapons of mass destruction. You can see why he would want to keep secrets. Barbouti died in 1991; there is speculation that he was assassinated by the Mossad.

A more realistic prospect for taking advantage of News Datacom's expertise was Reuters. And here Hundertmark came across the first warning signs of trouble. Kohlberg, the head of Yeda Research, which held a 20 per cent stake in News Datacom, called Hundertmark in London on 10 March 1988 and said he had been checking Michael Clinger's background. The two men arranged a confidential meeting at the Sheraton Hotel in Jerusalem, where Kohlberg told Hundertmark that Clinger for some reason was not able to enter the United States, though he held a US passport and had lived there for most of his life. Clinger was the logical person to send to the United States to visit Reuters to press their case, but he resolutely refused to do so. Several weeks later, when Hundertmark raised the US Reuters trip with him, Clinger casually asked if another NDS exec could handle it.

This was troubling because Clinger had become in effect the man running the Israeli operations of News Datacom. Seven months later a former partner of Clinger's gave Hundertmark court transcripts of a US lawsuit the Securities and Exchange Commission had brought against Clinger in July 1987, charging him with defrauding investors, falsifying accounts and insider trading. At that time Hundertmark had been busy working with him setting up News Datacom. Clinger had settled the case on a no-blame basis by agreeing to pay back $810,600 in illegal profits. All this would have then been water under the bridge, but Clinger never paid the fine. Instead he fled the country.

Hundertmark says he passed the transcripts to News International's lawyer, Geoffrey Richards at Farrer & Co, on 9 November. Hundertmark's feeling was that News Datacom appeared to have no cause for action against Clinger but he should remain under review. The matter was swept away because it was that afternoon when Rupert Murdoch phoned Hundertmark to tell him about his problems with Sky, and to ask him to attend the Thomson briefing the next day.

For more than a year Hundertmark had been looking for a use for this encryption technology. Now the penny dropped. Pay

TV was the perfect platform for News Datacom. Within days, Adi Shamir had developed a simple application to encode the Sky signal, which was broadcast from the Astra satellite. Sky would use the Thomson system to scramble the picture it broadcast. The signal would be picked up by each Sky subscriber's 24-inch satellite dish and fed into their set-top box. The video signal from the satellite would be seeded with encoded packages that would tell the set-top box how to unscramble the picture. But the set-top box would not contain within it the means to open those encoded packages. Instead, Sky subscribers would insert a News Datacom smartcard with a microchip mounted on it into the set-top box.

The smartcard would control access to the Sky signal by doing two things. First, it would check that this was a legitimate paying subscriber and it would inform the box that this was a legitimate News Datacom smartcard. Second, it would then instruct the set-top box on how to unscramble the picture. And that was the problem solved. The odds were about a million to one against anyone cracking the encryption algorithm that Shamir had provided to the News Datacom smartcard. In this system, all the secrets were in the smartcard. If, by some miracle, pirates and hackers did break the code, Sky could just issue a new smartcard with a different code on it.

While Adi Shamir developed the conditional access system that News Datacom would use, the programming of the huge headends that would run the system for Sky from its subscriber base in Scotland would be done by the young man who had just been appointed News Datacom's chief technical officer. He had just finished his masters degree at the Weizmann Institute, studying under Adi Shamir and, like many of his new colleagues at News Datacom, he was Haredi—ultra-Orthodox and a religious nationalist. His name was Yossi Tsuria.

Yossi and the News Datacom team would do wonders in setting up this entirely new technology system for Sky. It was a remarkable achievement, but it would end in tears and disaster. And when it did, Rupert Murdoch would respond by hiring his own private spy agency. Rupert's ex-policemen and security officers and former spies would be put on a collision course with another group of young men who came from backgrounds completely alien to Murdoch's hunters. They were hackers, and sometimes pirates. The clash of cultures would turn ugly.

PART 2

The Hackers

He wasn't a criminal, he wasn't a lowlife. He was a geek, he was a nerd, somebody that was very talented, and I thought maybe we could work him into our organisation and control his . . . his . . . his hobby.

John Norris, about Chris Tarnovsky

San Diego, 27 October 2009

Half an hour out of San Diego I'm finding Karen Jacobsen a little irksome. I'm not blaming her. I could never have come this far without her. No, it's me. Right now the relationship isn't working. I want to move on, but Karen's stuck in the past. Fixated on that last unfortunate corner.

No one was to blame. No paint lost—so what's the problem? But it seemed to throw her. She didn't actually say, 'You stupid, *stupid* Australian'. But now she tells me she's recalculating. I think she's a very recalculating sort of woman.

It was the car hire people who introduced us. At the counter in the huge Hertz lot at Los Angeles International Airport. I said I needed a guide to get me down into the backcountry north of San Diego. So they gave me Karen, the infallible in-car companion. She came only with the Lincoln Town Car. Five minutes later I pulled out of the airport—my first time driving in the United States—on the wrong side of the road, at the wheel of this smooth black beast.

Karen knows the drill with foreign tourists. I happen to know she's actually Australian—a Queensland girl from Mackay on the Sugar Coast. Back in 2002 she was living in New York when her agent emailed her with a fabulous job offer. The good folk at Global Positioning Systems needed someone with just her tonal range and timbre to record 50 hours of driving instructions, to cover every possible highway crisis and navigational debacle that people who use satellite navigation systems can steer their way into, with or without the aid of the internal combustion engine ('Proceed along twenty-lane freeway, try to turn left *when you can*'). Ever since, she's been there for us.

Our relationship began well enough, as she directed me from the Hertz lot onto West Century Boulevard, then onto Route 405, the San Diego Freeway, which eventually feeds into Route 5 heading south. Down near Carlsbad she eased me off to the left onto Ronald Packard Parkway, and this is where things got a little sticky.

I was looking for the turn-off for a little town with a nice country club and views of the hills. Karen began telling me about the turn ten miles off. She updated as we got nearer, the warnings coming closer and closer until, at the very end, I knew that if she had had a siren she would have been sounding it. But, somehow, when I came to make that last-minute manoeuvre, I saw two possible ways to turn and I made the wrong choice.

She tells me tersely she is recalculating, which means the helpful little map of the streets around me suddenly disappears. In a 2010 media interview the real Karen said 'recalculating' was her favourite word: 'In your life you can always stop and recalculate and start all over again.' Which is a nice thought, only now I'm heading off into the unknown at 50 miles an hour, guided only by a voice in a little black box that's having a hissy fit. When she comes back to me a minute or so later, I've travelled several miles more. She just tells me to make my way back to where I was. She doesn't want to talk about it.

Two things emerge at this point. First, I'm really crap with tech stuff. That will become more apparent later. Second,

Karen Jacobsen is a paradigm for our whole culture's fumbling relationship with technology. It's our best friend: it promises us everything, to take us to the stars. But where exactly will we end up?

I'm in south California chasing a story that has tantalised me for a decade and a half. It is driven by an issue at the heart of the modern experience of technology: How can we keep our secrets? The fears, the passions and the violence that this question provokes is defined most clearly by the figure that threatens our secrets most—the hacker. That figure is portrayed alternately as a subversive activist or as a threatening foreign presence in our networks. More comfortingly, Hollywood traditionally treats the hacker as its favourite comic sub-character: overweight, poor social skills, incurably dweebish, distinguished by a fondness for pizza, beer and fart jokes. The hacker is the necessary high-tech accessory to enable the hero to breach the impenetrable fortress or find that missing name in the locked file part. But the hacker is no more than this in Hollywood.

In the northern autumn of 2009, a series of scandals that will radically change our perception of the hacker are simmering. While I am failing in my little tussle with Californian geography, WikiLeaks founder Julian Assange is flitting between Britain, Denmark, Iceland and Malaysia, fighting a secret UK court ban on a report about a toxic dumping disaster on the Ivory Coast that has hospitalised up to 100,000 people. In June, Assange picked up Amnesty International's 2009 New Media award for exposing hundreds of secret assassinations in Kenya. It's almost two decades since he was the target of an Australian Federal Police investigation into the Melbourne hacking underground and now he's almost a respectable figure, though that won't last long. October is also the month that Private First Class Bradley Manning, newly transferred to Iraq, arrives at Contingency Operating Station Hammer near Baghdad, where he has access from his workstation to the

Secret Internet Protocol Router Network as well as a mountain of classified US diplomatic cables.

In London, Rupert Murdoch's News International was still insisting that there was no evidence of telephone hacking by *News of the World* journalists beyond the regrettable incidents that led to its former royal editor, Clive Goodman, and private detective Glenn Mulcaire being jailed nearly three years earlier for hacking into the voicemail of members of the Royal Family. In hindsight News International's cries of innocence would prove a little disingenuous.

In Detroit, News Corporation's marketing arm was stoutly denying that it had repeatedly broken into the computer systems of a rival company as part of a strategy to drive the company out of business, despite testimony from a former executive who, according to News America, had stolen a confidential hard drive when he left their employment. Three months later, and days before jury selection in Michigan, News would quietly settle this case for $500 million. Naturally it proceeded to sue its former executive who had turned whistleblower, dunning him into bankruptcy for breach of confidence; however, in 2011 the courts would decide against the company because the non-disclosure agreement it had him sign was written in the wrong verb tense.

A common feature in these three storylines—WikiLeaks, the telephone hacking and the industrial espionage case in Detroit— was the anger and consternation that was the universal response from those who had been the subject of hackers, and the automatic resort to intelligence services, to police, to private security groups and, of course, to lawyers that the hacking threat triggers. To write about hackers is also to write about the people who hunt them. It is to plunge into the world of intelligence operatives—spies and ex-spies, former policemen and agents, the cloak-and-dagger world that is never far from the surface of corporate security.

Employing such men and women is not a neutral, stand-alone act. They change the lives of the people they pursue, and they also affect those who employ them. If an intelligence operative will do anything for his country, what will he do for his company? Corporate culture has changed merely by the need to ask that question.

The other disturbing feature of the hacking narratives that were unfolding in 2009 was that two out of the three involved arms of Rupert Murdoch's News Corporation. And here I was, lost in the feeder towns north of San Diego, on the trail of a much heftier hacking scandal. This was no hapless bugging of celebrities, or hacking into gritty industrial marketing businesses. It was corporate spying on the high wire. No less than three separate billion-dollar lawsuits had spun off this saga, making it arguably the biggest industrial espionage case in history. Almost every major satellite broadcaster in the world had accused the Murdoch empire of breaking the law to cripple its rivals. In the endless debate about the future of the communication economy—the doomed cashflow models that drive mainstream media, the battles for shrinking market share—this was the dark side. This was the side of the media business where there were no rules—high-stakes corporate cybercrime, the bleak face of a truly subversive future. The man at the centre of this decade-long legal firestorm lives in a quiet street a dozen or so turns off the Ronald Packard Parkway. Actually it feels like several hundred turns by the time I've made my peace with Karen Jacobsen, found a motel, and arranged a meeting. But finally here he is, limping into Starbucks. And what am I expecting? A Hollywood cyber nerd? A monster? A criminal genius? 'Von Rat', as he once liked to call himself? Before that, he was 'biggun', or just 'Von'.

This is the most confusing part of this mixed-up day, because Chris Tarnovsky is none of these things. He's breezy, he's excited, he's so damn likeable. His zest for whatever he is working on is infectious. Starbucks was his suggestion, his home turf, and he deftly orders a complicated beverage that includes everything except coffee. He has ADHD, which means he tightly monitors the coffee breaks. He's got a caffeine schedule. He's still hobbling after breaking his tibia and fibula in a motocross accident four months before. He shows me his other motocross war wounds— the fractured femur, the shattered wrist, broken collarbone. By my count Chris has damaged himself severely on his bike every other year since 2001, when he stopped working undercover. It's as if he needs the adrenaline rush.

He has recently separated from his Belgian wife, Sylvie, after eighteen years together. He blames the split on an accident two years before, when her nephew was killed by a stranger clowning about in a parking lot at a motocross park. He paints a lightning portrait of this stranger: 'Fatso. Kid's bike. Pulling wheelies. He can't pull a wheelie, so he's going . . . he's going fast, trying to make the wheel go up.' Then a quick sketch of the collision itself: 'This big hippo guy . . . hippopotamus, like 300 pounds [140 kilograms], probably. He . . . hit him. Killed him. He knocked him to the ground so hard it cut the oxygen to his brain off. So his brain really . . . swollen . . .'

And that's the first 30 seconds of our conversation.

'You know, it's kind of, you know it's been hard . . . it's been . . . That lawsuit was tough. It's been . . . lawyers and crap. You know, I don't hack anything, I analyse them.'

Chris is barely with me. He is supposed to be visiting one of the children of his new girlfriend in hospital. In the course of 70 minutes he receives a series of calls asking where he is. Clients are calling as well, about the consulting work he does.

It's a noisy environment. And there's something going on with a woman who walks in halfway through—a lot of eye contact. Ten minutes later she comes across, looks at him and borrows my pen.

Chris is working on three or four conversations or thought processes at any one time. And he is compelling in each of them: 'I'm the mix of an introvert and an extrovert. I don't mind makin' like—hey! You know . . . for me to go up and talk to a girl. I'm a little shy. For myself. You know?'

I nod sympathetically. My first thought is: How much of what he is saying can I believe? It's the undercover thing—the years he spent living as 'Mike George'. He betrayed his friends, he helped have people sent to prison—sometimes at personal risk to himself. He lived with stories within stories. He tells me his life history and it sounds familiar until I realise I've read it all in the transcripts of the trial the year before. Of course the story is the same, but it seems too close. It comes out like a legend he has fashioned. Two years before, he was fired for lying to his employer. How did he live with it all?

'I'm a weird person from that perspective, I think, because like . . . I could wake up in my sleep to "Mike". You know, if you say "Mike! Mike!" And I'd wake right up. It's . . . it's weird. It's like the flick of a switch.

'My wife told me one time, she was like, "That's scary, you live like a double life, and you lie with such a straight face, you know, about it." And she was like, "How do I know you're not lying to me about . . . whatever?" And then I was like, "Well I can't lie to you without laughing." I mean, I can't. I can't tell a lie without laughing.'

And that's the endearing part about Chris Tarnovsky, his note of amused wonder. Whatever dreadful things he has done, or hasn't done, he will look you in the eye with an infectious grin that says, 'Hey look at me! Look at this cool thing that I'm doing!' It's disarming.

John Norris, Chris's formidable supervisor when he worked for NDS Ltd, lives 25 kilometres south of where we are sitting. Norris is genuinely scary, but Chris won't tell me the address.

'He's still with NDS—they never talk. When you actually meet him, ah, he has a very big heart, very nice guy. Very gentleman, very polite. Totally opposite of what you think he is.'

What about the story of Norris threatening to stuff people into the boot of his car, kidnap them and take them across the Mexican border?

'Did John say it? I don't know. It would be funny. I can picture him. I have no idea. No idea,' Chris laughs. 'But I mean he's against . . . these guys were hurting NDS pretty bad. I mean I give NDS credit—they're the only ones in the world that people fear.'

I ask him about the people who pursued him. He's cool with Alan Guggenheim, because he still hopes Alan will give him a job.

'I've met him and stuff, and we talk all the time—he's on Skype—to each other. He's a good guy.'

Ray Adams?

'I always found him kind of creepy.'

Gilles Kaehlin he first met in a London strip club.

I'm hoping Chris will show me the home lab where he works. But it doesn't come up. I don't think he wants to go there. I mention the police raid on his house, but he corrects me. There was no raid—a couple of customs people wanted to talk to him. I don't mention that I cruised past his house an hour earlier. I had made my peace with Karen Jacobsen, who led me deftly through the back roads into the dry foothills, ending up in a built-up street with a cluster of new houses. I drove past surreptitiously a couple of times. At least as surreptitiously as is possible in a black Lincoln Town Car, in full daylight, with the driver taking photos as he manoeuvres the car around at the end of an exposed cul de sac. I was completely invisible.

The lab is important because this kind of hacking is not about computers. It's about microchips—those tiny mini-computers that sit on strips of plastic and open your bank account or your gates, that sit in your passport or your phone. The things that everyone is betting the future on. Online commerce can only go so far without the bankcards, the debit cards, the digital wallets that will be the key to who we are, what we are, and what we can do. These smart-cards are hugely sophisticated devices, guarding their secrets—and your security—in layers of encryption and stealth architecture.

Thousands of banks around the world will attest that these cards are secure—those funds of yours that they are protecting are as safe as it's possible to be. But as Chris and a handful of smartcard hackers around the world will tell you, that's not saying much. How safe are these cards? Think of the comfort of being guarded by a couple of wet biscuits.

'I mean there's not a smartcard today that I haven't analysed. Well, there's never been a job I've taken on that I didn't finish. Which means I successfully analysed it. Which means I've pulled every part of the code inside it. I've never found a smartcard that I couldn't hack,' he tells me.

It's an aside, really. He's sweating on a call. He lets one from AT&T go to voicemail; but he's hanging out for one from Infineon Technologies, the big smartcard manufacturer. He's just cracked the new 'unhackable' Infineon chip and he thinks that must be worth something to Infineon—maybe seven figures as a consult-ancy fee. Infineon doesn't seem to value that he could get a million from selling the hack, no problem. Not that he does that stuff. (It turns out that Infineon never comes to the party. Three months later, he announces at a Black Hat hackers' conference that the Infineon chip has been broken. Infineon has some problems.)

Chris Tarnovksy, setting out to earn a million dollars a year as a security consultant, is a world away from where it all started. Back then it was all much, much more personal. On the hacking side, this is a story about a group of young men with a shared passion who became friends, comrades together on a grand adventure, only to find themselves players in the intelligence world. And it's about the men and women who pursued them. This is about friendships, and what happened to them.

Which is why I am prompting Chris with names from his past. How about his old buddies . . . How is Jan these days?

'Jan is a nice guy, but he's a pedlar,' he tells me with fine disdain. He has already written to me about Markus: 'Just because he has a PhD don't think he's legitimate.' He mentions Boris in Berlin: 'You know, I think Boris killed himself. Stefan told me he was mixed up with cryptology and the Russian mafia.'

And Plamen and Vesco, the pride of the Bulgarian ex-military?

'Those guys—they didn't even know how to use a FIB,' Chris says contemptuously. 'Plamen was smart in a way, but his stuff was just glitching.'

I murmur sympathetically. I have a vague idea of what a FIB is and look it up again later. He's right—anyone who doesn't know how to use a focused ion beam has to be some sort of moron. I hate to think of the debacle they could create with a sat nav. I'm guessing Karen doesn't speak Bulgarian.

I'm feeling like I'm in a remake of *Steel Magnolias*, where Mercedes Ruehl tells Shirley MacLaine: 'If you've got nothing nice to say about anybody, honey, you sit next to me.' Then I ask Chris about Oliver.

'It's funny because it's like we're twins,' he tells me. 'Except he's got long hair. My hair was long and then I cut it off. It messed around with my collar and stuff and it went wrong.' I tell him I had a moustache like that—don't ever shave when you're drunk. He pauses.

'I don't drink . . . No. Just kidding there.'

Oliver is a tall German with broad shoulders and the build of a footballer. Chris is maybe 30 centimetres shorter, lightly built. They're twins in the way that Danny DeVito and Arnie Schwarzenegger are dead ringers. Fish meets bicycle. I think Chris is still pulling my leg, but he's serious. He keeps coming back to it—he and Oliver are a breed apart from others; they alone inhabit a lofty realm.

'When we're together, we're kind of like two brothers. We fight with . . . we fight sometimes. But I don't trust him, as far as I could throw him.' Or, as he put it earlier, 'He's crazy and will probably get hung off the back of his boat someday.' I think deep down he hates Oliver still.

Old friends. Good times.

Avenue de la Chartreuse, 1972

A whisper of excitement rippled through the big house on Avenue de la Chartreuse. The boy had picked up on it, as he picked up on all the moods of the household. At three he was an acute observer, most of all with anything that involved his father, Renato.

It was 1972. His father was in his study in the family's ground floor apartment, surrounded as always by his papers and books. Nothing was said but, even with his back turned to the door, hunched over his desk, Renato managed to exude a buzz of satisfaction. The boy, Jan, had grown up surrounded by Renato's papers.

'It's like learning a language,' Jan recalls later. 'You never realise you learn it, since you learn it from day one.' He knew the smell of old manuscripts, the faded ink of seventeenth- and eighteenth-century scrawls, older parchments of centuries earlier from a world long gone, carrying down the years the last forgotten murmurs of the dead. Jan also knew the dire penalties for damaging the papers, for playing with them or re-sorting them. He bore the admonitions with fortitude, for this was his father's passion.

Two days earlier Renato had been at a little sale in Paris looking at odd lots of papers retrieved from deceased estates, handwritten pages from the age before the typewriter. Not for the first time he marvelled that French collectors took so little interest in anything written in English. On something between a whim and a hunch he bid on one of the auction lots, picking up a little parcel of pages for 120 francs. In the twenty-first century, this would be the equivalent of some 300 euros. Several of the papers he had been fairly sure about. There was a letter written and signed by the poet Byron. Another page had three or four lines of writing without a signature, but Renato recognised the handwriting as that of the Scottish poet Robert Burns. What had really drawn him was a three-page letter signed 'CD'. He thought he recognised the writer—Renato had an almost photographic memory for handwriting—though this was a younger hand than the examples he had previously seen. But it was too heady a discovery to be certain. He took the pages home to Grenoble, to the house on Avenue de la Chartreuse, where he could prove to his satisfaction, among his reference books and collection, that 'CD' was Charles Dickens.

Renato had thus found the first letter Dickens had written in his great thwarted love affair with the young Maria Beadnell. Renato sat and wondered at the anguish and delicious audacity of the letter, addressed to the daughter of a wealthy banker by an eighteen-year-old penniless legal clerk with limited prospects who wrote, 'Dear Miss Beadnell,' and proceeded to assure her of his passionate regard. He didn't know if he could ask her to marry him but, if she wished, he proposed to write a little poem for her.

This discovery—which was soon recorded on the front page of the *Times* in London—would cement Renato Saggiori's growing reputation as one of the leading autograph experts in the world. Jan understood little of this. What he knew was that his father was excited and happy, which was enough for the quiet little boy with the round eyes and the cherubic features. Jan was a strong-willed but self-contained child. His grandmother had once remarked on his readiness to play by himself for hours, without demanding attention from adults or friends. Recently his mother had found the three-year old standing beside the wall of his bedroom where he had written his name. Except the letters were reversed. He had produced a mirror image of his name in letters a metre high.

Was it a code? It would take more than a decade for his family to understand the significance of these strange letters.

The Saggioris were a family that followed their passions. Renato's father Giovanni had large landholdings around Venice, from which the family wealth came, but he had based his life around his interests in languages, electronics and his document collection. He translated Marconi's work into Italian, he was a professor of Esperanto. When Renato was twelve and studying French seventeenth-century history, his father went to his collection and produced a letter written by Louis XIV. Renato took the letter to school where it was an instant hit with his friends and teachers. He was hooked. He began managing his father's collection, buying and selling documents, and in the process discovering a rare letter by the astronomer Galileo. Giovanni's children split his three fascinations between them: his daughter became a language professor, his younger son worked in radio, while Renato made his living from buying and selling documents and providing consulting services to international collectors and libraries.

In 1969 Renato married an Italian woman who had spent most of her adult life in France, after the Germans destroyed her hometown during the war. Ultimately the couple settled in Grenoble in south-west France, where they built a four-level house as their home and divided it into apartments. With Jan on the way, they moved into the ground-floor apartment. Jan was born in 1970. His mother worked as a receptionist at a local computer company, so Jan spent much of his time as a baby and a toddler with his father, with whom he formed a tight bond. The quiet little boy became the close observer.

'It's enough with my father just to close his eyes, and I know what he feels, what he understands,' Jan says.

By 1977 Jan had a two-year-old sister and the family moved to the south of France near Avignon. They were there when *Stern* magazine in Germany and Rupert Murdoch at the *Sunday Times* in

London published the Hitler Diaries. *Paris Match* won the auction to publish the diaries in France. After seeing the first edition, Renato contacted the French magazine to tell it the handwriting was not Hitler's. The magazine's editorial director thanked him for the advice and said he would arrange a time when they could meet. Some three decades later Renato is still waiting. When Mussolini's diaries came to light in the 1990s—also fraudulent— Renato knew a little more about how to sound the alarm. On Jan's advice he issued a press release to Associated Press.

There was nothing of the post-modernist in Renato Saggiori. He had a voracious appetite for the secrets of history—for writers, for monks of the Middle Ages, for musicians, great leaders and villains. He believed the signature was the gateway to the soul, the authentic voice from history. He immersed himself particularly in the eighteenth and nineteenth centuries.

'I search not manuscripts but autographed manuscripts. I need to know the person who wrote it,' he would tell his son. 'I like the autograph because it is a manner, a way to speak directly with the author.'

He pursued Hemingway's drafts to see how he edited his manuscripts—'It is for me important to find the cancellation or the modification, what he modified in his mind, in his writing, so this is important to better understand the manner in which the person worked in his book, and his personality, the development, the process in his mind to write the definitive work that was published.'

He advised on Che Guevara's notebooks before they were stolen. He bought Tchaikovsky's musical scores to read his annotations, and looked into Voltaire's machinations with his publishers—the French writer wrote to one publisher saying he could not publish his next book because thieves had taken the manuscript, while on the same day he wrote to another publisher offering the draft, explaining that he would tell his former publisher it had been stolen. Renato's is the skill of the virtuoso.

'He can analyse handwriting just by looking at it, as a musician would listen to an orchestra and pick the different strands, the tones, the rhythm,' says a family friend. 'He can analyse every component that went into it.' In fact, the roots of the family name, Saggiori, came from *saggia*, 'to taste', and *ori*, 'gold'. It harks back to the Middle Age craftsman standing in the marketplace as the gold tester, attesting the gold coins were authentic.

'One of the stories that my father always tells is that a fake is a crime of history,' says Saggiori. 'Originals are important, fakes need to be thrown out. End of story.'

Some issues remain elusive. William Shakespeare is a mystery to Renato—how could one man apparently write so much, and yet leave so few traces in his own hand? Shakespeare left seven signatures, all of them different—'Someone who cannot write seven times in the same manner, his hand—it is very strange.'

The documents in Renato's collection went back to the eighth and ninth centuries, before the time when papers were signed by hand. His earliest signature was a paper hand-signed by Pope Paschal II, the great figure of the Middle Ages, in 1114. The depth of Renato's obsession with uncovering these secret treasure troves was matched by his loathing for the artificial and the fake: 'It's just burning the truth.' He became a one-man crusade, waging a 'war against the fakes'.

In 1985 Jan's parents moved again, to Geneva in Switzerland. For the next four years Jan boarded at a Catholic high school in Grenoble to complete his baccalaureate. He had been born in France, lived in France all of his life, but saw himself as entirely Italian.

'I was in the middle of a French school and I was Italian,' he says. 'So it taught me to fight.' He hated it. 'There were a lot of uncontrollable boys—people who think they are the centre of the world.' The experience affected him profoundly—to the extent that, when he turned nineteen, he renounced his French citizenship. This also removed his obligation to do military service, but for Jan it was a more personal rejection of his collision with the unappealing side of French culture: 'I didn't want to look like these guys in my school, who were badly educated by rich parents, *parvenus*, rich but without much education.'

The other big change during his high school years was that at fifteen, with failing grades for mathematics, his parents provided him with a maths tutor, who worked out within the first half-hour lesson that Jan had dyslexia. He saw letters and figures in reverse. This was the reason for the mirror image of his name he had put on his wall as a child. The son of one of the world's leading palaeographers was dyslexic. His tutor then employed methods for teaching dyslexics, and Jan would later score 16 out of 20 in the baccalaureate.

This episode helped to explain the shape his life was taking. For rare documents were not Jan's passion. Around the time of the Hitler Diaries affair, Jan had become enamoured of a Sinclair Spectrum computer in his Uncle Alberto's home. Alberto gave him the computer, and bought himself another one. It opened a new world.

'I was never the person who wanted to play with the computer, I wanted to do things with a computer.' In 1987 he got an Olivetti PC for his parents' company, and in 1989 he used his savings to buy his own computer, an Apple IIGS.

Pursuing technology was still within the family tradition. His father's imprint coloured the way Jan saw his world and there was also his role model of the expert collector. The important thing was knowledge, which should be shared broadly. It was appropriate for those who produce discoveries to receive a little reward, but the quest is not about money.

'It's always possible to discover something if you work at it with passion,' Renato says today. 'I told my son: when you are passionate about something, you must go over the limit, to go beyond what is reasonable, to persevere, to risk everything.'

His parents noticed that, when he visited them in Geneva on weekends, Jan rarely needed money. 'And we asked him in which manner did you have this. He said, "Ah, but I found that my friends need floppy discs and I found someone that sells for three what I can sell for five. So they ask me always for this, at a good price. So the teacher of the school asks of me, because I like very well the computer, to give one hour as teacher to my school friends during the afternoon"—and he was just fifteen, sixteen years old. And he got a little money . . .'

Jan took the teaching job because it was the only way he could have access to a computer. At nineteen he went to university in Geneva. By this stage he was importing computer components from Taiwan and Hong Kong for resale. He repeated his first year of university—the mathematics class defeated him—then settled into completing his business degree. It would be several years before he became aware of an exciting new area of computing that was just taking off in Geneva. There were programs that could be used with a satellite dish and a set-top box to decode the programs from the new wave of satellite pay TV broadcasters. One of the favourites for the hackers was Sky Television in the United Kingdom.

London, November 1990

In Jan Saggiori's world it had gone almost unnoticed that Rupert Murdoch was going broke. News Corporation was in deep trouble. From 8 October 1990 through to 5 February 1991, Murdoch and his lead bankers were negotiating furiously to refinance $7.6 billion of debt. Small banks repeatedly refused to roll over their debt and Murdoch would find his media empire just hours—or even minutes—away from collapse. One of the key decisions that helped make his escape even remotely possible came on Friday 6 November, when News announced that Sky was merging with its competitor, BSB. The new service would be called British Sky Broadcasting.

In the welter of news stories about the merger, no one picked up on an obscure legal development in the United States. The Securities and Exchange Commission had run out of patience over Michael Clinger's refusal to pay the $814,000 fine for his insider trading case. On 12 November, a New York grand jury issued an arrest warrant for Clinger, who was now running News Datacom in Israel.

Bruce Hundertmark had been quietly pushed off the scene a year earlier. Hundertmark had got Sky off the ground with an encryption system, but had fallen victim to the rivalry and infighting that marks Rupert Murdoch's court. Among other things, Hundertmark had clashed with the new head of News International, Gus Fischer, who wanted to appoint a friend of his, Tom Price, to run News Datacom from London. Price had no tertiary or technical qualifications; but he had sold paint and finishing products internationally for twenty years and was 'as honest as the day is long', Fischer told Hundertmark.

'I said it might be difficult to accommodate a non-technical, albeit experienced paint salesman, in a high-technology business,' Hundertmark testified later. But by May 1990 Hundertmark was out and Price was in. In practice that meant Michael Clinger in Israel was calling the shots.

From 12 November, Clinger was an international fugitive, with the US arrest warrant hanging over his head; but that did not seem to faze him at all. Meanwhile, he had engineered a switch in the company supplying the blank smartcards that News Datacom programmed in its Scotland processing centre to carry Video-Crypt. News Datacom was now receiving blank smartcards from a Californian chipmaker, Bharat Kumar Marya, whom Clinger seemed to know.

Punta del Este, 2011

Oliver Kömmerling is never quite who or what I want him to be. It's really inconvenient. More troubling, he is never where I want him to be. Ideally this would be in his dressing gown and slippers, curled up on the sofa, so that I could tickle him under the chin, offer him a saucer of milk, and ask him more about where he got all that money. But Oliver is not really a dressing-gown-and-slippers kind of cat. Oliver is a bad boy. I mean that in a nice way. Really. The one thing in life you never really want to do is get a major league hacker feeling snippy with you. If there was a protocol in conversing with them, you might want to mention their great personality. And then compliment them on their clothes and dress sense and the subtle colour balance that on other people might not quite hit the mark, but which on them works just neato.

Oliver is a bad boy in what he represents. For the executives around the world who run banks, credit card operations, telephone companies or mass-transit ticketing systems, who issue passports, who provide physical security, or who sell almost anything on the Net or in stores, if there is one face that should give them nightmares, it's Oliver. In the world of hackers there are software guys and hardware guys. Software hacking gets all the media. But the hardware specialists, who take apart the microchips that are used to secure most things in our lives, the little markers that authenticate who we are, and what we can do, are the ones to worry about most. You have a decent shot at shutting off a software attack, but a sophisticated hardware hack is almost impossible to beat. Oliver is the father of hardware hacking on microchips. He and his friend Markus Kuhn wrote the manual. It's not what he does, you understand, though you might ask questions of some of his friends. It's what he could do. He has stuck mostly to pay TV smartcards. It offers the best business model for hackers. But that won't always be the case. He can see the broader picture.

I wrote Oliver a couple of emails in 2009 hoping to catch up, which he deftly ignored. I tried again when I was in Europe the following year. I interviewed his friend Markus Kuhn and three days later Oliver emailed me back with his telephone number.

I picked up his message at Charles de Gaulle airport hours before my flight back to Australia. When I phoned, he was open to seeing me at his apartment in Monaco, but uncertain when that could be because his wife Vicky was in hospital with a back injury. He suggested we talk on Skype, which hackers like because it was thought at the time that it was hard for surveillance teams to decrypt. But it never happened.

Then in April 2011 he emailed me out of the blue, asking whether I was still interested in talking with him, mentioning he was moving to Uruguay. Yes I would like to talk, and why the hell South America? There was a subtext to this conversation that I would discover only months later. I continued blissfully ignorant. Meanwhile, he went on to describe at length the wonders of the coast at Punta del Este—the seals, the diving, the new 3.8 terabyte internet cable that had just been laid, and attached photos of the two fabulous villas he had bought on the beach, side by side. I knew from all of this that he was in deep trouble.

He conceded that Europe was too hot for him. He had a short hate list of those he blamed for his woes: Jan Saggiori ('that Swiss idiot who badmouth me all day long') and Alan Guggenheim ('I hate this f_____, he is the biggest snake I have ever met in my life'). If he identifies with anyone it's Reuven Hasak, and that sterling work he did in the 300 Bus affair. A national hero. Oliver himself is just like that. A simple, naïve man who got caught up in a war between big corporations. It's a bit rich. But what to say?

I've already mentioned the personality. I would compliment him on his dress sense and subtle colour balance, but it's hard to convey this with complete candour in an international email exchange. There's a part of serious journalism that requires basic weaselling skills. I'm crap at it. Couldn't weasel to save my life. As a conversation starter I mention secret handshakes and ask whether Ray Adams was a Freemason. He never gets back to me.

It's August 2011 and Oliver writes again, more agitated, complaining that a security company 'spies on our company, stealing internal reports, our contracts, and hires an Australian investigator to attack our mail server from within the US'. Gilles Kaehlin's court case was down for October, and I urged Oliver to go public, to tell his story to a journalist, explaining his whole role in the Canal+ case, how he and Gilles were the heroes of the hour. It didn't have to be me, it could be any journalist he trusts. Gilles must know hundreds of them. That last bit was a rhetorical gesture, completely disingenuous. I assume he knows I will bite my own arms off if he gives the interview to someone else. But that's what he does.

In late September he emails me—'Hi my friend'—to tell me he has just given an interview to the BBC. The rough tape of the interview runs for about two hours, his whole life story. *The BBC*. It's not the news I was hoping for, and Oliver isn't happy with the result. When it finally goes to air in March 2012, as part of a wider *Panorama* program, only 30 seconds of it appears. By then Oliver is seriously unhappy with the direction the BBC investigation has taken, and its focus on Ray Adams, who was Oliver's handler at NDS. He emails me at length to assure me that everything Ray did was tickety-boo. Eventually I get to look at the full BBC transcript, along with a bunch of other first- and second-hand accounts to add to my own exchanges with him. And there's a curious thing. It feels like Kevin Spacey telling his magical story in the 1995 film *The Usual Suspects*. Oliver is telling a history that seems to contain so many other people's stories that are now his. I can actually recognise some of the pieces—from Chris Tarnovsky, from Jan Saggiori, from Markus Kuhn. And maybe it really all played out like that. Happenstance. It's a wonderful world.

There was a time before, though, when Oliver was not yet master of the universe.

Riedelberg, western Germany, 1991

The boy had a troubled schooling. Oliver Kömmerling never seemed to fit in a classroom, his head always full of his own intense, private interests, most of which revolved around electronics and computers. His father, an electrical engineer, had installed a laboratory in their home in Zweibrücken in western Germany, ten kilometres from the French border. The child grew up tinkering. When he was young his parents called him The Axe, because of his lethal tendency, whenever something mechanical caught his eye, to take it apart, to figure out how it worked.

'But getting them back together was a different story,' he says. 'I destroyed, of course, a lot of things.'

He grew up acknowledging few rules.

'I had a lot of problems,' he says today. While other computer nerds got failing grades or just scraped through, Oliver got expelled from school after school. He found it easier to pursue his own study interests at home, where his parents had set up his own little workroom so he could fix televisions. So he went to school as little as possible. The only times when he was sure to turn up were on exam days. It was a constant source of grievance to the German school system. He was a bad example. By the time he was fifteen he was a daunting figure for any teacher—tall, broad shoulders, long brown hair; a young giant with a strange mincing way of speaking. On another boy it would sound effeminate. With Oliver it underlined a certain precision that would be the hallmark of everything he did. And his disdain for anyone who tried to tell him what to do.

It wasn't that Oliver was the smartest person in the room. He just didn't have a lot of patience for mere mortals who got in his way, who didn't share his passionate curiosity—mostly his teachers. Any exam that involved science or electronics of any sort was a breeze but he had to work out how to cheat his way through the rest. He passed the German intermediate exams by building a miniature radio transmitter that he hid in his ear beneath the long hair, while a friend of his outside told him the answers. He also got better at putting the things he disassembled back together. When he was fourteen, he bought an old car from the city dump and drove his mother mad by installing it in the Kömmerling garage for a year as he took it apart and reassembled it in working order. So then he had wheels.

By his final year he was on his fifth school and the principal was playing hardball, invoking a clause in the curriculum that could be used to bar students with an absentee rate of more than 20 per cent from sitting the final exam. Oliver's family went to court to fight the decision and won, after claiming time he had spent at his previous school. By the time Oliver had won the right to sit the exam he had lost interest. He was an autodidact. As a self-made man, he would later study for diplomas by correspondence.

He ended up without a school diploma, and worked as the junior in a staff of three in a pharmaceuticals warehouse. Later he worked for the local chamber of commerce, teaching computer skills to the unemployed—how to use database systems, spread-sheets and word processing. This introduced him to a whole new range of friends, and places to hang out. It was the late 1980s and a few fledgling pay TV operations had started up. Smartcards had not yet appeared on the horizon. Instead the flimsy encryption systems were built around a microchip stored in the clunky set-top box. It seemed a natural progression from talking about electronics to talking about television, to talking about using Oliver's know-how to watch the pay channels. One of Oliver's new friends in the satellite business asked him to have a play with the chip in the set-top box of a Swiss-German pay TV channel called Teleclub. Taking things apart was what Oliver did. As well as Teleclub, Canal+ had a French channel using an encryption system called Discret. There was a Dutch channel, and a BBC service. He was just playing around. He did it as a favour for friends. Along the way, Oliver had come into money.

'He dropped out of high school early, he doesn't have any degree whatsoever, and in his late teenage years he started a software company of his own,' says Markus Kuhn. 'One of the early things he did was some business software for pharmacies . . . Normal, off-the-shelf commercial software company.'

He was still twenty in late 1988 when he bought his first home in Riedelberg, ten kilometres from Zweibrücken, for 500,000 deutschmarks. From his bedroom window, France was just one large field away from him, a short distance to the east. The house said a lot about Oliver Kömmerling. It was a mark of both his confidence and his self-sufficiency. It was a rambling three-storey affair on a two-acre block, with another building behind it. The ridiculously low price Oliver had paid reflected the desperation of the seller—the property was worth twice or even three times as much. Oliver had bought the house for his new bride. In October 1988, when he was two months shy of turning twenty-one, he married Victoria Hautz, six years his senior. Oliver was reclusive and painfully shy with women. But he knew what he wanted. Lesser men might content themselves with a den or study, or a shed out the back. Oliver had an entire two-storey building behind the main house to pursue his passions. And there was a hot new satellite channel to focus his energies on—the British broadcaster Sky Television.

You can argue that the way Rupert Murdoch launched Sky was the perfect recipe to assure the rise of global piracy, not just of Sky itself but of every major satellite pay TV system in the world. But that's overstating it. The way Rupert Murdoch launched Sky was the perfect recipe to assure the rise of Oliver Kömmerling. Sky launched in February 1989 without any encryption. This was one of the strengths of the News Datacom VideoCrypt system, that the smartcards could be distributed later when they were ready, and the decoders could be reprogrammed over the air. In the meantime, a large community of people quickly grew used to watching Sky programs without paying. It's a little like news on the internet today. People get used to it, so it's hard to reprogram them not to expect it for free. When VideoCrypt started up late in 1999, only some of the Sky channels were encoded and, in the rush to produce the system, News Datacom had settled on a much simpler microchip than they had first planned. This change of plan was made on the basis that the smartcard would be replaced every three months or so, which would stop any piracy dead. But with Sky haemorrhaging money, that was never a likely outcome.

The Fiat-Shamir algorithm is a beautiful thing, providing an infallible way for the set-top box, or decoder, to verify that the smartcard fed into it was a paid-up subscription. But in practice the first VideoCrypt chips had limited power and were pathetically simple to break. For example, when a subscriber stopped paying their monthly fees, Sky would send out an electronic command to deactivate the card. The kill command was at 21 volts, while all other commands were at 14 volts. So, if you put in a blocker that stopped any 21-volt current flowing through the smartcard, you had free television forever. Or at least until Sky figured this out.

The high churn of Sky customers who hadn't renewed their subscriptions meant that there was a large number of Sky boxes and expired smartcards in circulation, which could be acquired easily by the growing piracy market. News Datacom stopped using higher voltage to deactivate cards and instead devised a kill command using software. The pirates put in a program to look for the kill command, and block it. Another hack looked for any byte of data that included the serial number of the smartcard, and blocked it.

News Datacom and Sky fought back by producing new versions of the VideoCrypt smartcards. The changes were incremental and often ineffective. This ever-increasing market of people who were used to watching Sky for free, and wished to keep doing so, were prepared to buy pirate devices to bypass the Sky encryption. Every time Sky made a change to the smartcard, the pirates' customers had to go back to the pirates for a solution, and they would update or replace the pirate smartcards—for a fee. It was a fabulous business model for the pirates. The longer this went on, the more wealthy and resourceful the pirate dealers became, and the more money reserves they had to pay hackers to find a way to defeat the next generation of smartcards. It was a business model that became more profitable the more Sky tried to stop it. And this was just in Britain. Across Europe thousands of people wanted to watch Sky as well, and pirating the signal was not illegal.

New York, 1992

Gus Fischer's friend Tom Price, who had taken over as chief executive of News Datacom after Bruce Hundertmark was forced out, had struggled, as Hundertmark had feared. He knew nothing about the technical side of what the company did, which limited him when it came to finding new customers, finding new suppliers for smartcards, or identifying countermeasures against piracy. But the Israeli staff tolerated him. Dov Rubin, now the sales manager, felt sorry for him. Rubin tried to keep Price informed about what was happening, but it was a courtesy—the Israeli team did not seek direction or permission from him for what they did. Price, from his office in England, kept up a barrage of requests for information. But often his questions were just ignored. His role was reduced to administrative tasks, rather than anything to do with the operations or technology—he helped to choose a company logo.

In effect Michael Clinger now ran the company. He managed to quarrel with almost everyone he ran into at News. The fact that the United States had a warrant out for his arrest changed nothing—Clinger continued to run News Datacom out of Israel, travelling throughout Europe on the company's business. The only concession to his equivocal status was that he travelled on forged passports, like any other self-respecting corporate executive who was an international fugitive.

In the year that follows Rupert Murdoch emerging from his debt crisis by the skin of his teeth, one of his great regrets was that the debt-override agreement he wrested from his banks meant he was blocked from joining a group planning to launch a digital satellite service in the United States. By late 1991 Hughes Electronics, a subsidiary of General Motors, had taken the lead, with plans to launch this operation as DirecTV in 1994. Murdoch lobbied Hughes to adopt News Datacom's VideoCrypt conditional access system and took a personal interest in seeing the deal done. He wanted constant updates. But putting the deal together was beyond Price's ability. News Corp's corporate counsel, Arthur Siskind, was blunt: 'He had the title but really was not running the business.'

Instead the Office of the Chairman in News Corp's headquarters in New York took an active role overseeing the negotiations with Hughes Electronics. Siskind made that very clear in a British court case a decade later. New York was running the show at News Datacom. Not Price. If it wasn't, then News Datacom would be liable to pay British income tax. The four members of the Office of the Chairman were: Murdoch; News Corp's crusty new chief counsel, Arthur Siskind; the finance director, David DeVoe; and Gus Fischer, who had just been appointed chief operating officer for News Corp.

But there was an old problem still in play—Clinger. The head of BSkyB, Sam Chisholm, hated him. Clinger refused to travel to the United States to talk to Hughes and so, by November 1992, News had cottoned on to the fact that their technology arm was being run by a fugitive. Clinger was locked out of the News Datacom offices. Siskind set about buying out the 40 per cent of the group owned by Clinger and the Weizmann Institute's Yeda Research.

Meanwhile, Leo Krieger, News Datacom's accountant, and Dov Rubin continued negotiating with Hughes over the DirecTV contract. Even so it was Clinger whom they continued to consult on a daily basis by phone to work out their strategy. When the deal was finally done—with the honours shared between the most senior people at News and the man on the run—Rubin complained that Price tried to take the credit.

'He was pulling an Alexander Haig,' Rubin told a British court later; in other words, trying to claim he was in charge when in reality all the key decisions were taken by others.

There was no attempt to have Clinger apprehended. News bought out the Clinger and Yeda Research shareholdings on 1 July 2002 after valuing the company at $25 million. Seven days later, after tripling the total price News Datacom charged BSkyB for smartcards, News revalued News Datacom at $43.2 million and transferred part of its ownership to a new offshore British holding company owned through the Cayman Islands. The newly appointed board was controlled by three senior executives from News Corp's head office: CFO David DeVoe, Siskind, and DeVoe's offsider, Jeffrey Leist. No more Michael Clinger.

At least that was the plan.

Riedelberg, western Germany, 1992

You should understand that serious computer nerds go for three kinds of television. You can forget about football, news and most movies. Care factor zero. What they are big on is science fiction, horror and porn, and not necessarily in that order. In 1992, a friend of Oliver Kömmerling's was using a pirate system for Sky that he had bought from a British dealer to record *Star Trek: The Next Generation* on videotapes he then distributed to his friends. By now BSkyB was using Series 6 smartcards from News Datacom, but the hacking was not aimed at the smartcard, rather it was at the microchip within the decoder box.

'And my friend said, "If you can copy the chip, everybody can watch it and we don't need to make tapes,"' Oliver says. So that's what Oliver did, out of plain curiosity.

At the time, Oliver had 100,000 deutschmarks of sophisticated electronics in his laboratory, which he used to take the pirate chip out of the decoder box and dump the code from it. Then he programmed a Futuretron Microchip that he bought in Munich and ended up with a better pirate system. It came to be known as the Ho Lee Fook hack, which was the exclamation that BSkyB execs are said to have used after they learned of it. News of the hack spread like wildfire, forcing News Datacom to issue Series 7 smartcards to all BSkyB subscribers.

Of course it didn't end there. Oliver's friends watched Sky for a bit with the chips he had reprogrammed. It turned out that Oliver had another friend, who had a job on the railway, who in turn had another friend, who was in the satellite business. He supplied satellite receivers and dishes to American forces in Germany. He had heard about Oliver and he came to see him with one of the pirate cards that England's leading dealer, Chris Cary, was selling for the Series 7 BSkyB smartcards. He wanted to sell the pirate cards on the US military bases. Oliver could solve all of his problems—in fact he had already hacked Cary's pirate card. It wasn't just curiosity, there was prestige here, a growing notoriety among German hackers on the BBS bulletin boards and ICQ conferencing channels. By this time Oliver's work had caught the eye of the British dealers who sold pirated BSkyB systems. They were always on the lookout for talent as Sky's increasing security measures slowly raised the bar for hacking. They told Oliver they wanted to meet him and sent him an air ticket. For a young man who had spent most of his life in a twenty-kilometre circle in Palatinat-Pfalz, this was the big time.

For one of the dealers who met him on that first trip, the striking thing was just how raw and provincial this diffident young German was. They did what they always did with guests. They took him to a strip club.

'I could see he liked one of the girls, he kept looking at her,' the dealer says. 'I ribbed him about it, and he denied it and got very angry.'

Oliver was flattered by the attention from the English dealers who were so interested in his hobby. There was no talk of money. He was ready to give his hacks away for free, which, given the way things turned out, it's nice to know. Looking back now, who would have thought?

Erlangen, September 1993

One thing that several thousand years of scientific advance has shown us is that the first requirement for any interesting piece of research—the sine qua non, necessary before all else—is a decent cover story. It's a science thing. Well, a science and money thing, but really the latter goes without saying. Even the simplest sort of science hardly ever comes on the cheap. So the first thing any scientist needs is a wallet.

As a rule scientists are pretty crap at anything to do with finance so it generally needs to be someone else's wallet. It seems to work better that way. That is, someone else needs to be convinced to put up the money to support any piece of research. It might be a university or a government grant or corporate sponsorship or something entirely different. Whatever it is, there is a wallet that needs to be convinced. You have to talk to the wallet. Generally this is the time to shoot high, to explain just why the future of humanity may be affected by the rather exciting little data set that you hope to produce here. Tactical discretion is an asset right at this point. Candour is not. There's no need to tailor the funding proposal too closely to what you actually propose to do. That only tends to undermine your credibility and, really, who needs to know. 'Big Picture' wins the day.

Which is pretty much how the Kuhn family ended up shelling out for a satellite receiver and dish in August 1993 at their home in Erlangen in northern Bavaria. Markus Kuhn's father, a professor of mechanical engineering at the University of Erlangen, had been convinced to buy the satellite dish as a research tool. His son would use it to listen to English programs on the British Sky Broadcasting system, to improve his English language skills.

Markus was certainly agreeable to this research plan. He may even have suggested it. In fact, after preliminary experimentation, he had already established that the most effective way to improve his English would be by watching the Sky One channel. It offered some particularly useful linguistic training. His father might have heard of the particular educational program: *Star Trek: The Next Generation*. Markus Kuhn at age twenty-two was not yet a Trekkie, but his modest research proposal offered him every opportunity to become one.

There's general agreement among Trekkies that, while season seven may not have been their show's finest hours, it nevertheless finished off the franchise with a flourish. Since 1987 *Star Trek: The Next Generation* had been kicking along as a revival of the *Star Trek* series. Seasons five and six had been, quite frankly, a disappointment—there was a feeling that the franchise had lost its way. But, from the moment season seven went to air on 20 September 1993, with the android, Data, falling under the control of the Borg, it was clear the show was back on track. Around the world, Trekkies were back in their element. When the double-length finale went to air on 19 May 1994, thousands of Canadian fans packed Toronto's SkyDome to watch Captain Jean-Luc Picard battling with himself in three different time dimensions to save the universe. Trekkies had seen nothing like this for years. Unfortunately, neither had Markus Kuhn.

At the start of September 1993, three weeks before *Star Trek: TNG*'s seventh season began, Rupert Murdoch's British Sky

Broadcasting began encrypting the Sky One channel. It became part of the Sky Multichannels subscription package. Up until this point the channel had been open to anyone like the Kuhns who had a satellite dish and a receiver. From 1 September you could watch the channel only with a BSkyB subscription. The encryption scrambled the picture, but the sound came through unaffected. Markus listened to several episodes with a scrambled screen but, while he could hear the essential English expressions—'This is not reasonable', 'Beam me up Scotty', 'She canna take it captain!' and the like—he found it to be a little less than the key linguistic aid he had hoped for.

Markus was philosophical. If he had to pay BSkyB to watch *Star Trek: TNG,* that is what he would do. He called BSkyB about a subscription, but Markus was toast. When the screen in the call centre flashed up showing he was telephoning from Germany, the conversation was virtually over. By law, BSkyB could not sell subscriptions outside Britain and Ireland. No matter how many times he called, or how logical the arguments he advanced to the BSkyB operatives, there was no way that Markus could watch his show. From the viewpoint on the other end of the line, he was just another unhappy German Trekkie.

But Markus Kuhn was not your average television viewer. In fact he hardly watched television at all. His life's course had been determined back in 1983 when he watched a German television show about how to write programs for computers. Several days later he was in one of his father's laboratories at the university when he noticed it contained the same make of computer featured on the television show—an old Commodore PET. At his urging his father photocopied the manual, which Markus then spent several afternoons studying before he began writing his first computer programs. He was eleven.

Soon afterwards, he realised his high school had the same computers as well. While they were reserved for senior students, he talked his way into the computer lab and was soon spending long afternoons programming. By the time he was fifteen he had won the West German national school computer science competition. He won it again the following year, 1988, and the year after that he headed a West German team that won the International Olympiad in Infomatics, a worldwide computing science competition run by the United Nations.

A computing science masters degree was the inevitable next step. However, here Germany's military service laws stepped in. Markus had escaped call-up at the end of high school, but the respite was brief. Two years into his degree he elected to do eighteen months' community service as an alternative to fifteen months in the army. Here again he was fortunate in finding a job at a neurological hospital where research groups were working on digital signal processing. They were delighted to find someone doing community service who knew quite a lot about computer programming and for him choosing the hospital was a no-brainer.

'Having Linux PCs with human brains connected as peripheral devices sounded more interesting than learning how to dig a hole in the mud and attach a mine at the bottom of a Soviet tank, which was the alternative program on offer,' he says.

At 22 Markus Kuhn was a composed, personable young man with a fiercely analytical mind and a dry sense of humour. His record already showed he was one of the most brilliant minds of his generation—he had never come up against a problem that he couldn't think his way through. But now, for almost two years, his life was on hold. He had plenty of spare time and little to engage himself with, except a television dish that, after two weeks, was exhibiting some fairly dramatic built-in obsolescence, thanks to BSkyB's new VideoCrypt scrambling process. Which was sort of annoying.

Today, as a Fellow at Wolfson College, Cambridge, Kuhn believes there are three essential requirements for a successful hacking, or reverse engineering. The hacker has to have the skill. He must have the time. And finally he needs the motivation. He finds there is nothing as effective a motivator as being really cross. All of these things came together for him in late 1993, the winter of his *Star Trek* discontent. BSkyB was about to take a bath.

Markus was not the first to hack BSkyB, as he soon realised. Most of the hacking traced back to three sources: in Ireland, England and Germany. Sky 03, Sky 04 and Sky 05 cards came and went, none of them offering much challenge to the pirates. Sky 06 was a step up again in sophistication. But it was Sky 07 that offered the most substantive resistance to hackers and pirates. Over Christmas 1992, reports began to emerge that a German hacker had popped the card. There were few details, except a reference to someone called Oliver. By the summer of 1993 this hack was available for the first time through pirates as a smartcard. So Markus Kuhn had a number of options open to him if he wanted to work on his English language research project with a pirate device. But that wasn't his way.

Kuhn is a theorist, so his first idea was to ignore the decrypting process and the smartcard and work out a way to unscramble the picture manually, by brute force. This is called an image processing attack (and when it comes to tackling a security device, it is always called an attack). He had a friend at the university who had access to a frame grabber—a piece of equipment that allowed him to record signal frames that were broadcast by BSkyB. He discovered how VideoCrypt was cutting the 625 lines in each PAL frame and swapping the ends about. He needed to reverse those cuts and there were some patterns already evident. For example, the cut could not be made too close to the edge of the screen, so the area to look for the cuts was reduced, and generally one line in a television frame almost duplicates the image on the line next to it.

So Markus sat down to write a computer program that reversed the cuts and matched up lines that were almost similar to each other. The process was fairly complicated, but in the end he had a program that gave him a slightly blurry image of *Star Trek: TNG*. The English language skills research project was back on track. The only drawback was that his 486 computer took about 30 seconds to unscramble each frame. PAL broadcasts 25 frames per second.

This is where the motivation and spare time became important. The friend who had loaned Markus the frame grabber was using a super computer at the university for a thesis on image processing. He was looking for research applications and shared Markus's view that *Star Trek: TNG* was really at the heart of the modern research project. The super computer, which was based on 88 computers running in parallel, reduced the time to unscramble the image to fifteen seconds. Eventually the two of them managed to get the super computer to manage about a dozen frames per second, which gave a watchable video feed. The sound had to be staggered to bring it into sync with the video. Eventually the two young men, both very pleased with themselves, managed to watch several episodes of *Star Trek: TNG*'s season seven on the super computer. And then life resumed again, and other researchers suggested alternative uses for the expensive equipment.

Markus had gone as far he could. He posted his software on the electronic bulletin board of a usenet group called alt.satellite. tv.europe (these were the forerunners of internet forums) and was surprised by the level of interest it triggered. A whole community of people were busy looking at VideoCrypt. There was a large piracy distribution group focused on BSkyB, but there were relatively few people who actually knew anything about the secret processes of VideoCrypt. When a pirate product came out, BSkyB would change the key codes for the cards or mount an electronic counter measure (or ECM), designed to permanently knock out the pirate devices. Several people now approached Markus to ask if he could help them with old pirate cards that didn't work any more because they had been ECM-ed.

'I was very excited about that, because I thought I had reached the end of what I could do with the image processing attack and I had already played around with what's going on on this smartcard interface,' Kuhn says. He knew how the card worked and he could talk to it with his computer; he just didn't understand how to get the right cryptographic answers the card wanted before it would decode the signal. But when he analysed a disabled pirate smartcard he had been sent, he discovered how the cryptography worked. During a long afternoon he managed to fix that card and now he had a pirate program that acted like a smartcard and could unscramble the Sky signal, but which ran on a computer. He sent off a copy of his new program to the people who had provided him with the pirate card. Almost overnight he heard reports that his software was being sold on street corners in London for £300.

Markus was stunned. He wasn't doing this for money, or to make others rich. Markus is a tech head, a scientist through and through. In March 1994 he published his software on alt.satellite. tv.europe, together with decrypted pictures from *Star Trek: TNG* as proof of concept. His software was called Season 7. Now anyone with just a few electronic skills could watch BSkyB for free. VideoCrypt was completely broken.

News Datacom finally moved. It had been planning to introduce its Sky 08 card, but that now seemed too close to the hacked Sky 07 card; too easy a proposition for hackers to break. Instead News Datacom rolled out Sky 09, another generation onward in complexity. The cards were distributed by early May and on 18 May BSkyB switched to the new cards, in the process pulling the plug on every pirate card or Season 7 hack in Europe. The timing seemed to be pointed at Markus Kuhn. The pirate screens were still black the following night when Sky One broadcast the double-length season finale to *Star Trek: TNG*, in which the three versions of Captain Piquard and the 'Starship Enterprise' shifted from those different times as they battled together to save the universe from deadly peril—as you do.

Markus never got to see the last episode. In fact he didn't see much of season seven. He had lost most of his original drive to watch it. Instead he was drawn by the intellectual challenge of solving a technical puzzle. But his software program was a game changer. The hacking of pay television in Europe was in the process of moving from the secret realm of a few pirate hackers to a legitimate field of study for academics, computer science students and electronic hobbyists. For them, as for Markus, this wasn't about money—it was an intellectual problem, a game against the designers of security software, and a way of learning about the field. There was also a view that any new technological development, including security, should be tested. Hacking a satellite broadcast that could not be watched in your own country was not illegal. So why not?

Kuhn's Season 7 program made him a rallying point for a group of people.

'I had some correspondence with a couple of people and we decided to set up a more private email list to discuss a bit more about the technical issues,' he says. Luca Bertagnolio of the University of Milano offered to provide hosting facilities for the email group, which was called TVcrypt. At any one time it had perhaps only 30 to 40 members, with perhaps a total of a hundred members over time. But they were the most influential figures in European satellite decryption. This was a meeting of purists, set up in the collaborative method that had forged German scientific advance since the nineteenth century.

It was also a group of boisterous young men. In the rarefied circles of European science schools, hacking satellite systems was the great game. It wasn't just VideoCrypt. There was also D-2Mac, the European standard developed by France Télécom that was used particularly by Scandinavian countries as Viaccess, including as a platform for several pornographic channels, which became important fields of research for some of the keen young minds. The Swiss company, Kudelski, through its Nagra division, had a range of encryption smartcards and the South African group, Mindport, produced the Irdeto system. But BSkyB and its flow of US programming remained the premier target.

The other consequence of Markus developing his Season 7 program was that he got to meet Oliver Kömmerling, the hacker whose pirate card he had broken to make his program. Late one night Oliver emailed him. Oliver had a diametrically opposed view about smartcards and the pursuit of knowledge. His was a darker vision. Markus was different. He was the spirit of Anti-Oliver. What they shared was a sense of curiosity. Implausibly they became friends.

Riedelberg, western Germany, 1993–94

The deal Oliver Kömmerling made with a friend of a friend in 1993 to sell pirate cards to US bases had changed everything. The pirate economy was a world away from the gentle pursuits of academia. In the piracy business, hackers were piece workers. Freelancers at best. They did a job. They got paid. End of story. But Oliver's new business partner offered him his own slice of the action: a half share of the profits. Piracy makes drug dealing look like a low-margin business. The modified chips cost 10 deutschmarks and sold for 300. The two of them cleared close to a million deutschmarks on that first venture. That was from just over 3000 cards.

'And I didn't even see a client. I didn't do anything at this moment. I didn't have to sell anything. He was just bringing shoeboxes of money every week. It was really starting like that, and from that moment I noticed that with a really small, er, effort, there can be a lot of money in that area,' he says today.

I know what you're thinking. Being a pirate must be an absolute tax nightmare. But if there was one thing the Kömmerling family understood, it was how to handle money. Oliver went to the family tax advisor, who told him just how dangerous it would be if he ever wanted to do anything with the shoeboxes. So Oliver began writing software invoices that would explain where this flood of money was coming from. He could hardly say it was courtesy of Sky or BSkyB, so he invented companies that he invoiced for providing software.

To regroup here. Chris Cary had developed a pirate smartcard to rip off BSkyB programming for free. Oliver Kömmerling had ripped off Cary's pirate card to make his own (which would be in turn cracked by Markus Kuhn). And Oliver was staying square with the tax man by creating fictitious invoices. Is there a moral issue here? Oliver doesn't even understand that question.

'Honestly I didn't think [about it] because for me it was just—I was focused on the technology, and what was in my mind, for example, after the first money arrive is immediately to buy more equipment, bigger pieces, to continue in this direction because for me, this was a little chip, but there were other chips which were more complicated.' The real question was, though: Was it legal? More to the point: Could Oliver get into trouble for it? Oliver was reassured by a relative who was a lawyer that there was a loophole in German law under which broadcasts were regarded as free—or, at least, watching them through piracy did not involve touching or stealing anything.

Oliver had grown wary of making cash payments, so he had his growing number of clients buy electronic equipment for him. The first year alone this came to 500,000 deutschmarks. The major hacks of BSkyB were still coming out of Britain and Ireland. But as News Datacom turned to more sophisticated smartcards, the game grew harder. The key to hacking smartcards was not to defeat the algorithms that did the encoding and decoding, it was to analyse the system and find ways to trick the smartcard and the decoder into thinking this was a legitimate subscriber viewing. Part of that analysis was a physical exercise, using Oliver's new electron micro-scope to trace the tiny circuits on the smartcard that VideoCrpyt used, after exposing the different layers of the card. This required more and more expensive equipment. All of which made Oliver's garage more and more important.

What this meant was that, on that fateful night of 18 May 1994—Dark Wednesday—when BSkyB switched to its Series 9 smartcard, turning pirate television screens dark across Europe and triggering howls of anguish from pirate Trekkies who would miss the *Star Trek: TNG* season finale, the only sound that Oliver heard was a cash register. This time around, though, he was not pirating some other pirate's card; this was his moment. Within a month he had popped the new chip in his lab and produced a pirate code. It was a stunning achievement, and there was only one place to monetise appropriately what he had accomplished. Oliver went to London.

He called a meeting of Britain's leading pirate dealers at the Dorchester Hotel and announced he would be auctioning off his code to the highest bidder. The auction was won by five dealers who ponied up £50,000 apiece, and Oliver headed home with a cool £250,000. Heaven knows what his tax advisor was about to say. He was going to need a lot of invoices.

From that point on, it was just a race against time to pump out the new pirate cards to meet the impatient queues already forming in pubs across Britain. It was legendary stuff, and it would have worked even better if Oliver's code hadn't stopped working ten days later. The screens went back to being blank—the dealers had done their dough, and they also had a bunch of very unhappy customers. They leaked Oliver's code to the TVcrypt email group, known as the List, in the hope that they could help them find a solution. What Markus Kuhn and his colleagues found was that Yossi Tsuria's programming team at News Datacom in Israel had added a new level of complexities to ward off the hackers. Markus called them 'nano-commands', but Yossi's team referred to them as DDTs . . . digital dirty tricks. These nano-commands could change the way the cards operated, and could target specific piracy hacks. By early August the List had come up with a working solution to get past the DDTs and reactivate the dead Sky cards.

But for Oliver, the battle against the countermeasures had become like a chess game against Yossi Tsuria—although at that point he didn't know who he was playing against. Long before TVcrypt had cracked the code, Oliver had discovered how the nano-commands worked and devised a commercial solution for those pirates who could still afford it—because of course it would not come cheap.

Piracy is a logistics game. How do you get enough material to sell? The easiest thing to do is to reprogram an official smartcard from the satellite broadcaster, such as BSkyB. The first solution involved a smartcard that was cheap and plentiful, and had quickly become the workhorse of the pirate industry; it used the PIC16C84 microchip. The tricky part was that the pirates were not just reprogramming Sky cards—Oliver had hacked that card so comprehensively that he could now reproduce his own program on another smartcard to mimic the Sky 09 card. It worked fine, though it would need to be reprogrammed regularly, whenever BSkyB ran its electronic counter measures (ECMs) to kill pirate cards. That was the entry level solution. But then Oliver took it to the next step.

He devised a tiny circuit board that had a battery attached with a tiny keyboard. It plugged into the card slot of the set-top box and used a Dallas 5002FP microchip that could be reprogrammed using the keyboard. What this meant was that, when BSkyB ran its ECMs, if you used this battery card all you had to do was call a telephone number and write down a series of digits from a recorded message. You typed those numbers into the keyboard of the battery card and, like a charm, it started working again. It was a beautiful thing. And Yossi's team at News Datacom were incandescent.

BSkyB had just spent £21 million replacing its Series 7 cards with Series 9. But this had bought them only a couple of months' relief from piracy, little more. By the end of 1994, BSkyB's official position was that there were 50,000 pirate cards in Britain. But John McCormac, who wrote *The Black Book*, a manual and history of European scrambling systems and hacking, put the real figure at 300,000. That represented pirate sales in the previous six months of more than £50 million.

This wasn't the only damage. The launch date for the first big US satellite broadcaster, DirecTV, to be secured by News Datacom cards was 17 June 1994. They were modelled on the Series 9 that card BSkyB had introduced the month before. Oliver held his auction of his Series 9 code in the Dorchester Hotel three days after the DirecTV launch. Both the American and British satellite systems would soon be completely exposed, thanks to Oliver. It was quite a buzz for the boy with no education.

'For me it was just excitement because—imagine, you are sitting there alone and you crack a system, and you do this and in your mind you have this kind of vision of a company with ten, twenty engineers, designing that system and it's you as a single person which takes it all apart like that. It makes you feel really great . . . You just feel good,' he says. And this was just the beginning. All over Europe pay TV systems were starting up and pirate entrepreneurs were calling for Oliver's services.

'After I understood that there's a lot of money in this I really organised it, and I look with the lawyers, what I can do and what I can't do.' The answer turned out to be rather a lot of the former. 'And why should I think that it was wrong? I mean, I'm not stupid. Whenever I was doing something I was looking what I was doing . . .' He says he didn't really care to be in the grey area. That was for other people.

'I mean, I was always open to what I can get . . . with some people I had the arrangement for—we share the profit. With some others

I had the arrangement that I have 20 per cent, because they have all the production costs and et cetera. And with other people I say okay, you just pay me one amount—and after, you do what you want.'

Today Oliver claims he never sold a pirate card in his life. But the fame he won from the battery card soon had the world beating at his door. It wasn't that he was the only hacker working on cards. He was just faster, and probably better than anyone else. Everyone wanted a piece of him. They wanted to pay for a piece of him. His friend Harold in Nürburgring, for example, would bring cards to reprogram. Then there was Bela in Hungary, Lars in Sweden, and another contact in Norway. In short order, Oliver found himself at the centre of a ring of a dozen people who became his distribution network all across Europe.

Oliver thought it was fantastic. They even gave themselves a name—ELAB Works, which translated as the European Underground Laboratory Group. Through 1995, while BSkyB was hiring private detective firms to chase down British pirates, Oliver's group in Europe reigned supreme.

Geneva, 1994–95

Jan Saggiori was beginning to think he wasn't really cut out to be a lawyer. His parents had grown used to having his bedroom and sometimes their lounge room filled with computers in various states of assembly from his importing business. Digital Equipment Corporation had tapped his programming and language skills to produce an Italian version of its banking software program, but it was just a sideline. He had finished his degree in economics and finance in mid 1993. But the University of Geneva's business school opened doors across Europe for its graduates—particularly through Professor Klaus Schwab's final-year class, *Politique d'Enterprise,* or 'company strategy'. Jan loved it. He found he had a talent for working in teams and organising them. And he found himself mixing in senior business circles.

Jan had been doing internships with Olivetti in Spain. His work caught Schwab's eye. His major project under Schwab's oversight was a management presentation for Olivetti, where he met chief executive Carlo De Benedetti (the owner of *La Repubblica* and who in time would become Silvio Berlusconi's great enemy) and Corrado Passera (appointed Italy's minister of Economic Development, Infrastructure and Transport in 2011). Saggiori was offered an internship by the CEO of Coca-Cola, but instead took a three-month stint at Intelsat in Washington DC in mid 1995.

'Jan was a very, very special student,' says Vittorio Mischi, who supervised him. He pauses as he struggles for the right words. Idiosyncratic would be a recurrent term to describe Jan. He had a grasp of technology that was way in front of anyone Vittorio had met. While warm to friends he had a sense of form and propriety mixed with a taciturn social style.

'He will write you an email or letter with your address and title, the date, formal salutations and signature, while the message itself may only comprise two words,' Vittorio says. 'Jan won't say three words when two words will do.'

Jan loved the work so much he later became the only student ever to do Schwab's course twice, repeating it for his second degree, when he made a strategy presentation to Nicolas Hayek, the charismatic founder of the Swatch Group. Hayek impressed Jan deeply as a role model.

'He was a very impressive person, really nice, who lived life at 200 miles per hour,' says Saggiori. 'He was a builder and was very positive, not a thief like so many sharks around.' By the end of 1994 Jan saw that a law degree was the next step on the way to a senior management career, but here he ran into a roadblock. He hated the legal mindset, and at that very moment he had found a much more compelling outlet for his skills.

Jan had installed a satellite dish and decoder at his parents' big house in southern Geneva in 1992 so the family could watch Italian television programming, much of which was free to air. In 1994, acting on a whim, he bought a pirate card for BSkyB. It was based on a PIC16C84 smartcard and it worked a treat. It opened a whole vista of English-language programming from Sky for the Saggiori family, right up until the day it suddenly stopped working. Jan couldn't understand it—what was the problem? He went looking for answers on electronic bulletin boards across Europe, on what was the precursor to the internet.

He ended up on John McCormac's bulletin board in Ireland, which was a major meeting point for pay TV hackers. Here Jan found a whole new group of friends with shared interests. He also found a piracy dealer in Dublin who provided the upgrades needed to reactivate the PIC cards after each round of electronic counter measures (ECMs) was launched by BSkyB. The dealer was being supplied with updates by Steve Bennett, a leading figure in British piracy circles who was close to Chris Cary. Bennett told Jan that he was downloading the files to upgrade the PIC cards from a source in Germany; but they were expensive and sometimes took a while to come, which upset his customers. Bennett welcomed Jan's questions. Pirate dealers were always on the lookout for hackers—those who did it for the thrill, not the money.

The issue was simple for Jan. He wanted to know how this thing worked: 'When there's a black screen, I want to understand why I cannot see it. And I want to understand the process behind the software doing it.' Bennett picked up on Jan's fascination, and his obvious programming skills. He gave Jan a copy of the latest upgrade file he had received from Germany, and here Jan's social and networking skills kicked in. He talked about it with his friends online. They looked at the code together and worked on disassembling it. This was no simple task—reverse engineering a pirate smartcard can be every bit as elusive as cracking the real thing. They apportioned out parts of the code. Jan had a knack for getting people to work together.

'It's my natural way. I gave it to my friends and they were happy and were giving me feedback on parts of the code. It was just teamwork, with nobody first, but everybody in it together.'

Then they had the code. Oliver's code. There was no more need for expensive upgrades for the cards. The question was, though, what they were going to do with it. And the answer clearly did not include plans to get rich from it. Jan's online nickname was ToySoft. It was his private little joke. He meant Soft as in software, and he added Toy to make it clear that this was all just a game. Nothing more.

At the same time Jan was following his passion, and in the process his law studies were taking a hit. He had a mainstream career to pursue, and he knew that he could work successfully with senior business figures across Europe with whom he was mixing regularly. More than that, he had grown up in a family deeply imbued with a sense of history and ethics. His father would walk through the towns of northern Italy with him and would rattle off the history of every street, almost every house, going back centuries. Jan had a larger world than just heading for the nearest money-making opportunity. Hacking wasn't illegal and he didn't see it as wrong. He would help his friends, and on occasion he would take a little fee for his costs. It was only fair, given his expenses. If anything he was a curator of ideas and knowledge. So, inevitably, he set up a website to carry the code he and his friends had hacked and re-engineered.

'I did it for enjoyment, for fun. Because it's not commercial for me. It's not to get fame—it's just to do something successfully and understand it and for the recognition you get, like a researcher. A guy will research and then he publishes in a magazine. Why not a website?'

He was soon collaborating with other leading hackers—like Voyager in Holland and Andy Kozlov in Moscow. John McCormac had introduced him to TVcrypt. The List wasn't the place to find things out, but it was a place to get contacts. It was with these contacts that Jan picked up another commercial pirate device, an unblocker, or 'Phoenix' device.

By late 1994, BSkyB was sending out kill commands to more than 200,000 cards a month, most of which had been distributed under its Quickstart program offering a cheap subscription for the first six months, which then usually lapsed. An unblocker reversed the kill command and brought the old card back to life—hence the name Phoenix. Jan extracted the code from the pirate unblocker, figured out how it worked, then created software on the computer to do the same thing. This went on his website too, along with the best of the other programs available.

'The Sky 09 card—I think I killed it. Because I released the software called Phoenix 2, and that software was reactivating any old card. There was nothing they could do. Every card around was going to be fully reactivated.' In the process, Jan made some powerful enemies.

Jan had dropped his law studies in favour of a computer science degree. His research thesis at the Univeristy of Geneva would be reverse engineering smartcards. His links with the business school continued. And at the start of 1995 Professor Schwab hired him to work in the logistics team for the World Economic Forum at Davos. His duties included looking after VIPs for some of the sessions, which is how on 31 January 1995 he ended up escorting the headline speaker for the session in the main room at Davos to the podium. Rupert Murdoch barely noticed the young man beside him with the reserved, deferential manner and wry smile. Then Murdoch launched into a spiel on the future of newspapers—he thought the European media business had way too many laws.

Riedelberg, western Germany, 1995–96

This was Oliver's time. As word of his hacking exploits spread, more and more people asked to join his distribution network. There was an entry fee—dealers had to pay between 50,000 and 100,000 deutschmarks. Though, as always, while he developed the pirate products, he never sold the pirate cards—there was always a cut-out, someone else who would take the heat if any problem arose.

On 31 October 1995 BSkyB deployed a new card, Sky 10, from Yossi Tsuria's crew at NDS. The card was the most sophisticated yet, with a second ASIC microchip added to the first microchip, to provide more security. This one was expensive and was supposed to be unbreakable. It was delicious. Looking back, Oliver can't stop laughing.

'They thought, "If we do this development, then we should be safe. I mean, it's not going to be so easy really to analyse the chip physically and reverse engineer that." And basically they are right,' he says, again with the high-pitched giggle. 'What was funny is that when—once I extracted the software I found some bugs, software mistakes, which allow you to modify an original card in a way that you could switch on all subscriptions and, er, it was so funny because only—the only thing we had to do is to tell people about it.'

Popping a card never took Oliver longer than three days. A security fence is only as strong as its weakest link. And he had found it. This was Yossi Tsuria's nightmare: his 450 engineers had produced an expensive card after years of research, and it was all brought to nothing—you could almost count the hours—by Oliver uncovering a basic loophole that had been left in the software. And then it was open season again for Oliver's people.

The fact that Sky 10 had two separate chips mounted on it meant that PIC cards would no longer work for it. But they could reprogram existing Sky 10 cards at will (these are called modified original smartcards, or MOSC). Later on Oliver produced a battery card that mimicked the Sky 10 card. And life was good. Oliver owned BSkyB. And that was wasn't all. Across Europe there were other pay TV operators, other encryption systems to crack. There was D2-Mac, which was used in France and Scandinavia; there was a later version of D2-Mac called Viaccess; there were Nagra's latest version, Syster, and South Africa's Irdeto. Oliver's ideal was his Omega card, a battery card that worked for all pay TV systems—the one card to rule them all.

Oliver was king of the jungle. But even the king will pick up when someone challenges his dignity and his position. Royalty can get snitty. Oliver was aware of various hackers who had pirated his own products. It was really deeply annoying, but he could live with it for the most part. Lately he had begun to focus on a hacker called ToySoft. He knew from the TVcrypt List that it was Jan Saggiori in Switzerland.

There had been the battery cards Oliver had provided to Steve Bennett in Britain that had stopped needing updates from him, thanks to Jan. This had cost him money. Then there had been Jan's publication of the Sky 09 codes on the web—but this had made Oliver more money when BSkyB had to move to the Sky 10 card, but that was hardly the point. Thousands of PIC cards that had been used by Oliver's Sky 09 code were completely useless. Now he heard that Jan had found a way to reprogram Oliver's old Sky 09 cards in order to use them for completely different systems running D2-Mac, the rival encryption program in Scandinavia. Jan was really starting to get up Oliver's nose. However, he had an idea about how to even the score.

These then were the different faces of hacking at the end of 1996: Markus, the principled academic who had made hacking acceptable in the course of building a career that would take him to Cambridge University; Oliver, the individualist/mercenary, a commercial hacker who miraculously kept his fingers clean and his police record pristine; and Jan, the taciturn, passionate management trainee with the head full of history, who pursued hacking because it was his personal fascination, his absorbing hobby. Oliver was an individualist, but Jan's mindset and his loyalty to friends made him a collectivist—for him, the hacking community was akin to a guild.

Hackers' allegiances lay with each other. Chris Tarnovsky was not yet a player; at this time he was assigned as a driver at a US army base in central Germany and loathing it. Oliver was the anti-Markus figure, with his singular focus on monetising everything. But life is usually more than simple binaries. The real anti-Oliver figure, it would turn out, was Jan Saggiori.

The world that had produced these men had already begun to change. Hacking's age of innocence was about to end. It started with an unwelcome surprise at a meeting in London in July 1995.

PART 3

Hunting Parties

I would not accept criminals around me but if somebody in my environment does pirate products who am I to judge him? Or you? We were both doing the same now we are on the other side. Can we really judge them. Can you? I can't. Would make me feel arrogant.

I can't judge what's good or bad so I leave it to my lawyer.

Oliver Kömmerling to Jan Saggiori, May 2011

London, July 1995

Abe Peled knew the job was too good to be true. There had been a question swirling around in his head ever since that first approach. Rupert Murdoch had asked for an interview with him in May 1995. Peled had flown to London from Israel to see the head of News Corporation in his office at Wapping. Rupert had been in headhunting mode, which is to say he was at his most charming. All sorts of topics across world events were discussed before he came to the point. Peled had been in too many power interviews in his days as vice president for research at IBM not to know the style. His IBM job had turned out to be a lot about selling things to people. It took a lot of chutzpah. Or a hide like a rhinoceros'.

Peled could also turn on the charm in his deep, heavily accented English. He was a raconteur. But he could tell a story with an edge to it. Like Murdoch, he could make some of his most combative, barbed comments as an amusing aside, an afterthought. And he wasn't afraid to tackle an issue head-on. Now, after the preliminaries, Murdoch was offering him a job to run NDS, his Israeli technology arm, replacing Tom Price the former paint salesman.

Why were they having this conversation? Why was Murdoch getting involved in such a tiny part of his empire?

'Why me?' Peled asked bluntly.

'Because the future is digital,' Murdoch told him.

It was the magic line. Peled now knew that Rupert was serious about wanting him because those very words came from a book Peled had published ten years earlier. Books about digital signal processing don't get a lot of play in bestseller lists. Whoever had put together Peled's dossier to brief Murdoch had managed to get hold of a copy and actually read some of it. Which in turn meant that Murdoch might really be serious about this, with some idea of just how far this new technology would propel the world forward.

It turned out that Murdoch had always believed that encryption was the key to the digital future. He had sent people around the world to look for the best encryption technology, and he had found that the very best was being done by Professor Adi Shamir in Israel. It was another example of Rupert's unfailing vision and foresight. At least that was how Peled told the story later. With the right man in charge of NDS (the new name for News Datacom), this was just the beginning.

As the two men talked, a vision of the bright future stretched before them. Rupert Murdoch's global pay TV empire then stretched from BSkyB in Britain to Stream SpA in Italy, and then across all of Asia through Star TV to Foxtel in Australia, Sky in New Zealand—and Murdoch was just getting into stride. News was investing in a string of new platforms across South America; in the United States Murdoch was partnering with long-distance telephone giant, MCI, to launch American Sky Broadcasting. The single element that drew this vast empire together, that provided security for its operations, that in the end made sure the whole system worked, was NDS. Murdoch was such a passionate advocate that he had convinced General Motors to use NDS for its DirecTV launch. But for Peled it was much more than this.

The NDS set-top box was the door into hundreds of millions of homes around the world. Peled wanted to use that door to sell a whole suite of interactive services feeding off that set-top box. It would be worth billions. Peled's visions were even grander than Murdoch's, but both men were in agreement on one thing—that the success of NDS would prove pivotal to News Corporation's future.

It was happy timing because Peled's career was then in hiatus. He had been born in Romania in 1945, four months after the end of the Second World War in Europe. His parents migrated to Israel when he was thirteen and, as a young adult, he had completed an electrical engineering degree at the Technion in Haifa, graduating just in time to serve in the Israeli army in the Six-Day War. From there he had become an officer in the Signal Corps, which meant classified encryption work while he studied part-time for his masters. In 1971 he went to Princeton to do his PhD, and then joined 'Big Blue'. He was at IBM for nineteen years, the last eight years running the troubled politics of its research division. Then in August 1993 he left to return to Israel to run business development for an Israeli investment firm, Elron Electronic Industries. He said he made the move to be closer to his family. But 47 is a dangerous age to make life decisions. Peled had discovered, it seems, that at heart he was a passionate Israeli. It was a massive step down in the world. Peled didn't even run Elron—he was having to answer to a chief executive who had his own ideas.

Almost two years later, the religious/patriotic sentiments remained, but now he was running his own little fiefdom in News Corporation. And at first it had all gone so well. He had started work on 1 July, with a general introduction to the staff at the NDS offices in Jerusalem. It had been cordial enough. Days later he had flown to Australia, to attend the annual News Corporation management conference on Hamilton Island on the Great Barrier Reef. That was the weekend when the British opposition leader

Tony Blair made his pitch for Murdoch's support. Blair's speech was impressive, but it was the assurances he gave Murdoch on future Labour Party policy in a private meeting that sealed his bright future.

Murdoch was then in the middle of buying out the remaining 36.4 per cent stake that the Li Ka-shing family owned in Star TV in Hong Kong for $346.6 million. The deal was made public on 19 July, just five days before the White House announced that Murdoch's investment bank advisor, Stan Shuman, had been appointed to the President's Foreign Intelligence Advisory Board. It's hard to know exactly how Murdoch reacted to the news that his favourite News Corp director now had access (even if he could not share it) to all CIA and state department intelligence reports—for example, on ticklish subjects like Chinese trade relations . . . in the same week that he doubled up his bets on Star TV. In my mind, at least, the words, 'Well that's pretty handy,' would probably be a good start.

Peled flew back to London after the Hamilton Island conference to find that News Corporation's chief legal officer, Arthur Siskind, wanted to see him in his office at News International. Siskind had a few matters to talk through, but he started off with generalities, which was a warning signal in itself. Siskind didn't do small talk—he was a stocky, dogged figure who peered at the world with great suspicion and looked like what he was, an attack-dog New York lawyer. And remorseless. He could argue a point for days in any corporate negotiations, to the point where the other side's lawyers wanted nothing more than to get out of the room. Now he told Peled there was a problem. It was Michael Clinger and sex. And at this point Abe Peled felt the first tickle of the hook in the trap that had been set for him.

Little had been heard of Clinger since his departure from NDS in 1992, but he had been busy. Apart from defrauding almost everyone he had ever done business with, the former NDS chief had a wandering eye. He had left his wife, Niva Von Weisl, when she was pregnant—for another woman. He had then divorced Niva and remarried. But, just because he was divorced, didn't mean that anyone could touch his ex-wife.

Leo Krieger, NDS's chief accountant and Clinger's best friend, didn't get it. Krieger fell hard for Niva and left his wife and six children to move in with her. Clinger was furious. It became an obsession. He painted the word 'Adulterer' in Hebrew on the wall of his ex-wife's Jerusalem house—no small thing when you lived in the Orthodox community that made up much of the senior ranks at NDS. When Krieger and Von Weisl took a vacation in Spain, Clinger followed them. The ex-husband was threatening violence and Krieger began fearing for his own safety. At least, that's what he told Gus Fischer, because Krieger now took steps to take Clinger out of the picture.

Krieger met Fischer in London in March 1995 and told him that Clinger had been stealing millions from NDS for years. The fraud was based around the supply of blank smartcards. Clinger and an accomplice still at NDS had manoeuvred to ensure that only one supplier—Catalyst Conductors in California, owned by Clinger's old friend Bharat Kumar Marya—met NDS's security requirements for supplying the blank smartcards that it programmed for BSkyB in Britain and DirecTV in the United States. Marya inflated the price of the cards by £1 and split the secret profit with Clinger. After 19 million cards, that's a lot of secret profit.

But now the game was up. Or the game would have been up if Gus Fischer had not fallen out with Murdoch and resigned days later. So, once again, News Corp failed to follow up on allegations against Michael Clinger. But he had no shortage of enemies. On 31 March an Israeli lawyer, Abraham Nantel, flew to London for a secret meeting at the Four Seasons Hotel with two News executives, and repeated the same claims about Clinger's fraud. This time alarm bells rang in New York and Arthur Siskind became involved.

Everything happened quickly from then. Siskind hired Argen Security, a private firm founded by a former spy that had an uncanny ability to extract confidential information . . . starting with the bank accounts of Clinger's secret holding companies in the Netherland Antilles, the British Virgin Islands, the Channel Islands, Bermuda, Liberia and Panama. They discovered bank transfer details, telephone records and restricted court documents relating to Clinger.

'We know everything about him,' Siskind boasted in 1997. News was able to obtain the details of Clinger's marriage settlement, which was locked in an Israeli court safe, and even the cost of the $250,000 Swiss glass staircase he had installed in his $1.5 million home in Jerusalem.

For some of the investigations necessary in Israel, Siskind also hired Shafran, a security firm run by three former Shin Beit agents—Rafi Malka, Peleg Radai and Reuven Hasak. They had developed quite a reputation. They had had a minor walk-on part in the US Iran–Contra scandal, and there had been some unseemly and hurtful claims made by Likud Party figures in the 1988 election that Shafran had been wiretapping their phones for the Labour Party. But nothing had come of that. They had security links right to the top. When Israeli Prime Minister Menachem Begin was assassinated in November 1995, it was Rafi Malka, the former operations chief, who headed the first review of how Shin Beit had allowed this to happen.

Siskind authorised cash payments to Clinger's former friend, Leo Krieger, for bodyguards. And Abe Peled was brought on board. Peled had been thinking of this new job as a springboard for international expansion, but he belatedly realised the real reason he had been hired was to clean up a disaster zone. Rupert hadn't mentioned this at the job interview.

Siskind now told him that at least one of the executives who had been so welcoming to Peled only days before was still secretly working with Clinger on the fraud. Peled would have to continue working with the man without giving any hint of his suspicions while the undercover investigation continued. Meanwhile NDS was facing a pressing deadline. BSkyB was due to switch over to the new Sky 10 cards on 31 October, which meant that Peled was dependent upon getting supplies of the new cards, which for the moment could only be obtained via Clinger's good friends, Marya's Catalyst Conductors.

Could Peled manage this? Did he have an option? It was in this meeting of minds in July 1995, between Peled and Siskind, two singularly aggressive and determined players, that a bond was formed that would reshape not just NDS but much of Rupert Murdoch's global satellite empire. And it would tie the runaway Israeli operation even more closely to the Office of the Chairman in New York.

Siskind would become obsessed with pursuing Clinger.

'It's become a personal mission of Arthur's,' Murdoch said later.

For Peled, as his vision of the dream job cratered, it would be impossible not to feel a deep sense of betrayal, one that focused on the threat Clinger's treachery posed to NDS's future. His job had become a moral imperative—to right what was wrong. It seemed like Peled was working once more in the secret world of his days in the army signals division. Reuven Hasak became an invaluable guide and a close friend. He was a fount of stories about security operations. What soon became clear to Peled was that the biggest threat to NDS's future was not Michael Clinger—it was piracy, which now posed an existential threat to NDS's future. VideoCrypt had become the most hacked conditional access system in the world—in Britain, across Europe, in the United States, Canada and Mexico. Hasak was Peled's guide through this new landscape. Because, for Hasak, piracy was just another sort of security problem. And security was what Hasak's people were good at.

If there was a point where the whole NDS operation started to go off the rails, it was probably here. Of course it's easy for me to say that, typing away while eating burnt toast and surrounded by dirty coffee mugs, years after the event. You note these turning points only in hindsight. Arthur Siskind was pursuing an international fraud run by Michael Clinger, and his agents would end up with information about the fraud from sources and techniques that can only be wondered at. For both Siskind and Peled the hunt would be deeply personal. Clinger must be made to pay. But soon that emotion and commitment, as well as the logistical infrastructure at both men's disposal, would be turned against not only the commercial pirates but student hackers around the world as well. And the game would become far murkier.

Security is about enforcement, but first of all it's about information. You run the internet searches and patrol the chat rooms but in the end the key is HUMINT—human intelligence gathering. You need informants. But to run informants, you need agents and you need controllers. It's an intelligence network.

The first move would be to set up a permanent operational security division at NDS. In fact they already had a security officer—an ex-Shin Beit agent called Roni Segoly—but this was just a start. Hasak was now permanently seconded from Shafran to run the new security division. In Britain, BSkyB had turned to using private investigators to hunt down pirates; but Hasak could do better than that. He hired a former Scotland Yard officer with a tough reputation.

Ray Adams had resigned from the Met on health grounds in May 1993, citing a bad back. Since then he had worked for Pinkerton detective agency. In January 1996 Adams was hired as NDS's head of operational security for Europe. To head the US operation Reuven hired John Norris, who had kicked around for twenty years in the private security business, before becoming a security consultant for DirecTV in late 2005. The Jerusalem office would be run by Avigail Gutman, a young woman in her late twenties, who was discreet about her training but had impressed Hasak.

This was the A team. But, from an outsider's perspective, its pedigree was deeply worrying. At its head was Reuven Hasak, one of the world's most senior intelligence operatives, who came to News Corporation with a history of fabricating evidence and orchestrating perjury. In Britain, I think the kindest thing that can be said about Ray Adams was that his handling of his informant Kenneth Noye could have gone better. The question that is always levelled at informant–police relationships is, whether it's conscious or not: Just who is running whom? Some of Adams' colleagues had a more jaundiced view. The decision by the Crown prosecutor's office that there was insufficient evidence to bring charges against Adams entitled him to say he had been exonerated without a single aspersion on his character. But after two years of investigation, even though it had led to no findings against him, if Adams had opted to stay on in the Met indefinitely, that would have presented continuing challenges. In California the new recruit, Norris, brought with him a history of aggressive action against pirates—his nickname was 'The Cowboy'.

Hasak, Adams and Norris had no idea what they were about to unleash. The kindest interpretation of what followed is that they were ludicrously inept. In the mad days that followed, the most sane viewpoint, the voice of reason at NDS, would come from the former terrorist, Yossi Tsuria.

There would be a reckoning to be paid for this, but the three men who would trigger it remained oblivious. Meantime, Alan Guggenheim was about to become a consultant with Charlie Ergen's EchoStar satellite start-up in the United States, which used the Swiss encryption system, Nagra. Gilles Kaehlin had found someone else to annoy and had been exiled once more, this time to New Caledonia in the Pacific. And Jan Saggiori had just found a neat new way to trace smartcard serial numbers—he wasn't worried at all.

Grafenwoehr US Army Base, 12 March 1996

Chris Tarnovsky had the home-cooking thing down pat. The oven was on pre-heat to 150 degrees, his cookie tray ready to roll. A reek of acetone wafted through the kitchen of his army townhouse in central Germany as it melted inside a glass container he had balanced on top of the metal cookie tray. Mixed with the whiff of acetone was a more acrid aroma, from the liquid in an eye dropper perched beside the oven. It doesn't rate a mention in most kitchen routines, but the sharp bouquet of nitric acid is hard to miss. In Tarnovsky's world, you just had to say 'HNO3' and all hackers knew what you were doing. Chris was about to attack a smartcard. This one was the NDS VideoCrypt II card for BSkyB.

Attack. Now there's a word. While everyone else in the world might refer to attacking a card, or hacking it, the characters in this saga prefer gentler terms.

'You know I don't hack anything, I *analyse* them,' Tarnovsky told me in 2009. 'But I mean there's not a smartcard today that I haven't analysed.' *Analyse* is more an expression of neighbourliness—a social occasion, a little like dropping over for tea and crumpets.

Hacking is a foreign concept to Reuven Hasak as well. 'I know that they are running . . . technical research I call it, because I am not technical enough to understand what is research engineering, so I refer to [it] as technical research,' he testified in 2008.

Oliver Kömmerling shares their semiotic scruples.

'I wouldn't call it necessarily an attack, I mean . . . *attack* is not a safe word,' he says. '*Analyse?* Well, I mean, if I look into something on your car or your clothes I'm not attacking you—you can say I'm analysing you, or spying on you. When the doctor is making an analysis of your body, is he attacking you? . . . It's not an attack—an attack sounds like physical and it's not like that. But anyway let's skip that.'

In March 1996, the technical research in Tarnovsky's kitchen began with putting the card in the glass container and slipping it into the oven. Chris took it out after a minute and then, with the plastic pliable and the heat loosening the glue that held the card together, he used an Exacto knife to bend the plastic, and began to insert the knife from the top to the bottom of the card. As it cooled, the card stiffened and he returned it to the oven for another 30 seconds. He would take it out to work the knife a little further, and then he'd return it to the oven. Over and over until the micro-chip on the card came free. Then he worked the wire edges under-neath the microchip with his knife, excruciatingly aware that any false step would break the tiny contacts and kill the card.

Any smartcard has eight contact areas, which is the gold design on the front of the card, though only six of the contacts are used. The microchip sits beneath them and needs to be worked free. Tarnovsky put the microchip, still encased in plastic, back on the glass tray for another minute. Then he eased a drop of nitric acid onto the chip and closed the oven door as the acid began fuming. Another minute and the acid had turned the surface of the micro-chip a dirty brown colour with little bubbles. He used the knife to etch away the acid residue—sweating a little with the effort required to keep his hands steady, and not to push too far—before he tried another drop of acid. When he finished etching, the plate of the microchip (known as the 'die') was clear. He had made it through the first step. Or so he hoped.

But that was all he could do. From here on he needed access to an electron microscope. His friend Stefan could help there. In the early cards, this was all that was needed. For all their compli-cated designs, encryption routines and high-tech applications, there is no magic wand that tells microchips how to function. It's a physical thing that must be laid out in the two sets of memory built into the card. There is the read-only memory (ROM), which can't be changed and carries the base code of the card. And there is the electronically erasable programmable read-only memory (EEPROM), which can be reprogrammed throughout the card's life. The memory and the source code that runs the card are on the microchip as a series of microscopic binary circuits (meaning each section can have a positive or negative charge, representing a one or a zero). It is laborious and sometimes bewilderingly complicated, but if you trace all of those circuits and those positive and negative values under the microscope—the binaries—you can work out the operating instructions that make the card work. You have the source code. You can use that to extract the secret keys that will unlock the decryption, and you can reprogram the operating instructions to make the card do whatever you want. You own the card.

Smartcard designers know all this, which is why they have made the microchips harder and harder to take apart and expose. It's a war that is played out at the microscopic level, with security meshes and grids and multiple covering layers that hide the inner workings of the chip. That's just the first level of defence, along with internal timers and clock lines and checksums, which are all ways of verifying that the internal running of the microchip has not been altered by hackers, checking the timing of the signal, and whether the packets of data have been modified by a pirate attack. These would require a bit more equipment than an oven and a dropper of nitric acid. Tarnovsky's more immediate problem was to explain to his wife Sylvie, eight months pregnant with their second child, why their kitchen smelt like a chemistry class and cookies were off the menu. Unhappily, the operation had not been a success. As he recalled: 'Unfortunately the card is somewhat dead. I must have broken the clock line. It tries to send but no cigar.' Those wretched clock lines.

He told the List about it anyway. Hacking had become Tarnovsky's obsession. When he launched with characteristic gusto onto the TVcrypt List in November 1995, he was 24 and stuck in a dead-end army job. He had grown up in Nyack, New York, near West Point military academy. Like many hackers he had a dominant father figure—George Tarnovsky was an electrical engineer, designing computer hardware.

'He was kind of cool, he always kind of inspired me, basically,' Chris says. 'You know, he just always gave me the drive.' Chris was always working on projects, from little circuit boards with LEDs to building his own Apple 2 computer with components from China: 'I grew up with a soldering iron in my hand.'

Picture an intense child with ADHD, which is often interpreted as a problem child. A lonely child.

'I was always kind of alone. I always had friends, but I was always kind of like in my computer. I didn't want to go to college because I hated school. I barely got out of school. All I'd do is write software in class. I never did my homework.' He would go to summer school to make up the classes he flunked, 'And I took some college, but honestly college bores the hell out of me.' Somehow he ended up in the army. He wanted a break from everything his life had been.

'I just wanted to go off on my own. And the military seemed like . . . Let me try it. Let me see.'

He ended up working in signals on the intelligence side, after intensive training in cyptography, with a top secret/sensitive compartmented information clearance, working at Supreme Headquarters Allied Expeditionary Force (SHAEF) headquarters in Belgium in May 1990. He met Sylvie Berny at an artificial beach. He spoke no French and she had no English, but they hit it off and by 1992 were married. He was then transferred Stateside, to the headquarters of the National Security Agency in Maryland. When his term came up, he re-enlisted to get back to Europe; but this was the army, so it didn't work that way.

'I said, "Wait a second, you know, I have a TS/SCI." You know, top-secret clearance. That's a lot of money they incurred training me. So they shipped me to a corner of Germany. I *hated* it.'

Sergeant Tarnovsky found himself attached to the third infantry division based in Grafenwoehr, which needed an encryption specialist with a security clearance equal to the president's like it needed a fish on a bicycle. They made the best of it and made him personal driver for the battalion commander, Colonel Thornsvard.

'Biggest mistake I ever made. I'm sitting on my thumbs doing nothing, driving him around. It's time for him to go back to America and he's like, you know, "Buy my satellite system?" And that was it.'

For $175, the colonel sold Tarnovsky a satellite dish, a decoder box and a couple of dead pirate PIC cards for BSkyB. From there it was a familiar story. American soldiers jumped at the chance to watch US television programs carried by BSkyB and piracy was rife through the army bases in Europe. It wasn't illegal, and ads for pirate cards were in every issue of *Stars and Stripes*. The local dealer, Jim Pitts, put Tarnovsky in touch with his supplier, Helmut Dolber.

The German piracy dealer was all over him: 'I was technical. There weren't a lot of technical people out there back then. And he had so many problems with the system going down, he needed help.' Tarnovsky was able to reactivate Helmut's PIC cards, then he moved on to the new range of battery-powered smartcards that had just come out. He extracted the code for the battery cards—he had heard they were produced by someone called Oliver—and set himself up as the new supplier for local army bases. Helmut introduced Tarnovsky to another local hacker, Stefan Eisvogel, just south of him in Regensberg, who introduced him to Markus Kuhn. And there he was in November 1995 joining the List.

Sky 10 had just come out, which made his Sky 09 battery cards obsolete, so, while he waited for someone else to pop the new card, he did the only thing possible and focused on European porn channels instead. The Rendezvous channel was promising. It used the D-2Mac encryption system, which had already been hacked by Jan Saggiori. Chris now extracted keys for the Danish TV3 channel, which he released to the List. He lived life with an exclamation mark and had no sense of discretion—he wanted help, he wanted everything, right now! In mid December he discovered nitric acid: 'I am going to do it! (buy 1 liter of $HNO3$). I only want like 25ml though! What should I do with the rest? (Markus? Anybody? Need some?)'

It was March 1996 before he worked out how to use the nitric acid without killing the card, but he was rubbing people up the wrong way. He had just received a stinging public put-down from a Swedish member of the List, Per Goransson, when he received a helpful note from Jan Saggiori. Chris latched on to Jan like a limpet, coopting him into his personal campaign to crack the Rendezvous cards. And suddenly there developed one of these intense exchanges between hackers that can forge lifelong friendships. Jan was much closer than Chris to the action that was going on elsewhere to crack Sky 10, and Chris was desperate to be part of it: 'If we do dump the card I sure won't give anyone except us the keys. People are real assholes on the List lately!'

He began phoning Jan regularly. Part of the bond came from being underdogs, not part of the Oliver Kömmerling cabal. Oliver had his Omega card. Chris dreamed of making his own Ultima card, which would carry solutions for multiple pay TV systems. Everything else in his life became a distraction from his intense online sessions. Everything. He confided to his new best friend: 'So you are Toysoft?? I always wanted to be "VONRAT ASSOC." (That's "TARNOV"sky backwards! Just something my Dad came up with a long time ago.) Cool.'

Tarnovsky's new colonel had told him he was too smart to be driving a Humvee around Germany. He convinced him to take an early discharge. Tarnovsky was due to fly back to America on

4 July and he was determined to take as much pirate software as he could, particularly since he had learned that the NDS card used by DirecTV (also known as DSS—Digital Satellite Service) was based on Sky 09. Every day there was a new appeal from him to Jan: 'Can I get a copy of your program . . . Let me know if you have Algo [the algorithm] for DSS? I will need it. I am keeping silent about it since I will be watching and it is illegal [to hack in US]!'

He was particularly anxious to get Jan's latest version of his Sky 09 code. He would share this with nobody, it was just Jan and him. Really.

'It was not I who released the key nor leaked anything! I am totally out of contact!' Almost completely out of contact, as later he wrote: 'Oops. I gave Luca the stuff this weekend . . . I thought it was not so bad if only me, you and Luca have base code . . . I truly believe he will be honest.' That was Chris all over—excitable, running at a hundred kilometres an hour, very likable and just a little flaky as he horse-traded with Jan to swap smartcards and decoder boxes.

The new friends were mostly oblivious to the gathering storm overshadowing the world of satellite hacking. In Britain, Ray Adams had hired Detective Chief Inspector Len Withall, a twenty-year career officer with the Surrey Police, as his deputy. Their first target was Chris Cary's Irish company, Megatek. Cary had a battery card for Sky 10 on sale by April 1996, but what Cary didn't know was that Withall had planted an undercover informant to work in his British offices.

On June 20, Cary was arrested in a series of police raids on Megatek's English operations. The court process would take a while, but Cary would end up with a four-year jail sentence. Six days later on the other side of the Atlantic, police in the United States, Canada, Bermuda and the Cayman Islands raided 26 hackers and pirate distributors involved in pirating the new DirecTV service in an operation coordinated by John Norris.

The raids were just one part of Reuven Hasak's strategy. The first hurdle had been to convince UK and US police and security agencies to move against satellite piracy. Adams' and Withall's police contacts were useful here. In the United States, John Norris had hired a former US Customs and Border Protection agent and his manager of security was a former special agent with the US Secret Service. The Secret Service, in addition to protecting the president, is also charged with tracking counterfeiting operations. One of the great achievements of US cable companies had been to convince the Secret Service that anyone who produced a pirated smartcard or decoder was a counterfeiter. Norris would get very close to law enforcement. He would provide technical expertise, lab facilities, training; he even sponsored charity golf tournaments for them. By one account NDS also provided police officers with an email box for private correspondence.

The next move had been to convince prosecutors elsewhere—notably Canada and Europe—to join the fight, even though US and UK piracy was not illegal in those countries. This was a harder sell, but by no means impossible. With this support in place, piracy dealers in England and North America would be targeted, employing a muscular style of enforcement directed by Abe Peled's new employees.

'There's nothing like turning up at a hacker's home in the evening, preferably with a police officer,' Len Withall would say later.

It wasn't just police presence that NDS was relying upon. Ray Adams could play many roles, but he was really super at in-your-face unpleasantness.

'Ray Adams is like a policeman from the show *The Sweeney* in the 1970s—he likes to play the tough guy,' one dealer told me. Others at NDS had even less polish, and showed a serious capacity to frighten people. Hasak aimed to take out the key piracy dealers and to adopt an aggressive stance against small dealers. And then there were the raids themselves.

Having a police team go through your house with a search warrant early in the morning is a traumatic experience; but that was just the beginning, as Alan Guggenheim, the French engineer turned American management consultant, found out when he began dogging NDS's footsteps in 1999. 'They [NDS] used threats a lot, as well as money and other things in order to [recruit] pirates . . . Many, many, many pirates told me that and I have a tendency to believe it might be at least partly true.'

Private security firms traditionally provide physical security, or risk assessment, or they conduct investigations. What they don't usually do is set up permanent networks of informants. Even police operations tend to use informants on a more ad hoc basis, for a particular operation, rather than a directed long-term strategy. That seems more the province of an intelligence agency. In fact, something like the Israeli secret police, Shin Beit.

In 2000, Ray Adams spent several hours explaining to Alan Guggenheim the NDS strategy for creating networks of inform-ants around high-profile hackers and pirates.

'They would identify a target,' Guggenheim told me. 'And their goal was to have five people in their close environment; so, for example, family—like sisters, brothers, wives, parents—or close associates in the business—like a cashier or some clerk or someone or other in the store—and get these people on the NDS payroll and informing on what's happening around the target.' As Ray told Alan, they had dozens of targets, which in turn would require hundreds of people around them to be on the NDS payroll. It seemed extraordinarily expensive.

'I asked Ray if they always had five, he said no, sometimes we have one or two, but we like to have five,' said Guggenheim. 'You have to realise in the NDS system it's a mix of what they do and what they say they do and what they want pirates to believe that they do.'

Whether or not this is true, the fact that these claims floated about was effective in making people afraid of the new NDS, even if all this was perhaps merely run-of-the-mill intelligence work. But I think it was finessing Markus Kuhn that showed Reuven Hasak was running the show, because someone at NDS—and almost certainly it was Reuven—had figured out that blunt force would not work on Markus. That someone knew Markus wasn't doing this for money. It was his intellectual curiosity that made him so dangerous. In the first half of 1996 Markus had been completing his masters thesis by reverse engineering the 'unbreakable' Dallas DS5002 chip, which was being introduced for bank and credit card applications. The German information security agency was interested enough to set up a test case, to open an electronic vault they set up for him. Two hours later he faxed them back the twenty-digit code to open the safe, along with an annotated disassembly of their software—red faces all around at Dallas Semiconductor, and a $100 million bill to fix the hole in their chip and update the one million cards already in the field. In the summer of 1996 Markus was moving to Indiana on a Fulbright scholarship at Purdue University, but he was no less dangerous because he was out of Europe. So NDS tried a different tack.

Markus received an email. It read, 'Markus, we have never met. I think we know each other quite well.' It was from that legend of cryptography, Adi Shamir, who was still a consultant to NDS. Markus was suitably flattered by the attention. It was natural that Professor Shamir would introduce Markus to some of his colleagues at NDS. They too were interested in his ideas about cryptography, and suggested he might become a technical consultant. They asked him to write up his observations on the Video-Crypt system. They were thinking of doing something better, how would Markus do it? In hindsight Markus says he didn't realise how good the ideas he was passing on were. It was a one-way relationship: 'I would get a one-line email, "Do you have any thoughts on that subject?" and I wrote ten pages and, "Oh yeah, that's very good, do you have any thoughts on this subject?" And I would write another ten pages.' In hindsight he thinks he would have been better off publishing his replies as articles.

'I probably should have insisted on visiting them in person.' Markus doesn't say so, but there is an undercurrent that suggests that he feels he was taken advantage of. He shows no sign of being aware how closely NDS kept him under surveillance, or how intensely they debated the threat that he posed them. But perhaps Markus is just too polite to say so.

From the start, an NDS engineer, Perry Smith, had been a member of the TVcrypt List. But for Markus there was no conflict—this was about academic inquiry. Now Hasak's people began scrutinising everyone on the List . . . knocking on doors one by one. For example, Dieter Scheel was a high-profile German hacker, until the police came to the door even though hacking BSkyB was not illegal in Germany. Once they were in the court system, Ray Adams would drop by for a chat. He offered an end to the legal problems. And a little money. Perhaps that is what happened to Dieter. By the end of 1996 he was on Adams' books receiving regular payments.

Everyone would feel the heat from Hasak's team. But what they really needed was to catch the whale. They had to go after Oliver.

Riedelberg, western Germany, 1996

Police all over the world have a secret handbook that tells them how to do police stuff. That's my theory. They'll deny it, but I think it's the only explanation for why they all manage to do things the same way. Like when they stop you for a speeding ticket. No matter where you are, there's a way they get out of their car and saunter over on the backs of their heels. They teach that at the academy. And if you ever try a little humour to break the ice—an amusing aside, perhaps some witty commentary or a *hilarious* anecdote to ease the tension—they all have the same lip-tightening movement that tells you that this is so not a good idea. It's more like a facial tic. And then they give you The Eye. Stand-up comedy and police work are a dodgy combination wherever you go. I don't want to get into customs officers and airport security—it's a sensitive point.

Clearly there's a protocol that covers these things. For example, police raids. Serious ones only ever happen in the morning. And when I say morning, I mean 7 a.m. Any later and the target is likely to be leaving the house. Any earlier and it's going to be dark, and it's definitely going to clock up the overtime bill. Aside from the timing, there are two ways to run a raid. The first is to crash through with overwhelming force. The second is to have a couple of officers knock on the door, explain that they are making a little visit, and then signal the other dozen police officers waiting around the corner to pile on in. It's a little like asking 'Rabbit's Friends and Relations' over for morning tea.

Riedelberg is a rural community far out on the French border, which is perhaps why its police station never got the handbook. It was practically midmorning before a group of seven police officers came to the gate of Oliver Kömmerling's compound. His home was walled, with closed-circuit cameras covering the approaches. When the gate was finally opened, they drove up the drive to the main house. Across the field was a second building, but they ignored that. The man who opened the door to the house was in his underwear and dishevelled, giving every sign of having just woken up and not being very happy about it either. The lead officer took a moment to wonder what he had got himself into, then said they had a search warrant.

Oliver had been up much of the night working in his lab, and the moment to comprehend what was going on seemed to be slipping past him. What was this all about? The police officers wouldn't tell him. They told him a warrant had been issued by a court in . . . and the legal phrases just floated right past him.

The police team was in the house now, five men and two women, looking through everything. It was a typical middle-class home in a respectable area, with pictures of the two children at kindergarten on the walls. The sense of unreality grew as it became clear that, while the police were sparing no efforts in their search, they weren't completely clear what they were searching for. At something of a loss, the police inspector in charge turned to Oliver and asked, 'Do you have some kind of, uh, card?'

'What card are you talking about?' Oliver asked in return.

The inspector looked at his notes again. 'A smart . . . card,' he said in some puzzlement, experimenting with the sound of the new term.

'I don't know,' Oliver told him, and here, it must be said, he was not being entirely candid.

They knew it must be something to do with computers, so they took his wife Vicky's computer. And his four-year-old son's computer, which he used to play games. And that was pretty much that. As they walked out, the police inspector gathered what dignity he could, fixed Oliver with The Eye, and said enigmatically, 'I hope you understand that the search can be done in this way, or *another* way.'

He all but harrumphed. Oliver watched them drive away. At no time had they considered that the two-storey building across the field from the main house was on the same property, and thus also subject to the search warrant. It had never occurred to them that Oliver's reverse engineering lab was right in front of them. They probably didn't even understand what reverse engineering was.

Back at the house Oliver was putting the pieces together. Some time before, two men had made contact with his distribution group, with a batch of Sky 10 cards to be reprogrammed. Something about them had not seemed right.

'How the hell did you get so many cards?' he asked them. They mumbled something about collecting them through the post, in anticipation that someone would be able to reprogram them. Oliver hadn't believed them. In fact one of the two men, called Terry, was a private investigator working for BSkyB, while the other, Andy Coulthurst, worked for NDS.

The police had nothing on Oliver, he believed, though they could well charge him anyway. But his German partners were not so lucky. His friend Harold Steffes and his company, Heaven, were raided and Steffes was arrested on charges of hacking BSkyB. The police had found one of Oliver's hard drives at Heaven, but the files were encrypted. Today they're still in the police evidence lock-up, still encrypted.

And here was Oliver's problem: He didn't want to see his friend in trouble but a more pragmatic consideration was that, if his friend did a deal with the prosecutor, Oliver could find himself facing charges as well. Oliver had not got where he was by taking small gambles. He made an appointment to see the prosecutor.

While the prosecutor expected him to make a statement, Oliver was just fishing for information. In the verbal sparring that followed, Oliver learned that the most the police had on him was a document at Steffes' office that referred to sending 20,000 PIC cards to his address. The prosecutor had dropped this like you drop a winning card. And Oliver had breathed again. The prosecutor was bluffing. Oliver had not worked with PIC cards for some time but the explanation was simpler. His piracy network used codenames for each other, drawn from *Star Trek: The Next Generation*. Oliver was the leader, Captain Picard. If Oliver's partners were sending 20,000 to Picard it would have been money, not smartcards. In fact, he was sure he had a software invoice somewhere that would explain it. The police had nothing on him.

Oliver spoke to Steffes' lawyer, who was concerned, and Steffes' wife, who was frantic, and that contagion spread to Oliver's wife, Vicky. The walls seemed to be closing in on Oliver's group.

'I mean it was all very pushy and emotional at this time because I need to move and to act, so to sit at home and wait wasn't an option for me,' recalls Oliver.

His next port of call had to be NDS. He thought he could do a trade—he was the king of the pirates, he would offer his knowledge of the weaknesses of their smartcard in exchange for the release of his friend. Vicky told him he didn't know what he was doing. At this stage Oliver didn't even know who NDS was, or who was orchestrating the hunt against him. But he knew there had to be someone running the operation. He turned to a Pakistani piracy dealer in London called Huff, who came back with a name—a former Scotland Yard commander called Ray Adams— and a telephone number.

'I think you know who I am,' Oliver said down the line to London. Ray Adams was too old a hand to be drawn in like that.

'No, who is it?' he said.

'I'm the person you sent the police to in Germany.' And just like that, Ray Adams knew the whale was on the hook. But landing him would not be so easy. It would take time.

The first step was a meeting at Frankfurt airport. Oliver had a friend drive him the 170-kilometre trip. Adams showed up with News Datacom's German lawyer. And here was the first problem because, within minutes, Adams and Kömmerling had sensed something in each other's character that meant they could deal together. But Adams' first question was whether Oliver was The Man, the brains behind the Sky 10 hack. Oliver froze.

He had known the question was coming. But it was a question he couldn't afford to answer. If he said no he wasn't, then he had nothing to deal with. If he confirmed he was, then the lawyer could come after him based on his own statement. And here Oliver went off script.

He asked Ray Adams for his hand, and grasped it in a curious way. His index finger was bent back upon itself so that it nestled against Adams' palm. He told Adams to ask his question again; if he pressed his hidden finger against Adams' palm, he would be confirming his role in hacking Sky 10. But only Adams would know Oliver's response. And that was that. Oliver had sent Adams his own encrypted signal with his secret handshake, and the lawyer looking on could not say what had been communicated.

Adams was amused by the simplicity of this ploy. After they had talked on for another half an hour, he made his key gambit. In fact it had all been leading to this—tracking Oliver like a wild horse, beating the bushes and stampeding him towards the NDS corral. It was an old game, but it could still go amiss. Yet, when it came to the point, Adams found it was best to keep it casual.

'Could you imagine working for us?' he asked.

Oliver didn't hesitate. In principle yes, he said, 'But what do you really want? I mean, what does that mean? What do I have to do?'

The hurdle was past. And the talk moved on. There was Oliver's friend, Harold, to be considered. That would be difficult, said Adams. The public prosecutor had begun something; they couldn't just unwind it all and tell the prosecutor that it was all a big mistake. The meeting ended without resolution.

Back in Riedelberg, tension remained high. Months before, Oliver had booked to take a two-week vacation in Ibiza.

'The vacation was already planned and we wanted to go . . . it was all stressy situations, so I went with my wife and family there,' Oliver said. But Ray Adams now moved to a full-court press. He flew briefly to Ibiza with his wife, Inge, to see the Kömmerlings. The personal touch was to establish a link with Vicky. Perry Smith, the technical expert from NDS, also came to put Oliver gently through his paces. Two days later Adams called back to say Oliver had to fly to London for another session. The tickets would be at the airport. No, it couldn't wait until after the vacation. Oliver had to break the bad news to Vicky.

Oliver had made it through the first two rounds. This next encounter, in early 1997, would be the game decider. He was meeting Ray Adams' boss, the worldwide head of security for NDS. But Reuven Hasak had other things on his mind.

Jerusalem, 1995–96

Michael Cornelius Clinger was not going gentle into that long good night. Abe Peled and Arthur Siskind had dropped the boom on him on 14 February 1996, launching a civil action in the British High Court against Clinger and his cohorts claiming £19 million in damages from his fraud. The statement of claim was a model of its kind. An affidavit by Siskind listed in excruciating detail all the cash payments in and out of Clinger's bank accounts in Liberia, Jersey, the British Virgin Islands, Switzerland, Monaco and Luxembourg, showing how his ally B. K. Marya was siphoning cash and diverting 60 per cent of it to Clinger. It also contained extensive telephone records and a 45-page transcript of bugged phone conversations involving Clinger, which was produced by Leo Krieger—Clinger's most memorable line was his view about News management: 'You know, you have got to keep that in mind . . . we would not be doing what we were doing if they were particularly brilliant.' Meanwhile NDS executives who were suspected of working with Clinger were fired. It should have been game over. But Clinger, aged 45, snug in his new home in Saint Moritz, Switzerland, was still way ahead of them.

Abe Peled and Reuven Hasak had not been as successful in keeping their investigation as secret as they had hoped. Siskind had let the cat out of the bag just days after he had briefed Peled. When Michael Clinger agreed to sell his shares in NDS to News Corporation in 1992, he had insisted on retaining an ongoing royalty stream. But on 2 August 1995 Siskind told Clinger's lawyers that NDS was withholding further royalty payments, 'pending . . . investigation of certain matters'. On 10 September

1995, Clinger signed an agreement with the Israeli Tax Office to help them investigate what he said was a huge tax fraud by NDS. On Sunday, 17 September, Israeli tax officers raided Leo Krieger's home and took him and Clinger's ex-wife, Niva Von Weisl, in for questioning. Krieger was charged with not paying tax on $3.5 million he had received from News. He was released on bail of $1.37 million.

Krieger's starting salary at NDS in 1990 had been $48,000. But he had received hundreds of thousands of dollars in consultancy fees paid into an Amsterdam account. Clinger received much of his NDS remuneration via an account in Switzerland. (When I queried this with Siskind, he told me that this was perfectly normal because the two men had dual nationalities—as it happens neither of them are Dutch or Swiss—and the payments were for services outside of Israel.)

Clinger was just beginning. On 20 September in London, according to a News Corporation source, a lawyer associated with Clinger told a British lawyer for News that NDS would have tax problems unless they resumed the royalty payments. Four days later the *Mail on Sunday* reported that News was facing a tax investigation in Israel. The threats continued.

On 4 May 1996, William Lewis at the *Financial Times* wrote a sensational feature about a High Court case. He revealed the Israeli tax investigation and detailed how NDS, while receiving Israeli government grants for research and development, had channelled the profits offshore to tax havens and paid a major part of its executives' salaries into Swiss bank accounts. Lewis cited a critical assessment of NDS's tax position by a former Israeli tax officer, Arvi Alter.

This incidentally was how I came to be involved in following NDS, after chasing some Australian leads to the story. It was then that I discovered from a LexisNexis search that Clinger had been on the run for six years with a US arrest warrant outstanding. To me this was the most remarkable aspect of the whole outlandish tale—that News had employed an international fugitive as a senior executive and then given him money to go away. Lewis had not mentioned this in his article.

'Mr Lewis, who was aware of the indictment, chose not to report on it,' Siskind told me in a fax after I raised it. 'Mr Lewis appears to have accepted without question information provided by Mr Clinger, with whom he has been in contact since at least November 1995.'

It turned out that Siskind knew much more about Lewis than this. He could name dates and places where they had talked. Which in turn was how I came to be asking Siskind later that year how it was that he knew so much about Will Lewis's personal life and his conversations with Michael Clinger, and whether he had had a journalist under surveillance. Siskind's offsider, Genie Gavenchak (who, like Siskind, had formerly been a partner at Squadron Ellenoff Plesent & Sheinfeld in New York), replied that all that Siskind knew about Lewis came from surveillance of Clinger: 'We have not engaged in any illegal act . . . Our instructions [to our agents] are not to engage in any illegal acts.'

In mid 1996 Siskind maintained that, while he had on several occasions asked the Israeli Tax Office whether they were investigating NDS, he had been assured that they were not. All of that changed on 20 October 1996. At 7 a.m. on this Sunday morning, 75 Israeli police and tax officers executed mass raids against NDS's Jerusalem head office, its Haifa offices, its accountants and lawyers, and the homes of senior executives. Television cameras were on hand to record every moment of News Corporation's discomfiture. The police also held warrants signed on the evening of Thursday, 17 October, by the Israeli chief of intelligence, Daniel Vash, to hold for questioning seven current and former NDS and News Corporation executives, including Rupert Murdoch, on suspicion of tax evasion.

The raids produced sensational headlines around the world, with revelations that Israeli authorities believed NDS had failed to report $150 million of income. News Corporation furiously denied any wrongdoing, complaining of Israel's 'large and intrusive . . . public and extreme action', despite News always offering its full cooperation to Israeli authorities.

Arthur Siskind in particular took it poorly.

'Mr Clinger has the tiger by the tail,' he told me in a gritty Bronx accent straight out of Central Casting. Arthur and I really weren't hitting it off by this point, but he overcame what was clearly his growing personal dislike of me to clarify his intentions in regard to Michael Clinger: 'There is a message to be sent here. Despite the economics of the return, we feel strongly about people who seek to defraud the company . . . We will not allow ourselves to be extorted by anybody.' News Corporation's counsel was not about to take prisoners. In an ideal world, where media corporations stocked weapons of mass destruction, you could depend upon Arthur to press the button.

All of this would prove to be just a sideshow for the real action that was taking place behind the scenes after 20 October. Abe Peled's new problem was that, when the tax officers searched the NDS headquarters, they had found a collection of cassette tapes in a safe in his office. The tapes were telephone conversations involving Michael Clinger talking to his lawyers in Jerusalem, in London and New York, as well as conversations between Israeli tax officers, and journalists' conversations. This was evidence of wiretapping, which carries a ten-year jail sentence in Israel. According to documents filed in the British High Court, where Siskind would launch proceedings against the former NDS exec, in early January 1997 Clinger was called in to Israel's National Serious Crime Unit with his lawyer, former Jerusalem district attorney Michael Kirsch, to identify Clinger's voice in a string of calls on one of the tape cassettes, marked 23A. In an affidavit also filed in the same British court, Clinger claimed to have seen a fax taken from Peled's safe that was a transcript of one of the conversations on the tape; it was addressed to a London lawyer working for News and to Genie Gavenchak.

Arthur Siskind had put Genie Gavenchak on point to handle questions about the tapes and the faxes. She was clear: 'If any tape recordings of any conversations do exist, it is clear to us that Mr Clinger was responsible for making them. If any tapes were indeed found within our company's offices, they were planted there. Mr Clinger has failed to produce any evidence of this purported fax, other than his own word, the trustworthiness of which needs no comment.' Not only did both recipients of the purported fax deny ever having seen it, but Justice Lindsay subsequently ruled that it was unlikely that professional officers of the court would be involved in any breach of legal privilege.

Israeli police began pulling in suspects for the wiretapping. Abe Peled was high on their list, but News told them that work overseas would keep him from returning to Israel immediately. When he did return he was questioned for sixteen hours, while they shouted at his secretary in the adjoining interrogation room. But no further action was taken and Peled was cleared.

Then the police investigation turned to NDS's security firm, Shafron. They were determined to call in Reuven Hasak and Rafi Malka for questioning about the wiretapping. They too would be cleared.

London, late 1996

When Oliver Kömmerling met the man who would decide his future, Reuven Hasak was in the middle of a yoga session on the floor of the hotel room. He held the position for some moments before he climbed to his feet to greet the newcomer.

Reuven had other hackers he was thinking about hiring. One was in North America. But Oliver was the key—the man was a genius, way out in front of anyone else on NDS's horizon. Reuven didn't just want to hire him; he wanted to win him over. He and Ray Adams had upset Oliver's tidy world—they had created a climate of fear and anxiety to make him vulnerable. When you play this game, the last person to know they are being manipulated is the target. Conventionally the next step would have been to let him stew a little before making contact with him, but Oliver had jumped the gun on that, and in the process had altered the power balance slightly. But no matter. Now Reuven wanted to bring things to a head. He wanted Oliver's allegiance. He had established the threat; now he needed to change the picture.

Hasak was at his most charming. He had a little gift for Oliver—an NDS certificate, properly embossed and mounted in a frame to hang on the wall back home. It was an award recognising Oliver's success in screwing NDS around. Reuven liked the idea of fooling NDS. It was a private joke, a little touch to show that really they were all friends, with a little quiet stroking of Oliver's ego. In time Reuven would be all over Oliver—he would befriend Vicky; he would dandle Oliver's children on his knee in the big house in Riedelberg; he would hire Oliver's father, to keep the family bonds strong. Reuven was a natural when it came to running talent. This was just a beginning, here in the London hotel room.

Of course they needed to talk money. Reuven threw out some numbers. There were sweeteners and bonus arrangements, and the package took a little while to explain. Oliver would be a consultant, rather than an employee. It went unspoken that this freed NDS of any legal responsibility for him if he messed up. As for the little problem with the police, NDS had hired the best prosecution lawyer in Germany to pursue Oliver, and now they would hire the best defence lawyer to clear him. When he finished, Oliver said, 'Right.'

'Do you agree?' Hasak asked.

'Okay ... sounds okay, sounds interesting to me,' Oliver told him. But there were some conditions. He wanted the case against

Harold Steffes lifted. 'And another condition is that I don't want to work for you as a . . . how do you say, a mole.' Oliver would not go undercover to betray people.

'I'm helping you technically; I will help your development team. You can also get information from me, I don't have any problem with that; but you don't touch any of my friends.'

This was the real bottom line. The dozen people in Oliver's piracy ring were not to be targeted by NDS. 'If there is a problem with them, I deal with it. I will talk to them if they, for example, touch your system, I will take care that they will not do it.'

This was important for Oliver. 'I mean, I have some morals,' he said later. 'When you have a friend you don't just go and change your work so that you trash them. That is not really friends.'

And another thing—Hasak and Adams would hate it—but Oliver planned to tell his network about the new deal with NDS. 'I told, against NDS's will, all my friends that I'm working now for NDS because I trusted them . . . and that made me very, very valuable. I kept the network from before as an information source and that has proven excellent. I mean it was a goldmine of information for NDS because every one of these people was phoning me for everything that's going on everywhere.'

That's how Oliver, this hulking, unpredictable German autodidact, with the precise, high-pitched voice and the broken English, tells the story of that first meeting and of the deal he struck. Whatever Reuven and Ray Adams thought they had secured at the end of this meeting, in Oliver's mind it was quite clear. And it was clear from what followed that this was the way that it did in fact operate. Oliver and his friends had run Europe's most efficient piracy network. Implicit in Oliver's account is the assumption that henceforth the network would not target NDS products, but everything else was still fair game. Oliver's comrades would provide information to NDS about the network's pirate competitors. In return the network would expect, and would receive, support from NDS.

There's a certain logic to this from a law enforcement point of view. It's why so many police detectives around the world cultivate a relationship with illegal brothels. They reason that it's impossible to stop them anyway and, because they are illegal, they give police a direct line into the criminal milieu. Detectives need illegal brothels to exist to give them an information source. And, really, prostitution is a victimless crime, they say. At least that's the rationale that police have offered at various times. It is problematic in so many different ways.

Essentially Oliver is mounting a similar kind of rationale here. Except that with piracy you can't even pretend that it is a victimless crime. It's more like coming across a gang of robbers breaking into the house next door and congratulating yourself that they are not targeting you as well . . . perhaps even going so far as to give them a hand with some of the bulkier items—you have to give a little to get a little. You agree to it because the information you get about your own personal security is really invaluable. And then really it seems only a matter of time before Rupert Murdoch is accused of being mixed up with piracy.

Gary Larson has a cartoon from The Far Side that has a hunter's sniper scope framing two bears, with the cross hairs lined up on one of them. The bear in the cross hairs is looking down the barrel, giving his best weasel smile, and pointing at the other guy: 'Pick him! Pick him!' That's the Faustian bargain that Oliver Kömmerling was offering NDS. That moment in the hotel room would have consequences for media businesses around the world. That's the marvellous thing about moral courage—virtue is its own reward. There was a line in the ground and the conversation seemed to sweep past it and bear the participants effortlessly into the Elysian fields beyond, almost without noticing.

By Elysian fields what I really mean was a quiet little restaurant overlooking the river at Bray near Windsor Castle, just up the road from the NDS offices in Maidenhead. Oliver, Reuven and Ray met there in late 1996 to restore the tissues, and to wrestle to the ground just what Oliver was going to do for NDS as a consultant. And really the answer was staring them in the face. Oliver would help NDS set up a black-hat team in Israel—a team of engineers in Haifa that would attack NDS products produced by Yossi Tsuria's development team in Jerusalem.

'So the principal idea is they develop something, they'll give it to us before they put it on the market. We attack it and, if we succeed to attack it, we will give them back the results and so in this moment we can improve the technology,' Oliver said.

This would prove to be so not a good idea.

Andover, Massachusetts, July–August 1996

Chris Tarnovsky was having an identity crisis. It wasn't the first time and it surely wouldn't be the last. He would get better at the whole multiple personality thing, but right now he was in panic.

Sergeant Tarnovsky wasn't a risk taker, but the move back Stateside had been smooth enough. He had brought with him two infants and a Belgian wife who had bad memories of her previous stay in America, and he wanted some security. Back in April 1996 he had had a telephone interview with Ulvac Technologies at Andover in northern Massachusetts, and wangled an entry-level programming position. He had flown back to the United States on 3 July and got his army discharge on Thursday, 4 July. By the following Monday he had started the new job. The family was camping at a Residence Inn in Boston. A couple of weeks later they would move into a comfortable three-bedroom house they had found a couple of miles north across the New Hampshire border.

Chris was still at the hotel when he contacted NDS. In hindsight it had all been leading to this. Chris was undiscovered, unrecognised talent. In spite of his training in cryptography and his top-security clearance, he had spent three years as the colonel's driver in a line division. He had dabbled in hacking, but his was an institutional view of the world. He wanted recognition, and he wanted it from NDS. He had joined TVcrypt in November 1995 and four days after introducing himself to the List he had written a reply to a technical query from Perry Smith, the NDS programmer who Markus had invited onto the List. Chris had concluded with a dig at Smith's email address: 'P.S. This might seem dumb, but are you from ".il" Illinois? (Hehehe . . .)' It was an email that was all about saying 'Notice me!' But no one did.

In those frantic months before he left Germany, when he was befriending Jan Saggiori, Chris had another agenda. In particular he had asked Jan again and again for a copy of an EEPROM dump—the readout from the electrically erasable programmable read-only memory—from the NDS card used by the DirecTV satellite system. The P1 card, as it was called, was based on the Sky 09 card used by BSkyB, which had been hacked in Europe since 1994, though DirecTV was a digital system while BSkyB was still analogue, so the system had its differences. In the hotel in Andover Chris's first move was to send Perry Smith a copy of the EEPROM dump.

'Maybe this helps you guys,' he wrote. He didn't mention that he had got it from Jan—what would be the advantage in that? The inference was that this was Chris's work. It was one of the reasons NDS needed him.

You can read this as a personal betrayal, but I don't think it started out like that. That would come later. If you look through Chris Tarnovsky's life—behind the shadow of his father, the army, and then NDS—it's hard to know what he stands for, who is the authentic Chris Tarnovsky. Perhaps you see it best in the furtive and flawed acts of dissent that would signpost his life. But here it seemed harmless enough. Giving NDS a readout of its own DirecTV card didn't hurt anybody. Massachusetts was a world away from the European hacking scene.

In any case nothing happened. He got no response—from anybody. He wrestled with the EEPROM a little. 'Please help . . .

I am lost in never-never land!' he wrote to the List in late July. Was there a problem with his email which explained why no one was talking to him? And then, just as he realised that NDS was not going to get back to him, he went off the air.

On an evening in early August, days after he and Sylvie had moved into their new house, Chris received a telephone call from an English member of the List called Karl Gamble. Karl asked whether he could give Chris's telephone number to someone. It was a name he didn't know.

'The Canadian wants your help.'

Then nothing for a couple days. And then the telephone again, a lazy drawl coming down the line from the sweeping plains of Saskatchewan.

'It's Ron Ereiser. I hear you can help me.'

Kerrobert, Saskatchewan, June–August 1996

Conditional access describes any system that is designed to allow consumers access only to what they have paid for, and the world of conditional access runs at three speeds. Speed 1 is what most people in the industry work at, whether they are employees of the big conditional access firms—like NDS, or Nagra in Switzerland, or Irdeto in South Africa and the Netherlands, or Canal+ or Viaccess in France—or they are academics, hobbyists and researchers of different kinds. They're all smart, no question of that. But when it comes to reacting to problems, to planning and reaction time, it's all in slow gear. At Speed 2, the security operatives who work for the conditional access companies are a lot sharper, but it's a question of degree. And then there is Speed 3—the commercial pirates. It's hard to pick them up as they brush past you, because they moving at faster than light velocity.

If you want a definition of a microsecond, it's the time a serious commercial pirate takes to figure out what you have just said, to weigh it up, and consider the options dispassionately. *Click*. And then they have worked out their countermove. Generally this will mean coming at you from a direction that you never expect. It's not personal, it's business. When they make a decision, they know if they get it right they make a lot of money. Get it wrong and they end up in prison. It seems to focus the mind.

I'm talking about the smart pirates here. Admittedly there are few enough of those. For the rest, the industry is peopled by crazies, stoners and the truly weird—and that's before the Canadian biker gangs and the arms of organised crime move in.

Ron Ereiser carries the frustration of being smarter than most of the people around him. He grew up in Kerrobert, a town of 1200 people in northern Saskatchewan. It's prairie country, at the top of the vast sweep of North America's Great Plains that stretch from Texas up past Montana and North Dakota until you get to . . . well, a little past Kerrobert. The place has 75 days a year when it is frost free. They tell you this as if it is a good thing. And it's breezy. It's easy to assume that all of the wind comes piped in direct from the North Pole, but that's clearly wrong—there are warmer side winds in there that come from Siberia and Greenland. In February the temperature can get down to minus 40 degrees centigrade, before the wind chill kicks in. And that's your social life right there—'You either went to the bar, the hockey rink, or watched two channels of television,' Ereiser says.

By the time I met him, in the fall of 2009, Ron had long ago moved to the warmer climes of Victoria on Canada's west coast, off Vancouver. The island is absurdly picturesque, so much like a biscuit tin lid I kept imagining the whiff of cookies. Ereiser on his home turf is a slight man with a direct, homespun face, blue eyes and red hair, day-old growth on his cheeks, deliberately casual in jeans and windbreaker. He's good company. An easy man to underestimate.

We speak in a succession of cafés and restaurants. Everyone comes to talk to him in the end, and there is a cynical world-weariness in some of his responses. He talks about meeting

Guggenheim, with Alan's tape recorder showing in his shirt pocket. And the NDS meeting: 'Typical John Norris—he gets his recorder out and I say, "No, I don't want to be recorded." So he says, "Okay, I'll shut it off." He put it in his bag and I could see he didn't shut it off. He was just being John Norris. Then, when the meeting was over, he picked it out of there and said this is the so and so day, the so and so hour.'

Ron isn't a fan of John Norris. Now I gingerly take out the little dictaphone I bought in a vending machine at Seattle airport and put it on the table, showing him it's not recording. Towards the end I pull out a little iPod nano I have in a jacket pocket. It has a little video camera in it that I want to film him with. And I see the little flicker in his eyes as he realises that I have another recording device. *Click*. In that microsecond I understand that he has reassessed me. He sees that the tape recorder on the table was just a blind, that in fact I have been tricking him while taping him with the iPod. He has to put me into a new classification. He reviews all that he has said, concludes pragmatically that he can live with it—it's no better than he expected—and resumes the conversation.

All this plays out in the space of a heartbeat. And I really don't have the heart to tell him he's wrong, that I really am as hapless and hopeless a journalist as he first thought, that of course I haven't been secretly recording him. That would be unethical, and life is too short. I'm way behind the pace here—I'm not even Speed 1, and way too reluctant to acknowledge it. He'll figure it out soon enough anyway. In any case I want to ask him about how to talk to the man I'm going to see near San Diego two days later, Chris Tarnovsky. Ron has a few ideas.

Ron Ereiser was 21 back in 1980, when he and a friend opened an electronics store together. Four years earlier, American media maverick Ted Turner had transformed the American cable business by building an uplink facility to transmit his Atlanta television station, WTCG, to an RCA satellite. The satellite in turn bounced Turner's television feed down to cable operators around the country, who ran it on their cable systems. Before that, cable operators across the United States could only show videotapes, and programming received via expensive microwave links. But now any cable operator with an earth station could pull the signal down and re-broadcast Turner's superstation on their cable network. It was a whole new way of doing things. It made Turner a lot of money, but it worked just as well with any other programming— like Home Box Office, and a crazy news channel idea that Turner had called CNN.

At some point the penny dropped that it wasn't just cable operators who could pull down the programming from the satellite. Really, anybody with a satellite dish could do it. Ron's partner, Dale, raced out to see him one day, in raptures about a satellite dish he had just seen advertised . . . a dish that he had just ordered. It was $7000. They hauled it back to town on a trailer. 'We had to go over to the bar and get everybody to help move this huge thing,' Ereiser says.

And then they were on a streak. 'There was demand like you wouldn't believe for this kind of thing. People would pay eight, nine thousand dollars to get more than two channels. There's nothing else to do in the middle of Saskatchewan.' Then in 1985 US programmers started using a line-scrambling system called Videocipher to encode the satellite signals, and all the screens went blank. This was very depressing. It lasted several months, until an electrical engineer called Norman Dick in Victoria on the west coast wandered down to his local satellite dish dealer and bought an old system and used it to hack Videocipher. He sold the hack to some dealers across the country and everyone was back in business.

'You know it was fairly popular, so satellite TV became a main staple up there,' Ereiser says.

As well as servicing the local market, the Canadian hackers found a big demand in the United States, which they serviced from the Cayman Islands, the popular Caribbean tax haven. General Instrument introduced Videocipher 2, but that didn't take Norman long to break either. To put this in perspective: in 1992 it was estimated there were 500,000 Canadians with satellite dishes watching American programming. This didn't cost the United States programmers anything, because they couldn't sell to them anyway. But there were up to a million pirate dishes in the United States as well, mainly in rural areas where having a large satellite dish outside your home could pass without remark. The going rate was $15 a month to pirate dealers for code upgrades and $100 a year for hardware upgrades to beat the electronic counter measures. That's $280 million a year of pirate turnover in the US. Some estimates put it at twice that.

In 1993 General Instrument was about to introduce Videocipher 2 Plus, but was worried that Norman Dick would hack it as well. So GI targeted Norman with a series of raids by the Royal Canadian Mounted Police. GI Security did a deal with Norman: they wouldn't press charges or sue for damages if he agreed not to hack Videocipher 2 Plus. At least that was the approved version. It was also reported that it was around that time that Dick suddenly found himself in funds, enough to buy his own helicopter.

'And then along came the little dish,' says Ereiser. Rather than the three-metre installation outside your home, satellite television came with a discreet dish that could be bolted to a roof or a balcony. DirecTV launched its high-powered digital service in June 1994 and by mid 1995 DirecTV piracy was flourishing in Canada. Ereiser was part of a group of a dozen dealers called the West 3M group. They included high-profile dealers like Gary Tocholke in Winnipeg, and Herb Huddleston based in Grand Cayman. They were using a hack provided by Norman Dick—a battery card with a Dallas DS5002 chip based on Oliver Kömmerling's original battery card. By 1996 it was a thriving business.

What was the business like for Ereiser?

'Well you know, you look at it now and it's kind of like it was Mafia. But when I was doing it, it wasn't. We started selling big satellite dishes, and then Videocipher comes along—we've gotta sell this. And then little dishes come along—we gotta sell this. It was just like selling a TV.'

Yes, it was illegal in the United States; 'but in Canada there was nothing wrong with it.' Canadian courts had ruled that you can't steal something that you can't buy. DirecTV suffered no loss from Canadians watching its programs. Ron is struggling to make a distinction in a world composed of varying shades of grey.

'Today the business is way different. Way different. You do get a lot of criminals in the game right now. They'll do anything. We weren't like that. You know, there were rules to live by when we did it. And we probably lived by the rules a lot better than John Norris lived by his rules, I'll tell you that. I'd trust 98 per cent of the pirates back then a lot more than I'd trust anybody from NDS, that's true. That's just simply true.'

The first sign Ron Ereiser had that he was about to be raided was a summer night in June 1996. He was standing in his driveway outside his home in Kerrobert, talking to a friend who was a local police officer, when a van drove past slowly with three people inside, all looking out the window. It's a small town, you notice stuff like that. And only remember it later.

At 7 a.m. the next morning they were back with a warrant. Five police officers from out of town descended on Ron's store, with another half dozen at his home.

'I mean it was like a big bust in a little town, right? So they didn't even know what to take, what they were looking for. They really didn't know. There were no NDS people there. A couple of the police officers said to me, "I don't know why we're here, I don't know what we're doing."' They took away all of his satellite equipment and hundreds of smartcards. In all, Ron's inventory was down $150,000, and he counted stuff like that. By the time he got it all back, it would be out of date and worthless.

While the police posse was sorting Ron out, simultaneous raids were being carried out all over Canada, including one on the home of Norman Dick in Victoria. John Norris was part of this raid and he began to interrogate Norman even during the search. Two days later DirecTV and NDS issued a civil damages suit in the United States against 24 Canadian dealers for $14 million. Norman Dick, badly rattled by the raids and the court action, subsequently declared himself out of the piracy business. Meanwhile DirecTV had launched one of those electronic counter measures that NDS called DDTs, which knocked out all of the battery cards. And the screens went blank again all over Canada, with no one to fix them.

That was the end of June. By early August Ron, undeterred by all the legal action, was desperate to get a fix. The dealers talked among themselves: 'We need a big gun hacker from Europe,' was the consensus. So Ron found himself a website in England, run by Karl Gamble, that looked like it might offer him some solutions. Karl told him about a hacker who had just moved back to the United States, called Chris Tarnovsky; he told Ron he could get hold of Chris's number.

Andover, Massachusetts, August 1996

Chris was in Germany when the June 1996 raids rolled out across Canada and the Caribbean, but he had heard about them. Now this voice on the phone was asking him if he wanted to be a player.

'He said, "Can you help us?" And I was, like, "Yeah, you know, why not?" Chess game! Right on.' That's Chris talking about it in 2009. Actually chess was probably the last thing on his mind. Ron explained the spot he was in with Norman Dick and asked him if he could solve the problem.

Chris said, 'Yes I can.' Ron asked what he needed, and Chris told him he could use a satellite receiver with dual output on the line that runs from the satellite dish. FedEx delivered the dish to

Tarnovsky's home the next day, Saturday, along with all the coding software Ron had from Norman Dick. They hadn't talked about money yet but clearly this was Chris's chance to play in the first division.

'I was impressed,' says Tarnovsky. 'I was like—Holy shit! You know I'd never seen anything like this. I was very small-time in Europe. I'd never really made money. I'd made like five grand in all the time I'd dabbled in it. It was all pleasure.'

And then it hit him. He had been Chris the army crypto specialist, Chris the driver, Chris the amateur hacker, Chris the NDS job applicant. He could be all those things at the same time. Now he was Chris the commercial pirate, living in the United States and doing something that under US law he could go to prison for. And he had been writing to Perry Smith at NDS about a hack for DirecTV. Now Chris was recalibrating.

On 22 August he emailed Jan Saggiori, Markus Kuhn, Stefan Eisvogel 'and whoever else I deemed addressable', to say he was working on a new encryption system that could be used to keep the TVcrypt emails confidential. Would they help? It's 8.20 on a Thursday morning in Massachusetts and he's at work at Andover. And he's stewing on this. No one was getting back to him. Ninety minutes later he unloaded a barely coherent spray on the general TVcrypt List at the micronet.it address, headed 'Sad but true'.

'What it comes down to is this,' he wrote:

Perry.Smith.was.let.into.the.list.No.matter.what.he.says.of.trust. He.can.never.be.trusted.to.let.us.discuss.his.work.We.are.his. comprise [sic].for.his.hard., 'Oh shit'.. when.someone.does.a.fairly. good.attack.on.something.you.believe.is.secure@micronet.it, you. are.deadened.inside.yourself.Trust.me@micronet.it,
But@I.know.Nothing.is.secure.Especially.this.list,
it.is.obviously.the.PSMITH.acount.leaking.all.info.into.
NDC.. I.would.not.be.surprised.if. 'PerrySmith'.is.an.alias.made.

up.and.possibly.2–3.people.working.in.the.Soft-ware.lab.read.
these.,

I.believe.this.is.not@He.knows.no.one.here.and.is.very.bold.
to.honestly.send.his.real.name.over.the.air.to.millions.of.hackers.
Some.who.could.be.psycho.and.possibly.fly.to.IL.an

It stopped mid sentence. If it was a conversation you'd be thinking, 'Did I just say all that stuff *out loud?*' The internet age has revealed some terrific lifestyle combinations, and one of the biggies is alcohol and emails. But Chris Tarnovsky wasn't drunk. Maybe he pushed the send button a little too soon, but it's the intensity that is troubling here, using full stops instead of spaces between words because he wants his readers to know how.important.this. is. It's all about betrayal and payback, and when he says 'deadened. inside.yourself,' this is not a happy camper. He is perhaps talking about himself.

Half an hour later Jan Saggiori emailed him to say that Chris could count on him for help with his new encryption project. Chris seemed mollified—he wasn't being ignored. He replied to the smaller group, saying that any encryption program released in the United States had been tampered with by the National Security Agency: 'We need to seal all leaks. A major one is this "Perry Smith" character. Markus knows him best and invited him I believe. Markus, what's your side of the story please. No thesis needed, just plain English in the reply please.'

The emails reeked of panic. Tarnovsky seems desperately fearful that NDS and Perry Smith would catch him in his new work. He was also fearful that he may be blamed by the List for leaking material to NDS just days before. His emails were aimed at shutting Perry Smith out (and, as a member of the List, Smith would have received a copy of the 'Sad but true' email). At the same time he was pointing the finger at Markus for allowing Smith in. You can almost feel the pressure on Tarnovksy, one of the few times he was caught between his many faces. He handled it with little white lies that really weren't quite so white any more.

And there was a status issue. A certain high-handedness was creeping into Chris's email style. The brakes were coming off. Two weeks later he would threaten one of the List, Manfred, that he would release the keys to a system Manfred has cracked and put them on the Net. Manfred had better behave.

Meanwhile, Ron Ereiser had a new constant companion: 'I talked to him every day—a really hyper, hyper kind of guy,' Ereiser says. 'He seemed nice enough.' Ron and Chris spoke by email, or via IRC chat sessions on the internet, or by phone. It took two weeks for Chris to find a solution to the new DirecTV card configuration.

'When I got it, man, I was like, "Yes!" I couldn't believe it. It was awesome. So awesome. But I'm persistent. I tell everybody: "I'm not the smartest rock out there." But I persisted, you know, and so, with enough time, I'll fix it.'

Tarnovsky emailed the new code to Ereiser and the battery card was working once more. The North American piracy industry was back in business. A month later Ereiser flew Chris and Sylvie up to Calgary for a meeting. Chris was still basking in his achievement, and was keen for more of Norman Dick's codes so that he could make a new master program for pirate cards, called a bootstrap, that would be easier to update. He told Erieser that people always promised him money in Europe, but he never really made any.

'There's a chance to make some money here,' Ereiser told him.

'Well if I can make $20,000 on this, I'd be happy,' Tarnovsky said.

There was the niggle. Ereiser was fighting NDS and the government in court, and in any case he had a chronic dislike for parting with money. Tarnovsky would have been better asking for $100,000. By starting small, he had typed himself as the journeyman hacker. It made for resentment when he ramped up the demands later. But, from his perspective, Ron was the one making all the profit from his work.

'At first he didn't want much and then it got to where he—you couldn't put enough money in his pockets,' says Ereiser. He estimates he channelled between $80,000 and $120,000 to Tarnovsky over time, though he can't be too precise because the money didn't all come from him. Tarnovsky later swore on oath that it was $40–50,000. But Chris wasn't just dealing with Ron. He ventured onto the IRC internet chat channels early on, using the nickname 'biggun'. His DirecTV fixes won him an instant following.

'Everybody, you know, praised him,' says Ereiser. 'People were sending him what he called donations. Money was coming in to him.' He was a celebrity.

'People didn't even believe the file was out when it first got fixed,' Tarnovsky says. Now everyone on the North American bulletin boards were talking about biggun, the secret identity he cherished to himself. Some time along the way, Chris figured he needed a 'legit' persona as well. He called himself 'Arthur Von Neumann' (a play on Von Neumann computer architecture used for some smartcards), or Von Rat—the name he had once confided to Jan Saggiori. Or just Von.

'I have never told a soul that I'm biggun,' Tarnovsky says. 'Biggun was always like, "Hello everybody," puts the file out, or whatever. You know I was always Von, and I was an asshole. So they were always saying, "What the fuck! Who the fuck is he?" So Von was always my persona. You know? And it's the opposite to how I really am.'

Jan Saggiori had introduced Chris to a Canadian hacker in Edmonton called Al Menard. The two became fast friends, with Tarnovsky sharing his new battery card code and his bootstrap code with him. Menard later took the unusual step of writing to Jan to thank him for the intro.

'Things have been going great and Chris is a cool dude, Thanx 10,0000,00 times over for introducing him,' Menard wrote on

3 January 1997, having just launched a new website and thinking Jan might like to look at it. It was called DR7.

Tarnovsky had become blasé about NDS.

'I'm teasing NDS, throwing them EEPROM dumps and stuff,' Chris tells me in 2009. By which he meant he kept emailing Perry Smith. 'So I just kept in touch with him, and then he says I want you to meet this guy Roni Segoly. And that's how it started. They knew I was close to the biggun figure.'

In late 1996, Reuven Hasak's people were on the move. They had secured Oliver Kömmerling in Germany. In Canada they had stomped on the West 3M piracy group in June, only to see it revive. Now they were coming back for another approach, beginning with Ron Ereiser. Ron's Kerrobert Satellite and Cellular had a website and on it in late 1996 he saw a comment had been left by someone from Israel called Roni Segoly. He figured he was NDS, and sent him a reply. Segoly wrote back, would you be interested in meeting with me?

'I said okay,' says Ereiser. 'And John Norris showed up.'

Saskatoon, Saskatchewan, November 1996

Saskatoon is 250 kilometres miles east of Kerrobert. If Ron Ereiser had wanted to make an impression, he would have driven 500 kilometres east to Calgary, in Alberta. But this was business. Let Roni Segoly come to him. And really, he shouldn't have been surprised that Norris was with him. He knew Norris from the Big Dish days.

John Norris was in his mid fifties but looked younger, six feet one tall, a little overweight at 100 kilograms. Norris finished high school in 1963 and four years later was in Vietnam. He had a two-year tour as a combat intelligence officer and a platoon leader. By the time he left the army in 1973 he was a captain in military intelligence.

He had taken a job with a San Diego retail conglomerate called Wickes Corporation as manager of corporate security, but was laid off when Wickes went into Chapter 11 bankruptcy in 1982. He took a stint at Fluor Corporation as field supervisor of investigations, then left to join a furniture company called Furnishings 2000, where he ended up vice president of security. He says he left when they went bankrupt, which was September 1990. Then he joined another San Diego company, the Videocipher division of General Instrument, where he was field supervisor of investigations and later manager of security before he was laid off.

His next job was at Miramar naval air base, the site of the navy's air combat training school that inspired the 1986 film, *Top Gun*. Norris was described in a 1999 profile of Reuven Hasak and NDS by Israeli financial paper *Globes* as a former high-ranking naval intelligence officer, spawning a decade of colourful newspaper bios. In fact Norris's job was a little less glamorous—he headed the 60-man private security force that guarded navy surplus stores that were destined for retail sale.

After two years guarding naval stores he was headhunted back to GI by Jim Shelton, who, as head of Videocipher, was taking a far more aggressive position against pirates, using undercover agents and running sting operations to trap pirate dealers. In a 1994 *Wired* article Norris decribed himself as Jim Shelton's 'trigger man', as head of special projects. He said he had notched up more than 100 convictions of pirates, citing recent cases where he had testified, helping to secure prison sentences of up to three years. 'All these guys were thumbing their noses at the system, and now the system is coming back and whacking them,' he told *Wired*.

Putting pirates in prison was nothing personal: 'I don't feel good or bad about it,' he said. 'It's up to the justice system to decide what they deserve. I merely provide help gathering and presenting evidence. And I will sit down and drink with any people who have been arrested through my testimony, and they'll say I acted like a gentleman. Many of them respect what I've done, because I didn't take it personally—I dealt with them in a proper way.'

It's a modest self-assessment for a man whose nickname was the Cowboy. Shelton left GI in 1994 and Norris moved on the following year, when he began consulting for DirecTV, then NDS. Which is how he came to be sitting down with Ron Ereiser in Saskatoon. There was the little thing about the tape recorder, but this was never going to be a meeting of minds. Ereiser is deeply bitter about NDS and particularly John Norris, and his comments need to be understood as such. NDS Security return the sentiments.

'He had a bit of a rep, because he worked with GI, because he was security,' Ereiser says of Norris. 'You've got to watch him—he'll do anything. He talks real nice to your face and two seconds later he's stabbing your back.'

'He's a liar, he's a criminal,' Reuven Hasak has said on the public record about Ereiser. Norris hasn't made any public comment about Ereiser, but he has confirmed he tried to hire him.

Ereiser later swore that 'John Norris basically told me—Norman Dick was our head engineer for the battery card . . . He told me that if I informed on Norman that I could continue to do what I do, and they would pay me $10,000 a month.'

'I'll get back to you,' Ereiser told Norris. But Ron wasn't interested. 'It struck me as kind of odd that he . . . that I'd be sued for doing something that they think is wrong, yet they're going to allow me to keep doing it and pay me to do it—pay me while I'm doing it.'

In an affidavit Ereiser has asserted that during this meeting Norris tried to persuade him to try hacking DirecTV's rival satellite broadcaster, EchoStar, which had begun operating in March 1996. When he spoke to me in 2009, Ereiser told me his customers had little interest in EchoStar, that they didn't have the programming to make hacking them an attractive commercial proposition. He also claimed that Norris asked him to send a message to Norman Dick: 'Well you can tell Norman that he can hack the Videocipher signal with GI, because the guy you made the deal with . . . has gone now, so Norm can do it.'

Much of this may be dismissed merely as verbal sparring between two people who didn't like each other. But then Norris floored Ereiser. Norris asked him about Chris Tarnovsky. Ereiser was dumbstruck.

'I didn't even . . . usually I have a pause, but I was flabbergasted they knew about him. Why I don't know—all they had to do was check my phone records.' Ereiser stumbled something out and the conversation moved on. He didn't know how Norris knew about Tarnovsky, but he hoped it was just a name to him.

Meanwhile NDS had taken the hunt to the Cayman Islands. In his 2008 court testimony, Ron Ereiser described what happened next. Gary Tocholke, who alternated between living in Winnipeg and Grand Cayman, was first. Norris and Hasak arranged to meet him at a restaurant in George Town, the capital of the Caymans. Hasak arrived dressed in Israeli army fatigues, but it was Norris who took the lead. He accused Tocholke of working through Mexico. 'If we ever catch you in Mexico, we'll throw you in the trunk, and haul you over the border,' he told Tocholke. 'What are you going to do?'

It wasn't a pleasant exchange. But Hasak and Norris were playing on Tocholke's home turf, in a restaurant owned by a friend of his, who had agreed to let Tocholke set up beforehand. He had installed a hidden camera to catch the conversation. He now had video of Norris threatening him. Score one to the pirates.

Herb Huddleston was another pirate based in Grand Cayman; he'd fallen out with his secretary, Lisa.

'John Norris . . . offered her money to steal information off the computer at Herb's office, which was the accounting for the battery cards, which is a crime in the Cayman Islands,' Ereiser was to allege later. But Huddleston got wind of it, and arranged for Lisa to call Norris back and ask for more money, which she wanted to be tax free. Norris suggested she open a bank account under her maiden name to keep it secret. According to Ereiser, 'The police were informed on the island, and John left shortly thereafter, and I'm sure, if he ever shows up again, he will be arrested.' Score two to the pirates. Norris was not asked about Ereiser's claims when he himself gave evidence in 2008.

The Royal Canadian Mounted Police (RCMP) had charged the dealers caught up in the June 1996 raids with pirating DirecTV, but the pirates were winning here as well. While the Canadian state courts took slightly different positions on what was legal and what wasn't, everyone agreed it was illegal to pirate the Canadian broadcaster, Bell ExpressVu. However, Canadians by law were not permitted to subscribe to DirecTV in the United States. This meant that Canadians who pirated the DirecTV signal did not damage DirecTV, or deprive DirecTV of income. They could watch it for free (through piracy). It was only illegal if they paid for it. This remained the position until 2001.

On the other hand, there was a flourishing 'grey market' in which Canadians were actually paying for DirecTV subscriptions by using a phony United States address. This was definitely against the law, the Canadian courts found. And it was happening with the covert approval of DirecTV. So it was DirecTV, rather than the pirates, who emerged as the villains.

The pirates had turned the tables on DirecTV and NDS by portraying the piracy charges brought against them by the RCMP as a challenge to Canadian sovereignty by US corporations. Now they attacked the legal basis for the June raids.

'I wonder if this investigation is in the public interest of Canada or really in the interests of News Datacom (NDS) and DirecTV,' Justice Craig mused in a brutal judgement in British Columbia, in which he threw out the search warrants used against the West 3M group and ordered the police to pay the pirates' legal costs. 'DirecTV has duped the RCMP,' he ruled.

In Ereiser's own case the highest court in Saskatchewan, the Queen's Bench, found in May 1997 that searches of his home and business were excessive and unreasonable. DirecTV had been operating 'a thinly veiled scheme to circumvent the laws of Canada by accepting subscription fees directly from Canadians provided that they maintain a United States address'.

The pirates had won a remarkable set of legal victories. It's perhaps little wonder then that Ron Ereiser was distracted, that he lost sight of what would prove to be the real threat looming before him.

London, 1996–97

In hindsight, Ron Ereiser believes that right after meeting with him in Saskatoon in December 2006, John Norris jumped straight on a plane to go to see Chris Tarnovsky. Actually it was a little more elaborate than that. Once Perry Smith had introduced Tarnovsky to Roni Segoly, the NDS man suggested Chris meet him in London. He would send over the air ticket. This was not a warning-off meeting for a troublesome hacker. This was a recruitment session. Of course John Norris was there.

'I didn't like him,' says Tarnovsky. 'At first. When I met him I didn't like him. But he's—he's a very nice guy. When you actually meet him, ah, he's . . . very big heart, very nice guy. Very gentleman, very polite. Totally opposite of what you think he is. But you hear that because of all the pirates.'

Norris didn't like Tarnovsky at first either. He didn't trust him; he didn't want to be involved in supervising him; he didn't want anything to do with him. He was all for whacking pirates. Tarnovsky should be in prison, he thought. He said it openly. 'If he's going to continue being active in illegal stuff that he's not telling us, then we are going to hand him over to the FBI,' Norris warned. It was left to Segoly to play good cop to Norris's bad cop routine.

We know about this meeting because in 2008 there was a critical court case, EchoStar and Nagrastar v. NDS, heard in the US District Court in California. The four-week trial offered a brief glimpse into the secret world of pay TV pirates and the agents who chase them; it is the only time when a string of NDS, Kudelski and EchoStar executives and a string of Canadian pirates have given evidence on a witness stand. They told their stories in their own words, which complement the email exchanges, documents and court exhibits. Even so, sometimes the picture was still tantalisingly incomplete. In the end, what exactly was decided at this London meeting became moot. Segoly testified that, 'The nature of the proposal that we gave him [was] that on [a] short time plan he would continue to be an informer, and on the longer time it would be NDS full member of team as a developer.' But what exactly happened next became shrouded in mystery, because no one at NDS who gave evidence at this trial could remember. There's a six-month blank. They couldn't even put the finger on when NDS started paying Chris Tarnovsky.

Reuven Hasak suggested to the court, 'Late '90s . . . maybe '96, '97 . . . No, not '96 for sure—'97, I guess. '98. I don't know. I don't remember.'

Chris Tarnovsky, who really should know, told me the first meeting definitely wasn't 1996. 'No, '97—'97. So, like . . . a bit like June of '97. No, no, May of '97.'

Norris only talked about hiring Tarnovsky in mid 1997. Certainly DirecTV knew nothing about it. Dov Rubin, the head of NDS Americas, met Tarnovsky but said, 'I had a hard time pinpointing the date. It must have been sometime in 1998.' This vagueness is puzzling, because NDS in its pre-trial filings in the 2008 case is more specific: 'In or about January or February of 1997, Tarnovsky was retained by NDS as an exclusive consultant to assist NDS in its efforts to combat satellite television piracy.'

What can be said for sure is that, from the first weeks of 1997, while he continued providing fixes to Ereiser for his pirate cards for DirecTV, Tarnovsky's email style changed. On 29 January he wrote an angry email, as biggun, to Reg Scullion, a Canadian pirate dealer whom he accused of stealing his code for pirate DirecTV cards. Tarnovsky pretended, entirely unconvincingly, to be a student living in Europe—a French speaker who made what looked like deliberate English spelling mistakes, though his French phrases were too atrocious to be treated seriously. And he threatened Scullion with informing on him to NDS, or News Datacom: 'I give you the TV and I can remove the TV . . . I may just give the source to NDC. I am sure they will purchase it from me, and if I agree to stop, your world stops also.'

Scullion had been a pirate for sixteen years. He could recognise the sound of an informant. From this point, Scullion assumed Tarnovsky was on the NDS payroll.

Geneva, December 1996

It was the end of a difficult year for Abe Peled's new broom at NDS. Reuven Hasak's recruits had come out swinging, with raids on Chris Cary's pirate organisation in the United Kingdom and the West 3M pirates in North America. But the court decisions in Canada had overturned months of work. Whatever had really happened in the Cayman Islands with Gary Tocholke and Herb Huddleston, NDS had ended up with egg on its face. The pirates had shown themselves to be horribly unpredictable. I think we can use the word, *devious*.

It was certainly a solid effort by the Canadians, quite the little repartee. But really, if you're looking for industrial-strength devi-ousness, for way-off-the-end-of-the-beam trickiness, you know there's only one place to look. When it comes to sneak factor, I think the British have always set the bar. And so the year ended with a covert move by Chris Cary that went several long steps beyond Machiavellian.

A little set-up here. By the end of 1996, Cary had long since cracked the Sky 10 card used by BSkyB. He had it all down pat. But he had a logistics problem. The difficulty was that NDS had mounted not just one but two microchips on Sky 10 to make it harder to crack. This included an ASIC chip, whose only purpose was to frustrate hackers. Of course it didn't for long, but the problem for pirates like Cary was to find enough disused cards with ASIC chips mounted on them for him to reprogram. They were in scarce supply.

How to solve the supply problem? The solution was simple. Cary passed a copy of his pirate code to Jan Saggiori in Geneva and asked him to release it on the Net. For Jan, the decision was a no-brainer. He knew there were a dozen other websites that would release the codes for Cary if he turned him down. Saggiori had dropped his law studies and begun a computer studies degree—his thesis would be on cracking pay TV smartcards. Jan posted the code from Cary on his website on 22 December, just in time for Christmas. Then on 28 February he posted the Season 10 program and source code (in the tradition of Markus Kuhn's Season 7 program for the Sky 07 card), which allowed anyone with a home computer to emulate a Sky 10 card to decrypt BSkyB's transmissions. Jan disguised the source, announcing that the codes and programs had come from Romania. In 1995 Jan had killed off the Sky 09 card by posting its codes on the Net. Now he had done the same for Sky 10. The card was irrevocably compromised and would have to be replaced.

This was just what Cary had been banking on. Now that everyone had the Sky 10 code, piracy levels would simply explode. BSkyB would have to replace all of the Sky 10 cards in circulation with a new generation of cards, Sky 11. That meant millions of outdated Sky 10 smartcards would be dumped—and each of them carried an ASIC chip. They would be easy for pirates to pick up. So, by feeding the code to Saggiori in this manner, Cary had ensured he would have the huge new source of ASIC chips that he needed, for nothing.

While this seems hugely wasteful and destructive, it's just pirate logic. It's capitalism without the brakes on. What is clear is that

Cary had a contemptuous disregard for anything that NDS would throw up in its next card. The starting point of his strategy was that he would be able to crack Sky 11. It went without saying.

And this would go down in history as just another example of tortuous pirate logic, except that the timing made it something else completely. Jan Saggiori's codes, which were posted in February 1997, ran smack into the middle of the biggest US media war in decades.

PART 4

EchoStar Wars

I am also less concerned about it 'cause I have tape recordings, mails and reports about this issue. The request to crack nagra came from the kangaroo's company when he had a fight with Charlie about the CA system. I know and can proof who did it inside the Company . . .

Oliver Kömmerling email to Ron Ereiser, 2 November 2002

Denver, Colorado, April 1997

Two media billionaires eyeballing each other—one of the scariest sights in the world. Two crazy visions of the world running headlong into each other, with neither side giving a millimetre.

Rupert Murdoch had this wild dream of a broadcast empire that would reach right around the world, from New Zealand and Australia, through Asia, Europe, Latin America, and of course North America, fed from satellites 35,000 kilometres above the earth in geosynchronous orbit. It would be a seamless global platform, and NDS would be the thing that would hold it all together, that would secure it, that would provide the technology base to allow Murdoch to pump all of his Fox programming down through his set-top boxes. Perhaps only half a dozen people around the world understood at this time just how ambitious Murdoch's plans were. One of them was now sitting opposite him. But he wasn't playing ball.

Not for the first time, Rupert Murdoch was reminded how frustrating it was to be in a room with Charlie Ergen. The man was slippery as an eel, completely unreasonable. And so cheap. Rupert had phoned him the first week of February and offered to buy his company. He knew Ergen was weeks away from running out of money. But Murdoch had his own problems. He and his partner, MCI, the long-distance telecommunications group, had two satellites and a licence for one of the only orbital slots above the United States from which a satellite could reach all of North America. Yet MCI now wanted to drop its partnership with Murdoch, leaving him with a lame duck satellite venture. Buying EchoStar from Ergen would help Murdoch jumpstart the process and get him back into the game, but Ergen didn't want to sell.

They haggled it up and down, then turned it into a merger of equals. News Corporation and EchoStar would both end up with 50 per cent of the merged operation, which would be called ASkyB. While Rupert Murdoch knew that his half share naturally meant his people would be running the show, Ergen somehow believed his half share meant he would be calling the shots, which was really a wacky idea. The conditional access system had almost been a stumbling block. Murdoch had insisted that ASkyB would use NDS, while Ergen had seen no sense in changing from the Nagra system that EchoStar already used, produced by a Swiss company called Kudelski. When it looked like a deal breaker, Ergen agreed to switch to NDS, as long as the system was secure and economical . . . by which he meant bargain basement.

The deal was announced with huge fanfare on Monday, 24 February 1997, when Murdoch's people promoted it as a cable killer. Preston Padden, Murdoch's aggressive Washington lobbyist who had become head of satellite operations at News Corp, promised the cable companies would be calling for Dr Kevorkian, begging for euthanasia. 'Our goal is to come to market with a television product so superior, and a consumer proposition so compelling, that a substantial number of 70 million households stop writing their cheques to their current service—usually cable— and start writing them to Sky,' Padden said.

Then of course Ergen and Murdoch sat down to renegotiate the whole deal over again. NDS was still a sticking point. Ergen had given away nothing when he signed the agreement to accept an NDS conditional access system if it was secure, because he knew DirecTV was widely pirated. But Murdoch had a trump card to play that Ergen did not know about prior to the talks. Late in February, DirecTV had begun sending out a replacement NDS smartcard to its subscribers. The new card, P2, was not in use yet and so it had not been hacked; thus, when DirecTV switched over to the new system in July, the system would be completely secure.

The timing was a little awkward. Peled had had his sixteen-hour interrogation by Israel's serious crime squad on 2 March. In the end no evidence was found that linked Peled or Hasak or anyone at NDS to the tapes found in Peled's office safe. Where they came from was a mystery. But the investigation was a distraction. Hasak meanwhile was orchestrating Oliver Kömmerling's recruitment, as well as the curious new relationship with Chris Tarnovsky.

The head of NDS Americas, Dov Rubin, was project manager for the merger with EchoStar. He conducted a three-week feasibility study into how EchoStar would switch from Nagra smartcards. But by April the merger negotiations were in trouble. Murdoch's technology advisor, Greg Clark, asked Rubin to prepare a memo outlining the weaknesses in the Nagra system and why NDS was better. Rubin was invited along to the next meeting to put the arguments in person at EchoStar's offices in Denver on 17 April. Preston Padden was there along with Rubin and Clark on the News side, together with Rupert Murdoch, Arthur Siskind and News Corp's finance director David DeVoe. On the opposite side of the table were Charlie Ergen, legal counsel David Moskowitz and the president of EchoStar Technologies Corporation, Mike Dugan.

Rubin moved into his presentation. Yes, DirecTV had been hacked; but there was a new card out that would fix that. NDS had gone through all this with piracy of BSkyB in Britain. 'And about a year or six months before that, before this meeting, we produced a card, a smartcard, which overcame all of these problems,' Rubin testified in the witness box in 2008. 'In fact, that card is still . . . and that system is still secure to this day. So, although we were hacked in '97 at DirecTV, we had the confidence to know that we were on the right path . . .'

It's a wonderful story. If only Rubin had been right. But BSkyB wasn't secure. As Rubin gave these assurances, pirate cards had been available for Sky 10 for at least a year. The difference was that they were commercial pirate products, not the semi-public posts of TVcrypt. Commercial piracy was more damaging, but less visible, allowing NDS to deny there was any problem. In Denver, the $2 billion ASkyB deal was coming down to the wire. It was in this charged atmosphere that Jan Saggiori in Geneva posted on his website the season codes for Sky 10 he had received from Chris Cary on 28 February. He said they came from Romania, but really it didn't matter where they came from. NDS could not claim to have a card in service that had not been hacked, and Charlie Ergen knew it.

This is where the meeting in Ergen's offices on 17 April teetered out of control. Charlie was fixated on keeping Nagra. It was less expensive, and it hadn't been hacked. Then Ergen signalled to Mike Dugan, who walked across to the bank of television screens on the wall. Dugan had a pirate card that he put into the decoder, and suddenly the screens across the wall were playing DirecTV programming.

'Look—it lights up like a Christmas tree!' Ergen told Murdoch.

There was a stony silence. The executives' gaze switched to Dov Rubin. He had nothing to say. Preston Padden stormed out of the meeting, leaving Murdoch behind. Padden resigned days later, and the deal collapsed. It left Charlie Ergen in desperate trouble, trying to find bank funding to stay in business. He called André Kudelski in Switzerland. 'Staying with Nagra has cost me a billion dollars,' he said. 'I hope it's worth it.'

Murdoch had his own reasons for needing to get out of the EchoStar deal. Padden's rash words on 28 February had struck fear into the cable industry, which called the merger 'Deathstar'. Suddenly Murdoch was finding that cable companies were balking at carrying Fox channels, just when he had spent billions launching Fox News and Fox Sports. It was one of the rare occasions when Rupert Murdoch faced total, crushing defeat. If he took the cable companies head on, he now realised, they would break him. He couldn't beat *everybody* in the American media industry at the same time, which had been Plan A. He needed to get out of the EchoStar deal, and the NDS dispute would serve as a cover. But he would need to eat a whole lot more humble pie than that. All the old animosity towards Rupert Murdoch as the obnoxious outsider had been dredged up again. He now had to make an abject approach to the cable companies to allow him back into the circle of trust, and actually persuade them to buy his satellites and US orbital slot for the cable companies' PrimeStar satellite operation. And maybe they might carry his programs.

It's one of the most under-reported periods of Rupert Murdoch's life. The previous October he had launched Fox News, then went to war with Time Warner to try to force it to carry the news channel on its New York cable network. Simultaneously with the EchoStar deal, he was negotiating to buy the Los Angeles Dodgers baseball team and Pat Robertson's Family Channel. Fox Sports was fighting with Disney on one side of the country, while on the other side it was buying up half of a cable network from Cablevision for $850 million. In short, the content side of Murdoch's empire was steaming along. But that wasn't where his heart was.

Rupert Murdoch had a dream of a global satellite empire and in February it had been finally within his grasp. Now it was gone and his whole position in North America was under threat, thanks in part to Charlie Ergen and his complete pig-headedness about using Nagra. So Murdoch had cut his losses.

There has never been any doubt that Rupert Murdoch will do whatever he needs to survive. I think the only logical conclusion to draw from his 60 years at the helm of News is that Rupert Murdoch must be indestructible. He'll always find a way out of the most dire predicament. It's so reassuring for the army of people around the world who make their livelihood writing about him, or analysing his every move, or trying to second-guess his latest tricky manoeuvre. 'He's a gift,' as one US lawyer told me.

But billionaires are dangerous people to humiliate. They brood. They remember.

Hong Kong, 1 July 1997

As the rain set in, the crowds swirling along the Kowloon waterfront became impassable. The celebrations had kicked into high gear after President Jiang Zemin declared on the stroke of midnight of 30 June that Hong Kong was returning to Chinese sovereignty after 156 years as a British colony. The handover was being celebrated at a host of sumptuous parties across the city for the local ultra-rich, whose numbers were swelled by thousands of A-list visitors from around the world. But down at Kowloon the police had cordoned off the streets, and the maze of alleys and lanes were a solid mass of people. The streets held hundreds of thousands of celebrating Chinese, and one elderly westerner dressed in the soggy, bedraggled remains of a dinner suit.

Rupert Murdoch had ducked out of the tedious official speeches at the Hong Kong Convention Centre, where he was one of the 4000 VIP guests, the moment President Zemin finished his speech. He jumped into a taxi and headed through the harbour tunnel towards his room at the Regent Hotel. But the crowds blocking the roads cut his trip short several blocks away from the Regent.

He climbed out of the taxi and promptly got lost in the crowds and the maze of streets. The rain was intermittent; the heat was constant and oppressive. For two exhausting hours, one of the most powerful men in the world tried to find someone who could give him directions.

Bruce Dover, describes this scene vividly in his book, *Rupert's Adventures in China*. Dover, who was Murdoch's advisor in China in the 1990s, was at his own party in the Regent when he was asked to come to the concierge desk. He was then escorted downstairs to identify a wet, bedraggled westerner, who had just arrived with no room key, no mobile phone or wallet, no identification. Clearly in too dishevelled a state to be granted entry to an international hotel, the blow-in was asking Dover to vouch for him.

I like to think about Rupert in those two hours when he was lost, way out of his comfort zone, exposed to the noise, the smells, the colours, the raw vitality of the Hong Kong street. Most of us have occasions when we lose our direction. And then we find it again. It takes five minutes. Or half an hour. Usually it's in a car, so we can have a little hissy fit in private. But two hours in a Hong Kong crowd is something else again. And the incredible thing about Bruce Dover's story is that when he sees his boss—the bow tie long since disappeared; the soiled black piece of material slung over his shoulder that surely must have once been a dinner jacket—Rupert's mood is *exuberant*. He's had the time of his life.

'What an adventure!' he tells Dover. 'Been out there for ages, trying to find my way, walking up one dead end after another . . . Couldn't seem to make myself understood to the locals when I asked for directions . . . I'd ask three of them where the hotel was and they would all point in different directions.'

That night in Hong Kong Rupert Murdoch is at a turning point. He's about to begin his epic bid to outrun the sun. He is 66 years old. In eight months he will be 67, the age at which his father died with secondaries from prostate cancer. He is feeling his mortality. He has had a wretched six months in North America—the cable guys just killed him. His wife Anna wants him to slow down, to retire, and that's the kiss of death to his marriage. And then he has this experience in the crowd in Hong Kong, a reminder of the raw energy of Chinese culture. It happens a day after Bruce Dover hosted News Corporation's cocktail party at the Regent, where Dover has brought in the Star TV staff from Shanghai. Dover recalls introducing one of the staffers to the boss that night. 'Meet Wendi Deng,' he says.

You can be as fanciful about this process as you like, or not at all. But if you look at Rupert Murdoch's career as different phases, something happens here. You have Rupert as the student up to 1952; Rupert as the Australian empire builder up to 1968; then Rupert as the Fleet Street newspaper baron who perversely lives in New York and dabbles in US media assets. That lasts up until 1985, when he makes the great gamble to buy Twentieth Century Fox and the Metromedia television stations, in order to launch the Fox Television network. Everything else follows from that.

In London he moves his newspapers to Wapping and overturns the entire British industrial relations system in the process, all of it to be able to pay for his Fox network in the United States. Then he buys two-thirds of the Australian newspaper industry as a debt restructuring deal (it's related to junk bonds from Michael Milken for the US television stations, but that's a whole different can of worms). He doesn't like the media laws in Britain, so he launches his own rogue satellite television operation, Sky, upon which Prime Minister Margaret Thatcher smiles graciously. Then he does the next logical thing, which is almost to go broke in 1990.

Sky becomes BSkyB; then he does a huge deal to buy British Premier League football rights, simply to stop BSkyB losing money. And then he keeps doing that—buying up sports rights around the world. He creates Fox News, Fox Sports, Fox television programming. Have I missed something?

But from 1997, that's about it. There will be a lot of talk, a lot of column inches about his grand plans. He finally buys DirecTV in 2004, then has to sell it. He wastes $3 billion on a vanity purchase of the *Wall Street Journal*. He is full of plans to use MySpace to exploit the internet, which turns into a plan to save newspapers from the internet. For a decade and a half News Corporation will keep doing what it does, but better and better. Yet there is not much new here. If you compare it to the tumultuous half century that came before, News is almost in suspended animation.

There's another thing. From 1997, the skeletons in Rupert Murdoch's closet are much harder to ignore. There is a new note—a darker seam that runs right through Murdoch's empire. Or maybe it was always there, and is now just more visible. It's in the late 1990s that journalists and private investigators at News International in Britain spin out of control with telephone and computer hacking.

In 2000, News Limited in Australia orchestrates a strategy that prompts the Seven Network to launch a massive legal case claiming $1 billion in damages from moves which Seven claimed forced its pay TV channel, C7, out of business. Seven will lose the case and end up with $200 million in legal costs, but a year of testimony uncovers just what a grubby business Murdoch runs in Australia.

It's 2002 when News America Marketing begins its campaigns of dirty tricks and industrial espionage that will force Murdoch to pay out $650 million in damages to settle cases brought by its competitors.

In 2009 the Murdoch family trusts have to pay out A$77 million for a tax avoidance scheme after they sell ten shares in a family company to News Corporation after listing the ten shares on the Bermuda stock exchange to sidestep paying stamp duty. It's one of a string of tax cases.

And then there is NDS.

Southern California, May–August 1997

Ron Ereiser was working on something tricky and John Norris didn't know what it was. The clock had been ticking from the moment in February 1997 that DirecTV began sending out the new Period Two smartcards from NDS (known as P2 cards), to replace the first-generation cards that had been so extensively pirated. DirecTV would finish switching over to the new cards and shut down the P1 system on 7 July. The question was how long it would take the Canadian pirates to crack the new card. So what was Ereiser doing?

The first part was predictable. Ereiser and his confederates wanted to lock in their in-house hacker.

'Okay, so basically the card swap's coming,' says Tarnovsky. 'And they're basically saying, "Hey, why don't you move down to Grand Cayman? We'll give you a million dollars. You hack the DirecTV Period Two chip, you support it from within the Grand Caymans. Everything will be great. You can live on an island."'

Chris flew down to Grand Cayman with Sylvie in April 1997 to meet Herb Huddleston and Gary Tocholke to discuss it. 'The Cayman Islands is great for a vacation,' he said. 'It smells a little bit. But it's very expensive.'

Tarnovsky is a fidget. He worried that he might not get the money. He had previously asked Ereiser for a $2000 oscilloscope, but Ron had told him to buy it himself.

'It seemed like I got money from them when I bitched,' he told me. He worried about being caught by US Customs. He worried about John Norris—'because I had heard about him by then, of course,' he testified in 2008. And that's a nice touch, because he was already an NDS informant. The issue he was struggling with was whether he was going to turn on NDS. He flew back to New Hampshire, but talks with Ereiser seemed to be stalling. He was back at work when John Norris called him.

'I heard you're in the Caymans right now,' Norris said.

'I wish,' said Tarnovsky.

'You want to come down to Nashville? You want to see me?' said Norris.

'Sure,' said Tarnovsky.

'I've got a ticket waiting for you at the airport in New Hampshire tonight.'

And that was that.

'I've gotta go,' Chris told Sylvie. He called in sick at work and he was on the plane that night. In Nashville, Norris gave him the NDS pitch. The salary would be $65,000 a year, a $10,000 loan that could be forgiven over two years and $14,000 in moving expenses. The last bit he had to break to Sylvie, because part of the deal was that the family would move to the San Diego area, near Norris, so that he could keep control of what Chris was doing.

'Well I don't know about this,' Sylvie told him. That was until they flew out to California.

'We were like—Whoah! We love it! This is paradise out here! We'd go to the beach and stuff for a week, meet John and his wife for dinner. It was great.' They were never going to leave. They bought a house in San Marcos, just north of San Diego, for $220,000.

Reuven Hasak flew Tarnovsky to Israel and gave him some lectures on how he had to stop acting like a pirate, and told him some of his own spy stories. And here was the tricky bit: this was an undercover operation that meant several things. First, Hasak and Norris had decided Chris couldn't tell anyone that he was moving to California. Because that was where DirecTV and NDS were based, the Canadians would immediately suspect that he had joined NDS. Chris told Ereiser's group that he wasn't going to the Caymans because he needed to look after his father, George. Chris's cover story was that he was moving to live with George in Manassas, Virginia, on the outskirts of Washington. Chris got a postbox in Manassas that redirected his mail to San Marcos, and a Manassas telephone line that automatically rerouted to him in his new home. No one from New Hampshire was going to look him up and no one at Manassas, except his family, would be expecting him. The Tarnovsky family had just disappeared between the cracks. All of this was for Chris Tarnovsky's personal safety, Hasak would say later.

'The piracy world is a violent world. And it's not what people tend to think—that it's a white-collar crime. It's not white; sometime it's very black. And we know of examples where people were threatened . . . And we know that . . . we knew that, if Mr Tarnovsky will be exposed, he might be—no, he *will be* under potential risk.'

Hasak went one step further: 'I didn't want him to be on [the] NDS payroll,' he said. 'And we found another company from News Corp, which is nothing to do with . . . The pirates don't have any interest in it.'

Tarnovsky would not be employed by NDS—at least, not according to his bank account or his tax returns. Instead, he was being hired by Kesmai Corporation, an online gaming company that News Corporation had bought the year before. NDS would reimburse Kesmai, but nobody was to know this. It was certainly news to Nick Laiacona, who ran Kesmai's online team in Charlottesville, Virginia. He had never heard of Tarnovsky when I asked him in 2008: 'It was ten years back, but I think I knew everybody back then. It was a pretty tight-knit company.'

Perhaps it's not surprising that no one told Laiacona about the new recruit because he was a line manager and this was a book entry, shuffling accounts within the News Corp group. But somebody had to know. It does not seem likely that this sort of arrangement could be sorted out directly between Reuven Hasak and Abe Peled and the Kesmai management. Did it have to be approved out of News Corporation's head office? If so, the natural place for that to be done would be the Office of the Chairman, possibly through News Corp counsel, Arthur Siskind, or the man who had to sign off on the group's accounts, News Finance Director, David DeVoe. Both men were on the NDS board. And both had been in the EchoStar offices just days earlier for that humiliating moment when Charlie Ergen had derailed the ASkyB merger with the pirate DirecTV card.

As Hasak acknowledged, while he could take some precautions, the risk in hiring a commercial pirate hacker was not just that he would be unmasked by pirates, but that he would release confidential information to his pirate friends. Setting up Tarnovsky's job cover through Kesmai would mean that the decision to hire him may well have involved the highest levels of News Corporation, possibly through Siskind and DeVoe. The Office of the Chairman would continue to take an active role in overseeing NDS, through the new head of News Interactive, James Murdoch, and the News Corp exec who oversaw NDS, Chase Carey. In 1999 News would sell Kesmai and Tarnovksy would have to find another cover, which would also have to be arranged by the Office of the Chairman. This time Tarnovsky ended up working as a curious adornment to the noble minds who toil in the book publishing industry. He joined HarperCollins, which by then was part of Lachlan Murdoch's empire. Lachlan and James Murdoch would both end up as NDS directors.

Tarnovsky was therefore safe from scrutiny, if pirates in Canada had the capacity to check his US bank accounts and tax records. But his links to NDS were also invisible from people closer to home. NDS's biggest customer, DirecTV, had no way of knowing that the man who was their biggest piracy headache now worked for NDS. Neither did US Customs and state narcotics police.

Montana, June–August 1997

John Norris had done everything he could. By hiring Chris Tarnovsky he had deprived Ron Ereiser of his best hacker, taken him out of the hunt to crack the P2 card. Now he followed this up with his law enforcement contacts.

'I appeared before a grand jury [in Great Falls Montana] after Roni Segoly and I met with the U.S. Attorney to demonstrate the technology,' Norris wrote later. An arrest warrant was issued for Ereiser, 'but since we are "only talking about television" the US government will NOT extradite Ereiser to the U.S. from Canada,' Norris noted in disgust. Nevertheless it was another way for NDS to ratchet up the pressure, in addition to the US civil damages case in which NDS was suing Ereiser and his partners for $17.7 million.

But Norris had missed something. Ereiser had gone cold on the idea of moving Tarnovsky to the Caymans to hack P2, even before Norris decided to hire Chris full-time. Ereiser had begun to suspect that the job was beyond Tarnovsky's talents. 'When I met him he only had one skill, that was writing code,' Ereiser said. 'To fix ECMs and stuff. He had never physically got into any card, ever.'

Before they stopped talking, Ereiser asked Tarnovsky for the name of a hacker in Europe with hardware experience cracking smartcards. Chris passed on the request to Jan Saggiori, who gave him the names and a phone number for two Bulgarian hackers: Vesselin Nedeltchev, who was known as 'Vesco', and Plamen Donev. Chris then passed the phone number to Ron Ereiser and that was the last he heard of it. Both men had a background in cryptology with the Bulgarian military. They had hacked Sky 07 and a bunch of other cards.

Ereiser gave their names to Herb Huddleston, the Cayman Islands-based pirate, who flew to Bulgaria to meet them in their hometown, Kazanluk in central Bulgaria. He was impressed by their technical skills; they were impressed by the amount of money he was offering. There is nothing like the whiff of six and seven-figure payments to engender universal bonhomie and expressions of brotherly love. An overwhelmed Plamen phoned Jan to thank him and told him that, once they were paid, he and Vesco would give him $15,000 as a thank-you gift for introducing them to Chris. Sadly, this brotherly love had a short half-life—Jan never saw the money.

What followed reads like a spy novel. Huddleston's daughter and son-in-law worked at Montana State University (MSU). In May 1997, Huddleston contacted MSU's Physics department and said he was part of a joint venture by businesses in Bulgaria and Canada to research a video chip, and asked about using MSU's Image and Chemical Analysis Laboratory. When asked for technical information about the video chip, Huddleston sent an unmarked sample, a chip that had been extracted from a DirecTV P2 card. On 14 July Huddleston flew into Alberta from the Caymans with Vesco and Plamen, who were travelling under forged passports.

Huddleston hired a car and drove south over the US border into Montana, past Great Falls (where the grand jury had been sitting just weeks earlier) and down another 300 kilometres to the State University in Bozeman. There was a small hiccup—Huddleston ran into another car just south of the border, a minor affair that still required an accident report—but otherwise the trip went smoothly.

Once at MSU, Plamen and Vesco began work on the P2 chip. Their first goal was to dump the read-only memory or ROM, and the challenge here was that the new chip used by Yossi Tsuria's team at NDS had a microscopic security mesh built into it to hide the ROM from hackers. The only way to get past it was to use a focused ion beam (FIB) to punch through the mesh, peeling it off micron by micron, to expose the tiny circuit board beneath. What they needed was an ion gun. What MSU had was a Time of Flight Secondary Ion Mass Spectrometer, which is a FIB on steroids, a hideously complicated piece of equipment to measure . . . well, stuff that's a whole lot more complicated than popping a microchip.

Neither Vesco nor Plamen had ever used a FIB before, but that turned out to be just a minor inconvenience. Plamen could wing it. 'He's brilliant; he's at another level. He's one of the best hackers I've ever seen—he's up with Oliver,' said Ereiser. 'When he was finished, the university wanted to hire him.'

Dumping the ROM was the first step. Once the circuitry was exposed, they used the electron scanning microscope, and then an optical microscope to take photographs of the ROM circuit board. The way the circuits are set out, each value has a one or a zero. If you chart all of those circuits you get a binary code, and from that you can work out the operating code for the ROM. I know what you're thinking—it's just too easy.

The next step is the electronically erasable programmable read-only memory, or EEPROM. Unlike the ROM, you can't see it under the microscope because it's something that can be changed, or erased. A hacker has to find a mistake, a loophole in the ROM operating code, that allows him to dump the contents of the EEPROM. Then it spits out all the values of the EEPROM registers. And from *that*, you can work out the operating code for the EEPROM, which is the operating code for the chip. And it's only at that point that you have a shot at cracking the chip. You look at the operating code and you have to find another backdoor or mistake or loophole that you can exploit to take control of the chip itself. That's like finding a parking space in Sydney. It's not for the faint-hearted. And it might take some time to find it, but it's always there somewhere.

Dumping the ROM is the only part that requires the FIB and the million-dollar lab. The rest you can do anywhere. Huddleston drove Plamen and Vesco back to Canada, then they flew to the Caymans. Plamen sat up for four nights without sleep working on the software to run the hack, living mostly on cigarettes. They would bring food to his door and he would wave them away.

Then it was done. He had the P2 hack. Huddleston and Tocholke and Ereiser and all their partners were back in business. The card had lasted less than two months.

Maidenhead, England, July–September 1997

On 11 July 1997 Ray Adams was writing one of his reports to Reuven Hasak. It was a long discursive document that subtly grouped Hasak and Adams together as the real professionals on the team. He was a little worried about North America, where—no doubt for understandable reasons—he was afraid that some possible moves were being overlooked by John Norris in the hunt for the other big Canadian pirate, Marty Mullen. 'Why not, for example, let Alex and Mike run together on this one. Why separate them? I am prepared to let JN run the operation.'

'Alex' was Oliver Kömmerling's codename at NDS. Chris Tarnovsky was 'Michael George', or just 'Mike'. Alex and Mike. Neither of the two hackers knew that the other was on the payroll; they both thought they were the one and only. The JN line was a nice touch because even now Ray knew that Oliver only answered to him, not John Norris. If Oliver was working North America it would be Ray calling the shots.

'For some time there has been speculation about Kömmerling and the fact that he is no longer acting with the pirates. His withdrawal from the USA scene will serve to confirm the suspicions.' And then there was the Jan Saggiori problem . . . 'He knows that Kömmerling is with NDS.'

On 26 September Ray Adams, who is running a network of more than fifteen informants across Europe, has to write his weekly report for Reuven Hasak. He skips lightly across the mundane stuff . . . court prosecutions in the United Kingdom and Germany. There was a risk of blowback in one of them. He was thinking of hiring Chris Cary's sales manager, Steve Bennett, and his wife—but did he really trust them?

He had several operations underway. The first is in Germany: 'BF has not answered his phone for the past two days. His mother says he is working at university. I try every few hours. Plan is to see him next Tuesday with Chaim.' BF was Boris Floricic, a young Berlin hacker who was a close friend of Markus Kuhn and Oliver Kömmerling. Ray had plans for Boris. Chaim Shin-Orr was the head of the black-hat team that NDS had set up with Kömmerling at the Matam research centre in Haifa. Adams ran through his other agents: 'Diesel' (Dieter Scheel), 'Prince' . . . The next heading was more troubling: *The Bulgarians*.

'The latest email today from ILIAN says that he is concentrating on the Irdetto [sic] digital system,' Adams wrote. 'He has a full working hack. He lacks the cards and chips to put it on.'

Irdeto smartcards were used in the Netherlands, Germany and Italy, and in Australia by Foxtel Satellite, Optus Vision and AUSTAR. The cards for the different countries were linked, so any threat to Irdeto in Europe could threaten News Corporation's 25 per cent interest in Foxtel. But Adams presumably didn't know this yet. 'Ilian' was a hacker in Sofia. Adams was keeping tabs on him through Oliver. Ilian had approached Oliver's friend Bela in Hungary to supply him with chips, but the two had not been able to agree a price, because Bela wanted access to Ilian's hack.

'We can break the deadlock,' Adams told Hasak. 'The chips are Thomson F48. They are an old chip. I can buy them through an agent for about $11. This is a pretty good price. I may even get them cheaper.'

Adams didn't even know how to spell Irdeto, and now he was proposing to help pirate it. The question is where this idea came from—the old Scotland Yard copper, or from his agent, Oliver/Alex?

'Having say 1000 chips would make Ilian come running to Alex. Ilian says that once the Irdetto hack has launched he will concentrate on all the other European systems.' This would include Sky, 'so we must concentrate on this guy'.

If you look at the arithmetic, Adams was planning to spend $11,000 on blank smartcards for Oliver to sell to Ilian. The pirate cards would sell for $150 or more, which would total at least $150,000. The cost to the pay TV operator who was pirated would be some multiple of that, in revenues forgone. As a result, NDS might end up closer to Ilian and better able to stop him pirating Sky. NDS would get its $11,000 back. It could even make a profit. But the unnamed pay TV operator that would be targeted by Ilian could end up more than half a million dollars out of pocket. Law enforcement agencies can run operations like this if they have the knowledge and consent of the parties who will be damaged by it. When media groups like News Corporation do it secretly for their private gain, it begins to look like piracy—though back in 1997 it was not necessarily illegal.

What's most telling is that Adams merely includes this as a sidenote in his report before getting on to the main issue, which was that NDS was facing a crisis over the failure of its technology. How long before NDS began to lose customers because of the piracy?

'Our jobs are on the line. Maybe not yet but we are vulnerable.' The new Sky 11 card had not been hacked yet, but listening to Alex, 'I fear [it] is as weak as anything else we have produced.' Alex was not allowed to hack P11, so all that he could tell Adams was that the programmer was obviously a different person to the programmer for the P10 card—'there are lots of technical mistakes,' and the card 'is programmed against some of the rules'.

Really Alex hadn't looked at the card at all. Just a casual glance.

'When I speak with him he says that "I cannot look any more because you told me not to",' Adams wrote. He went on to castigate the complacency and overconfidence of the NDS engineers, whose shortfalls were being covered by the operational security team. The pirates would eat them alive. The answer, Adams argued, was to let Oliver loose. 'We must expand and learn. We have a willing teacher. Alex is available but entrapped. His imagination, his expertise must be brought into play.'

Riedelberg, western Germany, late 1997

Abe Peled had embraced Reuven Hasak's idea for setting up a black-hat team for reverse engineering. Peled was familiar with the concept from his days at IBM. NDS leased secure offices on the third floor of the Matam Advanced Technology Centre in Haifa, just back from the beach. The first job was finding the people.

'The basic idea of Hasak was to send me engineers. First of all to send them to Germany for me to check out to see if they are good or not, if they're talented et cetera . . . [and to then tell him] whether or not they could be suitable or talented for such a task; if they have the . . . the touch, to crack cards—to be in that spirit,' recalls Oliver.

They all came to Riedelberg to be overwhelmed by Oliver's reverse engineering laboratory in the house behind his home, just as Markus Kuhn had been overwhelmed three years earlier. Oliver had his own chemistry lab, complete with fume cupboard and chemistry benches and a low-grade clean room, for the acid work with the chips. 'If you look at his place, it's full of gadgets, of all sorts of things,' says Markus. 'He had pretty much every sort of instrument device that I had ever heard of. He had maybe two versions of it.'

The micro-probing station at the heart of the lab was based around four Karl Suss micropositioners, which manoeuvred the microscopic probes that Oliver used on the chips. Oliver had a Zeiss Axiotron 2 CSM confocal microscope, as well as a Mitutoyo FS-60 microscope mounted on a New Wave QuikLaze-II laser cutter, another optical microscope with CCD camera built-in and a modified scanning electron microscope. Then there was the obvious stuff . . . an oscilloscope, pattern generator, a logic analyser to record digital data and a computer with peripherals for card protocol interface handling, data acquisition. Just a modest little hobby room.

An NDS engineer, Chaim Shin-Orr, had been appointed to head the black-hat team; but it was an older man on the team, Zvi Shkedy, who forged the closest ties to Oliver.

'The first time that I flew to Germany . . . we found out a common language, chemistry, between ourselves,' Zvi said. 'So it was kind of an open channel of mutual appreciation and mutual way of thinking, creative, innovative, and so forth.'

'Zvi is a living calculator, I love this guy,' says Oliver. 'He taught me the fundamentals about statistics and I taught him all about the chips and how they work. Nicest guy I met in my life. We always shift the credit to each other. He always said in NDS meetings that he got all from me and I did the same.'

By mid 1997 Oliver was visiting the European trade fairs with Shin-Orr to pick out equipment for the Haifa lab. Then he was training the team in his lab. They peppered him with questions: How do you approach that? How do you attack the card? What are you looking for inside the card? Which locations do you go to? The most telling moment for Oliver was when one of the trainees looked at him and asked, 'Now tell me why you put the needle exactly here?' Looking back at him, Oliver realised he had no answer. You couldn't write down why he made the decisions he did, why he chose the locations he did for his attacks.

'It's an intuition, I don't know why,' Oliver answered him.

Zvi and the black-hat team analysed the NDS cards, including Sky 11 and Sky 12, but got little thanks for their efforts. By the time they were given each card, it was already in production, which was a little late to find out it wasn't very strong. Hitachi asked them for a report on one of their cards. Then they popped a pirate smartcard based on the Dallas chip.

Zvi Shkedy has a simple view on reverse engineering: 'First of all, it's legal. And the reason that it's legal is because it is necessary for the humanity,' he testified in the 2008 EchoStar case. He meant that it enables humanity to advance. 'By reverse engineering, you are looking at a system. For example, when you look at a bird and you ask yourself how the bird is flying, you invent the airplane. So this is kind of reverse engineering of nature, but it's the same applied also to technology.'

It's a fresh approach to the fusty legal restrictions on copying other people's ideas. Man's inhumanity to man . . .

New York, late 1997

For Rupert Murdoch, the show as always had gone on. After his defeats in North America he had switched his attention to Europe, where he was already deep in plans to buy into pay TV operations in Italy, France and Germany. Murdoch never looks back. The failed merger with EchoStar to form ASkyB would have been just a memory, except for the fact that the day after Murdoch finally killed off the merger, Charlie Ergen lodged a $5 billion damages claim in the US courts.

There seems a certain inevitability to the position in which NDS and News Corporation executives found themselves in late 1997. NDS was a product of the rapid decision-making that characterised Rupert Murdoch's empire, beginning with Murdoch's sudden announcement back in June 1988 that he was launching a new British satellite service, Sky Television, in just eight months' time. He hadn't even considered any need for a conditional access service for Sky. When he realised his mistake, it was a piece of outstanding innovation by Bruce Hundertmark, Adi Shamir and Yossi Tsuria at News Datacom that allowed Murdoch to introduce encryption to Sky on the run with the smartcards. But that staged approach also proved to be the perfect breeding ground for piracy.

It was bad luck that Michael Clinger became involved, but the checks and balances that save most corporations from runaway executives didn't work at News. You could argue that Murdoch was lucky he had only one Michael Clinger in his ranks (if indeed there was only one). Then in 1995, when News discovered that Clinger was still defrauding News Datacom, Murdoch's legal counsel Arthur Siskind hired Reuven Hasak.

The answers we get in life are often determined by the questions we ask. Or to whom we ask the questions. People see solutions through the prism of the way they have been trained. If you have a pain and go to see a general physician, they will prescribe tests and often a drug treatment. A naturopath will give you a different answer. If you see a surgeon, they will tell you they need to cut. Mention it to a manicurist and they might not be much help with the pain, but you will end up with a wonderfully buffed set of nails.

If you ask a spy to help with a security problem, you end up in a whole new universe. NDS now had dozens of informants, undercover agents, internet monitoring operations and a black-hat team reverse engineering its products. The focus of the security operation had expanded from pursuing Michael Clinger to targeting pirates in Europe and North America. And now it took what must have seemed like the next logical step.

A management decision was taken. The black-hat team would not just target NDS chips, or do work when requested for outsiders like Hitachi. Zvi and Chaim and Oliver would now turn their sights on the cards made by NDS's competitors. These competitor systems were Viaccess, a card made by France Télécom, used in France and the Scandinavian countries; the SECA card made by Canal+, used in France, Spain, Italy and Asian markets such as Malaysia; and the Nagra card made by Kudelski in Switzerland, used by EchoStar in the United States, Bell ExpressVu in Canada and Sogecable in Spain. And then there was Irdeto, which seems to have been Oliver Kömmerling's personal responsibility in his lab in Germany.

Oliver has been emphatic over the last decade that the request to target Nagra came from News Corporation, after that humiliating debacle in Charlie Ergen's office in April 1997. NDS's view was that it had stronger cards than its competitors but they were on high-profile platforms that everyone wanted to watch. Higher demand translated into many more pirates focused on breaking NDS cards. This gave the mistaken impression that they were easy to hack, whereas the inferior cards of NDS competitors survived simply from lack of demand. But was this a fair assessment of the situation?

'There was a—a request from News Corporation to have a look at, ah, [the] EchoStar system, whether or not this is, ah, really safer or just nobody pays attention,' according to Oliver. 'What they wanted . . . is to have a report about the security which they wanted to use in the negotiations of whether or not which systems to be chosen, to have a document which they can give to EchoStar and say "Look, it's the same as yours and what are you complaining about our system?"'

When Zvi Shkedy was asked at the 2008 EchoStar trial why NDS reverse engineered its rival's smartcards, he said there were two reasons—to use the information to improve NDS products (though NDS used an entirely different type of chip) 'and to assist marketing'.

Kömmerling had regular access to senior executives at NDS, including Abe Peled. Oliver may well have been told that the order to hack Nagra came from News Corporation, but that does not prove that it did. He wasn't there when the decision was taken. The hack would require a major outlay of resources by the black-hat team, so Peled clearly needed to have been a part of the decision. The command lines in Rupert Murdoch's empire have always been short. NDS was part of News Interactive, which by this time was headed by James Murdoch. Chase Carey, News Corporation's co-chief operating officer, had oversight of NDS. He reported to Rupert. There is certainly no stronger evidence than this hearsay, but is it possible that somewhere in this short chain of command, there was a Thomas à Becket moment: 'Will no one rid me of this tiresome smartcard?'

In pre-trial court filings in the 2008 EchoStar case, NDS gave a different reason for why it decided to hack EchoStar's Nagra card: 'The primary reason was to prepare material in anticipation of litigation or for trial.' NDS gave this explanation in a response to interrogatories from EchoStar in November 2005. NDS did not say which litigation or trial it was anticipating, but the $5 billion damages claim against News by Charlie Ergen at EchoStar was the only lawsuit on the horizon (this was a separate action and unconnected with the 2008 trial). The News Corp legal strategy certainly seems to have been broad-based, as NDS proceeded to reverse engineer not just the Nagra card but SECA and Viaccess as well.

A legal strategy suggests a different decision-making process. News Corp's chief legal counsel Arthur Siskind and his offsider Genie Gavenchak were defending the case against EchoStar, as well as running the High Court case in England against Michael Clinger. It should have been their call. Thus, if it was a legal decision to hack Nagra, then the decision would have to be made within News Corporation; in fact, possibly within the Office of the Chairman. It also makes the whole operation invisible. If the primary reason for the hack was 'to prepare material in anticipation of litigation or for trial', then the process is covered by legal privilege. There will be memos and reports and other documents prepared for the lawyers that relate to how the decision was taken and how much was known of the operation by senior News Corporation executives. These are sacrosanct, which means News cannot be forced to reveal them.

Two comments can be made. First, it was not illegal to reverse engineer the products of competitors, if you took appropriate steps to safeguard the technological secrets you discovered. Laws across the world make allowance for this. But secondly, in this case, it seems a desperately reckless decision. It would involve the active assistance of the world's leading pirate hacker, Oliver Kömmerling, whom NDS previously had been trying to send to jail, who had done a deal when under threat of prosecution, and who maintained close links with his former partners in piracy. It came just after NDS had hired Chris Tarnovsky, who had been involved in piracy acts in the United States that carried a prison term. If this operation went wrong, then NDS and News Corp faced serious legal risks.

If you look at the three incidents—the confrontation in Charlie Ergen's office, the elaborate charade to pretend that Tarnovsky was employed by Kesmai, and now the decision to reverse engineer Nagra with Oliver Kömmerling, the common thread is that the Office of the Chairman, in News Corporation's handsome offices on Avenue of the Americas in New York, may have had a hand in any of them. If so, this was not just Abe Peled's responsibility. Had NDS become the pet project for Rupert Murdoch's personal team?

Toronto, November 1997

The storylines at NDS Operational Security were starting to tangle up. The decision had been made to reverse engineer cards, but doing this would not be simple. The first problem was to get hold of samples of the cards—blank ones from the manufacturer first of all, to practise on; then actual cards issued by the pay TV companies. Both SECA and Nagra used smartcards made by SGS-Thomson Microelectronics, which was in the middle of negotiating a deal with NDS and BSkyB to build the new set-top boxes for when BSkyB went to digital in 1998. Thomson was happy to provide blank cards to NDS and on 20 October its UK man emailed Adams: 'If you could detail your requirements then I will be pleased to assist.'

Adams emailed Oliver early on Tuesday, 21 October: 'Give me urgently a description of all the chips we want as samples.' Oliver replied with the specs on the Wednesday afternoon, 22 October. What they needed was the card used by Canal+ for its SECA card, plus the card then being used by Nagra. This was all very mundane, except that organising the wherewithal to hack NDS's competitors was unfolding right at the same time as NDS had decided to send Oliver on a *mission*, to go undercover in Toronto.

Called Operation Duck, it was Ray Adams' idea and, given the timing, it was perhaps the silliest thing that NDS had done to date. As with so much that would happen in the Murdoch empire over the next decade, it only made sense if those involved believed they would never be called to account.

Oliver and Vicky flew business class from Frankfurt to Heathrow and then to Toronto, arriving on Tuesday evening, 21 October. They were joined in Toronto by John Luyando, a wheeler-dealer in piracy circles who had worked with Oliver in the past. His NDS codename was Jellyfish and John Norris had a great scorn for him. The prize that Kömmerling was offering to pirates in Canada was a hack for DirecTV's P2 card. He had called Ron Ereiser about it but Ron already had his hack, thanks to his Bulgarians, Plamen Donev and Vesco.

The goal of Operation Duck was for Oliver to program some DirecTV cards for local dealers and use this as a stepping stone to get to Marty Mullen, who was one of the two biggest piracy dealers in North America. Back in August Oliver had spoken on the phone for almost an hour with Mullen, who would later testify that Oliver offered him a hack for EchoStar, but Oliver denies this (in Mullen's deposition in 2007, he claims he had been told by NDS lawyers that this was part of a sting operation by Oliver and NDS). Mullen, though, had his own hack for P2 cards and NDS dearly wanted to know who Mullen's hacker was. In fact the hacker was Norman Dick, who had worked for Ron Eresier and the West 3M group before he had ostensibly 'retired'. He hadn't needed to use a lab or a FIB to break the P2 card. He had just gone back to the P1 card, which he knew well. He assumed that there would be more than one backdoor into the card and—because he knew programmers generally don't fix what isn't broken—it was likely the undiscovered holes in the P1 card would still be there in the P2 card. And so it had proven.

By 25 October Oliver had been in Toronto four days and had programmed a swag of pirate cards, using a program he had ripped off another pirate hack. And he had been paid a lot of money. That evening, he met with two piracy dealers in a car and programmed a few cards for them with his portable programmer box to demonstrate that it worked. The following night he received a call from a friend in London, a partner in his old piracy ring, who was sleeping with a woman who worked for Federal Express. 'He told me, these guys [from the previous night] sent a parcel to Larry Rissler,' Oliver recalls.

Rissler was a former FBI agent who headed the Office of Signal Integrity—the operational security division—of DirecTV, and he had been hunting Oliver for some time. One of the dealers Oliver had met was a Rissler informant and he had despatched a reprogrammed smartcard by FedEx to his boss. The parcel would be with Rissler early the next morning—if it wasn't already there. Oliver hit the alarm button.

He booked out of his hotel with Vicky and Luyando and took a cab ride in the middle of the night twenty miles to the US border, crossed it and booked into a motel on the other side, along the southern Lake Ontario shore. But this was the wrong move because, while piracy might not be illegal in Canada, in the United States you did jail time for it. Forty-five minutes later, Ray Adams called. He said they had to get out.

In Los Angeles, Larry Rissler had already picked up that Oliver was heading into the United States. He had entered Oliver's name in the US Customs database and flagged him with a Search and Detain order. For Rissler, Oliver was a glittering prize. For years he had been Enemy Number One for DirecTV, the man who consistently hacked and broke their cards for the pirates. Now it was only a matter of time before Oliver was picked up. But here, in his moment of triumph, Rissler made a mistake. He made a courtesy call to John Norris, to let him know what was happening. It would have been hard not to show a little satisfaction that DirecTV had beaten NDS to the punch.

Norris said it was wonderful news. He didn't tell Rissler that Oliver worked for NDS, or that this was an NDS undercover operation. He just put down the phone and sent an urgent message to Adams, who then got on the phone to Oliver.

'Adams phoned and told me to go—go quickly,' Oliver said. 'So I had to wake up Luyando, and tell him, "Come, we have to leave".'

Then the three of them—Oliver/Alex, Luyando/Jellyfish and Vicky—left everything behind in the motel room—computer equipment, money orders, clothes—as they headed south and east, away from the border. They booked into another motel, only to panic when they saw police cars go by. They were back on the road, looking for a new place to hide.

'We did that twice. In the third motel we paid cash.'

Oliver was continually on the phone to Adams. He hadn't even touched the smartcards, he said, so there were no fingerprints. He hadn't personally programmed the card, even if it was his decoder the Canadians used. And if there was a print or a DNA trace of some kind, there was no continuity of evidence to say it was the card that Alex's decoder had programmed.

Adams was continually emailing Hasak in Jerusalem. It wasn't a criminal offence to reprogram cards in Canada, he said. A good lawyer should get him off. Adams argued with the desperate eloquence that graces a man who is fighting not just for his agent, but for his own job. This was a tricky situation that required managing, he said magisterially. Of course it seemed completely clear that this whole mess was the fault not of Adams, but of his colleague John Norris, who had alerted them to the airports alert Rissler had put out.

'I am well ware of these provisions and know better than anyone their strengths and weakness,' Adams emailed furiously. 'A stop and detain alert is really a pathetic provision. It means that we have no evidence against this person ONLY suspicion so please stop him and if he has anything with him detain him and let us know.'

The arguments went back and forth as they struggled with the logistics of getting Alex out of North America. It would have to be from an airport with low security, and not a direct flight to Germany. From Jerusalem, Hasak hosed Adams and Norris down when the infighting grew too ugly. In Norris's view, this operation to make contact with pirates had been Adams' bright idea, riding roughshod over the North American operations. Now the blame was all Adams'. Norris had always been contemptuous of Rissler at DirecTV.

'He's a nice idiot,' Norris had told Oliver before the operation. When he was really snitty, Norris called Rissler a speechwriter. But the worm had turned.

'The only possible evidence that could ever have existed to connect Alex to the card was what was on his PC,' Adams later wrote to Hasak, reviewing the episode. Adams had Oliver/Alex reformat the drive and then disassemble the laptop into two parts, each of which was posted by two different courier companies to two different addresses in Germany. But Oliver still had to walk through those airport gates.

'Alex had absolutely nothing with him,' Adams assured Hasak later. Oliver did not even have a credit card and Adams had two lawyers on standby ready to get him out of trouble. 'There would have been absolutely no legitimate grounds for detaining him for a second . . . Nothing existed technically to connect Alex to the card in either Canada, the USA or Germany.'

So Oliver was home safe. That was the end of it, everyone walked away clean . . . except that Larry Rissler was seething. He knew someone had tipped Oliver off and his list of suspects was very short. He fronted Norris, who denied any link to Oliver. In reality, Norris had made sure he didn't even know Oliver's real name—he was just Alex to him. Rissler accused Norris of hiding the fact that Oliver worked for NDS. Rissler's chief source in the pirate community claimed to have proof that Oliver worked for NDS and his accusations became more and more insistent. According to an Adams email tendered in the 2008 trial, Norris lied straight faced, telling Rissler that Oliver had no connection at all with NDS that he knew about. The row was escalating to the point where the future of the NDS contract with DirecTV could be at stake—and that would mean the future of NDS itself.

Five days after Oliver flew out, the pressure grew too much. The Cowboy blinked. Norris told Rissler that he was right—Oliver was one of their people. Adams was incandescent.

'We discussed this,' he raged, that 'under no circumstances must we tell Larry Rissler that Alex works for us. It was an absolute priority. That decision was made and we all acted on it . . . Despite whatever table thumping Larry Rissler may indulge in I knew that there was absolutely nothing that LR could do about Alex . . . My frustration is that we went to great lengths to protect Alex and then give away our greatest secret to someone we do not trust.'

That was the problem. It was DirecTV that wasn't trustworthy. It had come to this. A hacker on News Corporation's payroll was on the run from police in two countries. He virtually had to be smuggled out of the United States. If he had been caught, the repercussions for NDS, for News Corporation and for Rupert Murdoch in the glare of publicity were potentially disastrous. The first question would be how News Corporation came to be involved in what looked like criminal piracy directed against NDS's biggest client, DirecTV. Whatever their ultimate intentions, in order to mount this sting operation NDS had been pirating DirecTV— peddling software codes and stealing the signal from their best customer, without even telling them.

None of this troubled Ray Adams in October 1997 as he struggled with a much simpler issue. Why—*why*—had Norris come clean? It was so simple. 'All we had to do was stick to our story and deny.'

It would become a familiar legal strategy: Deny, deny, deny . . .

Calgary, November 1997

'So Ron calls me and says, "You know what? The fucking Kraut is in Canada right now, doing cards with Mullen, Marty Mullen!"' This is Chris Tarnovsky, talking to me years later. I do wish he would tell me what he really feels about Oliver.

'I'll never forget that—I was in the backyard of my old house. So I said "Damn!" You know?'

Tarnovsky had become a little obsessive about Oliver. It wasn't because Oliver was a rival in NDS, because he didn't know that. And it wasn't because Oliver's escapade in Toronto had made Chris's position more dangerous, because no one told him about that either. And it wasn't that he got on badly with him, because he had never met him, never interacted. He just didn't like Oliver.

'Chris Tarnovsky is jealous of everybody, of every engineer,' says Ereiser. 'You know there's Plamen in Bulgaria, who can work circles around Tarnovsky. You know he's always been badmouthing in on everybody.' Ereiser had used a second programmer, known as 'Axa', as back-up for Tarnovsky. 'He was doing fixes at the same time Chris was doing them for me, and [Chris] was always trying to get at this guy, you know—he just had nothing nice to say about any other guy who could do any coding or anything. You know he always called Oliver . . . "Something Fucking Kraut". You know, it's just the way he was.'

Ereiser, of course, is not Chris Tarnovsky's greatest admirer. But in late 1997 Tarnvosky, using the nickname 'Coleman', had begun badmouthing Oliver in European chatrooms, or so Oliver believed. Norris had to tell him to knock it off.

Norris, though, slept with the calm serenity of the morally virtuous. He had discovered candour. He had told Larry Rissler that Oliver worked for NDS. Now he let him know NDS had a second hacker on the payroll, a young man named Michael George. Ray Adams' greatest beef over Norris telling Rissler about Oliver was Ray's certainty that Rissler would share the information with his informants. But, of course, Norris's candour was not entirely a matter of choice. After the Toronto debacle, NDS had had to give DirecTV an assurance it would not run any undercover operations without telling Rissler for the next two years.

It was in this new spirit of glasnost that Norris raised the next topic with Rissler. He described it as a tactical play by NDS, and it had the codename, 'Operation Johnny Walker'.

In mid November, Ron Ereiser called Chris on his phone line in Manassas, Virginia. The line diverted the call to Chris in California without Ereiser being any the wiser. For Ereiser, nothing had changed. Ron asked Chris to come to Calgary for the weekend to meet with some of the other pirate dealers. They had a problem with their DirecTV P2 hack: 'Would you help us support the card?'

Tarnovsky said no problem. A year after leaving the army, Chris was looking more the part of the pirate hacker. He worked from home, was growing his hair long and pursued his passion for heavy metal music and his growing guitar collection. He also had the eternal pirate's suspicion that he had been short-changed.

Calgary was Tarnovsky's first face-to-face meeting with most of the West 3M dealers, as they filled him in on their troubles. It was the first time he heard of Plamen and Vesco. Chris was startled to learn that the West 3M dealers had sneaked them into the United States to do the hack just days after the grand jury had issued warrants for the dealers (although they lied to Chris, telling him they used a lab in California). But the Bulgarians had later proven to be trouble. After they quarrelled, Vesco had flown home. Then Plamen had a meltdown and flew back to Bulgaria soon afterwards, accompanied by Herb Huddleston, who had become his mentor. When DirecTV ran its first electronic counter measure (ECM) soon after the pirate cards appeared, Plamen had got the cards back up and running. But when a second ECM came through, Plamen couldn't be contacted. He was prone to bouts of deep depression. 'You didn't know, if you had an ECM, if he was not going to answer the phone for three days or not . . . so we got pretty worried that we weren't able to keep the customers up,' Ereiser told me.

In mid November Huddleston was in Frankfurt with Plamen, meeting with Oliver Kömmerling, whom they hoped to do a deal with. Meanwhile Chris agreed to be West 3M's back-up hitter. His first job was to provide four reprogrammer boxes that the pirates could use to fix the cards killed by the latest ECM. They knew that NDS had made the connection between biggun and Tarnovsky. This time they would call him 'Joe'.

Chris had gone to Calgary with Norris's blessing—in fact, this was to be the start of Operation Johnny Walker. But Norris had warned him to be particularly wary of one pirate, who was said to be linked to a Hells Angels affiliate. After he arrived, Chris made a bad slip-up while complaining about his connecting flight to Calgary from Dallas—it had in fact been his connection from San Diego. The pirate picked up on this, taking Chris aside to grill him on how, if he lived in Virginia, he had flown to Calgary via Dallas.

'He threatened to break my legs or my knees or something, some part of my lower body, if he ever found out I was a narc,' Tarnovsky testified in 2008. He didn't doubt for a moment that the pirate meant it. 'Other individuals in Canada that dealt in this piracy issue, the dealers, had their legs broken and beaten up. There's been some bad stuff going on up there.'

The easiest answer to give was that he was coming from Texas because his mother lived there. Tavnovsky's inquisitor swept straight back into negotiation mode. 'You know, it's pretty scary when a guy just pulls out ten grand, in hundreds, puts it on the table and says, this is for the past, then pulls out another wad of ten grand and says this is for the future,' Tarnovsky says.

Chris let the $20,000 burn a hole in his pocket over the weekend, until the pirates broke it to him that he couldn't take that much across the border. He kept $10,000 and left the rest for the pirates to post as money orders, split between his father's address in Virginia and his mother's address in Texas.

'Of course, then it took Ron Ereiser months to send it to me,' says Tarnovsky. Ereiser testified that on at least two occasions he sent money to Tarnovsky hidden inside a PlayStation game—once to Tarnovsky and once to his father. In any case, Tarnovsky flew home from Calgary with the $10,000 and the lower part of his body intact. The relationship with Ereiser had a bit of niggle, but the pirates accepted he was one of them.

'You know I just couldn't believe that he actually was informing on me the whole time,' Ereiser said later. 'I talked to him absolutely every day. You know like friends, we talked family, we talked everything, just—it absolutely blew me away. That's why I never caught on, because I just never dreamed . . . There were red flags right everywhere, when I look back, but I just trusted him.'

Up to this time, John Norris had had no idea how the West 3M group had hacked the P2 card or who their hacker was. But Norris was the one person who didn't trust Tarnovsky. He lived less than 25 kilometres from him and spoke to him by phone and emailed several times a day. One of the first things he did when Chris returned home was to wire him up to a polygraph machine and ask him just what he had been doing with DirecTV pirates.

Meantime Operation Johnny Walker was under way. NDS Israel was already working on the four programmer boxes that Chris had agreed to provide for the pirates. They would work like a treat as they spat out pirate cards, up until the moment when DirecTV pulled the plug on them with an ECM when they would all die. The pirates then would end up poorer, and they would need Tarnovsky more than ever to fix this new problem.

Geneva, December 1997

Christmas was looming and Jan Saggiori was surprised by an old friend. Chris and Sylvie Tarnovsky were back in Europe to spend the holiday break with her family. Chris found the family sessions interminable and announced a sudden need to make a flying trip to Switzerland to see Jan, in the grand Saggiori home in southern Geneva. Chris was actually en route to Israel, but he didn't mention that to Jan.

They went to dinner in a restaurant. After nearly three years of emails and phone calls, this was the first time Jan had ever met Chris face to face. He had not heard much from the American of late; he found his friend a little changed in his interests, but recognisable in his manner. They still shared the same passions. In the dwindling circle of hackers that Jan could trust, Chris was a friend, and Jan had a streak of intense loyalty to his friends. 'We were talking about each other as brothers because we were willing to exchange everything,' Jan said.

Jan had just finished his computing science degree. His friends noted a new seriousness about him as his attention switched to what he would be doing after university. His thesis had been about hacking conditional access smartcards, and part of his presentation had involved installing a satellite dish and receiver in front of his thesis markers and demonstrating a variety of hacking approaches. He had focused his efforts on the D-2Mac system, which left him little time to look at the Sky 11 cards. Anyhow he knew his days as a smartcard hacker were numbered. A new European community directive was coming in from July 1999, which would finally make pay TV piracy illegal, even if it was directed at another country's pay TV service. And that would be that. In the meantime he had set up his own private company, SSS, to work as a technical consultant.

Chris was eager to hear everything that had been happening in Europe. He was a little more pushy than Jan remembered, pressing Jan to provide him with a pirate system for Canal+ for his in-laws in Belgium. On that, Jan was non-committal. Jan told Chris he was disappointed with Plamen and Vesco after they had welshed on their promise to pay him for their introduction to Chris and to Ron. Chris had not told Norris of his role in procuring the Bulgarians for Ereiser—indeed, identifying the West 3M hacker had been a major reason Norris had despatched him to the pirate dealers meeting in Calgary the month before.

Tarnovsky was happy to renew his gripes about OFK (as in Oliver-the-Fucking-Kraut), but Jan told him he had had a rapprochement with him. Oliver had a hack for Sky 11, Jan told Chris, and pulled out 22 Sky 11 pirate cards that Oliver had sold him for his friends. As Jan sat there talking, he had no idea how much interest NDS was focusing on him. He had become a regular feature in the weekly reports. NDS had a codename for him—he was 'Hannibal', and he would become an obsession.

By November Ray Adams had decided to recruit Jan, and had sent to Geneva an NDS informant called 'Angel' to check whether he was working on the Sky 11 card. Angel, who already knew Jan, reported that Jan was 'well connected but not a threat (neither a hacker nor a financier)'. Nonetheless, Ray and Avigail Gutman prepared a brief of the questions they wanted Chris to put to Jan; this was their next step in trying to recruit Hannibal.

This was something new for Chris Tarnovsky. He was already playing a double role with Ron Eresier and his group, but now he was setting up one of his friends. Perhaps he didn't care. Perhaps he thought recruitment was not the worst thing in the world. When I asked Chris in 2009 whether deceiving Jan was difficult, he shrugged it off. He and Jan had grown apart. What was Jan like?

'Just like a Joe, an ordinary Joe. A software guy,' he said. 'He's a pedlar. He's a nice guy but he's a mama's boy.' Chris broke off to make a crack about Jan still living with his parents back then, in a big house with an elevator.

'He wants to be in the middle, and he wants to make money off the middle, off the transaction. So he'll take it, he'll take the transaction, and he'll take 20 grand or something. Like the P2 crack. I didn't get crap. I didn't get any money from that, for introducing the Canadians to the guys in Bulgaria.'

Was Chris that dismissive of Jan in 1997, or did this come later, after Jan became a threat? Chris's report confirmed that Jan was working exclusively on D-2Mac systems, with no interest in hacking Sky 11. It wasn't a hostile report; it just said that Jan wasn't a player.

But those Sky 11 pirate cards in Jan's possession caused surprise at NDS Israel. When Avigail Gutman put her monthly report together for the operational security team on 28 December, she flagged as a priority for follow up: 'What is the origin of the card given by Oliver K to Jan Saggiori?'

By early 1998 Ray Adams was ready to attempt to recruit Jan. It was a practised manoeuvre. First, you get close to the target—very close. You surprise them with how much you know about them, who they know, what they have done, why they are in such deep trouble. The most powerful ingredient in this is suggestion. It's a bit like a card trick—if you keep throwing out cards with reckless abandon, your audience in the end believes that you must hold all the cards. You make them frightened, and let them stew on it, then at the right moment you suggest there might be an alternative. They don't have to go to jail. In fact, there might be some money in it for them. This had worked dozens of time for Adams. But it didn't work on Hannibal, simply because Jan refused to allow Adams to get close enough to work his magic.

Adams called Jan at his home, politely enough, and suggested they talk. Almost invariably, curiosity will win the day, and the target will want to know at least what it is about. Not Jan Saggiori. He refused point blank.

'I won't see you and, if you come to my house, I will call the police and tell them there is a thief breaking into my property,' Jan told Adams.

And that was that. Hannibal was secure under Swiss law. Without personal access to him, Adams could work no magic.

February 1998

Canadian piracy circles were abuzz with the latest sex scandal. It had split Ron Ereiser's West 3M Group. John Norris was in heaven. The stories centred on Herb Huddleston, whose secretary Norris had tried to bribe in 1996, according to Ron Ereiser's testimony in the 2008 EchoStar trial. Norris is a sensitive man when other people's feelings are bruised. He does glee really well.

'Our friend HH has been tossed out of his home by [his wife] Tootie,' Norris emailed Adams in late February. 'Tootie threw his laptop across the room and destroyed it. HH is sleeping on the boat . . .' But this was just the domestic news. The real kicker was Herb's problem with Plamen Donev, whom he had been mentoring.

Norris had heard a whisper that Herb might have got Plamen's 24-year-old girlfriend pregnant: 'PD and HH are no longer on good terms.' Plamen had not taken the news well and had trashed Herb's rental car. Huddleston was heading back to Bulgaria the following week ('he travels on a US p/p/ and appropriate calls have been made'), and Herb proposed to bring the pregnant ex-girlfriend home. Plamen was back working with the West 3M group, which had expelled Huddleston, who was now expected to team up with Vesco.

By 1 May, Norris was reporting further details. Plamen was stuck in Bulgaria, after Canada twice refused his work visa for 'untruths and deception'. Herb seemed to be back at his base in Grand Cayman, making up with Tootie ('I may have to let her know about the Booger girl'). Norris boasted that Chris Tarnovsky 'can presently run circles around PD . . . PD is in dead calm water.'

On 1 July Ray Adams arranged for the newly founded Bulgarian Association Against Copyright Theft (BullACT) to raid Plamen's apartment in Kazanlak. It was the NDS modus operandi—to work through a copyright organisation that they controlled. ('We pay a retainer to FACT in London each year,' Adams wrote in 1999. 'This gives us access to their investigators and prosecutors any time we need them.') Police marched out of Plamen's apartment with his computer, his nine mobile phones, radio transmitter, two satellite phones (and some of these items were still in working order); his laptop stored in the elevator service room; 63 smartcards for pay TV services all over the world; $10,000 in a wad of $100 bills; two large flower pots containing 34 cannabis plants; Herb Huddleston's business card, and a pass for Arsenal football club. It was really rotten luck for young Plamen.

Later, Ray's job would be to tell him he sympathised, and that perhaps there was a way Ray might be able to help him.

Haifa-Bristol, May–June 1998

On 10 January Oliver Kömmerling flew into Tel Aviv to join Chaim Shin-Orr's black-hat team at Haifa to work out a plan of attack for three reverse engineering projects that confronted them. Oliver stayed a week at this time, but he would return from time to time at critical points in the months ahead. In fact, the Viaccess chip was no challenge at all, but the other two—the Canal+ SECA card and Kudelski's Nagra card, used by EchoStar—presented a sterner test of their unique skills. They would focus on the SECA card first.

Canal+ and Kudelski had taken different approaches to card security. The most important question that any conditional access company has to decide is where on the smartcard to keep its secrets. The Canal+ approach was to keep its secret keys in the ROM section of the card. They made this very hard to get to, and it could not be reprogrammed by pirates. It was a good system, but it meant Canal+ had all its eggs in the one basket. If you cracked the ROM, then you had the card.

The SECA card was based on a Thomson card and it proved difficult to crack. A smartcard is like a tiny computer: when power is applied, it boots up using the system codes (also known as the system ROM) that the manufacturer (in this case, Thomson) has built in. Once the card is booted up, it executes the instructions in the normal ROM, which has the SECA code. The black-hat team and Oliver destroyed a lot of cards in the process of trying to extract the ROM. While they retrieved the SECA part of the ROM, they were not able to extract the system code section of the ROM.

The black-hat team didn't really need the ROM system code to be able to hack the SECA card, but their efforts convinced them that they needed to upgrade the equipment they were using in order to tackle the Nagra card. Later that year NDS would lease a $1 million focused ion beam machine, but for now they would need to find a hospitable university with a FIB, just as Herb Huddleston had done at Montana State University. They didn't have to travel that far though—for £2800, Bristol University was very understanding.

Shin-Orr emailed Adams on 22 May with the details: he had booked rooms at the Aztec Hotel in northern Bristol and the university confirmed they would have access to the FIB—'Right now the plan is for us to have the machine for ourselves starting Friday morning.'

At low power, a FIB offers picture resolution down to 5 nanometres—just by way of comparison, a human hair is between 50,000 and 100,000 nanometres wide. The more important aspect of the FIB for the NDS team was that at higher voltages it became a sculptor's tool. You can shave off any surface you want, micro layer by micro layer. Oliver joined them in Bristol and under his direction, Shin-Orr and Zvi Shkedy punched holes through the microscopic security mesh that protected the Nagra card's five ROM locations, located a section of the card called the 'instruction latch', and applied two micro contacts that induced the card to spew out everything in the ROM.

When Kudelski designed the Nagra card its designers had taken a different approach to Canal+. Nagra used a different Thomson chip but while Canal+ stored its secrets in the ROM, Kudelski put its secret keys and subscriber information inside the electronically erasable programmable read-only memory. This was a section of the card that acted like a ROM, but it could be written over and reprogrammed—roughly like the drive in your computer. This approach makes the whole system more flexible—Kudelski could rewrite its software to fix any holes found by hackers to a far greater extent than Canal+ could with the SECA card.

The NDS team managed to extract the Nagra ROM codes, including the system codes for the card, without incident. From here it became a software problem. This was the job of David Mordinson, a Russian-born engineer who had been hired by NDS the previous September specifically for his reverse engineering skills.

It was Mordinson back in Haifa who pieced together the ROM binaries that Zvi and Oliver had extracted, and reconstructed the machine code that ran the card. Then he had to find the weaknesses in the system that allowed him to dump the code for the EEPROM. And then he had to take the EEPROM dump and reconstruct the code that ran from it. And then he had to find a weakness in the EEPROM code that allowed him to take control of the card. (The witnesses in the 2008 EchoStar trial were taken through all this, and some of the jury made heavy weather of it. My favourite moment was when Mordinson was explaining that a logic analyser was something he used to record digital data and Judge Carter instructed the court officer: 'Okay, Mr Ken, would you help the gentleman who's asleep back there in the yellow and wake him up. Thank you. Counsel, next question, please.')

It took Zvi and Oliver one month, from the end of May, to pop the card. It would take Mordinson another four months to complete the hack, but, by the time he had finished, he knew more about the Nagra card than anyone at Kudelski. His hard-won insights would end up costing Nagra and their client EchoStar about $1 billion.

London, February–June 1998

There are moments when being Rupert Murdoch is a very complicated business. Running a global media empire requires not just operating in multiple time zones but in effect living in parallel universes. In each country he must pursue different corporate, political and sometimes personal objectives. Just keeping track of them all might stretch a lesser man. Not everyone understands that. Sometimes people's reactions to the prospect of doing a little business with Rupert Murdoch can be quite hurtful.

On 22 February 1998 the *Sunday Telegraph* in London wrote about a book deal that HarperCollins had with the last governor of Hong Kong, Chris Patten, and the *Sunday Telegraph* seemed to get *completely* the wrong end of the stick about the whole affair. It suggested that Rupert Murdoch had canned the book after trying to tone down Patten's harsh criticism of China's communist leadership, as some sort of effort to curry favour with China. While it was true that Chinese officials didn't really like Patten—whom they had previously described as a 'perfidious whore', a 'drooling idiot' and a 'tango dancer'—the ultimate truth was, as HarperCollins insisted in a leak to the *Mail on Sunday*, that the Patten book was dumped because it was 'too boring'.

Unhappily, this was not how the rest of the media saw it. The *Telegraph* ran a copy of a memo written on 20 January by the head of HarperCollins UK, Charlie Bell, who said he was 'extremely worried' by the decision to 'relinquish rights' to the book, although he conceded: 'KRM [Keith Rupert Murdoch] has outlined the negative aspects of publication which I fully understand.'

Murdoch faced a media storm when he flew into London in early March, and was forced to give an interview to Raymond Snoddy of the *Times*, in which he said the furore about the book was just a 'cock-up' and it was all the fault of HarperCollins management. The point here was that, just because a decision was made in one part of the News Corporation empire, it didn't mean that Murdoch was behind it. These people had let him down. Three days later HarperCollins settled Patten's damages claim and issued a grovelling apology. Meantime Murdoch said he had full confidence in HarperCollins executives.

There was another episode that February that triggered fewer headlines, but was just as disappointing. Back in November 1996, the Independent Television Commission (ITC) in Britain formally called for applications for new digital terrestrial television licences. This would be a new digital service broadcast from ground stations rather than a satellite; but, as a pay TV service, it would be a direct competitor to BSkyB. Murdoch's vision for Britain was to have one pay TV broadcaster, which would be controlled by News. He was a fair way towards achieving this when the tenders closed in January 1997, and the leading contender was revealed to be British

Digital Broadcasting (BDB), in which BSkyB, Carlton Communications and the Granada Group each held a one-third stake. One of the selling points for the deal was that NDS would provide the set-top box and the conditional access system.

It all seemed so neat. But then the meddlesome European Commission insisted on putting its oar in, making a long submission to the ITC that suggested that allowing BSkyB (in which News Corporation was the 37.6 per cent controlling shareholder) to have its foot on both digital and terrestrial pay TV was anti-competitive. As a result, in June 1997 BSkyB was forced to withdraw from British Digital Broadcasting, leaving Granada and Carlton to go it alone with a 15-channel pay TV service that they would call OnDigital.

This was unfortunate. But what put BDB at war with News and BSkyB was its decision that OnDigital would not be using NDS for its encryption and set-top box. Instead, on 20 February 1998, the eve of the furore over the Patten book, BDB announced that it would be using the SECA conditional access card from Canal+.

'We chose SECA because it's a proven system,' BDB's director of operations, John Egan, said. 'The NDS system used by DirecTV in America has been pirated. NDS was offering us a new system, which was not yet available or demonstrable.'

There are certain events that ignite News Corporation and its various arms. There is a grievance, the sense of a wrong being done, a line is drawn in the sand and the empire goes on the attack. It's a familiar phenomenon in Britain and Australia, but only recently has Fox News given News Corp the clout to do it effectively in the United States outside of New York. In early 1998 News could feel the digital universe in the United Kingdom slipping out of its grasp and it went on the offensive.

BSkyB's chief executive, Mark Booth, said: 'BDB have both regulatory and contractual commitments to ensure that their box is compatible with ours. If necessary, we will take legal action to protect the consumer.' In April that's what BSkyB did, issuing a writ against British Digital Broadcasting to prevent it from selling its set-top boxes and to force it to use NDS, to make its programming compatible with BSkyB. Abe Peled thought BDB's decision was simply the result of anti-Murdoch prejudice: 'Being associated with Murdoch also has its disadvantages. There are few people in this business who are neutral.'

OnDigital claimed there was no issue. SECA's technology had 'the capacity to be inter-operable with Sky's program services', a spokesman said. Through April and early May OnDigital and BSkyB were at loggerheads; although they reached a resolution in mid May, the bickering continued. And that's where the parallel universes come in.

It turns out that NDS's black-hat team was reverse engineering the Canal+ SECA card, and visiting Bristol University to work with the FIB as part of that project, at the very time when SECA was snatching a valuable client from NDS. Of course a lot of things were happening in May 1998.

Maidenhead, England, February–May 1998

From the very start there had been an issue as to what NDS would do with the technology secrets that Oliver and its black-hat team would obtain when their reverse engineering efforts were successful. On 3 February, Ray Adams, who was planning a trip to Germany, emailed ahead to Oliver. The subject line was 'Irdetto': 'When I come over I need a text from you explaining the Digital hack and the mistakes in the original card. It can be as technical as you wish. Ray.'

Back in September 1996 Adams had emailed Reuven Hasak about Ilian, a Bulgarian who had a working hack for the Irdeto system. Adams was proposing to provide Ilian with 1000 blank smartcards he could use to launch the pirate Irdeto product. It was late 1997 before European pirates began selling an Irdeto pirate product called Hornet cards, but in February Ray asked Oliver for a technical report, and he assumed Oliver was already sufficiently familiar with both the Irdeto card and the hack. Ray didn't say why he wanted this report.

On 3 May, Avigail Gutman in Israel sent Adams an address for a web page set up by UK hacker Chris Coe, which was on a new website called thoic.com, short for 'The House of Ill Compute'. Adams passed it on to Oliver the next day: 'Have a look. Thoic is my site. Ray.'

The website was a new initiative that Adams had come up with after he recruited a young hacker called Lee Gibling. Lee had been running a BBS bulletin board called The House of Ill Compute since 1992. Adams provided a server and the funds to convert Thoic into a website. It was a non-commercial site for satellite hackers, a haven for refugees from the many UK websites that Adams and his people had closed down.

In 2002 NDS would downplay its connection to Thoic, claiming that it had only made a number of payments. In reality, from the start Thoic was financed out of the UK budget for NDS security, much of which was charged to BSkyB. Gibling was being paid £5000 a month. By 1999 Thoic would be the most popular piracy website in the world, with more than 10,000 members. It even offered its users a Thoic email service, which they could use for their most confidential exchanges.

Gibling served several purposes for NDS. Thoic was a honey pot, a rich source of information provided freely by its members in the belief they were safe among friends. It was also an excellent platform on which to produce misinformation. It achieved these ends by providing piracy codes that allowed users to hack smart-cards. This was a delicate legal path.

'It is illegal to sell pirated satellite cards, period, if a subscription is available in the country of transmission,' Gibling said in an interview with a Latin American hacking website in June 1998. However, 'because we are based in the UK there is no current law to prevent us from selling or releasing codes for transmissions outside of the UK, primarily the Nordic market where D-2Mac is the primary encryption method. We do not sell cards—we give away information for people to update their cards.'

Thoic wasn't commercial and it didn't offer pirate hardware. Rather, it published codes to make pirate products: 'If the person who downloads those codes uses them in their own country, it is up to the individual to determine the laws in their country.'

While Gibling claimed that his website remained 'legal' because of this loophole, NDS would ensure that all links to Thoic remained hidden. This was important because the codes that were posted on thoic.com were for NDS's competitors, not for NDS itself.

'At the present time there is no commercial hack for Sky Television,' Gibling told a writer for a hacking website who interviewed him in June. BSkyB was switching over to digital very soon, Gibling said, so it would be 'commercially unsound' to commit large sums of money to break the card. 'We expect a new Sky 12 card to be introduced to the UK very soon.'

This was a classic Reuven Hasak play. Sky 12 was a phantom card that NDS was pretending to produce in order to convince pirates not to waste time on Sky 11. It also gave a pretext not to have NDS codes on the site . . . though in reality there was a low-profile commercial hack for Sky 11 in existence. (The twenty cards Oliver had sold to Jan Saggiori were just a small sample of the underground trading in the Sky 11 pirate cards.)

Gibling was the picture of unassuming courage in the face of danger: 'We frequently receive threats of litigation targeted towards the websites, but with our server based in California they can KISS MY ASS!' In reality, it was NDS that provided Gibling with his server.

Gibling's sales pitch was that hackers needed to be ready to hit Sky when it went digital, and they needed to work closer together, through Thoic: 'For too long now, everyone that has been working towards hacking the Sky 11 card has been doing so on their own with no success. United we stand a better chance of succeeding.' It was a marvellous piece of deception. But again, while NDS was securing valuable information, it was its competitors who were bearing the cost of the piracy that was triggered by the pirate codes published on Thoic.

NDS had become very interested in SECA piracy. On 29 July 1998 Andy Coulthurst, an electrical engineer working for Adams at Maidenhead, emailed him: 'With our ongoing interest in the SECA system which will be in use in the UK for Digital Terrestrial Television I thought you would be interested in the following site ... which shows already that someone is looking at hacking this system.'

Adams forwarded Coulthurst's email to Oliver and commented enigmatically: 'Who will be first?'

On top of the OnDigital face-off, May 1998 was another bad month for Murdoch for two other reasons. The news had just broken that he had left his wife, Anna. His deepening relationship with Wendi Deng was still a secret, but had provided an intriguing backdrop to the decision to drop Chris Patten's book. Then Murdoch faced another crisis in America. On 16 May the head of the antitrust division at the US Justice Department, an aggressive lawyer in his early fifties called Joel Klein, filed an antitrust suit against News. In the wake of the failed EchoStar merger, News now planned to sell its interest in ASkyB to PrimeStar, the satellite broadcast company that had been established in 1991 by the six major cable companies. Klein argued that the whole intention of the satellite licences originally issued to ASkyB had been to encourage competition with the cable companies and that selling them to PrimeStar was like setting a wolf to guard the sheep.

It was now clear that Murdoch's deal was doomed and he was stuck with an expensive satellite licence and two satellites that he couldn't do anything with. It was a humiliating and expensive defeat, which could all be traced back to Charlie Ergen, and his decision to stick with his Nagra smartcards. It was entirely coincidental that a week later Chaim Shin-Orr was finalising his arrangements with Bristol University to use its FIB for the black-hat team to hack the Nagra card. Of course the decision to hack Nagra had been made long before.

The news would get worse over the summer. DirecTV, which was NDS's biggest customer, had become increasingly unhappy with the level of piracy of its cards. Now DirecTV formally notified NDS that it had invited other conditional access companies to submit tenders to replace NDS when its contract expired later that year. The notice did not specify who DirecTV was talking to, but it wasn't hard to figure it out. Meanwhile DirecTV contacted the Kudelski group in Switzerland and said it would pay $200,000 to fund a feasibility study by Kudelski into how DirecTV could switch to using the Nagra card. The sale negotiations would be handled by a French-American in California who had become a consultant for Kudelski. His name was Alan Guggenheim.

London, summer 1998

Policemen may retire, but their old files pursue them. In April 1993, Ray Adams had been drawn into one of Britain's most controversial murders of the 1990s. A young black man waiting for a late bus in Eltham had been surrounded by half a dozen white youths and stabbed to death. The investigation of Stephen Lawrence's murder became an eighteen-year saga, dredging up along the way allegations of racism and corruption within the London Metropolitan Police until, in January 2012, two men, Gary Dobson and David Norris, were finally convicted of the murder.

But in 1998 charges against five teenagers, including Dobson and Norris, were dropped and the investigation was in disarray, with Sir William Macpherson conducting a public inquiry into the police handling of the case. On 4 June 1998 Ray Adams found himself facing questions before the inquiry. He was recalled for a torrid cross-examination by counsel for the Lawrence family on 16 July.

Adams' only role in the investigation had been to write a letter to the Lawrence family's solicitors, discouraging them from directing questions about the case to the investigating police and suggesting instead that they address any queries they might have to himself or to the Chief Superintendent. It was Adams' last day of work. The next day he took sick leave, and then medical retirement for chronic back pain.

At the Macpherson inquiry in July 1998, the Lawrence family's lawyers argued that as a commander, Adams was too senior to be handling family liaison, and that he had involved himself in order 'to influence the investigation so that the suspects named over the first weekend were not arrested expeditiously. A potential channel for such influence arises from Commander Adams' previous links with Kenneth Noye who in turn has links with Clifford Norris.'

At this time Noye was still on the run after stabbing a motorist to death in a road rage incident in 1996 (he would be arrested in Spain a month later, in August 1998). Adams was grilled on the stand about his past links to Noye, about the three-year corruption investigation of Adams (in which he was vindicated) and about his links with Clifford Norris (whose son, David, would eventually be convicted of the murder) and with another family member, by then deceased, also called David Norris.

Adams said he had dealt with the late David Norris as an informant; but he repeatedly said that he had had no contact with Clifford Norris, and that he did not know one of the suspects was Clifford Norris's son: 'He did not even know the name Clifford Norris or anything about him until a few months before he came to give evidence,' Macpherson stated in his report. It seems a substantial failure for Adams as head of the SO11 intelligence division for Scotland Yard, for him to say that he had never heard of Clifford Norris, who in the 1980s ran much of south London's drugs trade and had been on the run since 1988. However, while Macpherson found there were strange aspects to Adams' evidence, there was no substantiation of the allegations put to him in the long cross-examination and it was 'not established that Mr Adams did anything other than that which he told us that he had done', and that he had written the letter 'in order to be helpful'.

Adams emerged unscathed and once again vindicated. But there was enough publicity to raise questions all over again about his judgement in running informants. Adams' next crisis would involve his attempts to recruit a friend of Markus Kuhn and Oliver Kömmerling called Boris Floricic. On 12 July, Chaim Shin-Orr at the black-hat team in Haifa, in the middle of the Nagra hack, took time out to send Floricic a parcel: 'Hello Boris, here are the analog devices, good luck.'

Cambridge, March 2010

I took the train to Cambridge and a taxi out to the William Gates computer laboratory building. I had made the necessary arrangements the previous week, when I was in Berlin. Ross Anderson had built the computer science school into a major research centre for encryption. Anderson is 'arguably the world's foremost authority on computer security', as he was described at the 2008 EchoStar trial. He is a major intellect. I have his 900-page manual on security engineering. He's a fount of knowledge on a thousand subjects, if only I could find a way to tap into it. I would really like to talk to Anderson about NDS. (I had requested an interview with NDS, but they had suggested if I have queries I should raise them with the NDS PR person in Hong Kong. Following up on that for a substantive response would prove fruitless.)

I have come to Cambridge today to talk to Markus Kuhn, who's a senior lecturer and Fellow of Wolfson College. He had long ago finished his doctorate—his thesis was about how to eavesdrop on computers in another building by analysing the reflection on the walls from the computer screen. Markus is the key figure in understanding the academic hacker community in Europe. The whole *Star Trek* hack was his. He's the founder of TVcrypt. He knows the whole scene. I want to ask him about the history of hacking. I want to ask him about Oliver. And I really want to ask him about Boris.

Ahead of meeting Markus, I don't know how much I trust him. It's not that I suspect him of any ill will or underhand behaviour. Spend half an hour with Markus and you realise how absurd that sounds. But hacking and piracy is dangerous ground. In this small world, where everybody knows everybody, the ground is littered with trip-wires that set off alarms elsewhere. My assumption is that anything I say to him he may repeat to Oliver Kömmerling, with whom he remains relatively close. I want to ask Markus some specific questions, but only as part of a whole bunch of other matters, a broader inquiry to blur some of my purpose in coming here.

He's on sabbatical and is generous with his time and attention. He's happy to talk about the TVcrypt days. But Markus appears unaware of just how much NDS was worried about him, or how closely they were watching him. Their codename for him was 'Castor'.

In late 1998 Yossi Tsuria wrote an email creating a whole classification system of people who reverse engineer microchips, and their different motives. In reality it was all an elaborate argument that led to his conclusion that it was dangerous for Oliver to be talking to Markus. And Yossi was right. Markus had noticed that Adi Shamir had told him about a new way to hit memory locations on a chip with a laser, after Oliver had told him exactly the same thing.

A month after Yossi's warning letter, Markus wrote to Oliver: 'Hi Oli, yesterday we had visited NDS in Heathrow. I believe more and more that they belong to your customers. As a test I mentioned your name to Yossi several times and observed his reaction carefully ... he looked aside for a moment and his face showed an expression [as if your] name embarrasses him somehow. Many people are as easy to read as smartcards. So no more excuses.'

Reuven Hasak told Adams that Oliver should be as vague as possible and definitely should not confirm any NDS link, because Markus would tell Ross Anderson. Adams told Hasak: 'It is our belief that MK knows enough to be certain. He is a very intelligent man.' Anyway, they had concluded he was not a threat and they would just let the matter die: 'Also bear in mind that I have a source at his workplace.'

And this is where my sense of unreality comes from. I'm in Cambridge, with all its mystique, in a high-tech building paid for by Bill Gates, and Ray Adams was saying he had an *informant* here? Is it a student? Or a member of staff? Or a friend? I have a copy of Adams' UK budget for Operational Security for the December half year in 2000. In those six months Adams and Len Withall spent £1.05 million on 'Security information' (£44,856), 'Contacts' (£711,083), 'Informants' (£4,000) and 'Consultancy' (£290,067). That's equivalent to £2.1 million a year on spying, and that's not counting the salaries, expenses, travel and overheads of Adams and his staff. Ray Adams put it best in a report to Reuven Hasak in June 1999: 'You and I will stick to our strategy. What we need is support. In the main that is money, money, money.'

The lion's share of the outlay went to Oliver Kömmerling's company, ADSR, which received £671,000 in the half year. It's possible to track regular payments each month to sixteen sets of initials, and individual payments to two other people; plus dozens of payments where details are not provided. But this is just the UK/European budget for NDS agents and informants. If you add in seven UK staff and overheads, and then include budgets for Israel, for North and South America and Asia and Australia, it looks like Rupert Murdoch is spending in the order of $10 million a year on a private security force—one that doesn't detail much of where its funds go, which takes an unconventional approach to intellectual property rights, and which operates on what seems to be a special remit from the Office of the Chairman.

This private security force exists to spy. Ray Adams is explicit about that. In a 2002 PowerPoint presentation he made to describe the work of the Operational Security Unit, he refers repeatedly to Sun Tzu in *The Art of War*: 'Unless you are kept informed of the enemy's condition . . . a war may drag on for years. The only way to get this information is to employ spies, and it is impossible to obtain trustworthy spies unless they are properly paid for their services.' It was neatly done. One moment we're talking about Sun Tzu and the need for intelligence, and it turns out that really it's a plea for more money. 'To neglect the use of spies is nothing less than a crime against humanity. One who acts thus is no leader of men, no present help to his sovereign, no master of victory.' Of course there's much more—Sun Tzu's strictures that nothing should be regarded as favourably, or rewarded as generously, as intelligence: 'Subtly, very subtly, nowhere neglect the use of intelligence. It is the divine web. It is the treasure of the ruler.'

Markus Kuhn and Ross Anderson have written treatises on why security by obscurity is a really bad idea. But that's what I'm doing, here in England, tiptoeing through the eggshells, trying very hard not to be noticed, working on my winning impersonation of a limp lettuce, but without the aggression. I really don't want to attract attention from NDS or anyone else right now. And so I'm not completely candid with Markus. I hope he will forgive me.

I ask him a leading question about the stereotype picture of the tortured hacker. He tells me about his friend Boris.

Berlin, 1994–98

It was 1994 and Markus had just set up TVcrypt. His fame as a leading hacker of smartcard security had proved a mixed blessing. It meant strangers sometimes would send him very useful information. He could also be bombarded with all sorts of approaches. One of them came in a late-night telephone call from Berlin. The young man on the other end of the line was an expert at phreaking—making long-distance telephone calls without paying—but wanted to talk about pay TV card systems. Boris Floricic was 22 and invincible, irrepressible and endearing. He had reverse engineered the Deutsche Telekom prepaid phone card so that when you made your call and took the card out of the machine, it reset itself to be full of credits. This was handy, because Boris never believed in short phone calls. He and Markus would talk for hours.

'He was always calling me from some public telephone somewhere in Berlin with his printed circuit boards sticking out of the telephone,' Markus told me. 'So I learned from him a lot about how to break the public telephones and I think I was able to teach him a few things about the pay TV stuff.'

Boris was creative. Markus still tells his students about the ingenious method Boris developed for cheating the magnetic stripe cards used in the university canteen. Boris was also dyslexic, which left him reluctant to use email. 'If I managed to get him to write down something, then it had very adventurous spellings,' Markus said. 'It became quite clear that he is far more comfortable writing C code than German or English prose.'

Boris's father was Croatian and ran a Berlin travel agency. He lived with his German mother in Britz-Süd, a gritty migrant area near Schönefeld airport. His online nickname was 'Tron', after the original 1982 science fiction movie about the computer programmer who is trapped in the machine. Boris was a subversive, with an insatiable curiosity that gave him endless energy, but no interest at all in commercial applications of what he discovered.

'He was very energetic . . . very enthusiastic and a quite capable subversive hobby electronics person,' said Markus. 'He was very much—"It's here, I want to break it, with my soldering iron, let's get it out."'

Boris existed on the fringes of the group based around Markus and Oliver Kömmerling, which included Stefan Eisvogel and Chris Tarnovsky. 'I talked to him one time,' Tarnovksy told me. 'I almost hung up on him I was so pissed off that he couldn't speak English. One time he called me, or I called him . . . and that was it . . . Stefan Eisvogel told me he was involved in something like the Russian mob up there or something. So it's very possible that . . . I mean, NDS was talking to him, but it's silly to think . . .' Chris broke off and rolled his eyes. 'No, it's silly.'

How good was Boris? Markus answers indirectly: 'Of all the people I met in this TVcrypt area, the only ones I got personally more interested in and had a longer term relationship with were Ross Anderson and Oliver Kömmerling. I think Oliver stands quite out of the crowd and Ross Anderson who was my PhD father. And is also a somewhat illustrious personality himself. Yeah, Boris—I should mention Boris Floricic as well in that category.' Just three names on Markus Kuhn's honour role. Boris had to be smart to be there.

So there he was, 24 February 1995, aged 22, making his bow as he joined the List: 'Hello tv-crypt list! I would like to introduce myself here. My name is Boris Floricic . . .' And then he went silent for sixteen months. He had had a little legal problem.

On 3 March, just a week after he joined TVcrypt, Boris and a friend were arrested near a vandalised public telephone. Deutsche Telekom had upgraded its pay technology and Boris's view was that the sensible way forward was to have a look at the newly printed circuit boards in the phones. Fortunately these were quiet easy to get hold of, if you hit the phone enough times with a sledge-hammer. Boris had the circuit boards with him when the police picked him up.

'I was rather disappointed by that—I would have thought he is a bit more sophisticated,' Markus told me. 'He was happy to admit that this was his work—he's not the sort of person who would be into lying. He would rather proudly [explain] what he wanted to do with these printed circuit boards.'

Boris got a ten-month suspended sentence and the police took away his computers, though he managed to replace them. It was June 1996 when he made his next appearance on TVcrypt, when he had a public fight with Jan Saggiori. Boris wrote a peculiar email, which he said was a report on his pay TV hacking. He had two paragraphs about this, and then Boris had six and a half pages of codes for a particular pirate card. There was a story to these cards.

Smartcards, you must remember, are like little computers. You can program them to be one thing, to do one task. But if you reprogram them, they can be and do something quite different. Back in late 2004, Oliver had sold a hack to friends he had in Scandinavia, who used it to produce a pirate card for Sky 09. Jan Saggiori with his friend in Moscow, Andy Kozlov, cracked Oliver's card, which was a nice bit of one-upmanship.

But BSkyB replaced its Sky 09 cards with Sky 10 in October 1995, and at this point Oliver's old pirate cards became redundant. A new hack had to be done. But rather than throwing the old Sky 09 pirate cards away, Jan found another use for them. He reprogrammed them to work with a different system. He installed on the old cards a hack of the D-2Mac system that he had produced.

At one level, the old cards were scrap, so it made sense to find a new use for them. At another level, Jan was trespassing on what Oliver saw as his territory. For these were Oliver's old cards that had been turned. Jan had made some powerful enemies, not least at NDS, which could blame him for the final postings that killed off their Sky 09 card and arguably the EchoStar merger deal. What was he doing, I asked Jan in 2010 in Paris.

'Having a lot of fun,' he says. 'Not so much NDS and not so much Ray Adams.'

And Oliver's Sky 09 card?

'It's always good to have more keys, understand more systems,' he tells me, and pauses. 'And it was a way to piss off Oliver.'

Why?

'It was fun.'

But in June 1996, it was Jan's turn to be on the receiving end. Someone had cracked his D-2Mac cards (that used to be Oliver's Sky 09 cards) and given the codes to Boris, who emailed them to TVcrypt. Posting codes publicly kills any commercial value of a code, whether you are a pay TV company or a pirate. Doing it like this made it a personal message that someone was sending to Jan, via Boris, and he had few doubts as to where the codes came from. Jan believed Oliver was punishing him for reprogramming his old cards, and was using Boris as a cut-out. If anyone was upset about it, Boris was the one who would face the heat.

'Seems they are hacking your code now! Hehehe...,' Chris Tarnovsky emailed Jan. In response, Jan emailed Boris privately that the List was about explaining how solutions were found, not merely providing code dumps. Boris emailed the List again on 24 June, complaining about the many responses he had received to posting the file before singling out Jan: 'I want to excuse me by Jan Saggiori that I disturbe [sic] your tradings. I mean this really serious. But why you bash me for mailing something what I not developed myself.'

From the summer of 1996, Markus Kuhn was in the United States at Purdue University. In his absence the mantle of mentor for Boris in his pay TV hacking seems to have fallen on Oliver Kömmerling.

'I know that he has visited Oliver's lab in Germany once and basically stayed there a few days and was very excited about all the things that ... like a kid in a candy store thing,' Markus said. 'And Oliver thought, "Yeah, nice guy, let him play around with things." But I didn't get the impression that there was any sort of collaboration or so involving [Oliver].'

It was during this year that Boris began looking at the Irdeto conditional access system. On the weekend of August 8/9/10 1997 Boris was a speaker at the Hacking In Progress convention in the Netherlands. Actually he was part of a three-man panel session but, once he started talking, the other two panel members seemed superfluous. His friend Stefan Eisvogel, who was also attending, had earlier updated the List with a Who's Who from TVcrypt attendees. He ended, 'Now just where did I put Boris's Ideto CAM dump?' CAM stands for conditional access module, which is just fancy talk for the smartcard. Boris (or someone near him) had popped the Irdeto card.

A photograph of Boris at the hacker's convention shows a handsome young man, slim, dark-haired, brown-eyed, sitting at a table surrounded by half a dozen other young men, all hanging on what he is saying. A Dutch radio journalist interviewed him. Boris spoke at length about the incursions that intelligence services were making into the hacking world: 'It has probably become too hot to be doing this. When I was doing it three or four years ago, I was the first in Germany. I hack credit cards and GSM systems and such things only for one reason—to make it public, not to hurt anyone . . . it's a huge outrage that state organisations, agencies, and even secret services are active here, using their dubious methods to spy on absolutely everything.'

That sense of outrage about spying coincides with the period when Ray Adams was trying to recruit Boris. It was only six weeks later that Adams made his report to Reuven Hasak, mentioned earlier, that 'BF has not answered his phone for the past two days. His mother says he is working at university. I try every few hours. Plan is to see him next Tuesday with Chaim.'

NDS had become interested in Boris because of Oliver. He wanted to keep Boris out of trouble, Oliver said. 'In reality I had sent Adams to Boris because I wanted to get him out of the legal danger zone,' Kömmerling wrote to a friend of Boris's family in 2000. Boris had not conclusively rejected the approach, he said.

Ray Adams put a lot of thought into recruiting an agent or an informant. It was simpler, of course, if they could be raided and charged—at that point Adams would appear as their only hope of avoiding catastrophe. Cold contact was much harder. First Adams needed an information dossier. In 2000 when he set out to recruit Jan Saggiori's friend, Andy Kozlov in Moscow, Adams used Kroll security, a major international company, to dig up background information on Kozlov; he entrusted Kroll to make the initial contact and even requested them to administer a lie detector test on Kozlov. Adams operated behind mirrors: 'I repeat that under no circumstances must Andy Kozlov know the identity of the Company nor the name of Ray Adams at this stage,' Adams instructed Kroll.

In the summer of 1997 Boris was a year from finishing his electrical engineering degree when he was called about a job interview. Boris jotted the contact details down. The meeting would be in the reception at the swanky Hotel Kempinski in central Berlin at 2 p.m.; the contact name was 'David'.

'The David issue is of no importance whatsoever,' Adams said later. 'It was a name of the interpreter the first time I met with Boris.' It's curious, because Adams' emails don't feature many Davids. There was David Mordinson, but he had not joined NDS at this time. The only David that Adams corresponded with in Europe, and whom he described as 'my colleague in Germany', was David Miel of the private security firm Argen, which had done such sterling work chasing Michael Clinger.

'My meetings with Boris were innocent,' Adams said later. 'My meetings genuinely were to see if he would consider working for us when he had finished at university . . . I mostly met Boris alone. On one occasion I took an engineer with me.'

That would have been Chaim Shin-Orr, the head of the black-hat team in Haifa, at the meeting Adams arranged for Tuesday, 30 September, this time at the Hilton. In June 1999, Adams explained the meetings to German writer Burkhard Schröder:

'Boris was bright. Such people come to notice. NDS offers sponsorship at university and possible employment thereafter. This is normal business practice.'

He wrote this, I imagine, with a straight face. Perhaps that's the most marvellous thing about being in the spy business. There are always good reasons to nuance the truth. Whatever business NDS Operational Security was in, it wasn't providing sponsorship at university. NDS hired consultants—at least that is how most of the payments appeared in its accounts—which inevitably meant becoming an informant. Of course it was never packaged that way. And if Boris needed advice, with Markus away, Oliver would be the person in the pay TV hacker business he respected most. To whom he would likely turn. In any case, whatever Boris's feelings were, he kept the dialogue going.

He was now firmly on the NDS radar. His name popped up in various emails, by Avigail Gutman and others. They noted that he was linked to the Chaos Computer Club—one of the largest hacker groups in the world, firmly committed to the idea of the hacker as opposed to big business as well as the state. For them, hacking was not about piracy and commercial rewards. They approached hacking the way other people do mountain climbing . . . for the achievement, for the adrenaline rush, to show they can. Other NDS emails noted that Boris and 'Ice', another hacker, were staying with Oliver on the weekend of 13 March; that his friend Stefan Eisvogel referred to 'our East European friends' in an email to the List ('Perhaps any friend of Stefan's should become a friend of ours?' Avigail wrote).

And then there were the chips that NDS sent Boris in July 1998: 'Hello Boris, here are the analog devices, good luck.'

North America, June–September 1998

Reuven Hasak had made the arrangements. The black-hat team flew into New York in late June. It was a 35-minute drive from

JFK airport, north on the Van Wyck Expressway, skipping across the top of Manhattan then across George Washington Bridge and there on the left were the leafy avenues of Fort Lee. Hasak's criteria had been simple. He needed somewhere quiet and inconspicuous, where two visiting Israelis would not be noticed, which ruled out using an office. It needed to be a private home, an Orthodox family, people Hasak could depend upon not to talk about it. He quietly put the word out in the Jerusalem office that he needed to find a close family member of NDS staff who lived in the United States. He got a few names, and asked them to let their relatives know they would need to host some NDS engineers for a day or two. In the end he settled on a home in Fort Lee.

Zvi Shkedy and David Mordinson only knew their host as 'Eyal'. He had an EchoStar set-top box and satellite dish, which they commandeered. Shkedy with Oliver Kömmerling had extracted the ROM code from the EchoStar card in Bristol a month before, and Mordinson had extracted the EEPROM code. Now they needed to monitor the way the EchoStar receiver communicated with the smartcard, and with the broadcast stream from the satellite. Mordinson had built a device called a sniffer to do this. It plugged into the EchoStar receiver, where the smartcard usually went. The smartcard then fitted into the back of the sniffer, which would thus catch all of the messages between the receiver and the card. In an ideal situation, Mordinson and Shkedy would have been able to do this comfortably from the lab in Haifa. Unhappily, the EchoStar satellites were all perched in geostationary orbit somewhere above Wyoming, which was on the other side the world from Israel. If they wanted to monitor the stream, they needed to be under the satellite. They needed to go to America. Which is how they came to be making conversation at Eyal's house in Fort Lee.

As a social situation, it had its challenges. Your relation calls you from Israel and says you have to put up a couple of my colleagues for a day or two, or perhaps a little longer if needed, and you can't tell anyone they are there, or what they are doing. It doesn't make for a lot of easy small talk. And the visit did not go well. 'We experienced some difficulties,' Mordinson testified later. Whatever they were, they decided not to go back. There were technical problems hooking up the card, monitoring the data flow, then trying to talk to it. And then the card stopped working, which was so unexpected, and so disastrous that it took a while to sink in. Eyal had put them up, given them free reign over the EchoStar receiver. And now they had killed his card. Shkedy and Mordinson had no option but to return home—the trip had been a complete failure.

Then they re-grouped. For the first two weeks of August, Hasak treated the Kömmerlings to an all-expenses paid family holiday at the Club Med resort at the Red Sea town of Eilat, where Oliver indulged his passion for scuba diving in the spectacular waters of the Gulf of Aqaba. On their arrival in Israel the family was met at Ben Gurion airport by an NDS staff member, who shepherded them on to the shuttle flight to Eilat.

Everything was done to make this a smooth operation. Oliver would farewell his family at Eilat airport on 16 August as they headed home. He would spend a week working with Zvi Shkedy and David Mordinson in Haifa and then in Jerusalem on the Nagra hack. Oliver would be referred to by his codename Alex. Hasak made clear: 'Make sure A has a formal invitation letter from NDS (to avoid problems in NATBAG) [Ben Gurion airport]. Do not forget to destroy it when not needed.' Hasak was always good at the details. NDS did not need any overt links to Oliver on the record that might come back to trouble them.

The time with Oliver in Haifa was worth it though. Late in the week, Chaim Shin-Orr had an email from John Norris in California: 'Chaim, the field told our contact of their requirement for a second image of the code (for comparison purposes).' Shkedy and Mordinson already had an EchoStar smartcard from Chris Tarnovsky, who had taken out a basic subscription with a pay-per-view option to watch movies. Now they needed another EchoStar smartcard—and they appear to have called Tarnovsky direct, without going through Norris. Now Norris was repeating what he had been told by Tarnovsky about what Haifa wanted: 'They need to be absolutely certain there is not the hidden possibility of identifying the ID of the E* card that their code comes from, some kind of a "fingerprint" or a receiver's serial card (if a card has been paired) in the code that is developed. They can do this if they have a second card.'

Zvi and David had discussed their difficulties with Oliver. As part of the security measures, when a Nagra subscription was first activated, the smartcard was 'married' or paired with the receiver. From that point, if you put the smartcard into another receiver with a different identification number, then it wouldn't work. Mordinson had found a way to get around this, but the risk was that there was some tell-tale mark in the code that would let EchoStar identify which card it was, which would lead them to Tarnovsky.

Norris was finding difficulty following all this, so he had asked for more explanation. Chaim told him, 'The code I sent you in the past is only the ROM code (that is, the one irretrievably put in by the silicon manufacturer). As far as we know . . . all card-peculiar data is contained in the EEPROM.' It was in the EEPROM that Chaim's team feared there could be some distinguishing mark.

Chaim's email to Norris on 23 August disappeared from Norris's computer; however it was later found as a saved file on his hard drive. At the 2008 trial, Norris said he didn't remember the email exchange. Chaim was ill and did not testify. But two conclusions can be drawn from this email. First, while at this point the project to reverse engineer the EchoStar card was perfectly legal, NDS and the black-hat team were obsessed with leaving no traces of their hack. Secondly, Chaim explicitly refers to the EchoStar ROM code as 'the code I sent you in the past'. Even before the hack was finished, the codes extracted by the black-hat team were being shared with NDS staff in North America. That would be John Norris and, by inference, Chris Tarnovsky. Norris testified he did not recall ever receiving any codes.

Shkedy and Mordinson were heading back to the United States, but this time Hasak would not be directly involved. They would make their own arrangements. They flew into Baltimore in early September and headed for an old friend's house in Silver Spring, Maryland, on the northern fringe of Washington DC. Vered Anikster was e-commerce project manager for NDS Americas and the NDS representative on a US government body set up to advise on how US government agencies used public key cryptography. It was called the Federal Public Key Infrastructure Steering Committee. Anikster was on the Technical Working Group, which released a landmark report on 4 September 1998. There's a neat symmetry here: an NDS exec was working on a report to advise US government agencies and private companies how to keep their secrets, at the same time as his house was being used to reverse engineer a billion-dollar corporation, EchoStar—although in their 2008 testimony about the visit Shkedy and Mordinson made no suggestion that Mr and Mrs Anikster knew what they were doing.

Shkedy and Mordinson headed home to Israel with the information they needed—the Nagra/EchoStar hack was now almost complete. The time had come for a live trial. But, while this needed to be carried out in North America, Shkedy and Mordinson would not do it in the United States. That might be illegal. Instead there was yet another family and house set up to host them, this time in Windsor, Ontario. Of course, in the world of hacking, the most effective path between two points is rarely a straight line.

It went like this. Shkedy and Mordinson flew out of Israel across the Atlantic to Baltimore. They hired a car, and made the 40-minute drive across to Silver Spring to the Anikster house. Mrs Anikster handed them her family's EchoStar receiver, which they put in their car and then drove back to Baltimore airport. Shkedy and Mordinson flew with the receiver to Cleveland and hired another car. Then they made the three-hour drive around the southern shore of Lake Erie through Detroit and over the Canadian border to Windsor, where they moved into the basement of the contact's house and wired up the EchoStar receiver to the satellite dish mounted on the house. And here, there was a problem.

The reception from the satellite dish was pitiful—too patchy to hold a picture, let alone conduct fancy piracy testing. The basement where they were staying had a Bell Express satellite dish for its Express-Vu satellite broadcaster. Express-Vu also used Nagra cards from Kudelski, but the dishes were not compatible. Mordinson and Shkedy realised that, while they were going to Baltimore to pick up the receiver from the Aniksters, so as to avoid leaving any trail of what they were doing, they could have bought an EchoStar receiver dish at any Walmart store along the way. So, it was left to Shkedy to drive back over the US border to Detroit, to buy an EchoStar dish.

Mordinson finalised the EchoStar hack in the basement in Windsor, Ontario. He took the EchoStar card that he had, and put it into his reprogrammer; he then used his hack program to write new code directly onto the card's EEPROM. Mordinson reprogrammed the card with the image of the card he had from Tarnovsky, which he had on his computer. Then he took the reprogrammed card out and inserted it into the EchoStar receiver. And the system opened up like a flower for him. He had all of the channels, all of the pay-per-view offerings, without a subscription.

It had taken Mordinson months, but he had beaten the card. It was the end of September and it was time to head home. It would take another month for the two NDS men to write up their report.

Thousand Oaks, California, October 1998

Alan and Suzanne Guggenheim were facing a major life change. During eighteen years in the United States, Alan had carved out a lucrative career as a consultant. He had begun consulting for Kudelski Corporation in 1997. Now the pressure was on him to work full-time for Kudelski, though this would not happen until mid 1999. Part of the pressure was politics.

In May 1997, after Rupert Murdoch walked away from his deal to merge his satellite interests with EchoStar because of Charlie Ergen's refusal to use NDS, Ergen had called Kudelski's chief executive, André Kudelski, and told him, 'I've just lost a billion-dollar deal for the sake of your technology. I hope it's worth it.' Actually he said a little bit more than this. In the future, he said, he wanted to own half of the company that provided EchoStar with conditional access cards. So EchoStar and Kudelski set up a new company, NagraStar, in which they each owned a half share, which would provide the Nagra system for EchoStar.

NagraStar was an ugly beast from the beginning—neither side controlled it and each pursued conflicting objectives. Its owners were united chiefly in their reluctance to spend money. In October 1998, however, Ergen had his mind elsewhere. For more than a year his legal counsel, David Moskowitz, had been pursuing EchoStar's $5 billion damages claim against News Corp for walking away from the merger. In May the Justice Department had begun legal action to stop Murdoch selling his satellite assets to the cable companies' lame-duck broadcaster, PrimeStar. By early October it was clear that that deal was history, which left Rupert Murdoch and his partner, MCI, with an expensive satellite broadcast licence, a satellite uplink centre and four satellites that he couldn't use. It would be madness to start up a new satellite operation against three entrenched competitors. In any case Murdoch didn't have the money to try it. He had to sell.

Unfortunately for Murdoch there was only one prospective buyer. Charlie Ergen didn't become a billionaire by being a soft touch. He knew Murdoch was in a sticky place. When Murdoch was finally forced to come to him, Ergen would be waiting.

Guggenheim had no contact with Ergen—the EchoStar account was handled exclusively by André Kudelski. But Guggenheim saw huge market potential for the Nagra card in the US cable market, principally because it had never been hacked. Meanwhile the biggest account of all was ready to be plucked. DirecTV management had made it clear how much they disliked NDS, and how much they wanted to replace them. In late 1997, after seeing its P2 pirated within weeks of its release, DirecTV had commissioned an outside firm, TNO, to reverse engineer the P3 card that NDS was proposing to introduce. DirecTV didn't like the results. And DirecTV didn't trust NDS in the aftermath of the Oliver Kömmerling debacle in Toronto the year before. The relationship with NDS had become like a bad marriage. But ending it was no simple matter.

It fell to the NDS and News Corporation lawyers to spell out to DirecTV how much more painful the divorce would be. A conditional access system is the nerve centre of a pay TV business. Apart from encrypting the programming, it keeps track of the millions of customers, what they have paid, which channels they are entitled to watch. It all gets figured out in the set-top box. If you took out your conditional access provider tomorrow, you wouldn't have a pay TV business. It can take more than a year to make a changeover. And the key piece of software in DirecTV's set-top boxes that verified a customer's account? NDS said that was its own proprietary software. So no one could even look at the set-top box without the NDS say-so.

In April 1998 DirecTV agreed to extend the NDS contract, which was due to expire in September, for another year, on condition that NDS allowed DirecTV to call for tenders from others, which would involve sharing information about the set-top box. On 3 August, DirecTV sent out a Request For Information document to all of the major conditional access companies in the world asking for a proposal for how DirecTV could replace NDS. It was the biggest conditional access contract in the world and by October, Alan Guggenheim knew that Kudelski Corporation with its Nagra card was in the box seat. The only competition was the Irdeto system, which had been hacked for a year, and Canal+ with its SECA card, but the French were never in the race.

Guggenheim and Christophe Nicolas were due to make a major presentation to DirecTV management on 3 November. There were significant technical and logistical problems to overcome, but the feedback that Alan was getting from the DirecTV people he was dealing with was that, barring a disaster, the deal was theirs. Kudelski had it in the bag, and Guggenheim was already thinking of other North American systems he could sell Nagra to as well. But in the first days of October, a faint warning bell sounded.

Cheseaux-sur-Lausanne, October 2008

Security comes in many forms. The basis of encryption, and particularly smartcard encryption, is perimeter defence. You want to keep your enemy out. But when that doesn't work, you need an alarm system. Nagra's card developer, Karl Osen, built a tripwire into EchoStar's Nagra card. He had been looking for a unique phrase to put into the EEPROM code on the card, and EchoStar management came up with one: 'NipPEr Is a buTt liCker!' A trifle crude, and there are many stories about what it means. Some reports say the phrase came out of Charlie Ergen's office; some even say that Charlie had a dog called Nipper. Whatever the source, with every EchoStar card that was issued—and we're talking millions of cards—during the initiation procedure when the subscription details were written to the card, the EEPROM memory was amended to include the Nipper phrase. Osen even put it in twice, to make sure any hacker wouldn't miss it. Of course, no one had ever hacked the Nagra card. But heaven forbid if someone ever did, then they would find that magic phrase.

For a nerd hacker, this would be like hitting the mother lode. It was a secret too funny, too bizarre, too unique, to keep to themselves. It was the ultimate inside joke. And it was guaranteed to make the hacker do something stupid. They would have to announce it to the world. Or just to their tight circle of friends. It would get out. And Kudelski and EchoStar would know immediately that their system had been hacked. Of course the reality was that, while EchoStar had put the Nipper phrase into countless satellite systems in homes across the United States, no one would ever know about it, because it was unthinkable that Nagra would ever be hacked.

At the end of September Al Menard, who ran the DR7.com hacking website from Vancouver, set up a new web page to carry material on EchoStar piracy tools. On 7 October, according to documents filed by EchoStar in its 2008 case, someone calling himself Von posted a comment on the page, 'Who is Nipper? I do know a Ripper!' The comment was completely meaningless to all but a tiny handful of people around the world. Even at Kudelski's offices in Cheseaux in Switzerland, only a few people understood what it meant.

The tripwire alarm had gone off.

Events were now converging with a terrible intensity. John Norris and Ray Adams, after conducting a spectacular trans-Atlantic slagging match about how little trust they had in each other's agents, had somehow patched up an uneasy alliance, just as BSkyB launched its digital service on 8 October. In the United States, News Corporation was still technically contracted to selling its satellite assets to PrimeStar, the satellite broadcaster owned by the big US cable companies. But the antitrust lawsuit lodged by Joel

Klein at the Department of Justice meant that in reality the deal was toast. DirecTV was in the final stages of dropping NDS and signing up to take Kudelski's Nagra system. The key meeting would be in Los Angeles on 3 November.

In Haifa, David Mordinson and Zvi Shkedy were completing the first draft of the Headend Report, a detailed explanation of how to hack the Nagra card. In Edmonton, Al Menard was already registering a lot of hits on his new page about hacking EchoStar. The world overseen by Abe Peled and Reuven Hasak was facing threats on all sides. It seemed inconceivable that things could get worse.

The next crisis came out of left field.

PART 5

A Death in Berlin

Tron fights for the users.

Sam Flynn, *Tron: Legacy,* 2010

London, 4 October 1998

Adams had picked up on a new buzz in hacker chat rooms across Europe. Irdeto. There was a new hack coming for the digital Irdeto card used in Scandinavia, Greece and Arabia. It was also used by DF1 and Premiere in Germany; by both Stream SpA and Telepiu in Italy; and by Foxtel Satellite, Austar and Optus Vision in Australia. Adams had picked up an article titled 'Death of a System' about this new hack, posted on one of the hacker forums without a byline. He told NDS Israel about it and by the morning of 4 October, NDS Marketing was desperate to get a copy. Alan Guggenheim in California noticed the article as well, but ten days later. The article said the Irdeto card had been hacked for a year. Clearly piracy now looked to be heading towards a new level.

Adams had been watching the Irdeto hacks for eighteen months, he assured marketing. Most notably in September 1997 Adams had written to Reuven Hasak about a Bulgarian hacker, codenamed Ilian: 'He has a full working hack. He lacks the cards and chips to put it on.' Adams proposed to provide Ilian with 1000 blank smartcards to get him started, and as a means to get close to him. Whether it was this source or another, in October 1997 'COP' pirate cards began to appear, reportedly out of eastern Europe. COP cards were a rudimentary hack that Irdeto soon overcame with electronic counter measures. COP was soon followed by the Goldpeg card, which was far more effective—obviously the work of someone who had fully reverse engineered the Irdeto chip. That was soon followed by the Hornet card, which was based on blank cards with an Atmel chip.

The Hornet was ingenious—the work of a highly skilled hacker. The hacker needed to have reverse engineered not just the Irdeto chip, but the Atmel chip as well. That put suspicion on Oliver's old network. Oliver's friend Lars in Scandinavia had paid for part of the equipment in Oliver's lab and, at the same time as the Hornet appeared, Lars began selling a pirate card for a D-2Mac system in Scandinavia. It was called the Hightech card, and it was also based on an Atmel chip.

Several hackers I have spoken to believe both the Goldpeg and Hornet software came out of Germany, though this is not proven. Chris Tarnovsky goes further, crediting Oliver Kömmerling with the two cards.

'Well, he hacked Irdeto from day one,' Tarnovsky told me in California in 2009. 'I've got his source code. I have his source code for Irdeto, the earliest version . . . He gave me the dumps in 2001 . . . This would have been the very first Irdeto hack.'

Chris Tarnovsky is not a disinterested witness on the subject of Oliver, and in my interview he often seemed to be loose on detail. Some things he said I found difficult to credit. And having source code is not the same as producing a pirate card. It's reasonable to conclude that Oliver was familiar with Irdeto—when Adams asked Oliver to explain the Irdeto hack in February 1998, he told Oliver he could be 'as technical as you like'. Later that month Boris Floricic and a hacker codenamed 'Ice' were at Oliver's house for the weekend. Boris had had a dump of the Irdeto card since at least mid 1997, as his friend Stefan Eisvogel had noted to the List.

Tarnovsky said he knew friends stayed at Oliver's house: 'But what they were doing I don't know. Ollie won't tell you. He won't teach you anything. You'll be his . . . his bitch. So, you know, he'll put you on a task to do something that works with what he's up to, but you won't actually understand why it is he wants you to probe the bus, probe this wire on the chip, say.'

Oliver used young hackers to do the dog work on his hacks, Tarnovsky said, tasks like compiling source software from the microscopic photographs that showed the layout of the memory of a chip. Whether Boris or Ice worked like this isn't clear.

'I've never heard that Boris was involved in Irdeto,' Tarnovsky told me. 'That's the first I've ever heard of it. It's possible, but I've got this quote from Ollie—Ollie pulled it.'

What can be said is that the group of hackers and friends, of which Oliver was a part, had an ongoing interest in Irdeto, with varying degrees of knowledge. On 27 April, Avigail Gutman reported that 'Icecool' had put software on the Net for a logger that targeted Irdeto. There were sporadic references to Irdeto in the NDS emails; then in early October the marketing department showed heightened interest and even Reuven Hasak got involved.

While it's thought that the hacker behind the Goldpeg and Hornet cards was German, the piracy ring that distributed them definitely wasn't—they were Bulgarian and Belgian. The mix was an unhappy one. By October 1998 the group had fallen out and split into two groups, one in Belgium and the other in Sofia, Bulgaria. The Bulgarian group had launched a new series of Irdeto pirate cards called +1, +2 and +3. The three cards would serve different Irdeto markets. These cards were also based on Atmel cards, and seemed to be from the same hacking source as the Hornet card.

On 12 October one of Adams' people, Chris Le Maitre, picked up a new web page titled 'Dr Hornet's Web Site'. It claimed to be the official Hornet site and Le Maitre described it as 'reputed to be the work of a Belgian national who is believed to be the author of the Hornet software'. But the Belgian was just a dealer/ frontman. Adams quietly forwarded Le Maitre's email to Oliver marked 'FYI'.

When piracy groups break up, the separation agreements are real killers. After the Hornet group split, the Bulgarians were not happy campers. They had had to obtain new piracy codes for the +1, +2 and +3 cards, apparently from the same German source. Pirate sources estimated that more than 100,000 pirate Irdeto cards had been sold, at prices around $150. That made it a $15 million market at a conservative estimate. It was lucrative, but that meant that any code for the +1 cards could not come cheap. So the second cause of the Bulgarians' annoyance was that they had been forced to make a large commercial commitment, which they now needed to recoup. They were financially exposed.

It was in this volatile situation that the Bulgarian pirates read the article, 'Death of a System', that had attracted the attention of Ray Adams and Alan Guggenheim. 'A new hack that permits the switching on of official cards is about to be launched,' the unknown author wrote. This was based on a modified original smartcard (MOSC), though these had not yet hit the market. 'A design fault inherent in the design of the card allows dealers to switch them on. The cards are in limited supply which explains the recent crop of advertisements for official cards surfacing on the net.'

The card would be a body blow for the Bulgarians. But where was it coming from? Something was going on, although Adams didn't know what it was. He put an old enemy in the frame. 'Jan Saggiori is working on Irdeto,' he told Reuven Hasak. Saggiori had become useful as the bogey man he could blame things on. But he was mistaken.

Belgium, early October 1998

On a balmy October evening, Rolf Deubel was dropping by to see an old friend across the border. The hacking culture in Europe was a complex one. Rolf was a hacker, and a good one, but he had come at it from an unexpected angle. He was born in West Germany and later moved to South Africa. Rolf was best known for high-performance engines and speed. He was a champion racer—in the early 1980s he had won a couple of world titles in side-car motorcycle racing, before he moved on to world championship rally driving races.

In the high-octane world Rolf lived in, every little detail made a difference. In competitive racing, that key difference was electronic tuning: putting a microchip in an engine to regulate the oxygen–fuel mix for maximum performance. The cars that had it beat the cars that didn't. Reverse engineering the electronic ignition of a rival's engine had been an act of desperation on Rolf's part. It made him faster. It also made him a hacker.

The next step was phreaking—hacking the telephone system. And then Rolf wandered on to the pay TV scene. But here he was mainly a pirate. Having access to a good local hacker was invaluable for any dealer when it came to getting pirate cards back on line after an ECM had killed them.

'Satellite shops "sponsored" hackers with hardware, and in return received information and software for modifying stock standard smartcards,' Rolf Deubel told me in 2008. Sometimes the local dealer would pay a hacker a few hundred deutschmarks for software, which is all they needed to pay a few costs. If a dealer knew how to hack, so much the better.

It was an ecosystem. At the top were the big pirate dealers, and now European pirates were adopting the North American system. In North America, when a new pay TV card came out, someone would spend big money developing a hack. The pay-off was to sell it for hundreds of thousands of dollars to a few big dealers, who would onsell it to a string of sub-dealers, who in turn sold the hack to their own network of minor dealers.

At some point there would often be a falling out between different dealers, and someone would post the hack online. Once it went public, in effect both the hack and the original card were finished, because everyone could make their own pirate cards for free. The pirates weren't making any money, and neither was the pay TV company, so they needed to issue a new generation of cards. This was the cycle.

Rolf Deubel was one of those who operated in both worlds, he was a former hacker turned pirate. Which is how he came to be dropping by his friend Angelo Montaperto's pub in Belgium. Rolf got on well with Angelo, an Italian known online as 'Sandokan', or 'Sally99', or 'Dr Hornet', who used loopholes in the different legal systems throughout Europe to build a large business selling smartcards. Tonight Angelo had a favour to ask of Rolf. He had just bought a piece of software from a hacker in Berlin. It was a zip file, but he was having trouble opening it.

'Angelo is fully commercial oriented,' Rolf told me. 'Angelo received the software . . . but it was password protected. He asked me to crack it, which I did in one night over two bottles of Italian Lambrusco from Angelo's pub.'

Rolf recognised the source of the file. It had come from Tron— Boris Floricic, who was a friend of Rolf's. German journalist Burkhard Schröder later reported that the file had been down-loaded from Boris's server on Saturday, 3 October, though it could well have been later. Rolf saw nothing unusual in this. He knew that a friend of Tron's—let's call him 'Wilbur'—regularly used Tron's programs to make some money and to maintain connec-tions in the dealer world. The money was shared with Tron, who really didn't have a commercial bone in his body.

'Tron had put 99 per cent of all his development work on his FTP server, which he ran every night from 21 hundred hours until midnight. Everybody could download anything from there; I did as well.' In fact Boris had put the address of his server on the Net.

Anybody in the world could have done what the friend had done. It was the ethos of the non-commercial hacker. Knowledge is to be shared.

Markus Kuhn had written to the List recently about a loophole in the PKZip program for compressing files: 'It had a rather weak encryption algorithm and a guy called Paul Kocher developed an attack that if you know one of the files, if you know a few hundred bytes of the data in there already, then you can infer from that what the password is.' Rolf lived in South Africa, so his chief interest in pay TV piracy was Irdeto, which was owned by a South African company. He knew Boris had been working on Irdeto, and he knew enough about the system to make some educated guesses about some of the contents of the file. So by the end of his second bottle of Lambrusco, Rolf had broken the zip file open. The file save date shows that it was 9.13 p.m., Wednesday, 14 October.

The first file was a blocker program for the new Irdeto digital card. A blocker stops the broadcaster—in this case DF1 in Germany—from sending a command that kills a card that has expired. It also stops them using electronic counter measures to kill the card. The second file was a Phoenix program, which reactivates cards that have been killed off. The two programs were a big step towards a full hack. In fact they seemed to do the same thing as the MOSC pirate hack that had been written about in the 'Death of a System' article. And they were worth money. Rolf passed the file to Sandokan, who immediately onsold it to a bigger dealer in the Netherlands for 3000 deutschmarks, who in turn, onsold it to a major dealer in the United Kingdom. Rolf didn't know how much he paid. And that was the end of Rolf's role in the saga, for now. Henceforth he would be reluctant to discuss it.

Nine months later, when a contact in New Zealand, Bob Cooper from *SatFACTS*, asked him about it, he replied: 'It appears you already know about 80 per cent of the truth. I would not tell you much more because of the consequences from the Bulgarian Mafia . . . still want to live a bit longer.'

When a new hack emerges, news in the piracy world moves at lightning speed. Two days later, on Friday night, 16 October, Boris's friend Wilbur called him to tell him what he had done, and that his Blocker and Phoenix programs were now in circulation. It must have been an awkward conversation. Because now it looked like there would be trouble.

Berlin, Saturday, 17 October 1998

When Boris Floricic slipped out of his mother's house after lunch it was just on 2 p.m.

'Bye, I won't be long,' he told his mother. He was going to the ATM at the post office to withdraw the 500 deutschmarks he took out every week for his grandmother, using her bank card. He was wearing a blue-pink sports jacket over a T-shirt, black jeans and sneakers. Boris took his phone but not his laptop. At the door as he was going out he met a friend who wanted to borrow some equipment for his studies, and they walked together to the post office. Bank records show Boris withdrew 500 DM from the ATM at 2.26 p.m. When the two friends parted, Boris headed off in the direction of the U-Bahn underground station. He didn't make it to his grandmother's.

Later that afternoon a café owner in the strip of shops in the square opposite the Britz-Süd U-Bahn station, two and a half kilometres south, saw Boris at a table, having a beer with two burly men he described as east European. It was an odd grouping. For one thing, Boris didn't drink alcohol, so the men who ordered the beer could not have known him well. They were having an animated conversation and Boris did not look happy. They left together in a dark car.

Boris didn't come home that night.

North America, 17–21 October

Rupert Murdoch's divorce had turned ugly. On Saturday, 17 October, the day Boris disappeared, News Corporation announced that Anna Murdoch had resigned from the News Corp board. Later she made it clear Rupert gave her little choice. Two weeks before, the first pictures of Wendi Deng had surfaced—on board Murdoch's yacht, the *Morning Glory*, in the Mediterranean with Lachlan Murdoch and the Italian prime minister Silvio Berlusconi. What had to date been relatively amicable divorce negotiations turned poisonous. Days later the *New York Times* published a sedate piece that Rupert Murdoch was living at the Mercer Hotel with Ms Deng.

With all the focus on the Murdoch family scandal, less attention was paid the next day, Sunday, 18 October, when News Corporation finally made the announcement that everyone knew was coming. Murdoch was throwing in the towel against Joel Klein at the Justice Department and formally pulling out of the deal to sell the ASkyB satellite assets to PrimeStar. The only surprise here was that the move had taken so long. It signalled that Murdoch and MCI were now free to sell their satellites and licence to Charlie Ergen. Of course that wouldn't stop News and EchoStar haggling for another month and a half over the details of the sale contract. Part of the deal would be buying the uplink centre, but Charlie Ergen insisted that would happen only after News had ripped out all of the wiring and equipment installed by NDS. There was some reason or other cited for this. It was so not personal. Really. Murdoch could only grit his teeth and take it.

Berlin, Sunday–Tuesday, 18–20 October 1998

Boris Floricic's mother, Hannelore, was frantic. Boris had said he would not be gone for long—he never stayed away without telling her. And he had left his computer behind. She had gone to the police on Sunday morning with Boris's father, Ivo, but the police told them they could not file a missing person's report until he had been missing for 48 hours. That would be Monday. Hannelore and Ivo went from police station to police station begging for help. The best chance of finding him lay in tracing his mobile phone. Later, that would be tracked to a general area of coverage covering the many apartment blocks near the Britz-Süd area. But late Sunday afternoon the battery on the phone ran flat.

When Boris's parents filed a missing person report on Monday, they told police that their son had been contacted by intelligence services, who had attempted to recruit him. The police were alarmed. They looked at Boris's court record and decided to seize his computer and issue an arrest warrant for him.

Apparently NDS had not been the only firm eager to recruit Floricic. 'This is a very sensitive area and the intelligence services are very interested,' Detective Thomas Kasbaum, one of the team investigating, said later. 'He received several specific offers of work, from German and international companies.'

By this time Boris's friends at the Chaos Computer Club knew he was missing. The CCC president, Andy Mueller-Maguhn, hired a lawyer to represent Boris in the police investigation.

Late that afternoon a friend of Boris emailed an alert to TVcrypt: 'Boris Floricic is missing.' Had any one on the List had any contact with him? 'His friends and parents are worried that something might have happened to him, as he usually leaves notes when he leaves for longer, and he also left all of his belongings behind.'

The stories kept on growing. Ivo, in desperation, phoned Oliver Kömmerling to ask if he had any idea where Boris was. Oliver suggested he call Stephan Eisvogel, he was closer to Stephan.

Haifa, mid October 1998

David Mordinson was struggling with an ethical dilemma, though that's probably overstating it. Perhaps it was just a question of taste, but Mordinson was a very serious young man. He was writing up the first draft of his report for Operation Headend. Mordinson and Zvi Shkedy had taken six months to reverse engineer the Nagra smart-card used by EchoStar. Mordinson was now distilling the results down to a 33-page report. It described the specs of the Nagra card, outlined its weaknesses, then provided a recipe for how to hack it.

It would be an elegant document, with references, tables and appendices—a classic academic paper, ready for peer review. Admittedly one section did not fit as easily with the elevated academic tone. When asked to read it out during his time in the witness stand in 2008, Mordinson almost squirmed: 'I apologise for the language that EchoStar inserted in the card.' But obviously it had to go into the final report. With an air of appropriate academic disengagement, Mordinson had typed: 'EEPROM locations E052 and F052 contain the text, "NipPEr Is a buTt liCker!" Putting aside the question of who Nipper is and what are his moral qualities, one should note that such texts are often used to store essential data. A more complete analysis will no doubt reveal that.'

Hidden essential data. It seemed the dignified way to handle it.

Vancouver, Wednesday, 21 October 1998

The new page devoted to hacking EchoStar on Al Menard's DR7 website had proven popular. One of the more high-profile posters on the page called himself 'Mr Bean'. On Wednesday, 21 October, Mr Bean renamed himself 'sWiss chEEsE pRODuC-tIoNs', explaining that the name was changed 'to avoid copyright infringement problems'. The mixed capitals were an arch reference to the random capitals in the 'Nipper is a butt licker' phrase in the EEPROM. Swiss Cheese itself was a reference to finding holes in the Nagra card, almost a nod to Stefan Eisvogel's description of the Irdeto card as being 'as full of holes as Swiss cheese'. That would point to a German source. The Swiss reference also dangled the prospect that it might be Jan Saggiori. But the original name, Mr Bean, suggested an English speaker, though perhaps one with European experience.

Whoever Swiss Cheese Productions was, they posted a zip file providing details on how to set up a data stream logger/packet decrypter, which it described as the 'first tool' towards a hack of the EchoStar system. Swiss Cheese promised to post two more tools on DR7 in the following days.

When EchoStar's lawyers asked Menard at a 2007 deposition who Mr Bean and Swiss Cheese Productions were, Menard said he didn't know.

London, Thursday, 22 October 1998

The rumours were running out of control. Late on the Thursday afternoon, 22 October, Adams received an email from Andreas Rudloff, who headed security at the Pay TV operations of German media company, KirchGruppe. Rudloff had heard of a 'strange problem', he wrote, with inverted commas.

'There seems to be a young hacker in Berlin, who has developed "hacksoftware" for digital TV systems.' Apparently he was not distributing the software but he was talking with his friends about this. 'Last weekend he has left his home together with two guys' and had not returned home, Rudloff wrote. Police were looking for him. 'As I have heard, the young hacker also knows something about the "Hornet-Card" and "Bulgaria" and "Russian Mafia".' There was a theory that his hack was against the interests of the distributors of pirate cards. 'If this would be the case they have different solutions to solve the problem . . .'

Rudloff didn't know if this was just a product of family and friends panicking. There could be other reasons for a young man to go missing in a town like Berlin, but Rudloff thought he should contact the police and see if he could help. Did Ray know anything?

Adams forwarded the email to Oliver on the Friday with a brief note: 'Everyone is talking about this.'

But Adams' information was already way out of date.

Britz Süd, Berlin, Thursday, 22 October 1998

In the last warm days of October it was still just possible for the colourblind, the overly optimistic and the very stout-hearted to believe the Berlin winter would never come; that by sheer bravado the city would shake off all insidious attempts to end its golden summer. Four days earlier the spiky fingers of autumn had gripped Berlin, taking average temperatures down to between 5 and 9 degrees from Sunday through Wednesday. It rained heavily on Wednesday night but the following morning broke fine and warm. By midday, temperatures in South Berlin would reach 17 degrees. And all was as it should be.

The green patchwork of parks throughout the city was a mass of yellow, red, orange and brown. In Neukölln in the south-west the regulars were out on the walking tracks. The paths ran everywhere, shadowing the major roads through endless belts of trees planted to muffle the traffic noise. Here and there the strips of green broadened into parks. Even in Neukölln, it would be conceded grudgingly, the trees were breathtaking.

Neukölln sits uneasily in the Berlin psyche. There's a sense that the area is uncomfortably anarchistic for a German city. Outsiders describe it as gritty or edgy, by which they mean it is full of poor immigrants. It houses a large Turkish community, but also has sizable Russian, Polish, Greek, Arab and Afghan populations. Just weeks earlier the city council had a sign, 'Neukölln—Place of Diversity', erected in the square opposite the U-Bahn station at Britz Süd, on the southern fringe of the municipality. The sign nestled comfortably alongside the large Turkish supermarket and the strip retail stores that bounded the square on three sides.

Britz Süd was built as a model housing project, based around the Horseshoe Estate—low-level apartment blocks built along U-shaped crescents. Row upon row of identical buildings are distinguished only by a vertical strip of coloured panels on each building—a thin column of red, orange or blue. It's not exactly a riot of colour but, when you're poor and you live in Britz Süd, how much individuality do you need? The corridors of trees were the great redeeming feature.

North from the U-Bahn station a strip of woodland follows Fritz-Reuter-Allee—only 20 metres wide at best, but within the canopy the traffic hum is hushed. The loudest noise is the crunch of your feet on the gravel and paving stones of the walking track, and all you can look at is the wonder of the trees, and the golden leaves. Which really is the point in this tableau. Within days the leaves will be gone, the trees stripped bare, the hidden corners of the wood-lands open to the outside world. But for now it is a world of mystery. It's hard to see three metres into the undergrowth, while the damp leaves on the ground mask any sign of tracks.

South of the station, across Gutschmidtstrasse, the path becomes a little park, perhaps 50 metres wide, behind the post office. The park runs up to railway yards. It is bounded on the west by a bus station and to the east by deserted dormitories that until recently had housed asylum seekers. During the day the tracks had regular traffic—cyclists and brisk walkers, for the main part, who are rarely tempted to venture off the path. But this is kiddie country. Two hundred metres north of the underground U-Bahn station is a school. Next to the post office is a youth club. The ones most likely to gambol through the undergrowth would be children. Which set a deadline for when the secret in the trees would come to light.

German schools break for the day at four o'clock. It was soon after four, as the clouds rolled over once more, that the first emergency call was made. But thankfully children are not the only explorers. An elderly man who followed his dog through the trees near the southern fence of the park found a body hanging from a drooping tree branch. It was a man in his mid twenties: slight build, with black jeans and T-shirt. His jacket lay on the ground beside him. Children had played in the area the previous afternoon, which suggested he had been hanging since some time Wednesday night. A belt that looked too long for his slim waist was looped around his neck in a complicated affair that was attached to a wire that had then been looped over a tree branch. It seemed an elaborate way to kill yourself on a wet, dark night. In any case the wire was too long or the branch too supple. The man's shoes were firmly planted on the ground.

It would be two days before the Chaos Computer Club broke the news in a press release: '*Tron ist tot.*'

Tron is dead.

Cambridge, 24 October 1998

Markus Kuhn was shocked and grieving. 'TVcrypt member Boris Floricic is dead,' he emailed the List on Saturday morning. He posted an English translation of a German newspaper article headlined, 'Police Investigators Do Not Believe in Suicide'. Markus had lost touch with Boris since he went to Purdue for the Fulbright Scholarship. From there he had gone to Cambridge to do his doctorate with Ross Anderson. He had caught up with Boris in September 1997 when he came to Berlin for an international radio exhibition— the two had stayed at Boris's father's house—and at the Chaos Computer Club Congress in Hamburg in December 1997.

'I didn't have the impression that he was . . . any trouble showing up,' Markus told me. 'He was very energetic, very . . . he certainly was never a depressed person, I've never heard that suggestion being made.'

Boris's death was a shock throughout the hacking community. So many people knew Boris, or had heard of him. Late on

Saturday, 24 October, Markus sat down to tell the List how he felt about his friend: 'He was by far the most skilled, ingenious, determined and creative embedded-systems reverse engineering expert that I have ever met. I always considered his ideas, his technical skills, and his energy to be both highly amazing and inspiring. I liked him not only because of his astonishing skills, but also because of his very open and helpful nature, his honesty, his sense of humor, and his reliability . . . He was always full of life and energy and I never saw him in any depressive mood. Therefore, the theory that he might have committed suicide is extremely difficult for me to believe.' And even if he did, he said, someone with Boris's creativity would not have hanged himself on a tree in the middle of a dark park.

The shockwaves in the secret world were only beginning as news of the death spread from Germany to London, to Tel Aviv, across the globe to California. If you want to be fanciful about this, consider for a moment, the gears of a huge international security operation frozen, paralysed by a fear of discovery—a fear of what might emerge as collateral damage from a police investigation. But that's fanciful, and in any case anything like that would have been just for a moment. Then their equilibrium would have returned. What, after all, did they have to fear from the body in the wood? Let the German police make what they would of it.

NDS was more focused on a whodunnit that was unfolding on the other side of the Atlantic.

North America, 23 October–3 November 1998

In two days, Swiss Cheese Productions had blown up the Nagra card's reputation for being impenetrable. On Friday, 23 October, the day after Boris's body was found, Swiss Cheese posted a lengthy text file with detailed information about the packets of information in the EchoStar broadcast stream 'taken from months of research'. The next day, Saturday, Swiss Cheese made the big hit.

It posted a copy of the EchoStar EEPROM, including the 'Nipper is a butt licker' text. And if Swiss Cheese had the EEPROM, they must have the ROM code as well, though that was not published. Swiss Cheese included some public keys to the card (public keys will decrypt a signal but typically they are replaced at least every month). Overnight the Nagra card went from inviolable to an endangered species.

On Monday, 26 October, Al Menard posted, 'Swiss Cheese Group has just released a EchoStar Blocker package to me and asked that I pass on to everyone and it is available in the EchoStar Tools section.' Menard subsequently said that EchoStar had heard of the new blocker device and tried to make some changes to make their card more secure. But Swiss Cheese Productions was on top of it and had added a new text file to the site that explained how to overcome EchoStar's changes to the card.

It was the next day, Tuesday, 27 October, that David Mordinson in Haifa finished the first draft of the Headend Report, that set out the EchoStar hack (the final version of the report was completed on 1 November). Later that Tuesday, in southern California, Chris Tarnovsky received a flame mail, all in angry capital letters, from Oliver Kömmerling's friend, 'Yianni' (John Luyando, codename Jellyfish). Yianni began: 'DEAR MR BEAN SORRY VON'. It went downhill from there as Yianni complained that Von had sold him out. 'YOU AND RON ARE TOO HOT TO PLAY WITH . . . WITH JOHN N AS YOUR FRIEND . . . I WANT TO BE KING OF IRC SO EVERY ONE KNOWS YOU ie BG, VON, VONRAT, BEAN, NOW SWISS GROUP.' Tarnovsky forwarded the email to John Norris, who called Yianni a nonentity and a goof when he sent it on to Hasak and Adams.

Because of legal restrictions Chris Tarnovsky was never able to be asked at the 2008 EchoStar trial whether he was Swiss Cheese Productions. I'm sure he would have denied it. But no more was heard of Swiss Cheese.

On 29 October, two days after Yianni's rant email, Ron Ereiser found himself in an internet chat session with Tarnovsky, who had dropped out of working on DirecTV for him months before. Ereiser, in order to needle Tarnovsky, claimed he had a hacker who had cracked the ROM of the EchoStar card. Tarnovsky demanded that he share a small part of the code with him, and he would be able to tell him if it was the real thing. Then he realised that Ereiser was just messing with him.

But this was a real issue. Did Chris Tarnovsky post the EEPROM on DR7? The expert witness for NDS at the 2008 EchoStar trial testified that he examined all EEPROM images supplied to him by the Haifa black-hat team, and there were differences from the Swiss Cheese posting. Against that, the NDS email records are full of instances where the source of files is disguised.

Shkedy and Mordinson testified in the 2008 trial that Tarnovsky never received the Headend Report, nor any of the Nagra or Canal+ source codes obtained by the black-hat team. Shkedy sent Oliver Kömmerling a copy of the Headend Report, because he was a key member of the team. But Shkedy and Mordinson were not privy to what information their boss, Chaim Shin-Orr, might have passed to Norris or Tarnovsky. Chaim was too sick to testify but, as previously noted, his August email to Norris, about obtaining more EchoStar cards, read in part: 'The code I sent you in the past is only the ROM code (that is, the one irretrievably put in by the silicon manufacturer).'

Norris said he didn't remember the email, which disappeared from his computer but was found later as a saved Word document. The metadata on the Word document showed it was written by Chaim and saved on Norris's computer on Sunday, 23 August 1998, at 1.39 p.m. It appears to have been sent to Norris as an encrypted attachment. The email begins by referring to a Mr Strong. 'I don't know who Mr Strong is, and I don't know who wrote this e-mail,' Norris testified. He didn't understand any of the references in it, either. He wasn't aware that the chip ID listed in the email was a card registered to an EchoStar subscription in the name of Chris Tarnovsky.

Had Norris ever seen the Headend Report?

'I don't recall,' Norris said, a position he maintained after vigorous questioning by the judge in the jury's absence.

'I would encourage you, if you have any ability to retrieve any additional information from your computer [about the 23 August email], take any kind of forensic search, to do so. Because the results are going to be devastating. I'm going to encourage you to go back, make the effort.'

To be fair, Judge Carter was admonishing both sides here, but Norris was the witness on the spot. Unless both sides lifted their game, he warned, 'I'm going to turn counsel loose because of what I consider, frankly, unwillingness to comply with the earlier discovery orders. And in watching some of the depositions, I'm absolutely astounded that some of these people who thought that this was a game didn't understand that, when it got to federal court, the chickens were coming home to roost.'

Norris: 'No games here.'

The position remained: Norris remembered nothing about any ROM code. But if Norris was all at sea about whether he or Tarnovsky received a copy of the Nagra ROM code, as the email states, how would he have any idea about whether the US team was given the EEPROM as well? It would be odd if he could remember.

Los Angeles, 3 November 1998

There are moments in life when the sky falls in on your head. Alan Guggenheim's moment came in a break during a project meeting with DirecTV in Los Angeles. Officially it was just a status update—a chance to show some PowerPoint slides, make some presentations about the steps involved in DirecTV switching its conditional access system to Nagra, and another chance to network with the DirecTV team. Christophe Nicolas was there with another three members of the team from Cheseaux-sur-Lausanne. In Alan's mind the deal was already done. DirecTV wanted the change; the Nagra product was way out in front of the others.

Alan and Christophe were sharing a coffee with Ray Kuhn, the technical director of engineering at DirecTV. Ray was in his forties, a little plump, a reassuringly solid presence with his yarmulke and warm smile. Alan liked him a lot.

'The breaks were a time when you can relax a bit and kind of probe each other, and work out where we are, how are we doing, what do you think of this and that, and what are your main concerns,' Alan told me. He and Christophe considered Kuhn one of their best technical contacts at DirecTV. 'Ray was probably among the technical team at DirecTV, one of the ones working most closely with NDS. He was very friendly and I liked him and we talked about many things.'

It was over the coffee that Kuhn began talking about security issues with the Nagra system. Had they looked at the set-top box and how easy it was to circumvent? Part of what Kuhn said next seemed incomprehensible. In later conversations, DirecTV execs would tell Alan that there was a fundamental hole in their system that couldn't be fixed. But what were they talking about? The Kudelski team knew nothing about any hole in the card.

Guggenheim remembers vividly the crisis meeting he had with Christophe after the DirecTV presentation was over. Both men were shocked by the conversation with Kuhn.

'Christophe after the meeting and for the following days and weeks was totally convinced that Ray had given him a signal that somebody knew how to hack our system. And that that somebody might very likely be NDS. And that information obviously was something that Christophe did not know.'

Today Kuhn denies sending any such message. But all through the summer the conversation with DirecTV was about how secure their system was. Were they sure it wasn't going to be hacked? Christophe had seen the IRC posts about Nipper days earlier. Alan didn't know what it meant, but Christophe told him. 'That's a proof that somebody has had the EEPROM code of our system, of our card.' Now, given all the rumblings, Alan wondered: Was there really a hack out there? Why are people saying there is one? Why is DirecTV saying there might be one?

Alan and Christophe had seen the Swiss Cheese posting. 'It said, okay now we have reached that level, where the system is not 100 per cent safe any more, because the EEPROM code is known.' It was a bad blow but, while the system was certainly damaged, it wasn't a pirate hack. There was still no way to write pirate code into the EEPROM. There was no hole that they knew about. EchoStar and NagraStar claimed in their 2008 lawsuit that on 3 November DirecTV told Kudelski representatives not just that their system had been hacked, 'they provided detailed non-public information of a highly technical nature concerning how the system was attacked'.

How did DirecTV know? Where did the Swiss Cheese code come from? Looking back at the sequence of events that converged in the days before 3 November, I think even the most dyed-in-the-wool NDS loyalists would concede that, on the surface at least, NDS is the most likely suspect for leaking the codes. The News Corporation company had spent six months working on a pirate hack for the Nagra card. The final version of the Headend Report by Mordinson and Shkedy was completed on 1 November. It would later become clear that Chris Tarnovsky had a copy of the Nagra ROM code and, if he had that, why would he not have the EEPROM as well? What would be the rationale to give him one but not the other? The timing couldn't have been better. The code was released when the fate of NDS hung in the balance. It truly happened in the nick of time.

According to NDS court filings, when the black-hat team reverse engineered the Nagra card, 'the primary reason was to prepare material in anticipation of litigation or for trial'. The NDS and News Corp legal teams were defending EchoStar's $5 billion damages suit over the failure of the ASkyB merger. NDS was also considering suing DirecTV, in the event that the NDS contract was not renewed. The legal team was also involved in the bruising negotiations to sell ASkyB's satellite assets to EchoStar. Then there is Oliver Kömmerling's account—that the reverse engineering was done not to help the lawyers, but to assist the marketing department. But it only helps to inform marketing about problems with a competitor's product if they go ahead and tell customers about it. Is this what happened with DirecTV?

NDS had knowledge that no one else had, and intense motivation to use that information—by posting it on the web, and by briefing DirecTV. But really, how likely is this? Would a major company like NDS, a special project of Rupert Murdoch, a subsidiary with a special relationship with the Office of the Chairman, really try to sabotage a competitor's product? EchoStar and Kudelski eventually came to believe that they did, but how much credence should one give to a competitor? It would be nice to point to sworn testimony by NDS executives that they didn't do it; but the reality is that they were never asked about it in court. By the time EchoStar lodged the lawsuit that came to court in 2008, anything in 1998 was beyond the statute of limitations.

Nevertheless, enough was said by the NDS lawyers during the 2008 trial to be able to understand their position. They said the codes posted on DR7 were either the product of pirate hackers or hobbyists, or they were released by an embittered former employee trying to damage EchoStar.

The first argument has its problems. It would have required a world-class hacker to have spent six months hacking the Nagra card, as NDS did, using sophisticated and expensive equipment.

If they had finally managed to achieve what, as far they knew, no one else in the world had been able to do, why would they give away the codes for nothing—that is, for no financial gain and no recognition? It seems bizarre, frankly. A self-effacing hacker is an oxymoron. Later it would emerge that there were several ways to hack the Nagra card, but the selfless, modest hacker conjured up by this scenario used the same approach as the NDS team did, at exactly the same time.

The second argument, that this was an inside job, is the perennial claim made whenever a card is hacked. It's also hard to disprove. But the story that unfolded in the following three years seems too long and too convoluted for this explanation to appear plausible.

The probabilities, at least, put NDS in the frame. There was even a certain restraint to the leak. At the very beginning, it wasn't piracy. It was just publication of Nagra trade secrets on the DR7 website, but not a full hack. But it was sufficient to help blow up the DirecTV–Kudelski negotiations. How much was keeping the DirecTV contract worth to NDS? In the following decade NDS revenue from DirecTV would total $1.27 billion. If you looked at the timing, the motivation, the opportunity and the money, it looked bad for NDS . . . the company spends six months cracking a card and then days later it's on the Net.

Even if NDS was completely innocent and this was all a ghastly coincidence (or a very happy coincidence, depending upon your view) it would look ugly for NDS if the timing of the completion of Operation Headend should ever emerge. Thankfully, it seemed unlikely that anyone would ever know about Operation Headend. That was where all the trains, planes and automobiles that Reuven Hasak had insisted upon proved their worth. Who was ever going to connect a house in Fort Lee with another home in Maryland, and a basement in a house in Ontario? There were no loose ends in North America that could put it all together. The only people who knew all the answers to this mystery were in Israel and Germany.

But this was where it might get sticky. Because Germany was now the focus of another whodunnit that was entirely unrelated to the Nagra card or to NDS . . . except in this: a murder investigation can take the strangest turns. If the police investigating the death of Tron began looking at pay TV pirate circles in Germany, that could lead to Oliver Kömmerling's friends, which could lead them to Oliver. And what was Oliver doing through 1998? He was working on projects with the NDS black-hat team.

Berlin, November 1998

A week after Boris's body was found, the mystery surrounding his death was deepening, beginning with the police inquiry. The findings of the autopsy, which was not conducted until Friday, 23 October, the day after he was found, pointed strongly towards suicide. The report cited three grounds.

First, there was bleeding in the muscles of his throat. This is characteristic of the shearing force produced when the body is suspended by a rope or belt, and is different from the mark of a strangulation.

Secondly, there were no signs of any other cord or ligature on his neck other than the three-inch belt that he was found hanging by (he had pliers in his pocket which were matched to the cuts on one end of the wire that looped over the tree branch, though no comparison was made with rolls of wire in his father's garage to trace where the wire came from). Actually the wire arrangement was another loose end—how on earth did Boris manage to tie the wire and the belt? He might have been a brilliant hacker, but he was terrible at any kind of knot. But this was beyond the range of an autopsy.

Thirdly, there were no physical signs that he had been moved after his death, nor were there signs of a struggle. He had his phone, his wallet and his grandmother's money. The conclusion was that he had died in the wood and, if he was murdered, he must have been standing there unprotesting while his killer set up the wire arrangement in the tree. And while his feet were on the ground, simply hanging by the belt would have constricted the supply of oxygen to his brain. He might have seen two men on the Saturday, but that was several days before he died. The time of death was put at one or two days before he was found, based on the presence of fly eggs on his body which take 48 hours to hatch.

'You can say conclusively that the post-mortem points to suicide,' said Detective Thomas Kasbaum in the first days. 'There are no clues that point to murder; no grounds for suspicion.'

Klaus Ruckschnat, the head of the third Berlin homicide unit, told journalists, 'We have found nothing: no defensive injuries, no traces of violence effects, no drugs, nothing. If it was murder, then it was perfect.'

The mystery was why an eight-man homicide squad headed by Ruckschnat and Kasbaum was assigned to investigate the death when the autopsy evidence was so overwhelming. Deaths of hackers had become a sensitive issue in Germany, after the apparent suicide nine years earlier of Karl Koch, who had been part of a hacker group selling US military secrets to the KGB. Koch was addicted to cocaine and in the grip of paranoia when he killed himself in a forest in southern Germany in 1989. That association meant Boris's death caught the attention of the security services. The Chaos Computer Club was pressing for an investigation, and Boris's death had generated media interest across Europe. For all of these reasons it was politic to investigate the death, despite the investigators' own strong assumption that it was a suicide.

There is no suggestion that the police investigation was anything other than competent. After three years German officials concluded that it was suicide, based almost entirely on the autopsy evidence and their inability to find any evidence that anyone had a motive to murder Boris. Something happened on the Saturday afternoon that led him to stay away from home for four days and then take his life in a fairly bizarre way. Burkhard Schröder, the journalist who wrote the 1999 book about Boris's death, argued that Boris killed himself because he was anxious about being forced to do national service, because he was dyslexic and because of disappointment that his Irdeto hack software had been released on the Net so he would not receive kudos for it.

Boris's friends had to re-evaluate the person they knew. What would make a young man of 26, who had set up a busy schedule of work to do and people to meet in the week of 19 October, disappear for five days and then kill himself? Dyslexia is associated with higher rates of depression and suicide, but he had just finished his degree, which seemed to undermine the suggestion he was frustrated by difficulties communicating. The biggest cloud on his horizon was the prospect that he might be forced to do military service, which he found an abhorrent prospect; but there were other options, as Markus Kuhn had found. Sure, he liked violent movies (as did way too many computer nerds his age), but his friends found it difficult to accept a finding of suicide.

Andy Müller-Maguhn at the Chaos Computer Club flatly did not believe it. When Boris's family was allowed to see his belongings in 2002, a year after the investigation was completed, it was Müller-Maguhn who measured the length of the belt and the buckle holes and proved it was much too big to fit Boris's waist. If he had not been killed with his own belt—what had happened to his belt? It's a fairly basic oversight by the police, which in turn raises questions about the thoroughness of the rest of their investigation. It looks sloppy.

The belt had been a major part of the argument for suicide—who stands around while someone takes your belt out of your trousers and sets up a hangman's noose in the middle of a wood? But if it wasn't his belt, that argument fails. If anything, it points the other way. If you are going to commit suicide, why get hold of someone else's belt? There are a range of possible explanations for the bleeding in the neck muscles if Boris were killed somewhere else—as just one example, if he were held down in a chair and throttled with the belt from above and behind.

The strongest remaining argument for suicide was that the body showed no sign of being moved—but here the science seems more equivocal. After the autopsy further DNA tests were cancelled, perhaps as a budgetary measure. While the tree trunks showed marks where someone had climbed it, no attempt was made to establish whether there were corresponding marks on Boris's shoes or clothing, or DNA traces or fingerprints on the pliers used. Stomach contents showed that Boris had eaten a meal of spaghetti and salad several hours before he died. But Boris never ate salad. It was why his mother put basil into his spaghetti. Her recipe was unusual enough for her to be able to identify it, if further tests had been made. But the police dismissed the suggestion.

What did this mean? Müller-Maguhn suggested an alternative reading: that the killers were professionals. They killed Boris on the Saturday evening, but kept the body chilled. By Wednesday the hue and cry about his disappearance had grown to such an extent that they needed to make it look like he killed himself. The refrigeration would have produced the dried-out appearance on his skin described in the autopsy. Changing the apparent time of death distracted attention from the Saturday meeting. It gave them their alibi.

Unless it was a totally cynical exercise, the fact that the police investigated the death for three years indicates that they envisaged the possibility that Boris was murdered, that the evidence from the autopsy was not as conclusive as they claimed. One of the fundamental problems for them was that they could find no evidence that someone had a motive for murder. What isn't clear is how far they were able to pierce the dark side of telephone and pay TV hacking.

How much did they know about what Boris did? How much were they told? His laptop was encrypted, which means there would have been little help there. The police didn't even take his laptop's power adaptor, which suggests they threw in the towel earlier rather than later. It seemed only a matter of time before organised crime made inroads in Europe, as it had in North America, and yet police in Europe were still reluctant to see pay TV piracy as a crime, let alone something that people could be murdered over. It appears that the police best able to understand Boris's pay TV hacking were not consulted for the investigation. So what was the most qualified person in Europe—former Scotland Yard commander Adams—going to tell the Berlin homicide squad?

Boris's parents had found the NDS invoice that accompanied the chips that Chaim Shin-Orr sent Boris on 12 July.

'He was an exceptionally talented engineer,' NDS spokeswoman in London, Margot Field, told the *New York Times*. NDS had wanted to hire him as a consultant, but they couldn't move forward because Floricic hadn't yet graduated or completed his compulsory military service. The firm's last contact with him had been in June.

'Consultant' was a wonderfully wide term that covered all of NDS's undercover agents and informants. Of course it was one thing to give clever answers to the media; the police were a different matter. How much did the Berlin detectives need to know about Adams' network of seventeen agents and the debate within NDS over whether any of them were involved in piracy or moved in pirate circles? This is not to suggest that any of the seventeen were linked to Boris's death. But did police need to know the background?

In the meantime, Adams seems to have been concerned about the possible Bulgarian connection and to have been busy with his own inquiries. He got in touch with his friends at BullACT in

Bulgaria. In an email with the subject line, 'Murder', they reported to him on 11 November that mountaineers the previous month had discovered the skeleton of Nikolai Iovchev in a precipice near Shumen, some 100 kilometres from the Black Sea. He was seventeen years old when he disappeared on 7 February 1997.

'There were rumours that the boy had been abducted by hackers who had made him work to them,' the BullACT researchers wrote. 'The boy was considered to be a computer genius. Possibly this is the guy you are looking for. If this is so, please confirm it, so we could proceed with this case or look for another one. As it concerns our current target's case, we are still awaiting for further instructions . . .'

Adams has never explained why he wanted details of a hacker murdered in Bulgaria, or who told him about it, or how this was linked to 'our current target's case'. In the next two years he would intensify his investigations into Bulgarian piracy circles, using private investigators from Argen GmbH.

Suddenly it seemed that NDS was concerned to get Oliver out of Europe for a couple of weeks. He travelled to Israel, on 15 November, to work with the Haifa team and then to visit Jerusalem. Possibly Adams was also concerned to provide Oliver with extra cash to fund additional security. Adams sent Oliver a strange email at 3.20 a.m. on 5 November with the subject line 'Pay':

Do not forget to include an item:
To reimbursement of money paid on behalf of NDS for special
software . . .
£10,000
Ray

Adams didn't expand on what the £10,000 was for.

What does all this mean for how Boris came to be found dead in a park?

'I think it's an 80 per cent chance that he killed himself,' Oliver Kömmerling said in an online chat in 2011. If it wasn't that, Oliver argued that Boris was murdered by criminal elements in the phone-hacking business: 'It was the Vietnamese guys screwing him [because] he gave the Telefon cards for free.'

In the days before Skype, Germany's large foreign communities provided a strong demand for long, free telephone calls. Earlier in the year, Boris had worked with others at the Chaos Computer Club to demonstrate how GSM phones could be hacked, after a US article described how it was theoretically possible. Oliver believed the phone cards remained vulnerable, despite claims that the hole had been fixed. Someone like Boris could endanger the pirates' profit margins if he publicised loopholes.

But others have cast the net wider. A newspaper report in November 1998 claimed that Boris had been contacted by Italian mobsters the previous year, wanting him to pirate the Irdeto-based pay TV operations, but Tron had refused.

'Boris could be so damn stubborn,' his father said. 'If someone tried to force him to do something he was opposed to, he wouldn't do it.'

Oliver is scathing about the theories of the Chaos Computer Club, which he dismisses as baseless speculation. His frustration boiled over in an intense internet chat exchange he had with Jan Saggiori over five days in May 2011. At 2.54 in the morning on 25 May Oliver began talking about Berlin: 'Look. According to Google I murdered Boris.'

'There is nothing on Google,' Jan replied.

Oliver said that recently someone had set him up to meet with Andy Müller-Maguhn to talk about Boris: 'I could not believe what kind of stories they created for themselves. Idiots. They prefer to sit in the dark and create imaginary stories.'

And then Jan asked Oliver why he hired two bodyguards. Oliver did a double-take: 'What's this again?'

'After the death of Boris,' Jan said.

'JAN you make me smile,' Oliver replied. 'I had never body-guards. What for? Look. You make me curious.'

'Okay, you told me when we met in Germany,' Jan said.

'I had a guy working for me,' Oliver told him. 'But not a body-guard. I don't need bodyguards.'

'You told me that you had two bodyguards for few months after Boris's death, and they were paid by NDS,' Jan said.

'Okay. You mix that. NDS wanted me to have some but I told them this is stupid. It was a [Ray Adams] game to get me under control and frightened. He always used such situations. Fear. If you can get somebody scared he belongs to you . . . Anyway I am armed. I shoot in a club. And at home. I am not afraid. I never felt that way . . . [and] I had always good relations with everybody. Companies and pirates.'

Jan Saggiori stands by his claim that Oliver told him in 2000 that NDS had paid for two bodyguards in the months following Boris's death. Oliver does not deny that Ray Adams wanted to do this, but says he refused it. If so, this may put a new complexion on why Adams wanted Oliver to make a claim for £10,000 for 'special software' and the rushed appearance of the trip to Israel.

Ray Adams did in the end talk to the Berlin homicide squad. But what did he tell them? It's not known. Did he tell them that he ran a network of undercover agents? When he said he wanted to hire Boris, did he spell out just what that would involve? Did he mention, for example, that Boris's friend Oliver had been busy working with the Haifa team on reverse engineering EchoStar's Nagra card in North America? Did he mention the murdered hacker in Bulgaria he was investigating, or the furious row he had had with John Norris three weeks before, over Norris's claim that Adams' agents were too close to pirates? Did he mention anything about hiring bodyguards for Oliver Kömmerling?

It needs to be noted that there has never been any credible suggestion that NDS itself was involved in Boris's death. But there are serious questions to be asked about News Corporation, its subsidiary NDS and its employees and agents. What obligation does an international media organisation have to assist police in a murder investigation? Where is the line drawn, when choosing what information is relevant and what is not? Who decides what should be disclosed and what shouldn't? When does the decision to withhold information on the grounds of relevance become more than just a company preserving its trade secrets and intellectual property? When does it become a cover-up?

PART 6

The Long Pursuit

Looks like Foxtel is well and truly hacked!

The hack is available 'on the card' for digital—cable will follow soon. Opens all channels including PPV and adult.

I have been offered the software. The hack is on genuine cards not DPSC.

The software is available commercially. Circa 5k US dollars.

Lee Gibling, founder of The House of Ill Compute
in ICQ chat 3 June 1999

San Diego, New Year 1999

It had been a busy time for Chris Tarnovsky. Back in October 1998 he had passed to John Norris a copy of a TVcrypt email from New Zealand, which had led to Ray Adams tracking down Chris Cary, the sometime British pirate radio DJ known as Spangles Mundoon, turned BSkyB pirate. In July 1998 the UK Court of Appeal had confirmed a four-year sentence for Cary for a £30 million card operation, but he had escaped from a low-security prison and fled the country. On 8 October Adams sent a smug email to Reuven Hasak: 'I have found Cary . . . sssssshhhhhush. Ray.'

Cary had been living in Saint Johns, Auckland, under the name Chris Broady. Adams hired a local security firm to keep Cary under observation. On 26 November Adams briefed UK police and the New Zealand organised crime squad arrested him on 7 January. NDS staff privately requested copies of the television news reports, to enjoy Cary's discomfiture.

Some people just can't get away from their job. At 4.26 p.m. Christmas Day 1998, at his in-laws' home in Belgium, Tarnovsky was busy forwarding an email he had just received from Vesco. It was a harmless Christmas greeting, except for the 'cc' list of email addresses of recipients. John Norris forwarded the email to DirecTV, where Larry Rissler recognised two of the addressees were at Montana State University, where he knew Herb Huddleston's daughter and son-in-law worked. Norris and Rissler had found the lab where Vesco and Plamen had cracked DirecTV's P2 card.

By 6 January John Norris was chasing down the accident report from the vehicle collision Herb and the Bulgarians had been involved in near the US border, to find out the false name Plamen had been travelling under. He was also preparing to go to the university with a lawsuit in his hand: 'We expect to speak to the asso. professor who apparently hosted Pman and allowed Pman to use University equipment.' Vesco's email to Chris would trigger many things, but Christmas cheer did not figure high on the list.

Paris, March 1999

Rupert Murdoch was making another of his grand plays that refashion the media landscapes of entire continents. He had been talking to Telecom Italia about buying its Stream pay TV business in Italy, which was losing money heavily. But he put that plan on hold when another opportunity arose—to merge BSkyB with Canal+, now controlled by Jean-Marie Messier's Vivendi Group. Talks ran hot in the first week of February. Murdoch was making all the right noises. He was suddenly a fervent European.

The French financial newspaper *La Tribune* celebrated *le Nouveau Rupert*: 'The ogre Murdoch, the enemy of European culture not so long ago, is now becoming the linch-pin in the creation of a major audio-visual group in the name of safeguarding the very same European culture.'

It lasted barely a week. Murdoch broke off talks in March after Canal+ chief executive, Pierre Lescure, insisted that he would be chief executive of the merged group and Vivendi the controlling shareholder. Lescure told *Libération*, 'We will have the leadership or there will be no agreement.'

Murdoch walked.

Eighteen days later, someone put the ROM code for the Canal+ SECA smartcard on the internet. The security system that safeguarded the huge Canal+ pay TV arms in seven countries in Europe, together with the fledgling OnDigital operation in Britain and the Measat Astro system in Malaysia, was now hopelessly compromised. The results were catastrophic.

In the next two years, piracy levels for Canal+ businesses in Italy and Spain would go from nil to more than 30 per cent. That figure accounted for hundreds and hundreds of millions of dollars a year that were directed away from Canal+ by the piracy operations. Five years later, Canal+ had moved from operating in seven countries to just one. Extravagance by Vivendi's Jean-Marie Messier and overspending by Canal+ management played a major role; but the rise of piracy, based on the leaked codes, starved the business of revenues—of oxygen. At one point in 2002, Canal+ was said to be a week away from financial collapse.

This time, unlike the Nagra/EchoStar files posted by Swiss Cheese five months before, there could be no mistaking where the leak had come from. Not that anyone noticed. The eyes of the media were focused on the other side of the world, to Rupert Murdoch's country property, Cavan, near Canberra, where on Saturday, 27 March, Lachlan Murdoch was marrying supermodel Sarah O'Hare. Media were kept well away, but a media crowd is rotten at keeping secrets. By the next day Australian newspapers were reporting on the tension between Anna and Rupert, whose divorce would not be finalised until June. Anna made a speech that began, 'And now I have the microphone, and I know one man in the crowd is nervous.'

It was during those hours, on the other side of the world in Vancouver, where it was still Friday, 26 March, that Al Menard posted the SECA source codes on his DR7 website.

Geneva, 26–28 March 1999

After completing his second degree in 1997, Jan Saggiori started two businesses. One was a smartcard security consultancy and distributor; the other company, started with friends in 1998, developed a SIM operating system for GSM telephone cards.

Early in January 1999, Chris Tarnovsky contacted Jan, wanting to arrange a big order of smartcards—10,000 blank PIC 16C622 cards from Microchip—through his UK business. Chris knew Jan's UK company could produce the cards under a licence. He told Jan the order would come from a friend, Al Menard.

Menard wired $10,000 to Jan's UK partner, Lester Wilson, as a deposit and Wilson began assembling the blank cards. But by early March, Jan was beginning to have misgivings. The only reason Chris would want 10,000 blank smartcards would be because he was making a new pirate card—and it was most likely EchoStar that Chris and Al would be pirating as the DR7 site continued to be the centre for EchoStar piracy.

Jan was no longer involved in piracy, but his role as the source of the cards would make him the chief suspect if Menard used them for piracy, which was illegal in the United States. But how could he cancel the order? By March, Jan had told Wilson to go slow on the order. Later he would tell Wilson to inform Menard that the card production had failed.

This was the uncertain position when Menard emailed Jan on 26 March, to tell him to look at the news section on DR7. It was the source code for the SECA card of Canal+.

'The contributors only ask that you acknowledge its source and enjoy,' Menard told Jan. Menard had wanted a European site to post the files—'after sending 4 emails with no response when my site needed help with hosting (I also offered to pay good money for hosting)' he had decided to do it alone, just on DR7.

It was after one o'clock on Saturday morning, 27 March, in Geneva. Jan went straight to the DR7 site and downloaded the

SECA zip file. He forwarded the files to his friend, Andy Kozlov, the hacker in Moscow, and they began to examine them. Just before one o'clock on Saturday afternoon he emailed Menard back, asking if he knew how to download the flash chips inside the Canal+ receiver box. In Vancouver it was 3 a.m., and Menard didn't reply. He didn't get back to Jan later in the day either.

Now it became tricky. Jan had a sense that there was more information, if he could just prise it out. There was some leverage on Menard to get back to him, because he still wanted the 10,000 blank cards he had ordered. But asking how to download the chips in the Canal+ receiver was too much of an ask. Perhaps Al didn't even have it. So Jan set his sights on Chris Tarnovsky, who he assumed was directly involved in the posting.

Jan phoned Chris on Sunday evening Geneva time, 28 March, for what would be one of the most important conversations of his life. It was just after midday in California. He had worked out what he wanted to ask Chris. But he took his time getting there. He felt a strong personal link with Chris. The two rarely emailed these days, but they spoke often on the phone.

Jan had developed an incredibly sensitive nose for picking out people who worked for NDS. He had picked Oliver as an NDS agent in mid 1997. When Chris Cary's former sales manager, Steve Bennett, had posted on TVcrypt in October 1998 after a year's absence (when he had been cooperating with NDS) it was Saggiori who raised the alarm about Bennett's bona fides. But Chris Tarnovsky was Jan's blind spot. Surely they were too close, had shared too much, for Chris to be playing a double role? It was natural for Jan to confide in him some of his recent troubles. Chris wasn't just a trusted friend, he was outside Europe, outside the loop. Jan could use him as a secret-keeper. At least that's what he thought.

Tarnovsky took it all in and passed it on to John Norris that evening. By nine o'clock that night Norris had written to Ray Adams and Reuven Hasak summarising Chris's account of his conversation with Jan. By Monday morning, Adams had forwarded Norris's email to Oliver in Germany. But how much of what Chris told them about the conversation could be trusted?

In the account Chris gave to Norris, Jan had started by telling Chris that one of his contacts had seen Oliver in the United Kingdom with an NDS executive, and that he was '100 per cent certain' that Oliver was responsible for the Hornet Irdeto cards. Jan went on to talk about the campaign that Ray Adams had been running against him. He told Chris that Adams now had a private investigator working in Switzerland to try to compromise him. The snippets kept coming. Oliver was communicating with Ross Anderson and Markus Kuhn at Cambridge, Jan said, and the three of them were getting money from Adams not to hack BSkyB. (NDS was a sponsor of the department, but Jan was wrong about Anderson and Kuhn.)

Finally, Jan mentioned that he had a secret manual that showed how to get into the 'bootstrap' code of a leading smartcard. He didn't want to send Chris the manual—he seemed too eager for it. But he would send Chris an attachment that came from the manual, along with an Atmel non-disclosure agreement. Jan hadn't signed an NDA and Chris thought he must have got the manual from Oliver.

To this point, Tarnovsky's account of the conversation isn't disputed. What happened next is where accounts differ. Jan had dangled a few carrots in front of Chris. Between the two of them it was always quid pro quo. Now he talked about the Canal+ code that had been published on DR7 two days before. He had been looking at it, and he had realised that the file skipped the addresses for some of the source code inserted by the manufacturer, SGS-Thomson, at memory location 2000. This was system code and actually made little difference to being able to hack the card, so it was a harmless little request Jan was making: Did Chris have the missing code sequence?

Jan had asked a critical question. They had wandered into an area where such questions could be asked, and Chris was happy to show how much he knew. Jan testified during the 2008 EchoStar case about the conversation that followed: 'He [Chris] told me he was not able to have the Canal+ ROM 2000 address because that part had been lost during extraction of the code.' But he had the ROM code for the Nagra card, which was also an SGS-Thomson card, so it was the same as the SECA card. Would that do instead?

'Do you want that part of the code?' Chris asked Jan.

'Yes, because that's the missing part,' Saggiori replied. 'If that's the same or similar, I'm very interested to have it.'

Jan understood Tarnovsky to be telling him that he had the whole Nagra card, but he wasn't going to ask him for it.

'I didn't want to ask too much. I wanted to ask him something that he could give easily.'

At the end of the conversation, Chris emailed the Nagra ROM code from his von@metro2000.net account to Jan at 1.36 p.m. California time. The email read: 'Good news from up north here. Enjoy, keep for you please . . . extremely top secret!' The code was an attachment to the email encrypted with PGP, an encryption program whose initials stand for Pretty Good Privacy.

The way PGP works is that the message was encrypted using Jan's public key (which all of his contacts had) and could only be decrypted by Jan using his private key. PGP doesn't just encrypt a message—it's a sealed record of that message. The email was proof-positive that Chris had part of the Nagra ROM code and that he was distributing it. Not just that, he had sent it as a replacement for the Canal+ code, claiming that they were the same at this particular memory register.

In fact Chris was wrong—the two ROM codes were quite different at this point. But by making that incomplete claim and substitution, Chris was tying himself to both codes, the Nagra and Canal+. He sent the Nagra code as a substitute because he had the Canal+ code (just not that particular part of it). He was admitting—and demonstrating—that he had access to both codes and he was distributing them. His conversation with Jan showed he was directly connected with the release of the Canal+ code on DR7... and put him in the frame for the Nagra code releases on DR7 as well.

It was by any reasoning an immensely silly email to send. He had just given Jan a smoking gun that could bring NDS down. Chris doesn't see it like that. He denies ever sending the email. What he told John Norris later that night was that Jan had mentioned 'there was a recent post to the internet that divulged the Sekka [sic] code. Jan is angry as he wants to benefit from this code somehow and does not want it public.' Jan had told him that it was posted in the United States 'but apparently came from someone in Europe who has problems with one of the European web site administrators'.

Over time, Tarnovsky would give other versions of this conversation. This version clearly does not square with Menard's email statement to Jan that it was Menard who had been trying to get a European website to publish the code—in fact, offering to pay them to do it (and why Menard would be paying someone to give away free software he never made clear).

In terms of what was said, it came down to Chris's word against Jan's... except for the PGP email. It couldn't be explained away. NDS claimed the email was a fake, and at the EchoStar trial they had their independent expert examine it. NDS can't have liked what their expert told them because he was never called to testify—the jury never knew of his existence.

It was left to Chris Tarnovsky to explain why he believed the email was a fake. The header of the message, showing the route the email had taken, couldn't be challenged.

'I believe that the entire header area would be legitimate,' he testified. 'However, the remainder from the "Good news from up north here, dot, dot, enjoy," to the end of the e-mail I believe has been fabricated.'

US law restricted the power of encryption programs that were publicly available in America, which meant that government agencies could crack encrypted email traffic—something that Chris himself had pointed out to TVcrypt in August 1996. But that limitation didn't apply to programs produced outside North America. US regulators couldn't crack the international version of PGP. That meant that once Chris encrypted the file with the international version of PGP, no one in the United States could read it—in fact no one in the world could decrypt it, except Jan Saggiori with his private key.

Sending the contents of an email like this from California presented Tarnovsky with a stark choice. He could have chosen a domestic encryption program, which might have been intercepted and read by US authorities, or he could have chosen one that couldn't be read but, if intercepted, might land him in prison. Tarnovsky's defence was that he clearly would not have used the international version of PGP, because that would be *illegal*.

Riedelberg, western Germany, 26–31 March 1999

The first that Oliver Kömmerling knew of the SECA code being on DR7 was a call from Canal+. François Carayol—the head of Canal+ Technologies, the division that developed and operated the SECA Mediaguard system—was on the line.

'He was really, really angry,' Oliver said later. Carayol had arrived at a client meeting, only to find that NDS marketing had beaten him to the punch. 'The client told him he had just had a meeting with NDS people and they were really smashing the system because it was hacked.' The proof was all over the DR7 site. 'In his mind, uh, I got the impression that NDS [was] completely responsible for that kind of thing.'

Oliver was going through one of his periodic bouts of unhappiness with NDS management. There wasn't enough to do. On his trip to Israel the previous November, he complained that the Haifa lab had hired a FIB and was doing all the work on the latest hacking technique, called glitching, while he was left with the lame-duck tasks. His unhappiness had left him open to an approach from Canal+, who wanted to hire him. But now the posting of the SECA codes on DR7 were to bring those discussions to an abrupt halt.

The first thing Oliver noticed when he looked at the DR7 post was the misspelled attempt to link it to a German source, 'das deutches [sic] underground'. If the hacker was German, then Oliver was the leading suspect. No wonder Carayol was upset.

Then Oliver began a forensic examination of the files, looking for any clues that might tie it to a source. The file itself couldn't be traced, but he went on to compare it with the copy of the SECA ROM code that Zvi Shkedy had sent him the previous summer, once the reverse engineering had been done. And then Oliver spotted the connection. He called Shkedy and urged him to compare the ROM codes on DR7 with the SECA file they had managed to extract.

'So? It's the same file, but the ROM is the same in all of the cards.' The penny still hadn't dropped for Shkedy.

'That isn't really the point,' Oliver told him. 'Now look at the time stamps.'

The SECA binary file extracted by Shkedy was called 'Secarom. bin' and the file was last saved on 6 July 1998 at fifteen seconds past 4 p.m. When Oliver had looked at it earlier, 'the file from us and the file from the website had exactly the same timestamp, to the second. It would be impossible that two people on this planet can read out the same file at the same second. The timestamp was like a fingerprint.'

Now Shkedy made the same connection. 'And then he was quiet, because it was obvious to him immediately that it was our file,' Oliver said later. 'And then he said to me, "I need to make some phone calls."'

Oliver now made an agitated call to Reuven Hasak.

'His issue on the phone was the code, the ROM that he extracted in Haifa, was published on the Net. And now he's going to be exposed to the pirates that he works for NDS,' Hasak testified in 2008. 'And he mentioned also a time stamp.'

In Oliver's mind, it was child's play to prove that the code came from NDS, and then his whole role would spill out.

'You have to understand that the world of piracy is not ideal world,' Hasak testified. 'It's world with lots of money, violence, weapon, things—ugly things. So sometimes people can be under severe risk if they . . . if pirates or people knew the pirates doesn't like them.'

This was five months after Oliver claimed that Ray Adams had wanted him to hire two bodyguards in the wake of Boris's death.

'I have to look into it because, you know, you are very excited,' Hasak told Oliver. 'Calm down, I'm going to look into it, and I'll call you back.'

Hasak put down the phone and called someone from the technical department.

'What's a time stamp?' he asked. When the technician explained, he asked, 'When there's a time stamp, is something 100 per cent proof?' He was satisfied when the technician told him, 'It's a proof, but not 100 per cent proof.'

Hasak called in his partner at Shafran, the former operations chief of Shin Beit, Rafi Malka, to investigate security at the Haifa lab. Malka reported security was good but had a few loopholes, Hasak testified in 2008. Then he reported on the investigation to NDS chief exec, Abe Peled.

And that was pretty much that. The time stamp wasn't proof. Someone else must have been using a focused ion beam to crack the SECA chip at the same time that NDS did. But the odds against two programs being created at the same minute in a twelve-month period is 526,000 to one. For it to be the same second, the odds against increase to more than 31 million to one. This is what is meant by saying it is not 100 per cent proof. But for all intents and purposes it is proof, as Abe Peled would have realised.

There were two other explanations: that someone had extracted the codes from the stand-alone computer in the Haifa lab where they were kept, or from Oliver's encrypted computer. But no one has seriously argued this. Alternatively, someone else used the FIB to crack the SECA chip, then released it for free after doctoring it to frame NDS with a fake time stamp. It's not hard to doctor a time stamp. The problem is, if they were inserting a fake time stamp, how could they possibly know which date and which time to use? You could only get that by looking at the original NDS file.

'The second part of the story I got from Tarnovsky himself,' Oliver told the BBC in 2011 as part of an interview that was not broadcast. 'I had a later meeting with him where he told me more or less how . . . Tarnovsky told me that he was given the code by NDS and he didn't really know what to do with it.'

According to Oliver's account to the BBC, it was at a dinner with Norris and Hasak that Tarnovsky raised the matter of the Canal+ code that had been given to him—it was no use in America. 'Tarnovsky say, "I cannot really use it, or I can dump it on the internet." And in this moment there was not a straight [response]—"No, don't do this, it's crazy," or something like that. It was more like, "Do what you want." Tarnovsky was saying, "Should I do this? Should I do this?" Or "What do you want me to do with it?" . . . Chris just told me it was not an order, it was a . . . a gesture, like an "I don't care" gesture.'

'He said to me it was a kind of nodding, or something like that.'

Hasak, Norris and Tarnovsky have given evidence denying any such exchange. In any case, for many years no one knew anything about the time stamp that linked the DR7 post to NDS. And meantime Oliver was the obvious suspect.

Thousand Oaks, California, December 1998

It was one month after Alan Guggenheim and Christophe Nicolas's somewhat disturbing conversation with Ray Kuhn over coffee at the DirecTV offices in Los Angeles that Nicolas called Guggenheim from Cheseaux to tell him there definitely was a hack. It was clear some people were using a battery card to watch EchoStar illegally. Nagra would have to do a countermeasure.

Both men were shocked and upset. The whole selling argument for Nagra—to DirecTV and other potential customers—was that its cards were not hacked. Guggenheim had been targeting the big ten telephone companies, and was starting to make progress with cable companies . . . Comcast, Cablevision, Charter.

'I thought I had already got DTV, I was really winning it. We were on a roll,' he recalls. Now everybody was asking him the same questions: Is Nagra secure? What are these rumours? What's going on?

From the start, Nicolas and Kudelski Corp CEO André Kudelski suspected that a competitor had cracked the Nagra card. Who else but a competitor would go to the trouble to crack their card, then give the EEPROM secrets away for nothing? That put Canal+ or NDS very much in the frame.

An alternative line of thinking was that it must be someone who had access to advanced programming tools developed by the chipmaker SGS-Thomson. That was what the first countermeasure was designed to test, André Kudelski told me in 2009. The ease with which the pirates defeated the countermeasure convinced him that the pirates must have the SGS-Thomson tools. And only half a dozen companies in the world had access to them. The second countermeasure killed off the battery cards. But the war was only just beginning.

'A lot of things were happening which were mind-boggling and Nagra was totally in the dark,' says Guggenheim. 'Nagra did not know how the hackers were doing it. And obviously they didn't know how to fix it, because when you don't know how it's done it's hard to fix.'

DirecTV execs were telling Guggenheim there was a fatal flaw in their card that made it impossible for them to resecure the system. But the Nagra team had no idea what they were talking about. By early 1999, EchoStar was screaming that it wanted the problem fixed. But how do you fix a bug that you can't even find? The mood at Nagra must have been close to panic.

'They had no idea where the hack was coming from; they had no idea what the hack was; they had no idea how to fight it,' an EchoStar source says.

In December 1998, just as the EchoStar battery card appeared, DirecTV began negotiations with NDS about an extension to its contract; but Guggenheim believed Nagra was still in with a shot. So Guggenheim found himself sitting down with a blank piece of paper to map out a security strategy. Nagra had never needed one before. Guggenheim's background as a military staff officer and the counterintelligence work he had been involved in after the assassination attempt in Guadeloupe made him decide he needed to treat this like a war.

He proposed setting up a technical intelligence organisation, with a listening network to monitor what was happening on the piracy forums, what was being said in the chat rooms. EchoStar and Nagra agreed, but approved a budget of only $50,000. The listening network would consist of Guggenheim and his wife with a standard home computer.

At the same time Guggenheim was talking to regulators . . . to the FBI, the CIA, the Secret Service, the DEA, a string of US attorneys, city and county police, customs, sheriffs, local police in Canada and the Royal Canadian Mounted Police. But NDS was always there before him. Norris offered superb technical back-up for the police. If they confiscated pirate devices, an NDS lab would process them for police—even if they were EchoStar pirate devices. Guggenheim found he got to look at them only after NDS had.

It was natural for him to discuss his problems with Larry Rissler at DirecTV. Rissler had been in the FBI for 25 years, was smooth, very polished, with thinning grey hair. 'He was very open, from the very first day—he had the attitude that the more people fighting piracy the better it would be.'

Guggenheim decided that he would swap notes with NDS. That didn't seem to be a problem, despite the conspiracy theorists at Cheseaux.

'Most people at EchoStar did not think that NDS could have done it,' he said. He didn't believe NDS was involved—NDS had too much to lose to do something like that. 'And I also thought it was kind of an excuse on Nagra's part,' he said. 'It's easy to blame the competition, rather than to look at your own bugs or mistakes.'

John Norris was certainly approachable. Guggenheim had met him at a trade fair and they agreed to meet up. Norris was a little abrupt, but he provided some helpful names of law enforcement officials to talk with.

Rissler and Norris believed in pursuing aggressive legal action against pirates. By 1999 DirecTV piracy was in the double digits and Guggenheim estimates it was probably in the 20 to 30 per cent range. That would be between 500,000 and a million homes across the United States. That's hundreds of millions of dollars of revenue a year lost to DirecTV—and a $100 million pirate industry.

'Just going through my neighbourhood—if I looked at the neighbours, the four or five neighbours, several of them had a DTV pirate device at home—everybody had it, it was really bad,' Guggenheim says.

EchoStar and Nagra were of one mind in that they didn't want to take the litigation route. Neither side thought it was effective and it was *very* expensive. It was also about perception. Nagra had a reputation as being a hard, complex system to crack. By April 1999 the battery cards were history and there was a full hack on sale, a 3M pirate card (3M is short for Three Musketeers, which was an original that had been reprogrammed to take all programming for free—one for all and all for one). However, as yet there were still very few Nagra pirates. With a piracy rate between one and three per cent, it made sense not to go the legal route—that would publicise that it was possible to hack Nagra.

As Guggenheim kept talking to DirecTV, it was more and more obvious that the hacking was hurting Nagra's prospects of picking up the DirecTV contract.

'However, they really wanted to deal with us. So they were telling us where the problem was, trying to understand it,' he said. In side conversations, after meetings or during coffee breaks at conferences, they would sidle up to ask Guggenheim whether Nagra was making any progress in finding out who was doing it, or who did he think it was. 'And that's where several of them hinted—they said it looks like it could be an attack by one of your competitors and it could be an attack by NDS.'

Guggenheim remained sceptical. He was struggling to make sense of what his intelligence activities were throwing up. North American piracy had a clear pattern. It was a high-stakes game, because those caught selling pirate cards in the United States faced court action and jail time. Given the high risks and the huge investment involved in producing a new hack, the dealers who had financed it would immediately try to recoup their costs by selling rights and territories to the hack among the dealers and sub-dealers. But the EchoStar hack had begun with a free EEPROM dump on the DR7 website, and then further technical information. And the pirate cards were only being sold by a small network of dealers. The economics of the EchoStar piracy didn't make sense.

The heart of the piracy was in Canada, and it seemed to be centred in Edmonton. Larry Rissler gave Guggenheim the telephone number and the codename of a piracy dealer in Edmonton called Mike, who he talked to. But Guggenheim had simply stumbled across an undercover sting operation that NDS was running and he was ultimately introduced to two law enforcement officers working with Mike, and a customs officer, with whom he developed a strong working relationship.

Meanwhile with each month the prospect that Nagra would win the DirecTV contract receded further and further. 'The message I got from them in early '99 was that, well, it looks like NDS is launching a very strong legal attack. All the lawyers are screaming at [DirecTV's parent] General Motors and menacing to make a big fuss and lawsuits and all that. And they said early on that we don't think we can go with the full option to switch to another conditional access provider.'

DirecTV funded a $200,000 scoping study by Nagra of the process of switching from NDS; but the real action was now between NDS and DirecTV over a new contract that explicitly allowed DirecTV to set up its own conditional access business in-house at the end of the new contract. The negotiations had been going on since December 1998.

Meanwhile, one day in the 1999 summer, Canadian Mike told Guggenheim that a big electronic counter measure was coming, and that it would kill all the DirecTV pirate cards that Mike had sold.

San Diego, July–August 1999

Chris Tarnovsky was crowing. 'They just don't have a clue,' he wrote to John Norris. On 6 July, NDS had dropped the boom on its latest pirate sting in Canada.

As long ago as December 1997, Tarnovsky had run Operation Johnny Walker, writing a DirecTV hack for Ron Ereiser's pirate group, which NDS had killed off at the end of the operation. That deal was undertaken with the approval of DirecTV, after the shambles of Oliver's Operation Duck in Toronto. But in September 1998, NDS had begun a new operation in conjunction with US Customs out of Blaine, Washington. It was called Operation Smartcard.net, and it involved Tarnovsky and Zvi Shkedy producing a new DirecTV pirate card, which they called the Eurocard. Through an undercover website, Customs officers sold 382 pirate Eurocards to individuals, and 3195 Eurocards to dealers.

The boom came down on 6 June 1999, when an ECM devised by Tarnovsky killed all of the cards. He was jubilant—particularly because pirates had been able to reverse an earlier attempt to kill the cards. Norris had a copy of an email Ron Ereiser had sent to Plamen Donev saying they had worked out that the ECM had corrupted part of the card known as the jump table.

'Negative Houston!' Tarnovsky wrote to Norris on 12 July, scotching that idea. 'They are very ignorant because nothing is ever as it seems when I write it :))).' The changes to the jump table were just a distraction to hide the real kill command. 'Hehehehe-heheh. I love it when a plan comes together!'

But six weeks later, on 23 August, NDS Israel reported that several websites were claiming that they were now able to repair Eurocards killed off by the 6 July ECM and Norris was forced to write a long explanation for what was looking like a total disaster. Originally Tarnovsky had produced a smartcard based on the hack of DirecTV that Plamen and Vesco had done at Montana University in July 1997. At the same time, another pirate hack, called the Vancouver or 'Van' Eurocard, had been produced for a 'deep undercover operative code named Myron'. After six months (which would have been around March 1999), the Van Eurocard had been reverse engineered and it was being sold in Canada under the name Ring of Steel.

US Customs asked NDS to shut down the operation and to kill all the Eurocards, both the Montana and the Van versions. Tarnovsky clearly believed he had achieved this in a way the pirates could never reverse.

'We were wrong!' Norris noted in his report on 23 August. Ron Ereiser and Marty Mullen were both using 'glitchers'—devices pioneered by Plamen—to reactivate the Eurocards and the Ring of Steel cards. As Norris ruefully admitted: 'The hackers have discovered how to repair the Eurocards :-(This is confirmed—not rumors.'

Norris was being as calm about it as he could, but the position seemed parlous. NDS had provided 3577 pirate DirecTV cards to US Customs and they could not be turned off. Not just that, the NDS pirate hack had been itself pirated and used to produce thousands more cards. At present they had no idea how to put the genie back into the bottle. The most worrying line in his report was this: 'there will be no problem with DTV, assuming the moratorium is over'.

The moratorium was the agreement that NDS had given DirecTV after Oliver's trip to Toronto—not to run undercover operations selling pirate cards in North America without DirecTV's approval. Norris's words reveal that DirecTV did not know about Operation Smartcard.net. Norris didn't even know whether the moratorium was over. It looked like a shambles.

On 13 August, NDS had signed a new four-year contract to provide conditional access security to DirecTV, to continue to provide the 6.8 million smartcards to DirecTV subscribers plus another 2 million new cards for customers that DirecTV had recently acquired after their purchase of PrimeStar. Now, eleven days later, Norris was discussing a secret NDS operation which, when it began in September 1998, seems likely to have been in direct breach of the moratorium agreement.

If they had been asked, NDS had the fig leaf of saying that this was a US Customs operation but, as ever, it was someone else who was picking up the cost of its operations. DirecTV pirate cards retailed for between $325 and $425, which meant the cards sold by US Customs were worth between $1.16 million and $1.5 million. Customs banked $516,000 from the sales, which meant that the pirate dealers they sold to cleared up to a million dollars from the deals. And that's not including the cards sold by 'Myron', or the sales from re-pirated versions of Eurocard.

But how do you calculate the damages to DirecTV? Earlier in the year, in another case, a Seattle court had awarded damages to DirecTV of $10,000 for every pirate card sold. On that basis, the compensation bill for the botched Operation Smartcard.net would be $35.77 million for the 3577 pirate cards sold, and that would have made it the largest damages bill ever awarded . . . if it ever came to court. This was another way of saying this was perhaps the biggest piracy operation ever detected—and the perpetrators were NDS and the US government.

Did they ever manage to kill the cards again? It would be nice to think so. The US Justice Department said nothing about Operation Smartcard.net until August 2000, when it bundled it up with an unrelated FBI investigation and unveiled it as a triumph in the battle against piracy. It had been the largest fraud investigation US Customs had ever undertaken that was unrelated to drugs. Eleven people in California had been charged. DirecTV commended the Customs Service, the FBI and the Justice Department for their 'aggressive actions against satellite signal theft'. Larry Rissler said the enforcement actions 'underscore the importance of protecting the intellectual property rights of DirecTV and our program providers'.

And really, at the end of the day, what else could they say? The episode was never explained. But by the following year DirecTV was preparing to sue NDS over the activities of Operational Security and its pirate hackers.

Kazanluk, Bulgaria, February–August 1999

Ray Adams had a new best buddy, and the former Scotland Yard man was almost squirming. In a few short weeks Adams had forged a lifelong link to Plamen Donev, former Bulgarian military technician, now one of the world's most threatening hackers. It was a little like watching the cat being romanced by the *Looney Tunes* skunk, Pepé Le Pew. Ray was the cat, and Donev believed he had never had a friend like him. There were so many things to say about life on Planet Plamen, beginning perhaps with the fact that NDS's latest recruit, who was on a visit in early July to head office in Jerusalem, was anti-Semitic.

Plamen was probably the most dangerous person in the world for NDS (apart from Oliver, who was on their side already). In the course of producing the hack of the P2 DirecTV card for Herb Huddleston and Ron Ereiser's group, Plamen had devised a whole new way of attacking smartcards, called glitching. It was a way of applying power to portions of a chip and measuring response times to deduce the values in the chip's memory. Plamen was brilliant in a comparable way to Oliver and Markus Kuhn, but he achieved his results without the fancy equipment—by ingenuity and determination.

Glitching had revolutionised smartcard hacking. NDS, like everyone else, had multiple generations of cards that had not been built to handle a glitcher. It was glitching that resurrected the Eurocards after Chris Tarnovsky killed them. Plamen might be too volatile to depend upon for the humdrum business of responding to countermeasures, as Ereiser had discovered, which had forced him to turn to Tarnovsky for that. But, as the danger man who could threaten NDS technology at any moment and who could blow a hole in the company, Plamen was in a class of his own. He was a bomb that could go off at any moment.

NDS had kept up the pressure on him since his apartment in Kazanluk was raided back in July 1998, ensuring his applications for a Canadian visa were blocked. In late January 1999 he had agreed to what became a series of meetings in Bulgaria with Adams, Hasak, Norris and NDS general manager Raffi Kesten. Norris played bad cop, Adams was Plamen's only true friend. They started with him on $5000 a month and said lots of threatening things to him. Adams somehow convinced him that he was concerned for him in a way that no one else in the world except his mother was. Plamen would be loyal to Adams forever.

But what to do with him?

Versions of Plamen's glitcher were now in use by pirates around the world. On 3 June, Yoni Shiloh, a senior NDS staffer in Haifa, wrote to Adams about a crisis meeting between Reuven Hasak and another senior Haifa operative, Dani Ratner, at which they discussed the threat to all current NDS smartcards posed by Plamen (whose codename was 'Pluto') and his glitcher: 'Because Pluto has created this device he could be of use in finding ways to counter it—both in the immediate time-frame, and in the long-term,' Shiloh wrote. 'Dani has been asked to decide whether PLUTO should be tasked with helping in this issue, and whether this should be done immediately.'

Australia, June–July 1999

Ray Adams had taken to referring to Avigail Gutman as 'the Jewish Mamma'. He didn't mean this as anti-Semitic. It was more misogynist: the good-humoured male dismissal of her as a homemaker. Of course, she would be a very good homemaker, there was nothing to be ashamed of about that. It was Avigail who remembered Oliver's birthday; who talked cooking recipes; who took photographs when the partners of NDS staff had babies (she used her email account aunt_abbi@yahoo.com for this); who was a young mother herself. Reuven Hasak was also her mentor, which is perhaps why Adams used the Jewish mamma line, to put her in a box well away from the world of the experienced intelligence operative inhabited only by Reuven and himself.

In any case, Reuven must have seen something in her because, when her diplomat husband Uri Gutman was appointed Israeli consul in Taiwan, Hasak made Avigail the East Asia chief for NDS Operational Security. In public she was the model diplomat's wife, serving on the board of charities to raise money for worthy causes. Privately her job was to set up an intelligence infrastructure from scratch, a whole new set of informants, targeting China as well as New Zealand and Australia. This turned out to be just at a time when piracy was about to explode in that part of the world.

Pirate cards surfaced in Australia just weeks after Boris Floricic's Irdeto digital code appeared on the internet in November 1998. At the start of 1999, almost four years after Australia's first pay TV business, Galaxy Network, began broadcasting, there was a great deal of blood on the floor, with the prospect of much more red stuff still to come. In May 1998, Galaxy's parent, Australis Media, had finally faltered into liquidation, leaving in its wake four main ways to watch pay TV in Australia. There were two analogue cable services run by telephone companies—Foxtel, which was half-owned by the telephone giant Telstra, with the other half owned by News Limited and Kerry Packer's Publishing and Broadcasting Limited; and Optus Vision, which was owned by Telstra's new rival Optus Communications. Optus Vision used an analogue Irdeto conditional access system, while Foxtel used Newscrypt, a variant of an old NDS system, which meant it had been hacked elsewhere.

But it was the two satellite systems, both using Irdeto digital, that hackers focused on. First there was John Malone's Austar, which serviced regional Australia. Then there were the 100,000 or so former Australis customers. After Australis collapsed, Foxtel had taken over the remains of its business, and its subscribers. The service was renamed Foxtel Satellite, and it still used the Irdeto system. Thousands of old Australis Galaxy cards had gone missing and the company's chaotic records did not show which ones were authorised. So when the Foxtel Satellite service was officially launched on 1 March 1999, it was a situation tailor made for pirates. They set to work almost immediately.

Rolf Deubel had had Boris's Irdeto program from the night he cracked the password on his zip file in Angelo Montaperto's pub in Belgium. Rolf was part of a loosely connected group of hackers sharing information about Irdeto on the Net. To them he was his online persona, 'MadMax'. 'Most of them I never met in person', Rolf later told me. It was called the Millennium Group and its effects were soon felt wherever Irdeto operated. The hack they had developed was given the name Cardwizard.

Irdeto used the same card to provide conditional access for all its customers, but different systems used different levels in the chip. This meant that the one card had the keys for all Irdeto systems built into it. Boris had unlocked the level used by Premiere and DF1 in Germany. Rolf set about breaking the other levels of the chip. It proved simple enough, though it was necessary to monitor the stream in each market to check the different way the Irdeto system would address local channels, then modify the software accordingly. It wasn't hard. It did mean, however, you needed to be under the footprint of the satellite. You had to go there, which is how Rolf began to work up his frequent flyer points. By February 1999 there was a separate hack for Irdeto in Italy. Rolf worked out the hack for Irdeto in South Africa. Australia was next on the list and he arrived here in May of 1999.

In fact, questions about Irdeto were coming from all over. On 29 April, Rupert Murdoch took a 35 per cent stake in Telecom

Italia's pay TV arm, Stream, in Italy. 'I hope someone told them that Stream is hacked,' Adams told Yoni Shiloh. 'Which leads to the question as to what if any is our relationship to them. If we start to help them fight piracy we will be directly assisting Irdeto.'

That was pretty much the dilemma facing NDS in Australia, where News Corporation owned only 25 per cent of Foxtel, though it provided effective control through appointing its chief executive, Tom Mockridge. By 6 May, the Cardwizard program was available on the Thoic website in Britain that Ray Adams had set up, run by Lee Gibling, who had opened up a whole Australian forum for card pirates. Thoic had another program, 'austr.crd', posted as 'Made by Antonio have fun!' which opened up all Australian channels on a basic card.

Just to note: at this point, NDS through its Thoic website was providing Australian hackers with the software to pirate Foxtel Satellite and Austar. (It would later emerge that the public version of Cardwizard posted on Thoic needed a minor modification to enable users to write directly to the card, but NDS did not know this when it was posted—there was never any suggestion that such files for competitors' products should not be published, though NDS codes were stamped upon.)

Avigail had obtained a copy of MadMax's Foxtel hack and arranged through Ray Adams for Oliver Kömmerling to rewrite the program to protect her source. 'It may even be to our benefit if these [Foxtel pirate smartcards] came out on the market first [before the MadMax cards],' Avigail told Adams.

A day later she wrote, 'A release from Europe sounds good.' In fact three weeks later, Lee Gibling at The House of Ill Compute was offering Foxtel commercial pirate software for US$5000. NDS says it was only trying to bring flaws in the Irdeto card used by Austar and Foxtel to the attention of Irdeto, and there was never any connection with piracy.

Meanwhile, MadMax was already in Australia. Rolf flew into Perth from South Africa, then headed for Melbourne, where he was to be met at the airport by his chief contact, whom he believed was a sixteen-year-old hacker called Kyle. Rolf didn't mind who he was or how old he was. Kyle seemed to know his stuff and to have a group of other hackers he would introduce to Rolf. But Rolf was in for a surprise, because it was the sixteen-year-old's father who met him at the airport. Kyle was the father, who had been using his son's email account to communicate with Rolf.

The father introduced Rolf as MadMax the magician from Germany to his small group of friends, the answer to their prayers.

'When in Melbourne I was in contact with about five to six people, but only through [Kyle],' Rolf told me in 2012. 'He was in charge and introduced the "magician" to his associates/affiliates. I did some cards for these guys (upgrade to full bouquet or re-enable dead cards). Made the .crd files right there.'

Through May and June, piracy in Australia exploded. Bob Cooper is an American who ran *SatFACTS Monthly*, a highly influential publication for hobbyists and the industry about developments in satellite broadcasting. In his June edition he wrote about the Australian situation: 'I would say they are out of control, beyond any reasonable level we would expect if the piracy card game was limited to a mere handful of hackers. The sheer volume of postings and information can only bring us to one conclusion— thousands of people must now be hacking the cards.'

A month later, Cooper declared the battle lost. 'It happened so fast . . . Austar and Foxtel jumped on the hackers by sending out electronic "card hits" beginning in late May. By mid June the ECM shots were running all but continuously.' At times the ECMs to kill the modified original smartcards (MOSCs) were coming 90 minutes apart. But over a 72-hour period, Rolf and his Millennium colleagues produced a blocker that shielded the cards from the ECMs.

'Austar and Foxtel never had a chance,' Cooper wrote. 'Australia is awash in MOSC devices.'

Paris, August 1999

In his forties, Roger Kinsbourg had found himself an accidental pornographer. He had worked previously in media in France, then with local television for minorities in the United States. When he returned to Paris in the mid 1990s an advisor linked to some banks suggested he try to turn around Rendez-Vous Television, a failing adult channel in Sweden that the banks were exposed to.

On a fine summer day in 1998 Ray Adams walked into Roger's office with an NDS colleague. Adams had the charm on. The group exchanged opening pleasantries, before Adams came to the point: 'Why are you the only company that has not been heavily pirated? You're not pirated at all.'

'That's a good question,' Roger replied.

'Yes, why? It means you must know something that we don't know.'

'Hmm, well, I'm not going to explain,' he told Adams. 'We are lucky.'

Roger took them downstairs to the bar in his office, and they drank a few beers and batted things around and it seemed to go no further. He didn't mention that he had hired a special consultant to fight piracy. But Adams would hear eventually that it was Jan Saggiori and he didn't like that at all. Jan had become an obsession with Ray Adams. Later he would tell Jan that he kept a picture of him on his desk, with bars drawn over the top of the photo.

Yet by mid 1999 Roger Kinsbourg had come to realise that running an adult channel might not be the career path he had once dreamed about. Recently he had also realised the world was changing and he faced some difficult decisions at Rendez-Vous. His whole dealer network across Europe was struggling to maintain subscriber numbers, which were less than 100,000. It was a shoestring operation. The only really profitable patch had been an all-too-brief period when Rendez-Vous was part of a German platform that paid little but gave him access to millions of viewers as part of a package.

Roger's new goal was to be on the Canal+ platform. He knew it would be no easy sell, but he wanted to show how helpful—how necessary—he could be to Pierre Lescure, Canal+'s boss. Roger still had his tail up from the memorable victory that Jan Saggiori had scored over some UK pirates who had targeted Rendez-Vous in April 1999 with a pirate hack created by Oliver Kömmerling. At the time, Adams had been trying to convince Roger to sack Jan and use NDS's services. But Jan had kept changing the codes for the Rendez-Vous cards every day, even twice a day, and in the end the pirates had given up.

Now Roger wondered whether he might not be tackling his problems the wrong way. In the past he had always deflected any queries about how Rendez-Vous, almost alone in Europe, managed to be free of piracy. The answer was clearly Jan Saggiori. Maybe Roger should be making more of that, and of Jan's expertise. How to leverage a skill like that? Roger rolled the idea over in his mind for a while. Then he called Geneva.

He wanted Jan to write a report about piracy. This would not be confined to Rendez-Vous—he wanted Jan to write the big picture, the definitive overview of how things stood across Europe . . . who was safe, who was toast, who was doing what to whom? And what should they be doing about it? He told Jan he wanted to show the report to Canal+ management, but it would go no further than that. What the report said, and the form it took, was up to Jan. Roger made it clear he wanted to do Canal+ a big favour because, in the end, he was going to ask for a big favour in return.

Jan came back to him with his report on 9 September. It was 1500 words, much of it in rough dot-point format. Roger made an appointment to see the executive he was negotiating with at Canal+, and he gravely passed over the document. The executive made interested noises, but didn't seem to give it much actual attention. Once Roger was gone, the executive quickly passed the report on to Pierre Petit, the old policeman who was head of security for the Canal+ pay TV business (though that was about to change).

Petit had heard all about Jan Saggiori. Really, the impudence of these pirates was breathtaking. The report went straight into the file. No more action was needed.

Cornwall, August 1999

Lee Gibling's NDS piracy site, thoic.com, was a cyber panopticon giving him 360-degree vision of almost everything going on in the piracy world outside of North America. He bragged that Thoic was downloading four gigabytes of codes and programs, which pirated NDS competitors to hackers around the world *every day*. For example, with the opening of his Australian MOSC forum, Australian hackers had begun using the Thoic web forums and email accounts to plan their hacking strategies.

But everything that MadMax/Rolf Deubel was writing through his Thoic email account was being monitored by Gibling and passed on to Len Withall, Ray Adams and Avigail Gutman. On 19 August Rolf was writing to UK dealer Joe Ibrahim trying to arrange a meeting to discuss the Australian market ('which I have now fully established and sales are going well'). On 21 August, Gibling sent an email with a subject line 'Jackpot!' It was an exchange between MadMax and 'Bond 007', a leading Australian hacker, that identified Bond 007 as David Cottle, with his company address in Sydney. (Cottle never worked for NDS.)

On Monday, 23 August, Ray Adams forwarded to Oliver Kömmerling an email exchange by Deubel in German. 'Translate this for Len please. It looks like a travel agency is planning flights for MadMax.' Rolf was in Vienna; he seemed to be planning a trip to Bangkok.

Paris, September 1999

Ray Adams was heading back to Charles de Gaulle airport for his London flight with the simple satisfaction of a job well done. He had come to Paris to see Pierre Petit—the Canal+ security man was quite endearing, in a harmless old French duffer kind of way. He thought the world of Ray. Petit was struggling to make sense of this whole new world of smartcard piracy, and he was hugely grateful for any scraps of information Ray could pass his way. In return, he shared with Ray everything he found out from his own investigations.

'Dear Ray. First of all, congratulation on the big work you did with your team,' Petit wrote to Adams on 2 September, before going on to give names, dates and full details of Canal+ operations. 'I am looking forward to seeing you in Paris next week and will let you know the date as soon as I have arranged a date with my colleague.'

The colleague turned out to be a former Renseignements Généraux officer called Gilles Kaehlin, who was security chief of all Canal+, which made him Petit's new boss. Actually the RG man seemed to have worked all over the shop. He was a thickset, muscular-looking fellow. He carried a certain wiry energy. You wouldn't call him polished at all. It was a little hard to get his attention sometimes. Then he would transfix Adams with a piercing glance. It was a bit off-putting. On one of those occasions Kaehlin had given Adams the look, and told him he could find out anything about anybody. And the damnedest thing was, looking at Kaehlin you believed him. These French . . . they played by their own rules.

Adams knew policemen like that. They were guided missiles. The trick was to make sure they dropped their payload where you wanted. That was Adams' cue to sketch out for the new man the identity of the hacker behind almost all of the new wave of piracy that was overwhelming Canal+ businesses across Europe.

His name was Jan Saggiori. He was linked to the pirates, he was linked to organised crime, and someone needed to take him down. If he needed any confirmation of this, Kaehlin need only turn to his colleague, Pierre Petit.

'I share your opinion of Saggiori and I openly indicated it to Gilles,' Petit assured Adams later. In the meantime Adams had the satisfaction of knowing Kaehlin was taking all his words in. He had a gleam in his eye. Adams knew that look. The missile had target acquisition.

Bangkok, September 1999

The job Rolf Deubel had come to Thailand for took very little time. Then he headed back to his hotel and slept. He was back at his contact's home the next morning. There were arrangements to discuss, fine-tuning of the piracy hack. It was all going according to plan when he realised there was a disturbance outside.

The house he was working in sat at the end of a cul-de-sac. Police cars are hardly novel in Bangkok. Rolf saw the police cars turn into the little lane and head towards the end. Each house they passed marked one less option for where the police were heading, until Rolf realised with a start that they were heading for his house. The police were coming for him.

And then there was a confused sequence where Rolf was trying to disconnect and shut down his computer, and the police were suddenly next to him, hindering him. And then he was in the police car in handcuffs. Other police were still at the house. Someone had picked up Rolf's computer and had the wit not to let it shut down. And then he was in a holding room in the police station, waiting. Waiting. All afternoon. Until there was action again.

Three foreigners walked into the room. They had his laptop. A young woman with dark hair who took photographs but never spoke. A hard-looking man who said he worked for Irdeto, Andrew Curle. And a nondescript man with an English accent. He introduced himself as Ray Adams. He knew all about pirating Foxtel.

'Rupert Murdoch is very unhappy with you,' Adams told Rolf.

It would take a long time before Rolf knew anything about Thoic, and in the long interrogation that night his mind kept circling back to wrestle over who had set him up. Was it his local contact here? Was it Joe Ibrahim in London? Someone closer to home in South Africa?

Rolf wasn't talking—but the information they sought was all in his laptop. The man from Irdeto played bad cop, while Adams was good cop, the one who sadly told him that he would be spending many years locked in a Thai prison. It really was quite grim. But Adams thought he might be able to help him. There might be a way out of this mess, if Rolf was prepared to help Adams out a little.

Rolf didn't take the bait straight away. Adams said he would catch up with him later.

It was the afternoon of the second day, after a rushed court appearance, that Rolf was put in a police truck and taken to Klong Prem Central Prison. The complex houses 20,000 prisoners in a number of different sections, which are themselves split up into a series of different compounds. As the truck pulled up outside one of the compounds, Rolf saw a line of prisoners shuffling outside. One of the prisoners had begun shouting and the guards baton-charged him. One of the clearest memories he would have of the prison was the sound the batons made when they hit the man's flesh. It seemed to go on forever.

Paris, October 1999

Gilles Kaehlin had Jan Saggiori on the line. It wasn't going well.

'Gilles who?'

If Ray Adams knew how to be the good cop, Kaehlin was master at playing the very, very bad cop. He knew exactly how to put suspects in their place, to convey menace, threat, indifference, anger, rage; how to frighten, how to project power, to wield the invincible arm of the French security apparatus. Kaehlin wasn't so good at being nicey-nicey.

He told Saggiori that he was the new head of security at Canal+. He wanted to talk to him about piracy.

'It's all in my report,' Jan told him.

'What report?' Kaehlin asked. He clearly didn't know what direction this conversation was taking.

'My report, just read it.'

'I haven't read your report, because I've never seen it.'

'Then why are you calling?'

Now *there* was a question. What was Kaehlin doing? At 44, he was at a career crossroads. After his adventure in the Caribbean in 1986, when the government had had to send a plane to Saint Martin to rescue him from the besieged police station, Kaehlin's bosses at Renseignements Généraux had found a new place of exile for him, but one closer to home where they could keep their eye on him. He was transferred to the labyrinth that administered French business records.

After revealing some politically explosive insider trading, Kaehlin had found himself transferred from Paris once more, this time to New Caledonia. By 1998 he realised he had reached the end of the line and he resigned from the RG and took a job with Canal+ after convincing its chief, Pierre Lescure, to hire him as head of security.

After listening to Ray Adams describing Jan Saggiori's leading role in the piracy, he knew he was dealing with a major criminal threat, one which justified the widest range of possible actions. He set his investigators off to build a full profile of Saggiori's life, his history, his business links. And naturally he tapped his phone. Kaehlin knew this game. As the mastermind of European piracy, Saggiori would slip up.

And here was the first problem, because the checks came back clean. There was nothing going on, over the Saggiori home phone or any of the multiple mobiles that he used. Even his past phone records came back clean. But if that was so, why on earth was Ray Adams so convinced Jan was dirty?

That was when Kaehlin reached out to Jan. He called him, told him he wanted to meet him to talk about piracy. And Jan refused. Read my report, he said.

It took some doing, but Kaehlin hounded Pierre Petit until he came up with Saggiori's report. Petit didn't think much of it. But Kaehlin finally sat down to read it. The report was a bald document, a few pages of dot-point notes, often not even full sentences. It began with BSkyB, and then turned to the hacking of Canal+'s SECA card. Jan's conclusions pulled no punches: 'You really must believe that it is part of a plan of NDS to weaken their bigger competitor in Europe. In effect, the situation of NDS in Germany seems very suspicious to me.' He went on to discuss Irdeto, Viaccess and Conax, repeatedly linking pirate software to a German hacker 'who is actually paid by NDS not to touch their systems'.

It was an all-or-nothing report. Kaehlin's only options were to treat its conspiracy allegations as serious, and launch a major investigation of NDS; or to agree with Pierre Petit, and dismiss it as just crazy talk. Kaehlin hadn't decided for sure which way he was going to jump. But he knew one thing. He wanted to talk to Saggiori.

The second phone call was a replay of the first. Kaehlin wanted to talk to Jan. The Geneva hacker wasn't interested.

'You don't understand,' Kaehlin said. He had checked out Ray Adams' claims against Jan and they didn't make sense, he said. He knew that Jan wasn't dealing with pirates because he had been tapping his phone.

'What!' Jan exclaimed, scandalised. Kaehlin realised that might not have been the best line to use. Now Saggiori was furious with him. Kaehlin tried to hose him down, while still insisting that he had to meet with him.

'I've already booked the flight,' Kaehlin said in the end, a little plaintively.

'Then I hope you will have a nice flight to Geneva, and enjoy some duty free shopping at the airport,' Jan told him, unmoved.

In the end, Jan settled for compromise.

'Go back to talk to Roger, because I don't really trust you guys,' he told Kaehlin. 'The one guy I trust is Roger.'

Let his boss at Rendez-Vous sort it out.

London, 22 October 1999

Exactly a year after Boris's body had been found in the little wood at Britz-Süd, on Friday, 22 October, the sky fell in on Ray Adams' head.

Pierre Petit called him about a meeting the two of them had scheduled for the following Tuesday. There was *un petit problème*. He told Adams that Kaehlin had gone wild about a report written by Jan Saggiori. It made the most scandalous claims about NDS. He had tried to tell Kaehlin it was nonsense, but Gilles wasn't listening.

What did the report say? Well . . . Pierre went through it quickly, but it would be more sensible surely if Ray could read it himself. What about if he emailed it to him?

Ray thought that was a good idea.

He had the report by that evening and then he emailed John Norris to tell him Canal+ had a report by 'Hannibal' (Saggiori's codename) about all the current hacks in Europe. Adams wrote: 'He is talking a lot about The GERMAN.' Hannibal also referred to their Bulgarians, and he was talking to Mike (Chris Tarnovsky) about the USA side of the SECA hack. 'He refers to Mike as my "blood brother".'

Was Mike actually talking to Hannibal, and just what had Hannibal told him, Adams asked Norris.

'I can tell you that the French Security Services and the German Police are investigating and that one of them is in touch with one of the agencies in the USA.' The Canal+ investigation was being run by a former senior member of the French security forces, who wanted to come over to see Adams 'for a whole day' the following week. Adams would have the document translated by next week. 'Briefly it says that the German did the SECA hack and that NDS paid for it.'

Norris definitely wanted a copy of Jan's report: 'My obvious question is, did the "GERMAN" do the hack and if so, how would Hannibal discover this?'

Kazanluk, Bulgaria, 23 October 1999

Adams had been wrestling for some time with a familiar problem . . . how to keep Plamen Donev happy and on the team, now that he was back in Bulgaria. Plamen had been assigned to find a fix for the 22 versions of the hack for DirecTV's P2 card. He did have an idea that might solve the problem once and for all, but no one was paying much attention to him. That crazy Plamen.

It was late Saturday evening, and still within the deadline Plamen Donev had imposed upon himself, that he emailed Asher Arbit at NDS Israel: 'Hi Asher, Here is the solution for the most of the hacks.'

There followed sixteen lines of coding, then a list to identify the 63 different hacks that the kill command would target. And that was pretty much that.

Maidenhead, England, late 1999

Ray Adams had been only slightly distracted over the weekend by an email exchange with Avigail Gutman, detailing her plan to provide an Australian hacker, David Cottle, with a device to pirate the Astro pay TV platform in Malaysia. She believed that pirating

Astro would distract him from his recent attempts to hack News Corp's Star TV. Cottle was a hobbyist working quite legally within Australian law. He didn't know it (and he never worked for NDS), but Avigail had high hopes for him, and had been resisting attempts by Irdeto security to lean on him.

'We do not want Cottle in jail until he has a successor for the Irdeto hack,' she wrote.

There was a nice symmetry: putting Rolf Deubel in a Bangkok jail for piracy in Thailand in September, then five weeks later planning to provide a device to promote piracy in neighbouring Malaysia. But Adams had a more serious matter to attend to—fending off the baseless Canal+ investigation. Andy Coulthurst emailed the full translation of Jan Saggiori's explosive report to Ray Adams on Sunday night, 24 October. Adams forwarded it to Oliver early Monday morning with a brief note: 'We must talk.'

In mid November, Norris and Tarnovsky held an emergency meeting with Adams at Heathrow airport to discuss how to discredit Saggiori. Canal+ needed to realise Jan was just a 'bullshitter and someone on a personal vendetta', Adams had told Hasak earlier. He would start influencing the thoughts of Canal+ in this direction; 'This must be subtle and discreet and come from others.'

Adams told Norris, 'I have a little plan to really shake things up.' A key part of this plan would be to include Saggiori in the lawsuit Norris was about to launch against Ron Ereiser and his Canadian pirate group over the hack of the DirecTV P2 chip by Plamen and Vesco at the University of Montana in 1997. Adams knew that Saggiori's only role had been to provide Chris Tarnovsky (who was at the time an NDS consultant) with the names of the two Bulgarian hackers. But Adams and Norris could wield the legal resources of News Corporation, a $50 billion media group, to crush Saggiori in a US civil suit. Exactly how would Jan begin to fight it? Having a $10 million damages award against Saggiori would completely destroy the credibility of his allegations against Adams and Kömmerling.

Oliver, meanwhile, was taking his own precautions. When NDS chief exec Abe Peled had dinner with him in early December, Oliver told him about the time stamp that linked NDS to the DR7 posting. Separately Ray Adams had told Peled about the time stamp and that Canal+ was now investigating. When Reuven Hasak found out, he was furious. He had explained to Adams before that it was he, Hasak, who decided what Peled needed to know. In particular, he didn't bother Peled with subjects 'which might embarrass him in the future'.

'So now, as Abe is aware of the complication we have with Hannibal/Canal/SECA, I am going to talk to him about it in our coming meeting,' Hasak admonished Adams on 4 December. It was all so unnecessary.

Jerusalem, 21 November 1999

A month after Plamen Donev sent Asher Arbit his program to kill off DirecTV pirate cards, Arbit reported back to Adams that Plamen 'has provided a very effective way of killing cards which will be almost impossible for the pirates to reverse'. That was the good news. However, he went on to say, 'Due to the politics of the DIRECTV situation, Raffi Kesten has prohibited any future kills. Therefore, this idea will probably never be implemented. So we should compliment Pluto and at the same time tell him that this idea will probably never be used.'

It was left to Zvi Shkedy, who had been copied in on the email, to ask, 'Reuven: Who, if and when we have to tell him?'

Hasak didn't shirk a tough call. 'Zvi, the first part of it should come from you and cc Ray and me . . . The second part NOT TO BE MENTIONED!!!!!!!'

Plamen—brilliant, driven Plamen—had pulled the rabbit out of the hat. He had found the magic bullet to stop DirecTV piracy, and he would get no credit, no acknowledgement. His idea would be ignored. To be clear here: three months after signing a new four-year contract to provide conditional access security for DirecTV, its biggest customer, which was suffering from hundreds of thousands of pirate smartcards, NDS had a solution from Plamen Donev that would eliminate much if not all of that piracy threat. And the NDS general manager, Raffi Kesten, according to Arbit's email, had decided for political reasons to prohibit any further kills that might reduce that piracy.

Relations between NDS and DirecTV had become poisonous. But what was there to gain from withholding a solution to piracy? Would it make DirecTV reluctant to switch to a new NDS card? Or was there a broader corporate strategy? In September 1999 General Motors had decided to sell its stake in DirecTV. News Corporation would be the logical buyer. The sale price would turn upon DirecTV's earnings. Killing off several hundred thousand pirate cards, hopefully turning a substantial portion of them into paying customers, could be worth a lot of money to DirecTV. It could add at least half a billion dollars to the sale price of DirecTV, and probably much much more. But NDS was sitting tight on that solution.

Thousand Oaks, California, and Edmonton, Alberta, 2 February 2000

Alan Guggenheim was thinking about the melting point of plastic. He assumed American Express didn't skimp when they made their product. The card he was holding in his hand certainly looked robust enough. But what he was about to do was going to cause a meltdown somewhere, and he hoped it wasn't in his pocket. If the bill ended up with EchoStar, he knew right now it would be a lost cause. Charlie Ergen was a legendary skinflint.

What Guggenheim hoped was that Kudelski Corporation, the other partner in NagraStar, would back his hunch here and pick up the bill—at least until the Swiss accountants figured out a way to bill it back to EchoStar. So was he feeling lucky? And really, why was he even wasting time with the question? Time and jet charter companies wait for no man.

The telephone call had come on a Tuesday afternoon from a police officer whose name he stumbled over: Detective Tony Caughell, Edmonton Integrated Intelligence Unit, Outlaw Motorcycle Gang Section.

'I think we have something for you,' Caughell said.

It took a little while to make sense of the words coming down the line from Edmonton. The words 'outlaw motorcycle gang' kept turning over in Guggenheim's head. Then it clicked. Dave Dawson—member of the Hells Angels, Edmonton chapter; operator of Discount Satellite, a shopfront that was the biggest dealer of EchoStar pirate cards in North America. He now had Caughell placed as well. Caughell had been part of a group of police officers he had met months earlier, a joint task force of Royal Canadian Mounted Police and Edmonton police officers. It had been just another fruitless meet-and-greet session, as Guggenheim remembered it.

Over the phone Caughell now told Guggenheim that, at three o'clock that morning, Edmonton traffic police had stopped Dawson's car for a minor violation. They had searched the car and found a pile of money and electronic gear, including what looked like a lot of pirate cards for EchoStar and Canadian broadcaster Bell ExpressVu, which also used Nagra. There was enough to take Dawson in and hold him for questioning. At the station, they had seen his rap sheet from his time with motorcycle gangs. The next step was to get a search warrant for his Discount Satellite premises at 170th Street, North Edmonton.

And this is where it all came sharply into focus for Guggenheim, at the moment when Caughell told him the reason for his call: 'We used to do this kind of thing with DirecTV and NDS, but, because we met, and you told us that you wanted to be involved, I want to give you advance notice. If you want, and if you can come to Edmonton quickly, I would like to associate you with the raid.'

Guggenheim was scrabbling to make sense of the bombshell that Caughell had dropped on him. Here was the thing: Canadian police never called Guggenheim or EchoStar when they were raiding a pay TV pirate. They automatically called John Norris's people at NDS on speed dial. It didn't matter which system was being pirated—most police and customs officers in North America didn't even know the difference between an NDS DirecTV card, or EchoStar's Nagra card. Even though Bell ExpressVu used Nagra, Canadian police still automatically called Norris.

The NDS people had strong links into US Customs and the Secret Service, as well as the Royal Canadian Mounted Police (RCMP); they had a US lab that could analyse any smartcards that were found. It was a source of unending frustration for Guggenheim, because it left him dependent on whatever scraps of information Norris decided to give him. NDS's Operational Security had a global budget of $5 to 10 million; Guggenheim had an approved budget of $50,000. Why would anyone call him? Was there a subtext here that he wasn't picking up on?

'Sure I'm very interested,' Guggenheim told Caughell. 'Let me see how I can get there.'

Caughell seemed pleased. The detective slipped the next question in smoothly: 'Would you like me to tell NDS about this as well?' And the real question was: Are you up to this?

'Well if you would do me a favour, I'd appreciate it if you didn't mention it to NDS for a couple of days,' Guggenheim said.

This, too, was acceptable to the Outlaw Motorcycle Gang Section.

'Suzanne!' Guggenheim called, reaching for the airline time-table. And that's when life got tricky.

Suzanne worked the phones, rummaging through timetables as the minutes ticked over, trying to find some combination of commercial flights that would get him from Los Angeles to Edmonton that afternoon. But there was nothing that would get him there before Wednesday morning. The search had already eaten up two hours before Suzanne started to look at chartering a private jet.

The quote from Xtra Jet International came in at 3.40 p.m. They had a Westwind seven-seater that would cost $9500 for the three-and-a-half-hour trip to Edmonton (complimentary snacks and beverages on board), or a Hawker for $11,900 ... and the Westwind wasn't available. Guggenheim had 50 minutes to hustle to Van Nuys airport for a 4.30 p.m. take-off. Arrival time in Edmonton with the time zone change was 8.30 p.m. Easy. All he had to do was pull out the plastic to pay for it. Getting to the police raid in time? Priceless.

Guggenheim felt he was on the brink of finding the answer to his whodunnit mystery. It had haunted him since that day in November 1998 when Ray Kuhn at DirecTV told him the Nagra card might have been attacked. It was like chasing a phantom. The first major wave of piracy after the battery cards had been pirate cards based on an AVR chip. These were effective, but fairly crude devices. It was when the E3M card came out in April 1999 that Nagra knew its system had been comprehensively broken. The E stood for EchoStar, the 3M meant Three Musketeers—all for one and one for all—pirate slang for saying you got everything for nothing.

The E3M was an original EchoStar card that had been reprogrammed so that it opened up all EchoStar programming for free—once you had paid the pirates the upfront fee for the card, which was up to $500. By January 2001 there were more than 100,000 pirate cards, which meant the pirates had earned more than $30 million—and EchoStar had lost many times that much in forgone revenue. The E3M was a hot new pirate product and everyone wanted a piece of it, but nobody knew where they were coming from.

Guggenheim told himself, 'One thing's for sure, I know that I can buy a card that works. So I know that it exists.' Yet that didn't take him far, because Nagra in Switzerland had no black-hat team for reverse engineering. The pirate card was encrypted so that Nagra couldn't uncover how it worked, or how the pirates had managed to reprogram their original Nagra card. Instead, Guggenheim concentrated on who was selling the pirate cards.

The DR7.com site continued to publish information about the EchoStar hack, claiming to be 'just an information site, we don't sell anything'. DR7 was based in Edmonton and eventually Guggenheim's team discovered it was run by someone called Al Menard. There were three main dealers selling the E3M cards, two of them also in Edmonton, and the biggest was Discount Satellite run by Dave Dawson. The way it worked was that you subscribed for a month or so to EchoStar—long enough to get an EchoStar smartcard. You sent it to the pirate dealers with $400 to $500, and they would return the card to you, reprogrammed into an E3M. Welcome to the world of free television.

Guggenheim's private investigators began testing the dealers, sending in EchoStar cards to be reprogrammed, timing how long it took to get them back, then comparing the different cards. They made two startling discoveries. Each of the dealers claimed to have their own version of an EchoStar pirate card that was better than the others—but Nagra engineers studied the different cards and found that they were all the same. The same programming meant the same engineer behind the hack. The second thing was that none of the pirate dealers programmed the cards themselves. The cards were all sent off somewhere. But Guggenheim didn't know where.

That was as far as he had got. Despite his initial scepticism, he was becoming more and more suspicious—based on his conversations with informants, DirecTV execs and police officers—that NDS was involved in the piracy in some way. On 19 January 2000 Guggenheim had been in Washington briefing a high-powered security firm, Investigative Group International, 'to determine any connection or complicity of News Data Systems (NDS) with Discount Satellite of Edmonton, Alberta in the "hacking" of EchoStar Communications Corporation's DISH network . . .'

They had sent him a proposal on 31 January outlining proposed investigations in North America and Israel, with field operatives charging between $100 and $350 an hour. And the sad thing was, Guggenheim knew there was no way that he would get a green light from Nagra in Switzerland or EchoStar in Denver for the sort of budget that was needed. He was at an impasse. Two days later, Detective Caughell had phoned.

Police and Customs officers met Guggenheim at Edmonton airport and whisked him past immigration directly to the Discount Satellite premises.

'They saw a ton of electronic equipment, a ton of Bell ExpressVu and EchoStar set-top boxes and cards, as well as drugs and cash,' Guggenheim says. He spent several days helping police compile an inventory of what had been found. There were piles of fresh EchoStar cards that customers had sent in, cards bundled up ready to be sent on to be reprogrammed, cards that had come back reprogrammed as E3Ms, ready to be posted back to customers. And all the records . . . shipping records, money received and payments outgoing.

'They were doing hundreds of cards, and it was expensive at that time. They were going for hundreds of dollars per card. I think at the time it was already in the millions. It was big business.'

It was Guggenheim's first look inside a piracy business. It confirmed what he had already concluded, that the pirate cards were coming from somewhere close by. 'We knew for sure that they were not programming in the building.' But there was no address for the programmer. So where to now?

Somerset, 3 February 2000

Avigail Gutman flew into Heathrow at 11.10 a.m. on Flight 162 from Tel Aviv with the brisk assurance of someone used to setting matters right. Adams and his offsider Len Withall were there to meet her and they immediately set off on the three-hour trip to Somerset. Lee Gibling was ready for them as the car pulled up. The House of Ill Compute was having a security audit.

Gutman didn't have much time—she was booked to fly out of Gatwick at 8.05 the next morning and, she didn't know it yet, the overnight hotel booking had been mixed up. But what she was in Somerset for didn't take long. Indeed, it was just as she had feared.

When Ray Adams set up Lee Gibling with The House of Ill Compute website in 1998, he had done a deal to share costs with the rival Irdeto company. NDS paid about £5000 a month in costs and Irdeto kicked in £1500. This didn't give Irdeto much more than a trickle of information and a nice warm feeling. In fact by late 1999 Adams was instructing Gibling to tell the Irdeto people nothing, though that didn't stop him slipping them tidbits of information from time to time.

By now, The House of Ill Compute was recording 1.8 million hits each day and receiving up to 2000 emails from hackers all over the world, and was still growing. But Australian hackers had become suspicious that Gibling was leaking material to third parties, perhaps even to NDS. On 21 January Avigail Gutman reported that her Melbourne agent, George, had become frustrated at being refused access to the closed Area 51 section in the Australian section of The House of Ill Compute. So he and a friend had decided to hack into Thoic's Unix server to find out what Area 51 was all about. Hacking in proved ridiculously easy. As Gutman concluded: 'If George can do this—ANYONE can, including our competitors and other hackers.'

The Thoic website, the emails and the online forums were not secure. The House of Ill Compute was a public relations, and potentially a legal, disaster just waiting to happen. This would have to change. Fixing the security leak now became a matter of urgency. The first priority was to take Irdeto out of the picture entirely.

In response to the concerns Avigail had raised, Adams now made his play to stay in control of the plans for Gibling:

- Lee should be exclusive. He costs us about £50k a year at present.
- He will be a 'consultant' as against employee with a contract and NDA [non disclosure agreement].
- He will be paid £2500 (or less) a month as salary. Running costs will be on top of this.

He would pay his own tax and NDS would shell out for a health scheme and pension scheme. It's the detail that is telling here. NDS would later claim that Gibling was merely an inform-ant, an attempt to keep whatever he did at arm's length. But the details of his contract, the arrangements to control how The House of Ill Compute was run, and the monitoring of all forums and emails show that this was merely a charade intended to hide the fact that Thoic was a website funded, controlled and effectively run by NDS for its own benefit.

Adams and Avigail had become unlikely allies, but it was Avigail who had Reuven Hasak's ear. For her, the first step would be to install firewalls on the Thoic server in the United States, with NDS staff in Israel implementing new security measures. This would be an interim step before taking the entire operation in-house, setting it up on one of NDS's own servers ('having spoken to Reuven, we may do this in the home of a family member in Sweden').

NDS staff already read the private emails sent through the Thoic email accounts of users of the site. But the method of transferring the emails wasn't secure. The whole business of spying on emails needed to be automated.

There was another safety precaution required for Gibling and his wife, Vicky, whose baby was due 1 March. It wasn't the risk from suspicious Thoic users that Gutman was worried about, but rather NDS's competition: 'To avoid approach by competitors and their agents, the source and his family will relocate and be given untraceable phone numbers. (Relocation will take place by the end of April.)' Meanwhile NDS should think about setting up an alternative site as an eventual replacement. In a further email Gutman apologised that her action plan should have been sent encrypted, but for some reason the PGP encryption hadn't worked and it was sent in the clear.

Reuven Hasak was by now becoming concerned about what would happen if NDS's role was ever revealed. Gutman reported that he had ordered that Gibling be told 'he should not deal with the "mails" nor remail or notify us of their contents' until the new security was in place. He also recommended they start planning a new in-house piracy site.

An intense series of encrypted emails between Gutman, Hasak and Adams followed. Remarkably, Gutman's project appeared to go ahead as planned—the firewall, the software for copying Thoic files for NDS.

On 1 March, the date that Vicky's baby was due, the Giblings and The House of Ill Compute moved to a new address in Truro, Cornwall, in England's far south-west. It was a frantic time. By June, Vicky had left her husband and moved out with the children.

Heathrow, 29 February 2000

Sometimes all of Ray Adams' worlds seem to be colliding. He kept running as fast as he could, tic-tacking back and forth, running multiple operations and counter-operations. Most days he loved it. But not this morning.

Oliver had come over yesterday for presentations at News International. The meetings had dragged on until 10.30 the previous night. Food had been ordered, but it hadn't turned up. Adams had got home, only to be woken by the nursing home that looked after his father, who had been found wandering around looking for his mother.

Now Ray was at Heathrow farewelling Oliver on his flight to Germany before he took his own flight to Scotland. There he was with Oliver in the departure hall, feeling like yesterday's breakfast, when Oliver's mobile phone went off. It was Roger Kinsbourg. He wanted to set up a meeting for Oliver with the top people at Canal+, but he was very vague as to what it was about. In fact it was mysterious. He said he would call back later.

Adams went into overdrive. He had been expecting a move of some kind from Gilles Kaehlin at Canal+ since October, when he first heard of Jan Saggiori's report. Ray had been lulled into thinking his campaign to discredit Saggiori had worked.

On 3 February, the day after Alan Guggenheim made his dash to Edmonton, NDS's lawyers had filed the lawsuit in Montana against Canadian satellite dealers Ron Ereiser, Herb Huddleston and David Truthwaite; it also included three names that NDS never intended to proceed against—Plamen, Vesco and Jan Saggiori. Ereiser emailed a copy of the lawsuit to Jan on 21 February.

In Geneva, the Saggiori family had come to realise that they were under siege. The telephone would ring at odd hours—local calls— but the line would stay silent. One day in January the fax machine in Renato's office began printing off page after page. It was a detailed report on Jan compiled by a French private investigator in Calais. 'It was a strange fax, sent by "error", or perhaps a menace, something that seems to be a threat,' Renato says. That was when Jan realised just how far NDS was prepared to go to take him out.

Now it was 29 February 2000, eight days after Jan had received a copy of the lawsuit from Ereiser. Ray Adams, standing beside

Oliver in the Heathrow terminal, felt the ground move under his feet as he thought about what to tell his prize agent to say to Kinsbourg when he called back. All his instincts were on alert.

'Don't go anywhere to meet him,' Adams advised. 'Insist that he comes to your home. And make sure he tells you more about what this meeting is about.' He had much more to say, but Oliver's flight was being called—and he himself was headed for Scotland.

Kinsbourg gave Oliver time to get back home to Riedelberg. Then he called him again and suggested meeting in Strasbourg, or at Oliver's house. He told Oliver that Saggiori was working for Canal+ under a six-month contract, but had fallen out with Kaehlin. Hence the approach to Oliver. Listening to Oliver's account of the conversation, Adams convinced himself that Kaehlin now believed that Saggiori was playing a double game.

The meeting was set for two days' time, Thursday, 2 March. Adams would fly to Germany on the Wednesday night.

'Apart from being there to watch, and hopefully record the team from Canal+ I want to be there to watch Alex. I do not want him doing any deals with Canal+ . . . On Thursday I will be hidden in his side office from about 11am through to when the meeting finishes.'

Ray Adams, former Scotland Yard commander, hiding in the next room. 'I will probably switch my mobile telephone off,' he told Hasak. The man was a born sleuth, one of life's natural crouchers. And that's where I'd like to leave him for a moment: at the crouch, waiting for Roger Kinsbourg and Gilles Kaehlin to rattle up the drive on 2 March, in those minutes and hours with nothing to do, when his mind could not help but turn to the other operations he was running. With the Bulgarians, for starters.

Plamen Donev had not seemed to fully grasp the cunning ruse that Adams and Norris were playing on the Montana court. NDS was pretending to sue Plamen and Vesco in order to be able to mount their case against Jan Saggiori. But Plamen couldn't help worrying that NDS really was coming after him for millions of dollars. So Adams was organising for both Bulgarians to come to England for a reassuring pep talk.

He had to find a way to get visas to the terrible twins, as Norris called them, and then to get them signed up to new contracts (a hefty pay rise for Plamen) so as to convince them that the Montana court case was a sham. He also had to get them back to Bulgaria, so someone could serve the court papers on them. Norris in the United States had already made the position clear to their lawyer handling the case. 'The Bulgars actually are not going to be defendants (they are now our consultants).'

Then there was Avigail. Her pet hacker, Sydney-based Bond 007, was completely unaware of her efforts to groom him to hack the cards of NDS's opposition, but her efforts had certainly been successful. Bond was working on yet another way to hack Foxtel and Austar in Australia, this time by reprogramming pirate smart-cards from Europe. But his supply of cards to work from was running low. On 1 March she asked if Ray could provide twenty or 30 cards that she could feed to Bond (indirectly, naturally) to help him complete the Foxtel hack. 'The idea being, of course, to delay their attempts to tamper with our StarTV system.'

Sweet child. Adams' new name for her was the 'Pacific Pin-Up'.

Maidenhead, England, 4–6 March 2000

Ray Adams was back in England, trying to shake off the sinking feeling that had gripped him from the moment that Gilles Kaehlin and Roger Kinsbourg had shown up at Oliver's house in Riedelberg. Kaehlin had been driving Pierre Lescure's big Citroën and had clearly forged a close bond with the legendary Vivendi chief executive—he frequently borrowed his car and he customarily used Lescure's special elevator to avoid observation when he entered and left the glass-fronted Canal+ offices on Quai André Citroën.

'I have attached a report that I think you should send to Gilles,' Adams wrote to Oliver from England on Saturday, 4 March, two days later. 'He will probably try to play a little game.' It was very important that Oliver taped all phone calls from Gilles. 'You and I will need to listen to it together.' Ditto for Kinsbourg's conversations. Of course it would be a big mistake to believe anything that either of them said. 'Remember that there was no need for them to say all those bad things about me.'

Kinsbourg had told Oliver that Adams was just an investigator and a spent force, while Kaehlin was a major player at Canal+ with the ear of Pierre Lescure. 'To say that there are people at NDS who do not like me and want to get rid of me is a strange thing to say,' Adams told Oliver.

As for Gilles' promises to put Oliver in charge of stopping the piracy, Adams commented acidly: 'Are we seriously saying that a $65 billion company is going to hand this responsibility to you . . . I think not.'

Adams was most troubled by Kaehlin's claim that NDS was close to UK satellite dealer Joe Ibrahim, who had phoned Ray from Dubai the moment he learned that police had raided his business. 'The story he gave you is completely false. There has never been any communication between Joe Ibrahim with myself or any of my staff . . . How could they trace a call from Dubai? It is all a lie.'

Adams was somewhat less definitive on this matter in an email to John Norris and Chris Tarnovsky: 'There is a war going on between Canal+ head of security—Gilles Kaehlin—and myself . . . GK has bribed people in the UK to give him the calls list from my telephones and others that he suspects are in contact with me. He recently quoted one call giving an exact time.'

This was just the sort of stuff NDS had been accused of doing. Adams was outraged. He paused only to send out urgent queries to find out Jan Saggiori's date of birth in order to help the process servers locate him to serve the Montana lawsuit on him ('he will go ape shit about me when he gets that news') and to put Kroll private investigators on the trail of Saggiori's associate, Andy Kozlov, in Moscow. Then he went back to devising curly questions for Oliver to bowl up to Roger Kinsbourg.

Sofia Airport, 11 March 2000

Rozalina wasn't there. It was a little before 2 p.m. when Plamen Donev and Vesselin Nedeltchev walked off British Airways flight 2892 from London, with the sheath of documents ready to pass to her. They waited as the crowd thinned. And waited, and waited. Till they were the last there. But she didn't show. They needed to call Ray.

The trip had gone smoothly up to now. Plamen and Vesco had flown to London on Tuesday, 7 March. Ray had put them up at the Castle Hotel in Windsor, handy to the operational security office. John Norris had flown over to see them and was staying in the hotel as well, for a little personal bonding. It was imperative to reassure them that the Montana lawsuit was a sham, as far as they were concerned. It must have helped that they were both getting new contracts with NDS, which they signed on Friday, 10 March, with a 25 per cent pay rise for Plamen.

Of course, to a jaundiced eye, this might have the appearance of providing financial incentives to take part in a deception of the US District Court for the District of Montana, Butte Division, so it was important to keep these two things—the money and the court case—completely separate.

It remained only to have a third party serve the court papers on Plamen and Vesco. Adams had emailed his two friends at the Bulgarian anti-piracy agency, BullACT, on Wednesday, 8 March, to ask them to meet the two men on their return. While they both worked for him now, 'as part of an ongoing operation I need to officially serve papers on both of them denouncing them in a civil case in the USA'. Would BullACT please serve the court orders on them for him? 'I can tell you that the case will not proceed further than this.'

There was a little hiatus here. Rozalina, one of the BullACT lawyers, wrote back to Ray on the Friday but, in one of those wacky mix-ups, she mistakenly sent him a PGP-encrypted email about a Chinese cancer medicine. It was in Bulgarian, and the only words recognisable were the reference in the last line to a 'Tai-Sheng Capsule (a novel and highly potent immune-potentiator)', which seems to have the same meaning in English and Bulgarian.

It wasn't the response Ray had been banking on. He sent a series of increasingly urgent emails to BullACT through Friday night and Saturday morning, explaining that his two Bulgarians were arriving Saturday afternoon. 'Could you meet them. They have the papers with them and [will] explain what you must do.'

It didn't work. Rozalina emailed Ray on the Monday that his emails had come after working hours, and that she had been shocked when the two hackers she had been pursuing previously for Ray had called her from the airport: 'The last thing I want them to know is my home phone number. So I was very angry when I met them.'

The feeling was mutual. Six weeks later Adams was emailing Plamen about a name for his newborn daughter when he made the mistake of suggesting 'Rozalina', 'a very pretty Bulgarian girl I met with'.

Plamen replied: 'By the way—I met Rosalina. She's not a good lawyer—she's just a fortunate vicious bitch . . . She looks like a con, she talks as a con and she's probably tricking you . . . She's probably better as a spy.'

Not a meeting of minds, then. But now they had been served with the court papers.

Maidenhead, England, 7–13 March 2000

Ray Adams wasn't sure whether to be puzzled by Jan Saggiori's latest gambit, or to congratulate himself on reading him so well. It was always better to go with the latter. On 5 March he had emailed

John Norris and Chris Tarnovsky that Jan might try to contact Chris after hearing about the Montana lawsuit. So it was gratifying that two days later Adams received a reply from Norris: 'Contact!' Jan was behaving just as he had predicted.

'What do you make of his short message?' Adams asked Tarnovsky. In particular, there was something about Jan asking for Chris's help in hacking a Spanish system called Via Digital.

Chris had got what Jan was driving at, though he didn't spell it out for Adams. Via Digital was a Nagra system. Jan was asking Chris's help with a Nagra system because he knew he had worked on EchoStar. It went over the head of Adams, who was unaware of the spectacular downside to his clever little plan to add Jan to the Montana lawsuit.

When the shock had worn off—after Ron Ereiser sent him a copy of the lawsuit on 21 February, which showed Jan as a defend-ant—Saggiori had begun to think about the list of defendants. All he had done was give the name of a Bulgarian hacker to Chris. So why wasn't Chris's name on the lawsuit as well? In the piracy world, there could only be one explanation. Chris—his blood brother, the old friend who had visited him with his family just three months before, who had stayed in his family's home—was a spy who worked for NDS.

Back in March 1999, when Chris had emailed him the portion of the source code for the EchoStar card at address 2000, Jan had assumed that Chris must have obtained it from Al Menard at DR7, who had got it from Oliver. But if Chris was working for NDS all along, then he would not need to get any file from Menard—he would get it from NDS. That didn't really matter, the salient point was that an NDS employee had sent Jan part of the code for an NDS competitor. This was economic sabotage, and the March 1999 email Jan held was the smoking gun to prove it. That email from Chris had meant little to Jan up to this point. The Montana lawsuit changed all that, because it revealed Chris's relationship with NDS.

Jan's latest email to Chris mentioned some online claims from American chat rooms that Tarnovsky was linked to DirecTV piracy, which Tarnovsky batted away in a reply on 13 March. ('I guess I am a famous guy? Hehe who knows.') It was all nonsense.

Saggiori wrote back the same day, assuring him that after all these years he knew better than to listen to what others said. He veered back to asking for details on the Spanish Nagra card, and ended with a PS: 'Some sources in Canada are telling me that you are behind the Echostar hack in USA. Just be careful, we never know to whom these words can arrive . . .'

Edmonton, Alberta, 15–28 March 2000

Alan Guggenheim's investigation was nearing the home stretch. He was working with a small private investigation firm run by former FBI agent Tom Parker. Parker's team had put Dave Dawson's Discount Satellite operation in Edmonton under surveillance after the 2 February raid, as Dawson immediately went back into the piracy business. Guggenheim was working with Bell ExpressVu—Canadian courts were far more willing to act against piracy against Canadian companies than US broadcasters.

One of Parker's investigators began a friendship with a woman who worked at Discount Satellite. Her job was to walk the packages of fresh EchoStar cards to the house nearby where the reprogramming was done. It was Al Menard's home. She described it as being like a fortress, with closed-circuit cameras on all sides. But she didn't give the address.

One of the clearest pictures of how the reprogrammer worked was given in 2008, when a Toronto hacker, Tony Dionisi, testified that Menard had flown to Toronto in 2000 and reprogrammed 50 EchoStar cards for a Quebec pirate dealer for $150 apiece. Dionisi said Menard used a stand-alone programmer; it was a dark-blue or black plastic box, with dimensions fifteen centimetres by five centimetres by five centimetres: 'It also had four or five push buttons which he had pressed in a sequence before inserting the card into the loader . . . Whatever sequence was used determined first off which file would be loaded, as well as if it was pressed wrong, the box would not work at all.'

Dionisi testified that, a week later, Chris Tarnovsky had called him and bragged about this new device he had built: 'He said that this box had buttons on it. I am not sure of the number. I think it was four, five. And that, again, if you pressed it a certain way, it would load a certain file. If you pressed it the wrong way, it wouldn't load it at all; and that it was also a what they call stand-alone, which means you do not need a computer to operate it.'

Tarnovsky later testified that he had built a device called a Stinger to communicate with smartcards; but that it had never reprogrammed EchoStar cards, and that plans to make it a stand-alone device were never carried out.

But back in March 2000, Guggenheim was beginning to see the finishing line of his investigation. The next step, his lawyers told him, was to obtain what is called an Anton Piller order from the courts—this would allow him to execute a private search warrant on Al Menard's home without warning and to seize any evidence. But, to obtain such an order, he needed direct evidence that Menard was involved in piracy.

His most complicated operation was now planned. Parker's agents would send a batch of EchoStar and ExpressVu cards with carefully recorded serial numbers to Discount Satellite to be turned into E3Ms. A team of three investigators would track the woman employee as she left the store to walk the cards across to Menard's address. When she picked up the reprogrammed cards, they would have the evidence needed for a search warrant.

Nearly eight weeks had passed since the 2 February raid, but Guggenheim's investigators were now ready to swoop. The operation was planned for 29 March.

Edmonton, Alberta, 29 March 2000

Guggenheim's people were in place. They had submitted the EchoStar and ExpressVu cards to be reprogrammed. Now the three-man team was ready to track the courier when she made the delivery to Al Menard that afternoon. In California, all Guggenheim could do was wait by the phone.

The news came earlier than he expected. 'I get a call: "Big problem. NDS and DirecTV just launched a raid on Dave Dawson's place, and they just trampled our case completely."'

Just after noon that day, with Guggenheim's team poised to track down the mystery source of EchoStar piracy, DirecTV and NDS had decided to seize the business to enforce a judgement they had obtained against Dawson months before. On 9 February, a week after the raid Guggenheim had participated in, they had quietly secured a court order to take over the business. But why were they doing it now?

'And that's it—it's over. They have seized all the equipment, all the stuff,' Guggenheim tells me. Everything he had worked for had been brought to nothing, just at the moment when success was so close. At the time he had been despairing: 'That was a terrible blow. A terrible blow.'

Days later, Al Menard left Edmonton and moved to Vancouver. And Guggenheim went back to basics. He knew Al Menard was programming all of the EchoStar pirate cards. By mid 2000 Guggenheim's informants had told him that the engineer behind Menard was a hacker known as biggun. Chris Tarnovsky. He lived in Virginia, in a town called Manassas.

'To this day I have a hard time to believe that [the Dawson raid] was just coincidence, because it was so convenient,' he says. 'It pushed my case at least six months back. And probably prevented us from really getting the full benefit of finding out who was doing what, and getting to sue everybody at the time.

'I think it saved Al Menard and Chris, and maybe even NDS, from a big, big, big lawsuit at the time.'

April–August 2000

Summer 2000 was just a blur. A series of frenetic snapshots.

Snap. Oliver Kömmerling had been offered 10 million French francs to work for Canal+, developing its next smartcard. In Britain, Ray Adams organised crisis talks with NDS chief executive Abe Peled. As Ray informed Avigail: 'There is a lot of politics and lots of interesting developments. Main one being that Canal+ (SECA) are chasing Alex as if he is the last Virgin on earth.' As a counteroffer, they proposed setting up a British company for Oliver/Alex—ADSR Limited, 60 per cent owned by him, 40 per cent owned by NDS. Oliver would then have his own laboratory in England. Adams and Kaehlin continued to battle over every piece on the game board.

Snap. Saggiori was still in Adams' sights. In April he was contacted by a friend in England, who asked him for codes to pirate OnDigital. He said he hoped to get a consultancy with OnDigital, and having the code would help establish his credentials. What the friend didn't say was that he now worked for Ray Adams. Jan downloaded codes from an internet site for OnDigital for May, which would expire at the start of June. Adams immediately used the codes that Saggiori had provided to his friend to denounce him as a pirate to Gilles Kaehlin.

Snap. Alan Guggenheim had now made Chris Tarnovsky his major focus. It wasn't hard to find people in the Canadian piracy scene who had sent money to biggun in the days of his DirecTV piracy. The address in Manassas was owned by Chris's father, George Tarnovsky. Guggenheim was still working with a private investigator who had been involved in the failed Discount Satellite operation and who also did investigative work for NDS. He told Guggenheim that the Tarnovsky house in Manassas would be difficult to put under surveillance.

Snap. It was 7 June and John Norris was in high spirits. The four Canadian pirates he had been pursuing in the Montana case had agreed to a settlement. He saw it as a big win. Now it was time to wrap up the minor details. What to do about Saggiori, he asked Adams and Reuven Hasak: 'Just to recap, we included Jan in the lawsuit in hopes it would give you leverage to impact Jan's relationship with Nagra . . . We (NDS-US and DirecTV) have no case against Jan although the lawsuit certainly impacted him somewhat. I think the biggest impact was the concerns his family has on their good name. When and if you can use the lawsuit to your advantage do as you see fit.'

'Fantastic result,' Adams emailed back. 'Jan is still playing silly buggers. He calls us the "enemy". Yet I have recently put him in a corner. He is starting to realise that we are in charge.'

Later that day Adams emailed Plamen Donev with the news that the Canadians had agreed to settle. He told Plamen he would receive a small bonus for his work. Plamen wrote back in some confusion that he had not done any work, and therefore had to decline the bonus. It raises the obvious question—whether the bonus was for his work or rather a reward for taking part in the legal deception.

Snap. It's a summer evening in Paris and there is an awkward table setting at the Hotel Nikko, across the Seine from the Eiffel Tower. Ray Adams is sitting on one side of the table with his prize agent, Oliver. On the other side are Gilles Kaehlin and Jan. They're making nice. Adams has played it that his American colleague, John Norris, is set on dragging Jan through the courts; but Ray thinks he might be able to work something out for Kaehlin on this one, in the interests of inter-corporate relations. Think of it as a very small favour.

The atmosphere between Jan and Oliver is frosty. Roger Kinsbourg has previously insisted that Jan meets with Oliver and they make up and shake hands. The two men comply, but they're not going to be lifelong friends.

At the end of the meal there is a slight change of plan. Adams is not quite sure how Kaehlin managed it, but Gilles is guiding his very good friend Oliver across the road to the gleaming Canal+ headquarters. Naturally they will use Pierre Lescure's private elevator. There are one or two people and some things that Oliver might like to see. No?

The invitation does not extend to Ray. As he brushes past, Kaehlin glances in Ray's direction and whispers in Jan's ear: 'Keep him talking. I have people still searching his hotel room.' Adams had left his laptop and papers in his room, but Kaehlin never told Saggiori what information they extracted from them.

Sydney, August 2000

Avigail Gutman was fretting about David Cottle, the Sydney hacker who ran the Australian board for The House of Ill Compute, unaware that it was an NDS front, or that he was being manipulated. Cottle had broken no laws; indeed, although he was useful to her, Gutman had a fine contempt for his hacking skills—in fact of any Australian hacker. But what about the European hackers that he was in touch with, she wondered to Ray Adams in January 2000. Ray was the very man to handle a problem like this.

'Getting his itemised telephone billing would tell us who he is in contact with abroad. Do you have resources to do that?' Adams emailed Gutman.

Now there was a thing. Technically that kind of stuff was *illegal* in Australia, Gutman told Adams delicately from her home in

Taiwan. Accessing private telephone records was illegal in Britain as well, but Adams seemed to manage it nevertheless. Two months before, he had obtained two months of phone records for 'Bill', the codename that NDS used for Canadian pirate Marty Mullen. Adams had told Norris that he would have his agent obtain a third month's records as well.

Ray certainly had a 'Can Do' outlook, which perhaps explains why Avigail in August 2000 confided once more in Adams her need to find out who David Cottle was talking to. This was not driven by her concern to monitor Cottle's Australian contacts, who were hacking Foxtel and Austar. Nor was it to find leads to the European hackers that Cottle shared files with. The issue that triggered Avigail's new approach to Ray was her fear that he might now be working with NDS's competitor, Irdeto, which Avigail was working so hard to displace from Foxtel and Austar.

Adams appeared to enjoy close relationships with law enforcement officers around the world. In January 2000, when he had been worried that Kaehlin would be checking Oliver's phone records, Ray had been able to assure Hasak: 'My friend in Deutsch Telekom will keep me informed.' In July 2001, when Mullen had a family vacation in Scotland, Adams was able to admonish Norris for not giving him enough advance notice: 'so I could not prime the Police at the airport to identify MM for us. If we had done that we would have known the car hire company that he was using and tracked him that way. Many UK hire company cars have built in trackers to prevent theft and we can access that system.'

How did Ray come to enjoy such remarkable access? Certainly he could draw upon personal contacts he had built up in his years at the Metropolitan Police. In addition he regularly conducted joint operations with local police. But questions would also be raised about a line entry in the NDS Operational Security budget for the United Kingdom.

Ray's deputy, Len Withall, a former Surrey police officer, explained it this way to NDS's accounts department in June 2000: 'In our budget under code 880110 there is an amount of money set aside for payment to Police/Informants for assistance given to us in our work.' Withall asked for a cheque for £2000 to be made out to Surrey Police. NDS later described it as a one-off charitable donation.

NDS ledgers and budget papers show that from June 1999 to December 2001, total payments from 880110 came to £15,023. That includes the £2000 cheque to Surrey Police. The rest of the money paid through what Withall and Adams variously describe as the 'Police/Informants Fund', the 'Police Informants fund', or a fund for informants was a series of cash payments to unlisted third parties. NDS vehemently denies making any payments to police officers beyond the cheque to Surrey Police.

Subsequent emails between Gutman and Adams on the matter of David Cottle were encrypted, so it's not clear whether Adams succeeded in obtaining Cottle's telephone records. But Gutman made no further requests for help tracking down Cottle's contacts.

San Marcos, Texas, 29–31 August 2000

Bennie started barking at the same parcel that the other drug dog, Xaduc, had identified moments earlier. Detective Mark Cumberland exchanged a glance with Ben Mewis, the manager of the Mail & More postal centre who had called him earlier. This was more like it. A positive reaction by two narcotic detection canines gave him probable cause—at least enough for a warrant to search the parcel. And then he would see what the man who had rented the postbox, Christopher George Tarnovsky—at least, that was the name on his driving licence—had to say for himself.

It was a mystery that had been gnawing at Mewis for a month now. San Marcos is a quiet Texan town midway between Austin and San Antonio. On 29 July a stranger—long brown hair, in his late twenties—had walked into the Mail & More office wanting to hire a mailbox. Chris Tarnovsky had a California driver's licence, but explained that he was a student at Southwest Texas State University. He was going home, and wanted to have his mail redirected. Any mail that came in was to be forwarded immediately via express mail to his home in San Marcos, California. He paid in advance, left his billing details and was gone.

Then the parcels started arriving. Large parcels, with electronic gear of all sorts inside, from all over, but particularly from Canada, addressed to CT Electronics at the Mail & More address. Mewis's staff duly forwarded the packages to California, but it didn't make sense. And then, on Tuesday, 29 August, a smaller parcel arrived. It had been sent from the town of Luling, 40 kilometres south down the San Marcos highway. Something about this particular parcel rang alarm bells for Mewis. He called Cumberland at the Hays County Narcotics Task Force and told him he was getting some suspicious packages.

'It doesn't make sense,' Mewis told Cumberland. 'He's receiving packages from all over and then having them directly turned around and mailed to a location in San Marcos [California] at a cost to himself. There is really no reason to have them sent to San Marcos, Texas, first.' Mewis told Cumberland he had been getting a package like this every day or every other day. It was costing Tarnovsky a fortune to have them forwarded to California.

Cumberland looked at the parcel from Luling that had triggered Mewis's call. The sender was someone called 'Von'. The southwest of Texas is not such a big place. It took Cumberland less than five minutes to discover that the sender's address in Luling didn't exist. And Southwest Texas State University had no record of a student called Christopher Tarnovsky. Cumberland and his partner, Sergeant Chase Stapp, called in the dog squad. But the dogs found nothing. They sniffed at the package, but it came up clean. Cumberland and Stapp left, asking Mewis to call them if another parcel came in for Tarnovsky.

Mewis phoned the next morning. Another package, this one larger, from 'Regency Audio' in Vancouver, addressed to CT Electronics, with a JVC CD player inside. This time the drug dogs responded to the presence of marijuana or other drugs.

Just after six that evening, Cumberland had his warrant and was opening the parcel. He took the CD player out of the box and unscrewed the top. 'Inside we located a brown envelope that was taped to the wires inside, and it contained money,' Cumberland testified in 2008. The CD player held US$20,100.

The next day there was another parcel from Regency Audio to CT Electronics. This one was a DVD player. Again the drug dog responded to the presence of narcotics. And again Cumberland obtained a search warrant. He took out the DVD player.

'When we took it apart, inside it was the exact same thing, same type of envelope taped to the circuitry the same way,' he said. This time it was $20,000.

Cumberland had a suspected money-laundering case, but following the leads would go way beyond the resources of Hays County. He turned the $40,100 over to the district attorney's office and referred the case to the Drug Enforcement Agency in Austin. From there the case was transferred to DEA Special Agent Nick Beretta. By late September Beretta had twice gone through Tarnovsky's rubbish bins in California and obtained his telephone records. He noted Tarnovsky had made 80 phone calls to Israel and 120 calls to Belgium. US Customs records showed he travelled overseas every three months.

Cumberland informed Tarnovsky about the two parcels that had been impounded (he was legally obliged to do so by 29 September). Tarnvosky then went to a lawyer in California for advice and told police in Hays County he had no knowledge of the money and disavowed any claim over it—Hays County could keep the

US$40,100. Later Tarnovsky told police that the mailbox had been set up by his brother-in-law, surname Bernie. But there were no records of a student called Bernie at Southwest State either. By October Tarnovsky clearly knew he was under investigation. But he didn't tell John Norris about it.

In the 2008 EchoStar trial, a string of text emails and online chat records were tendered as exhibits. They referred to 'Von'. In each case, Tarnovsky testified that the emails were fabricated, or that someone else had logged in to online chats using his Von persona.

In a September 1999 online chatroom 'Von' posted about an EchoStar hack: 'Yes, all you buttmunches bow down to me and send me your worldly possessions. I will lead you to the promised land at $350 a head. I'm the only person who knows how to hack Nagra's cards.'

EchoStar claimed that Tarnovsky had provided Menard with a programmer for EchoStar cards. In October 1999, Menard emailed Dave Dawson at Discount Electronics: 'I called von the phone and mentioned the problem . . . he told me that he is sending another box and we should have it this week . . . he's happy . . . thinks i killed this one from overuse hehe.' On 1 March 2000 Menard emailed Dawson: 'get some koin together I gotta ship to von this week.'

Tarnovsky set up the mailbox in Texas at a time when Alan Guggenheim's investigators were focusing on his Manassas address. Tarnovsky's mother lived in Luling, Texas, and he drove there from California to sell her his 1996 Pontiac on 16 August. So what was the mysterious parcel from Von in Luling that set the whole investigation off? Tarnovsky could have sent it for any number of reasons, but the simplest explanation is probably that he was just testing the system. With that much money flowing through the mailbox—particularly if there were any hiccups in the stream of parcels—it would only be natural to want to test the process yourself. It's the work of a single moment of paranoia, but it was enough to bring the entire scheme unstuck.

Tarnovsky has always denied any connection with the two parcels the police seized and says the string of other large packages posted to the Texas mailbox held no money. He accuses his former associate, Ron Ereiser, of planting the money in the parcels and then arranging for a confederate to give the police an anonymous tip-off. But that doesn't seem to fit the events.

It would be another year before police checked the DVD player and the CD player for fingerprints. These were then sent to the US Embassy liaison in Ottawa, then passed to the RCMP fingerprint database. It came back with a match: Mervyn Main, born 1969, with a record of petty crime and drug dealing from ten years before. He worked for Al Menard. Later Menard would describe him as a longtime friend who helped run the DR7 website and drove Menard around after he had surgery. This hardly looks like someone framing Tarnovsky. What it looks like is that Menard was secretly sending Tarnovsky large sums of money, apparently almost on a daily basis, as payment for the EchoStar reprogrammer.

By December 2000 the EchoStar piracy ring based on Al Menard was under pressure from all sides. EchoStar and Nagra had dramatically increased the number of electronic counter measures to kill the pirate cards. It was easy enough for the dealers to fix the dead cards, but the sheer volume of cards to fix and the number of ECMs was defeating them. At this point reprogramming boxes appeared for sale in piracy circles. Other dealers could now reprogram pirate cards. Guggenheim obtained one of the reprogrammers, which finally revealed how the pirate hack worked.

Other pirate groups were now muscling in on the action. Software was available on the web to reprogram an old DirecTV P1 card into a pirate EchoStar card. Tarnovsky showed Norris how it was done one day in November. Norris described it in an email to Ray Adams—something he would later regret.

By December the DEA had passed the Tarnovsky money-laundering case to US Customs, which was working with DirecTV investigators, who believed Tarnovsky was producing pirate DirecTV cards.

At 3.26 a.m. on 24 December, someone called 'Nipper2000' published the full EchoStar ROM code on a website called pirates-den.com. From this point on, all of the secrets of the EchoStar card were in plain view. Game over. Anyone with a minimum of technical skill could pirate the system. Tarnvosky was in Belgium with his in-laws at the time. He emailed Norris to tell him of the posting, with the subject line, 'Cat's out of the bag'.

Kazanluk, Bulgaria, 24 January 2001

Dani Ratner, NDS's chief security officer in charge of electronic counter measures, had it in his mind to do a kindness. He was writing indirectly via Ray Adams to Plamen Donev, the NDS agent he knew only as Pluto, to say thank you. He was sure that Pluto had heard of 'Black Sunday' three days before, when DirecTV had broadcast an ECM at the start of the NFL Superbowl game. It had killed off more than 200,000 DirecTV pirate cards.

'Guess how we actually kill them? Yes, you are right!!!!! We used your ideas,' Ratner wrote. It was the ECM that Plamen had devised in October 1999, the one that NDS had decided not to use because of the 'politics' of the situation with DirecTV. Fifteen months later NDS was finally using Plamen's technique. The delay—allowing more than 200,000 people to watch DirecTV illegally rather than paying subscriptions fees—had cost DirecTV up to $90 million in forgone revenue. And it had taken this revenue hit at a time when General Motors was readying DirecTV for sale, setting a price range for what by January 2001 was the only serious bidder . . . News Corporation.

Just over two weeks later, on 6 February, Rupert Murdoch would address the General Motors board, which would approve the beginning of a due diligence procedure to sell its stake in DirecTV's parent company, Hughes Corporation, to Murdoch's new satellite holding company, Sky Global. DirecTV executives were not overjoyed by this development—on 20 February Hughes chairman Mike Smith would walk out of a meeting with Murdoch. But back on 24 January, Ratner was keen to assure Plamen that those who knew he had been the chief architect of the Black Sunday ECM (and obviously NDS had ensured this was a very small group) praised his work and thanked him 'for the wonderful idea that make all of us happy and the pirate cardholders frustrated'.

Plamen's reply, when Adams passed the message on, seemed a little distracted. A few days before he had made the local paper, which had reported that, in the early hours of 16 January, 'an enraged drunk hacker' had been involved in an altercation and scuffle in a bar at the Hotel Palas, Kazanluk, with a DJ called Lyubomir. After bar staff separated the two men 'Plamen took out his gun Beretta and began firing at random in the bar,' the paper reported. One shot caught Lyubomir in the leg.

This would not be a good year for Plamen Donev. He had already written to his friend Ray about the difficulties having a newborn baby placed on his sleep and his work, and problems about building a house. By May his marriage was breaking up, he wrote: 'It is THE HELL here. My wife is a real garbage. I'm trying to get a divorce. She is trying to destroy me.'

San Marcos, California, 9 February 2001

Chris Tarnovsky was ready to head out when the knock came on the door of his bungalow on Poppy Road. Three men in suits were waiting outside. Two of them introduced themselves as Customs agents out of the San Diego office. The third man he knew—Ruben Romero, head of security operations for DirecTV Latin

America. They wanted to come in and talk about packages of money sent to Texas.

DirecTV security had been working with Customs for months investigating Tarnovsky, whom they suspected of being involved in DirecTV piracy. Customs was also investigating money laundering. Romero had come along to provide technical expertise. But this was not a raid; it was what they called a 'Knock and Talk'.

By this stage the agents were inside. Romero later claimed to have seen a card emulator, for reprogramming access cards, in the house. Tarnovsky told them he would talk with them later, but that he had to leave. His wife was about to have a surgical procedure.

Chris believed the whole operation was contrived by EchoStar, who had heard that he worked for NDS, but he appears to have been mistaken. Guggenheim and EchoStar had not heard of his Texas mailbox, and at that point had no idea he was a full-time NDS employee. The satellite piracy allegations came from DirecTV.

Eventually the three men left, after Tarnovsky promised to speak with them that afternoon. He immediately hit the phone. Norris was in Hawaii, but he soon got the ball rolling. When the Customs agents returned, Tarnovsky was with an NDS lawyer, who told them that Chris was an NDS employee, that all the equipment in his home that was connected to satellite piracy belonged to NDS, and officials were not to question him or search his home without a warrant and without NDS's counsel being present.

Norris was on the first plane back from Hawaii. Reuven Hasak was on his way from Israel. They joined NDS's lawyer Rick Stone at a meeting at the US Attorney's office in San Diego, where Tarnovsky was not present. Assistant US Attorney Richard Chang told them about the US$40,100 in the packages in the Texas mail centre the previous year. It was the first Norris had heard of it. Even so, NDS fought off any request to look at Tarnovsky's computers. They cited legal issues over the Customs agents' visit to his house on 9 February. Later, after EchoStar finally heard about the incident, NDS lawyers made a pre-emptive strike, going before the federal magistrate in San Diego to seek orders to bar any issue of a search warrant on Tarnovsky's house and to have court records related to it sealed.

'I was pretty upset,' Norris testified in 2008. Why hadn't Chris told him about money in the parcels? 'He said he was afraid. He was afraid of me.'

Norris considered firing Tarnovsky. Faced with allegations of drug abuse, Norris sent him to Scripps Hospital in San Diego for a blood test, which found no indication of drug use. DirecTV was now demanding that Tarnovsky have no contact at all with the next generation of cards that NDS was preparing for them.

On 16 February Norris administered a lie-detector test to Tarnovsky. He was only asked two questions: Since you have been hired by NDS, have you ever sold modified NDS Smart Cards? Secondly, since you have been hired by NDS, have you ever sold any NDS Smart Card secrets?

Tarnovsky wasn't asked about the money in the Texas mail account, or about his involvement in EchoStar piracy—or any of the string of other questions his behaviour gave rise to.

Tarnovsky had told Norris that someone—perhaps Ron Ereiser—had sent the packages to frame him. At this point there was no proof as to who had sent the packages from Vancouver. Hays County police would not lift the fingerprints on the CD and DVD players that would lead to Al Menard's offsider, Mervyn Main, until August 2001.

'I believed what he said—that he didn't expect or know who the money was sent from,' Norris later testified. 'It was plausible. It was believable.'

Vancouver, 8 March 2001

The hotel door opened and Alan Guggenheim found himself facing the man he had been pursuing for more than two years.

Al Menard walked gingerly into the room. Ron Ereiser made the introductions. Ereiser, who was in Vancouver between flights, had arranged to meet Menard at this hotel. Once there, Ereiser had invited Menard to meet Guggenheim in the room next door. Later Menard would claim it was an ambush, but he made no complaint at the time.

EchoStar had been a jump behind the NDS moves all along. Going into this meeting, Guggenheim had the disadvantage that he really had little to offer Menard as an inducement to come clean. Neither EchoStar on the one hand, nor Nagra on the other, would pony up any cash inducement to get Menard to change sides. They didn't operate like that. All that Guggenheim could do was to promise Menard that Nagra and EchoStar would not sue him if he could show NDS was behind the EchoStar piracy.

'For almost two years you were the only guy in the world who could do an EchoStar card,' Guggenheim told Menard. 'And, when you look at the history of satellite or cable television, that never happened before—never something lasted that long being in one guy's hands.'

Menard operated at pirates' speed, which was about five times as fast as the lawyers and regulators who were chasing him. Menard was *negotiating*, but he was up against someone who had been denied anything to negotiate with. In short order he told Guggenheim that he had never known or heard that NDS was behind the hack; that perhaps the hack was based on an internal leak from Nagra. If he testified for EchoStar, would that stop the Customs investigation of him?

'So how can your corporation protect me from that stuff?' he asked.

Any kind of deal for protection would have to be worked out with his lawyer. But 'Chris wasn't working for NDS a couple of years ago [when the EchoStar piracy began], I know that,' Menard said. 'I have a hard time believing NDS gave him the codes.'

'Did Chris give you the first programming box?' Guggenheim asked.

'Well I don't know about that,' Menard replied, and laughed. 'We'd better talk to my lawyer about stuff like that.'

Menard circled and circled, hinting at what he knew but then withdrawing, denying any knowledge while at the same time suggesting what it might take to make him testify.

'I'm still worried about things coming to me after this . . . Sounds like I'd be getting charged.' And then there was the issue of what NDS might do. 'I don't need lawsuits for 16 million shit.'

He wasn't going to testify against Tarnovsky. 'I don't think Chris should be arrested for anything. But if he's an employee of NDS, I'm not aware of it.'

Then he asked why didn't EchoStar hire Chris. 'I think if you ever offered him a regular job, he wouldn't turn it down . . . He's a smart guy obviously. I think it would be in your best interests to snap up something like that right away.'

It wasn't just a job for Chris that Menard seemed to be angling for.

'I don't know how I can help you guys without involving myself. And what . . . Are you guys gonna hire me? Then maybe I'd think about it. If I got a job from you guys, doing something on the Net? Sure I'd be open to an offer . . . I'd like a legit job. I've got my website, but I'd like to work for another one.'

He said he had to talk to his lawyer. It was a Thursday—he would try to be back to them by Sunday. Then Al Menard walked out. And that was the last they saw of him.

Days later Guggenheim was talking to Ray Adams on the phone, and Adams was describing with amusement the conversation Guggenheim had had with Menard in the hotel room. Adams had so much detail that Guggenheim concluded that NDS had somehow found a way to tape the conversation. Or that Menard himself was wired.

Zurich, March 2001

The Montana case against the Canadian pirates had had some hiccups, but was about to be settled. Adams was now under tight pressure to force some sort of concession out of Jan Saggiori. Norris had kept putting the responsibility back on him for bringing the action on Saggiori: 'We named Jan only to accommodate your efforts to make his life difficult and to give you leverage.'

On 16 November Adams told Norris, 'It is all window dressing to continue the action we have taken against him so far,' but he was afraid that unless Jan could be induced to sign 'some sort of document it will look as if he has won'.

Two days later he wrote to Saggiori: 'We have just over a week. The US lawyers are withdrawing the case against those who have signed the same agreement as I sent you . . . We could be faced with the position where you are the only one left and the rest of them give evidence against you. Please hurry.'

The plan against Saggiori had worked out well, he told Norris in March 2001, but now they must avoid any embarrassment in settling the case. Adams wrote to Saggiori: 'I intervened on your behalf because Gilles asked me to help you and to stop the case. At the same time I asked for nothing in return.'

Faced with the unlimited legal resources of one of the world's largest media companies, Saggiori signed an undertaking not to reverse engineer NDS products, while denying the allegations in the lawsuit.

Cornwall, April 2001

Lee Gibling's cover was blown. The House of Ill Compute was no more. Gibling's last email to Adams was 25 April. Shortly after-wards, reports of Lee's links to NDS appeared on the Modshack website, with copies of emails between Lee and Len Withall. Someone had obtained a copy of Gibling's hard drive, including

10,000 emails. The news was greeted with total shock in European and Australian hacking circles. And then the mood turned ugly. Adams' team was already in damage control.

'Mr Len Withall, who was Number Two, came to my house and we sledgehammered all the hard drives and everything else on computers,' Gibling would tell the BBC *Panorama* program a decade later. The records were destroyed, the paperwork carried way or shredded. At the end of the day there was no indication that The House of Ill Compute had ever operated in Lee's Cornwall home. Lee was gone as well. He was in the middle of a divorce and custody battle, but now had to go into hiding. By July, Withall was withdrawing £2000 in cash on the twentieth of every month for Gibling's support.

Recruitment, Summer–Fall 2001

Gilles Kaehlin had not given up on his attempts to win Oliver for Canal+. His first approach in early 2000 had galvanised Ray Adams and NDS chief Abe Peled to make a counteroffer. By September 2000, Kaehlin had come back with a new proposal. Canal+ would pay three million euros for a 20 per cent stake in Oliver's company, and would pay one million euros a year in fees to it for consultation work. Oliver would also receive between $1 million and $2 million stock options when Canal+ Technologies floated.

Oliver was asking for £500,000 a year for the first two years from NDS. Hasak and Peled came back with a package that was more like £300,000. But NDS would pay for the new UK lab at Maidenhead for him. Clearly it would need a chemical handling facility as well as a clean room; there would be the £600,000 Schlumberger focused ion beam, the £420,000 field emissions scanning microscope, the £220,000 scanning probe microscope, the £140,000 reactive ion etcher ... the list went on and on. Peled wrote a cheque for £2.8 million. That gave NDS 40 per cent of ADSR, with nothing for Canal+. Oliver held the other 60 per cent for no cash payment.

In June 2001, Oliver had dinner with Peled in London. At an earlier dinner, back in December 1999, Oliver had told him about the DR7 posting—that the SECA file had the same time stamp as the file produced by the NDS black-hat team in Haifa. When Kömmerling had dinner with Peled in July 2001, he told him that Tarnovsky had admitted to him that he had posted the SECA code on the DR7 website. 'He told me that they had a big fight, and they were both extremely drunk when they had that conversation,' Peled testified in 2008.

Probably part of the reason Peled was socialising with Oliver was to keep Canal+ from poaching him. Because, at the end of the ADSR incorporation process, Oliver had insisted that he be able to work part-time for other clients, including Canal+.

Meanwhile Gilles Kaehlin was never one to pussyfoot around when he wanted information. Where had the piracy come from? Who put the Canal+ codes on DR7?

'Many times, he push me with lots of questions,' Oliver says. 'And in this moment I didn't answer to him, I didn't lie to him . . . I said to him, "I cannot discuss it".'

Then in late July, Kaehlin asked to talk to Chris. Oliver phoned Adams in a panic. Ray Adams called Peled, who was on vacation in Ireland, and told him to phone Oliver urgently. It turned out to be a brief exchange.

'What he [Oliver] told me in that conversation was that Canal+ now know that it is Christopher Tarnovsky that posted the [SECA] code on the Internet, and they're looking for him, and I should hide him,' Peled testified.

'That's a completely preposterous suggestion,' he told Oliver. 'We have nothing to hide.'

Oliver went back to Ray. 'Maybe it's better we have a meeting in the UK so I can be present.'

So there Oliver, Gilles and Chris were on 14 August, sitting down to eat at Trader Vic's at the Hilton on Park Lane in London.

And then a funny thing happened that Oliver hadn't anticipated. Gilles and Chris spoke in rapid French for more than half an hour—leaving Oliver, who grew up on the French border but couldn't speak French, completely out of the loop. 'When we left, Gilles has a smiley face.'

So it was Tarnovsky who spilled the beans, in Oliver's account. But it's curious that, when I asked Roger Kinsbourg and his partner Elena Collongues-Popova in 2010 which language they spoke in with Oliver, they said French. When I went back to Kinsbourg in 2012, he said Oliver spoke 'a little French'.

Years later I asked Chris if he had any idea that Oliver would do a deal with Canal+ to testify.

'Uh . . . yeah, I knew he was going with them, I knew he was going with them, because he was trying to get me to go with him. He thought that I was on board. He was probably telling Gilles like, "No problem, we got him. He'll work with us" . . . So I knew it.'

Kaehlin says in his affidavit that at the London meeting he asked Tarnovsky if he knew anything about the publication of the Canal+ codes on DR7 in March 1999. Tarnovsky told him he had lots of information about this but he did not know Kaehlin well enough to tell him more. He was tired of working for NDS and would consider collaborating with Canal+. They agreed to meet again near Tarnovsky's home in California.

At the time, Tarnovsky was chafing over the restrictions that had been placed upon him in the aftermath of the Customs visit. DirecTV had insisted that Tarnovsky be blocked from any access to their cards. That ban was reinforced two weeks later, 28 August, at a high-level meeting in News Corporation's head office in New York. Norris, Hasak and News Corp deputy counsel Genie Gavenchak had a difficult meeting with DirecTV executives, who made it clear that the ongoing San Diego investigation of Tarnovsky was still a major issue. They hated the whole idea of recruiting pirates and giving them sensitive information. Tarnovsky's future was on the line, it seemed.

The September 11 World Trade Center tragedy fell two weeks later. EchoStar's Charlie Ergen had been due to meet with General Motors to discuss a rival bid for DirecTV, but the ban on air travel at that time meant it had to be postponed. Meanwhile, on the other side of the Atlantic, on 26 September, the chief executive of Canal+ Technologies, François Carayol, found himself at a conference in London sitting next to Abe Peled on a panel about the future of interactive television. Peled took him aside briefly after the session and suggested they discuss merging Canal+ Technologies with NDS. Just food for thought. Carayol soon heard that investment bankers for News Corp had approached Canal+'s parent, Vivendi Universal, about the deal.

Oliver had heard of the proposal when he had dinner with Peled again at Trader Vic's at the end of September.

'The dinner was about his concern that Canal+ want to buy NDS, destroy NDS, and what will happen to our joint venture,' Peled said. 'He told me that Chris Tarnovsky posted EchoStar code as well. Nothing more than piracy.'

This was now the fifth time that Abe Peled had been told by senior people within his company that NDS was responsible for leaking Canal+ codes (and now EchoStar codes as well), and that Canal+ was investigating. Oliver had told him about the leak in December 1999; days later Ray Adams told him that Canal+ was trying to prove that NDS was responsible for the leak—and Reuven Hasak had rebuked Adams for telling Peled about it. Kömmerling, who had the status of a vice-president within NDS, had told Peled that Tarnovsky had confessed to putting the Canal+ codes on the DR7 site in July 2000, in August and now September. Peled had discussed the allegations with Hasak, but on each occasion had decided to take no action to investigate.

Gilles Kaehlin had no such reticence. Just over a week later, on 5 October, Kaehlin was in Carlsbad, California, 30 kilometres from Tarnovsky's home, ready to do a deal with him to testify:

'Chris told me that he realised it would be extremely difficult for him to leave NDS, because he was afraid of certain NDS employees. But he didn't want to tell me more.'

And that's when Gilles suggested the secret handshake. He said he suggested 'a nonverbal method of communication, with which we were both familiar'. It was the same handshake, with the middle finger drawn back into the palm, that Oliver had used to signal secretly to Ray Adams in their first meeting in 1996 to confirm he had done the Sky 10 hack. Kaehlin in his affidavit said that Tarnovsky used this signal to confirm that NDS was responsible for the SECA code appearing on DR7. 'He also stated to me that the code had been sent to him by Reuven Hasak via John Norris by email for it to be published on the Internet.'

Maidenhead, England, October 2001

Ray Adams was beginning to think he was getting too old for this. He had played with the idea of retirement. He had had a little ultimatum from his friend, Sam, at British Telecom. He had had to tell her that he never meant to hurt her, but there was never any prospect he would leave his wife.

Jan Saggiori continued to frustrate him. In late October 2001 Adams wrote to him: 'I am disappointed in you. You are playing games and I do not know why... You have called me a lot of names, Gestapo etc. All I have ever said about you is the truth. Above all I stopped a prosecution case against you. Now you hint that you will be in one against NDS.'

But Adams had come perilously close to connecting the dots. On 23 October he wrote to Norris that ITV Digital were telling police that the codes for their service were posted on The House of Ill Compute, having been provided by the US hacker of SECA. They were trying to make the link to Tarnovsky. Adams wrote to Norris on 1 November that Saggiori, who was now working for Canal+, was saying some strange things about Chris, almost as if he had been in touch with him. Norris brushed off Adams' concern, preferring to major on how much more on the ball he was than Alan Guggenheim: 'Poor Guggenheim apparently does not have a clue.'

London, December 2001

Kaehlin flew back to Europe, confident that he could find a way to get Tarnovsky talking. He had carved his way through the Canadian pirate scene with an open chequebook. Besides a string of North American informants, he had relationships with pirate dealers across Europe. Two European dealers in particular had agreed to testify for Canal+, after insisting on some form of witness protection program. Kaehlin had briefed François Carayol on the investigation, as well as Canal+ chief Pierre Lescure.

Rupert Murdoch meanwhile had experienced an unexpected setback in his quest to buy DirecTV. While he had been sure the deal was in the bag, on 29 October General Motors agreed instead to accept a last-minute offer from Charlie Ergen at EchoStar. Murdoch was personally devastated. But the implications for NDS were more serious. Ergen would definitely replace NDS as the conditional access system for DirecTV, which would cut NDS's sales in half. It was the old nightmare, which added a new dimension of stress to the exchanges that would follow.

The stories about News Corporation angling to buy Canal+ Technologies had continued. François Carayol now decided to go on to the front foot. He reached out to Peled to set up a meeting for 12 December in Peled's London office, without telling him what it was about. Carayol walked in with Kaehlin and their California litigation lawyer, James DiBoise. Before they could talk about a merger, Carayol said, they needed to resolve the matter of NDS pirating Canal+. DiBoise had a diagram to show how the NDS scheme worked—in fact a whole presentation showing how the black-hat team had reverse engineered the Canal+ SECA card, then passed the source code to Hasak, who passed it to Norris, who gave it to Tarnovsky, who passed it to Al Menard at DR7.

Peled couldn't really have been surprised by DiBoise's claims, but he rejected them as completely untrue: 'We do not condone or engage in such actions.' He was, however, still interested in a merger with Canal+ Technologies if he could have a word with Carayol alone. In private, Carayol told him the merger talks could not proceed until they resolved NDS's industrial espionage.

'Mr Peled claimed not to know what we were talking about,' Carayol said later. 'But he said he would commence an investigation and get back to me with the results.'

Four days later, 16 December, Kaehlin was in Santa Monica to meet with Tarnovsky. Chris had been tempted by Kaehlin's proposal, but he was only now realising there were strings attached.

'Gilles is promising $2 million for lab equipment, $300,000 a year, and I'm like, "Great". And then all of a sudden, "If we employ you, you're going to go to Paris. We'll buy the equipment, but it's going to be in Paris." You know? That's really what he was getting to.' But Chris and Sylvie liked California. They liked the sun.

Financial security had always been an issue for Chris. He was under investigation by US Customs, the District Attorney's office and police in Texas; his position at NDS seemed to be under threat and DirecTV had cut off his access to their cards. The walls seemed to be closing in on him. If Canal+ took its case to court, Tarnovsky would end up as the villain of the piece. At worst, NDS could disown him as a rogue employee posting the SECA codes without NDS's knowledge. The fall guy. Kaehlin was offering him indemnity from legal repercussions. But would jumping to Canal+ be any safer? And Tarnovsky seems not to have meant that just in a financial sense.

Tarnovsky was undecided. Kaehlin turned the talk to the lawsuit Canal+ was planning.

'He promised to tell the truth to the court if he were called to testify but that he would not be the "whistleblower" on NDS's illegal activities, because he was too afraid for his life and for his family,' Kaehlin said in an affidavit three months later. 'I proposed we meet in London in January 2002 . . . to talk about our possible future collaboration.'

San Diego–Paris–New York, January–February 2002

John Norris was on to Chris. It wasn't really rocket science. Kömmerling had repeatedly warned Abe Peled that Canal+ was targeting Tarnovsky. The handy little diagram that Carayol's lawyer, James DiBoise, had handed Peled had shown all the steps between the black-hat team creating the SECA file in Haifa and it ending up with Al Menard at DR7.com. Tarnovsky was the obvious weak link. How else to explain how confident Carayol and DiBoise had been?

Tarnovsky was already intimidated by Norris. It didn't take much to stare him down, to force him to admit that he had been talking to Gilles Kaehlin. And then the News lawyers needed to spell out the facts of life to Chris.

'So I was like—you know what? The lawyers were like, "You either go with them or you stay with us. But if you're going to stay with us, you're going to have to write an email to him now and say, no more meetings." So that's when I wrote him that email and said, "Gilles, please don't send me any emails any more." That was at the lawyers' request.'

Kaehlin was uncharacteristically benevolent in his affidavit three months later: 'I regret this communication breakdown, because I consider Chris to be a decent young man who has been manipulated by NDS, and I would hope that we could renew our friendship in the future.'

On 9 January Abe Peled flew to Paris to meet with Carayol. It's hard to imagine Peled didn't have just a trace of satisfaction in his voice when he asked Carayol if he had any further evidence for the Canal+ case against NDS. Carayol assured him that he did, and explained a little more what Kaehlin had uncovered. Peled told him he was still interested in a merger with Canal+ Technologies, but he was not prepared to discuss the other matter.

Both men appear to have parted with a degree of contentment. Peled did not believe Canal+ had a case. Carayol had realised that, despite Tarnovsky's email to stay away from him, he hadn't told NDS about Oliver's plans. This suggested that Tarnovsky was still wavering, still playing both sides.

Now Carayol was ready to step up the pressure a notch. On 14 January he called the News Corp executive in the Office of the Chairman in New York who oversaw NDS. It was Chase Carey, who was also on the NDS board.

'He said he would talk about a merger, but did not want to hear about any claims,' Carayol testified later. 'I told him we needed to talk about the issue of NDS's wrongdoing.'

On 30 January Peled telephoned Carayol from New York. He was willing to discuss what he saw as the compelling strategic rationale for a merger. 'I'm not concerned or intimidated by your claims—your position is extortion,' Peled said.

Carayol was now ready to lodge his lawsuit. But he then learned that News Corp's general counsel, Arthur Siskind, had contacted the New York lawyers of Canal+'s parent company, Vivendi Universal, to discuss the case. There was another, unrelated deal going on. On 13 February, News Corp and Telecom Italia announced the sale of their Italian pay TV operation Stream to its larger rival Teleiu, owned by Canal+. It was not until late February that Siskind met with Vivendi's lawyers about the NDS case. Carayol had insisted on being present, as had Canal+ chief Pierre Lescure.

'Mr Siskind, like Mr Peled before him, said he would investigate and get back to us,' Carayol testified later.

Carayol was not the only one trying to negotiate—Oliver wanted to buy NDS out of its 40 per cent of his British company, ADSR. Oliver was in a fragile frame of mind, Adams told Reuven. While he had been trying to show he was a man of honour and integrity, 'the recent investigation by Sky reminded him that he is still viewed as a pirate. He is very hurt by this.' (In fact this was the first time that Adams had confirmed that, in addition to Canal+ and DirecTV, BSkyB had also investigated NDS hackers, including Oliver.) Now Adams said Oliver was massively stressed by the knowledge he would 'shortly be denounced alongside NDS in the world's media'. Particularly when 'the hack and the release by DR7 was not of his doing and casts totally unfair allegations upon his reputation. It is likely that the same will also happen with Nagra and possibly others.'

Oliver was aware that the court case would begin the next week and that 'media coverage starts thereafter'. So NDS should consider what Oliver's other options were. 'At the same time he knows the truth about what happened and he is aware of the totality of the evidence.'

Hasak's response was not encouraging. Yes, Oliver was valuable but he should not try to pressure Peled at the moment: 'You write that Oliver knows the truth of what happened. I would not take it as the truth; I would just take it as his assumptions.'

Carayol and the Vivendi lawyers met again in the News offices on Friday, 8 March, at Siskind's request. The following Monday, 11 March, James DiBoise filed Canal+ Technologies' suit in California claiming damages of US$1 billion against NDS Group and NDS Americas, and offences under the Racketeer Influenced Corrupt Organisations Act (RICO), which would allow Canal+ to claim triple damages.

NDS and Canal+ were at war.

2002

The story broke in Paris on Tuesday, 12 March. Two of the biggest media companies in the world taking each other to court is always a big story. But in such circumstances! 'In a startling lawsuit,' the *Wall Street Journal*'s account began.

'In a lawsuit that reads like a cloak-and-dagger thriller,' was the Associated Press intro. The idea that a major corporation could be involved in corporate espionage directed at a competitor, and that it could be caught out and sued, was huge. It made headlines all around the world. It was a knock-you-off-your-seat kind of story. Consider the threat that the lone hacker poses to society, to national security, to your private information, to your bank accounts. And then consider that the predator is not a lone hacker, but a $50 billion corporation—one of the biggest media groups in the world, employing its resources in industrial-scale manoeuvres to attack its competitors across the globe.

The news spooked investors, who sent NDS shares down more than 26 per cent, or US$6.05, to close at US$16.95 on the Nasdaq Stock Market. Months before, NDS stock had been above US$70. But there was a lot further to fall in the months ahead. The slide accelerated after DirecTV announced on 2 April that it was dumping NDS and was developing its own conditional access system.

The story confirmed all the stereotype pictures of Murdoch, the 'Dirty Digger'. If anyone would have a dirty tricks department in his empire, it would be Rupert. It read like a cheap novel, and that was the problem. It was too caricatural; it was too bizarre; too *out there*, to be conceived of. That incredulity played into the NDS response, which was loud and indignant. The lawsuit was 'outrageous and baseless', the company said and promised to mount a counterclaim.

The piracy problem 'is due solely to the inferior nature of Canal+'s conditional access technology, the failure of its business plan to contain measures to protect against piracy and its failure to deal with piracy once it began,' Peled said in a statement. The lawsuit was 'a blatant attempt by Canal+ both to deflect criticism of its new generation card, which is not believed to be state of the art, and to shift blame for its inadequate technology and its past losses.'

Two days in and Kaehlin's people dropped a bucket of files to the *Guardian* about Lee Gibling and The House of Ill Compute, including emails showing Len Withall approving payments to Gibling. The story was hackers. Secret payments. And spies. There have to be spies. On Sunday the *Observer* reported that the French Secret Service was investigating the damage to Canal+, a French company.

Within hours of the *Guardian*'s revelations about The House of Ill Compute on Thursday, 14 March, News International had engaged British master spin doctor Tim Bell. In a meeting with NDS corporate communications chief Peter Ferrigno on 14 March, Bell ticked off the steps News needed to take to pacify stock analysts, investors and government regulators. As for the media, Bell was blunt: Don't say anything.

'The only thing that might be useful here would be to get a very senior Newscorp executive—Rupert himself or maybe [chief operating officer] Peter Chernin, to refer to the lawsuit . . . and generally dismiss it as a frivolous or ridiculous attempt by a couple of media companies who are having some rotten financial results at the moment and trying to blame them on a successful competitor,' Ferrigno reported back to News executives on 15 March.

Rupert Murdoch and Chernin both stayed clear of the controversy. Lachlan Murdoch had joined his brother James on the NDS board just three weeks before. Other senior News Coproration execs on the NDS board included Arthur Siskind, Chase Carey and finance director David DeVoe. None of them were commenting, and there was no sign that they were aware of the company's covert activities.

The furore in the popular media blew over soon enough, supplanted by more compelling news stories. On 21 March a young girl, Milly Dowler, vanished while walking home from school in Walton-on-Thames, Surrey. Much later that would provide another side to News Corporation's unhappy experience with private investigators when the telephone hacking scandal broke.

Adams meanwhile was doing a little damage control. He had been in touch with Lee Gibling's number two at The House of Ill Compute, Nathan Savage.

'As we discussed you do not have any information. All you did was site design,' Adams wrote. He was also keen to send some money to Gibling, who was now living in straitened circumstances in southern Turkey. The argument about that went into April. Adams authorised a £5000 'loan' to Gibling, but the order was vetoed by NDS lawyer Ismat Levin. 'This is not in line with our discussion and is entirely inappropriate and very surprising,' Levin emailed.

'As you know I successfully kept this man away,' Adams replied indignantly. 'He is being actively sought by C+, private detectives, individuals and also more importantly by the BBC Panorama team re THOIC and ITV Digital. As we have abandoned him I fully expect that he will consider himself free to speak with whomever approaches him. I did not want this.'

Reuven Hasak quietly approved the payment and bumped it up to £8000. But this was just a side play to the main drama. The central issue in the lawsuit was the posting of the SECA code on DR7 in March 1999. But who was Canal+ relying on for evidence? Tarnovsky would not be testifying. That turned the focus on Oliver Kömmerling, who had been telling Reuven Hasak and Abe Peled about the posting for three years. Oliver kept up the pressure on NDS to sell him its 40 per cent in ADSR, but News Corp deputy counsel Genie Gavenchak recommended against it until the lawsuit was over.

Adams and Kömmerling were summoned to New York on 11 April, so the News lawyers could take witness statements supporting NDS. Kömmerling missed the flight. Instead he was with the Canal+ lawyers signing an affidavit confirming his knowledge that the file on DR7 came from Haifa, and that Tarnovsky had put it there.

DiBoise filed Oliver's affidavit with another one by Jan Saggiori, in which he described receiving the ROM file from Tarnovsky two days after the posting. His statement didn't make it clear what the file was. But it caused shock at Kudelski in Switzerland. The engineers recognised it was not ROM code for the Canal+ card that Tarnovsky had sent to Jan. It was the ROM from their own Nagra card.

The two affidavits made more headlines around the world. Previously the allegations, while colourful, had seemed to have no substance; now there was detail and substantiation. Peled moved immediately. Oliver discovered, when he tried to access the ADSR offices, which were leased from NDS, that his access card no longer worked. He had been locked out of his own company.

On 3 May, Reuven Hasak announced that Ray Adams had expressed a desire to retire from NDS and it had been approved effective immediately. Ray sent a reply channelling Oscar Wilde— that the announcements had been premature. His lawyers would discuss terms. But he was out.

Then the story sank below the horizon of the mainstream media. It was drowned out first by the financial crisis that was about to flatten Canal+'s parent, Vivendi Universal. Jean-Marie Messier's grand plan to turn a water treatment company into a global media empire had come massively unstuck. By June, just as Vivendi and Canal+, overwhelmed by debt covenants, were reported to be a week away from liquidation, Messier pulled a deal out of the bag to save the group . . . at least for now. On 8 June he agreed to sell Canal+'s Italian pay TV arm, Telepiu, to Rupert

Murdoch for one billion euros. The deal bought Messier enough time for the French government to organise a rescue of sorts. But it was a requirement of the deal with Murdoch that Canal+ drop its litigation against NDS when the Telepiu deal was consummated. So, for NDS, that was that legal problem sorted out.

Other dangers still threatened. DirecTV was suing NDS as well. It turned out that they had secretly sued NDS the year before, and made an equally secret settlement that they now wished to revisit. EchoStar and NagraStar were also suing NDS, but in a clever way, by applying to intervene in the Canal+ lawsuit before it was abandoned—which would safeguard the Canal+ evidence. In September 2002 two other pay TV operators—Sogecable in Spain, and MEASAT, the Malaysian company that operated the Astro platform—joined the lawsuit as well. The NDS share price was now under US$6.

That same month David Streitfeld at the *Los Angeles Times* reported that the US Attorney in San Diego had commissioned a grand jury and issued 21 document subpoenas against NDS involving allegations of high-tech sabotage. The investigation into Chris Tarnovsky's Texas mailbox and the shipments of cash had now come home to roost.

PART 7

End Game

We are surprised at the tone of your queries relating to the criminal proceedings currently before the court in Siracusa, Italy. Even a cursory review of the papers will confirm that NDS has been named in this matter as one of the 'injured parties'.

Amy Lucas, NDS public relations manager, 11 August 2011

Los Angeles, April 2008

Reuven Hasak was always going to be the star of the show. He might be older, and no longer the soldier–athlete, but he still had that same steady gaze and soldier's bearing that engenders instinctive trust in those who meet him. Reuven Hasak was 70 years old and what he resembled most as he stepped into the witness box in the courtroom in southern Los Angeles was everyone's favourite kooky uncle. He's endearing, in his occasional fumbles with English expressions and pronunciations. He's a little erratic. And he's funny. He has the court at times in gusts of laughter. Most of all he's forgetful.

This must be a strain sometimes, because bad memory or not, he was still Rupert Murdoch's top spy, still senior vice-president of Operational Security at NDS. Hasak and his staff have never been too deeply invested in written records, which is why so little had turned up in the court discovery process—they kept the important material in their heads. Hasak had a habit of making only oral reports, preferably in Hebrew, to Abe Peled, his boss at NDS. But now much of it he can't recall.

'I don't remember,' he told EchoStar's counsel, Chad Hagan. 'One of my weak points is I don't remember. Sorry.'

In old spies, it seems the memory is one of the first things to go. He says he doesn't remember 53 times, and another 53 times he doesn't know. No matter how hard he cudgelled his recollection, those lists and details escaped him. But at least he's open about the problem. I've heard testimony from senior media executives whose memory was so erratic I think they needed a seeing eye dog to find their way home. But it's not a total loss. Hasak remembers quite a deal about those who worked for him.

There are two sides to the man here on the stand. There is Reuven the intelligence operative, and he is formidable. But there is also Reuven the man. Listening to him, he divides the world into friends and enemies, and it's clear that you couldn't look for a better friend than Reuven Hasak. It's completely genuine. He's great at handling people. And perhaps that's what being a spymaster is all about—people skills. It's how he explains why so few safeguards were taken with Chris Tarnovsky. He wasn't going to put one of his agents under electronic surveillance; he wasn't going to bug his home. Because it was wrong, and because it would be counterproductive in terms of trust.

'Monitoring in his house, I think it's not a good system, and it's invading his privacy,' he says. 'I never did it in all my career. My own employees. I'm not talking about enemies . . . to . . . How do you say? Enemies, yeah. I mean, I never did it with employees.'

The case is about industrial espionage. For almost six years, EchoStar has been pursuing claims that NDS hacked its smart-cards, and that Reuven Hasak's Operational Security division released the codes to pirates in North America. It's only one of a series of claims that pay TV operators around the world have brought against NDS and News Corporation. But here in this courthouse in Los Angeles is the only time that Reuven Hasak will appear on the stand to explain just what NDS was doing when it reverse engineered all of its major competitors.

The first thing he makes clear is that he's not a technical guy. He doesn't use terms like hacking or reverse engineering.

'I know they are running "technical research", I call it, because I am not technical enough to understand what is research engineering, so I refer to [it] as technical research,' he says.

Was he involved in the decision to hack a competitor's product?

'I don't know about a hack—developing a hack. I knew about the—the technical research.' Any decision on technical research would be taken by the team in Haifa, who in turn reported to the NDS chief technical officer, a man called Yossi Tsuria.

Did Hasak ever become aware of allegations that Mr Tsuria was involved in terroristic activities?

'Forgive me for smiling,' Hasak interrupts gently. But now he's gone too far. Judge David Carter—himself an old soldier, who was huddling in dugouts in Khe Sanh when Hasak was still a raw Shin Beit agent—warns Reuven to answer the question.

'Yes sir. In 1981, when I was back in the service, I was in charge of . . . of exposing an underground against . . . a Jewish underground against the Arabs. We exposed them. Yossi Tsuria was one of the people who supported it. So he was not a terrorist, but he went to jail because of knowing of it and being a supporter. So the answer—he's not a terrorist. But I knew he was in jail, yes, and because of me.'

Then NDS hired him after he got out of jail?

'Oh yeah, sure.'

Judge Carter is now concerned. He shoos the jury away and talks to counsel about this quote–unquote terrorist who is part of this Israeli group to blow up the . . .?

'The Dome of the Rock,' the NDS lawyer supplies.

The judge is worried that the word terrorist might suggest Tsuria targeted the United States, 'when, in fact, this is an internal Israeli issue'. That needed to be cleared up for the jury. He'd like to hear a bit more about the gentleman who had been killed in Berlin, as well.

Reuven is asked what was it like to run this strange beast, NDS Operational Security? He was questioned about all those reports about technical research written for him by one of his senior staff, a former commander of Scotland Yard called Ray Adams, who was clearly one of nature's little worriers. His reports should be taken with two grains of salt, Hasak suggests.

'I don't . . . Much of it is just—how do you say it in English? Blah, blah, blah?' (Laughter.) 'You say in English also? Okay. Much . . . I'm not joking, I'm not joking.'

He's sitting pretty comfortably, but he's about to run into some turbulence. It's useful to take a look at the strange road that has led to this scene.

In the last months of 2002, NDS and News Corporation looked to be in as big a mess as it was possible for a multibillion-dollar corporation to get into—a perfect storm of billion-dollar legal claims, scandal, a grand jury investigation and endless waves of bad press. What followed was one of history's great corporate turn-arounds . . . or escape acts, depending on how you see it.

It began with a victory in Washington. Rupert Murdoch had been bitterly disappointed when Charlie Ergen at EchoStar had snatched DirecTV from under his nose the year before. Rupert's lobbyists had now convinced the Federal Communications Commission and the Justice Department to oppose the EchoStar/ DirecTV merger, which would leave only one US satellite broad-caster. Facing mounting opposition, Charlie called it quits in December and pulled out of the deal. From that point on, there was only ever going to be one buyer for the controlling stake in Hughes Corporation and its subsidiary, DirecTV.

On 9 April 2003, General Motors agreed on terms to sell its 34 per cent stake in Hughes to News Corp for US$6.6 billion. Murdoch's Republican links were again important as the

Securities and Exchange Commission approved the deal 3–2 on party lines. News' COO, Chase Carey, was appointed chief executive of DirecTV and one of his first moves was to kill off the DirecTV lawsuit against NDS and to introduce a new generation NDS card. Piracy was wiped out and the value of DirecTV soared.

The next problem was squaring off the deal to buy Telepiu from Canal+. That was finalised on 30 April 2003, at which point not only was the Canal+ lawsuit against NDS dropped, all the relevant files were destroyed and Canal+ was ordered not to disclose information about it. EchoStar's lawyers, along with the Spanish Sogecable and the Malaysian MEASAT group, had made valiant attempts to be accepted by the court as intervenors in this action, which would have allowed them to demand access to the Canal+ files and evidence. But all NDS needed to do was to keep lobbing challenges at every step, which meant that, when the Telepiu deal settled, after seven months the court had still not ruled on EchoStar's status. So the case was closed and all of the evidence was locked away.

The good news for NDS didn't stop there. If EchoStar and NagraStar's gamble to hitch themselves to the Canal+ lawsuit had succeeded, not only would they have had access to the Canal+ evidence, they could have used the start date of that lawsuit, 11 March 2002. Most of the claims they wished to bring against NDS had a statute of limitations of two or three years. So while the March 2002 date ruled out some of the early incidents, like the Swiss Cheese posting in October 1998, it freed EchoStar to base its case on that whole period from March 1999, when Chris Tarnovsky had emailed part of the ROM code for their card to Jan Saggiori, and when Alan Guggenheim believed Tarnovsky had been operating an EchoStar piracy ring with Al Menard on behalf of NDS.

Now that was impossible. Instead, EchoStar and NagraStar had to start all over again with a new lawsuit of their own. They lodged that on 6 June 2003. But now the three-year window of the statute of limitations only went back to mid 2000, in the last stages of the Menard-based piracy ring. None of Guggenheim's careful tracing of how the pirate network fed cards to Menard to be programmed, nor the raids on Discount Satellite, could be used. The EchoStar case wasn't looking good.

In the period of a few short months, then, most of the threats overhanging NDS and News Corp had been despatched. The one cloud on the horizon remaining was the grand jury investigation that had begun at Chris Tarnovsky's San Marcos mailbox. But that turned out happily for everyone, beginning with a change of scenery. The investigation was originally run out of the San Diego US Attorney's office. But News Corporation was successful in arguing that NDS Americas was based in Newport Beach, so the investigation should be handled not by San Diego but by Los Angeles. The case was transferred to California Central District and ended up with a young assistant US attorney, James W. Spertus. Later he would be criticised by EchoStar's lawyers for getting too close to News Corp and NDS, who were working with him on other piracy cases.

In late 2002 Norris and NDS lawyers sat down with Al Menard to talk about the pending lawsuits. Norris had recently had another crisis come out at him from left field, when three Canadian websites posted copies of secret NDS internal documents about the new Period 4 card that it had produced for DirecTV.

'My concern at the time was, do I have a leak in NDS?' Norris testified in the 2008 trial. 'My personal concern is—there goes my job if we do.'

It turned out that Menard had seen the documents posted online. He told Norris he could identify who was responsible for the leak. 'And damned if he didn't do it,' Norris said. 'And it worked. And the individual was identified by the FBI and prosecuted.'

The prosecutor turned out to be James Spertus, the assistant US attorney who would also be handling the NDS investigation. On

2 January 2003, Spertus made headlines around the country when he charged a nineteen-year-old university student in Los Angeles under the rarely used 1996 Economic Espionage Act. The student had been hired by DirecTV lawyers to help image thousands of pages of highly sensitive documents as part of their case against NDS. The copying was done in a secure room, which offered no way to remove the documents. It was completely safe—except for an internet terminal next to the copier. The arrest was a coup for the FBI and for Spertus.

More headlines followed. Back in October 2002, just after the grand jury investigation began in San Diego, the FBI had staged a series of raids on DirecTV piracy dealers in seven states. In March 2003, criminal charges, including breaches of the new Digital Millennium Copyright Act (DMCA), were laid against seventeen pirate dealers in Los Angeles. Spertus, who would handle the prosecutions, called it 'the largest undercover investigation of satellite theft devices to take place in the United States'. Later that year he would secure America's first-ever jury trial convictions under the DMCA.

The newspaper stories about this initiative talked only of the FBI and DirecTV, with nothing of the key role played by NDS, which was how Norris liked it. But inevitably it meant that Spertus liaised closely with Norris for much of the year in processing these cases. EchoStar lawyers would later suggest they socialised together. It must have made for some awkwardness, with Spertus working closely with NDS on prosecutions while at the same time he was heading an investigation into Norris and Chris Tarnovsky and Al Menard. Al was also an important witness in Spertus's other case, against the student who copied the documents.

It must have seemed even more awkward when, with the Canal+ and EchoStar and DirecTV cases still going, Spertus learned that NDS was actually planning to hire Al. Norris testified in 2008 that he had been impressed by Menard's research skills. He wanted to put Menard on a four-year contract—a $20,000 sign-on bonus then $78,000 a year, to spend 120 hours a month trawling the Net for NDS.

Norris could see how this might be misunderstood, that NDS was paying what turned out to be nearly $400,000 over four years to someone who was potentially a witness against NDS. So NDS counsel floated the proposal past Spertus.

'We were told it was okay,' Norris testified. Menard signed up on 1 April.

This is not to say that Spertus was anything less than professional in his investigation of NDS. On 21 April 2003, with the Canal+ case days away from settling, he applied to the court for an order compelling Canal+ to provide all copies of documents from the trial to the FBI. Meanwhile Spertus reached out to Oliver Kömmerling, whose evidence would be critical to any case mounted against NDS and Chris Tarnovsky.

Oliver had just managed to fend off some major legal action that NDS had launched against him in Britain over his switch to Canal+. He had arranged to take the family on a little holiday to Palo Alto, but he agreed to take a little side trip down to LA. Spertus arranged to put him up at a hotel at Marina del Rey.

'NDS was observing the hotel,' Oliver later told Jan Saggiori. The FBI picked him up in a car with dark-shaded windows. 'I felt like I was in a movie.' Some time later, when the car stopped, Spertus climbed in. It was only when he was sitting opposite that Kömmerling spelled out his position: 'Look, you want my help. Go start the case yourself. If you have the courage to start a case against Murdoch, I'll come and join. But don't start it on my back.' So there was no witness statement, no guarantee that Oliver would testify, if he was called, that Tarnovsky was responsible for the EchoStar and Canal+ codes that were posted on Al Menard's DR7 site.

Oliver had picked up $10 million from Canal+, and had set up a new lab at Sophia Antipolis, a technology park in the south of France. Gilles Kaehlin was part of his new company, CK2, which was owned by Canal+ via several intermediary companies in the Dutch Antilles. Oliver had bought himself an apartment on the waterfront in Monaco, where he moored his new cruiser. Shortly after Spertus tried to reach out to him, he had some more visitors.

'DirecTV was here on my boat offering $4 million a year to me,' Oliver said. The catch was that he would have to testify against NDS. He looked at DirecTV's evidence. He wasn't impressed—particularly since it now seemed only a matter of time before News Corporation took over DirecTV. He told the DirecTV lawyer, 'You're insane, you have nothing. You're all going to be fired when Murdoch takes over.' And they were fired, he claims today.

Through 2003, Spertus continued his juggling act. On the one hand, the criminal prosecutions of pirates who targeted DirecTV and NDS, which inevitably required a close working relationship with John Norris; on the other hand, the grand jury investigation into NDS and Tarnovsky, which slowly ran out of steam. On 3 February 2004, Spertus wrote to NDS that he had closed the investigation into Tarnovsky, Menard and NDS.

'Based on the information and evidence gathered as a result of the investigation, this office has concluded that there is insufficient evidence of wrongdoing by NDS to seek criminal charges.' NDS and its employees had been completely exonerated. By May, Spertus had taken up a new job as director of anti-piracy operations for the Motion Picture Association of America.

That made 2004 a pretty good year for NDS. Meantime EchoStar and NagraStar kept bowling up different versions of their lawsuit, and the courts kept slamming them back. Their case involved showing there was a conspiracy between NDS, Tarnovsky, Menard and the Canadian pirate dealers such as Dave Dawson; but much of their evidence of piracy was inadmissible because it related to a period before mid 2000, when the statute of limitations kicked in.

'It completely killed us—our strongest evidence was based on an earlier period,' Guggenheim told me in 2012.

Guggenheim had had several meetings in London with Oliver, who had played him some of his taped telephone conversations from 1999 and 2001, where he told NDS executives and lawyers about NDS's piracy links. Ray Adams also indicated he was prepared to testify, but he wanted protection, Guggenheim told me. Protection can be another way of saying money.

There had been some unpleasantness over Adams' departure from NDS in May 2002. Reuven Hasak had promoted Len Withall as new head of UK Operational Security and asked him to drop by Adams' house in Windsor to pick up his NDS phone and his laptop. Len called Ray in puzzlement several days later.

'You're fooling me,' Len said. Apparently there was something wrong with the hard drive in Adams' laptop.

That would be because he had swapped over to a new hard drive, Adams told Withall. He had some family photos on the drive he wanted to keep for sentimental reasons. Was that a problem? Adams was graciousness itself. It would be no trouble to return the hard drive. Why didn't Len pop over the next morning? Withall duly did this, only to hear a tale of calamity.

Adams had put the hard drive on the front seat of his wife's car, and some local petty crim had smashed the window and stolen everything they could reach on the front seat, including the hard drive. It was gone and he had had to file a police report about it.

Hasak didn't believe Adams' claim that the hard drive had been stolen. 'He gave it to somebody. After we are finished with this case, I am going to go after Ray Adams and sue him, yes,' Hasak testified in 2008 (though four years later NDS had still taken no action against Adams).

Adams' hard drive contained more than 14,000 of his work emails, some dating back to 1997. At some point Canal+'s security chief Gilles Kaehlin obtained a copy of the emails on a pair of

CDs. And later still, Kaehlin provided a copy of those CDs to Ron Ereiser in Victoria, Canada, who by that stage was working for an arm of Canal+. It was in early to mid 2004; Ereiser testified in 2008. Kaehlin didn't say directly where he got the emails from.

'My understanding was—and I never asked any more questions—that he had a court order to download e-mails off the NDS server which had to do with the court case he was involved in,' Eresier said.

Ereiser testified that, when he looked at the CDs, he found emails between Norris and a Royal Canadian Mounted Police officer who had his own email address on an NDS server. The RCMP officer referred to two of Ereiser's businesses which they raided.

'And it also said that they found some information at one of them about Oliver Kömmerling, some emails or something,' Ereiser testified. 'And John [Norris] instructed the police officer to get rid of that stuff before it went to court.'

On 17 January 2005, Ereiser met Alan Guggenheim and former FBI agent J.J. Gee, who had headed NagraStar's security since 2001, at Vancouver airport and passed them a copy of the CDs containing the emails. The Adams emails, together with other documents from Kaehlin, were a bombshell. They transformed the EchoStar case. They provided details of a number of questionable NDS operations, and they formed the basis for a revised statement of claim against NDS. The statute of limitations problems were still there, so the EchoStar lawyers focused on the only known incident within their restricted time window. They claimed that Chris Tarnovsky was responsible for posting the whole EchoStar code and piracy instructions on the Net on Christmas Eve 2000.

The case ground slowly on. NDS launched a furious counter-claim that EchoStar had illegally obtained stolen information, that it was not coming to the court with clean hands, and that all copies of the emails should be declared highly secret and accessed only by counsel.

EchoStar was scheduled to get a deposition from Chris Tarnovsky on 3 April 2007. Three days beforehand, NDS fired him. Stunned, Tarnovsky called Al Menard. Al was gone from NDS as well. His contract had not been renewed. Norris and Hasak and Abe Peled had stood by Tarnovsky and Menard for seven years, through the customs investigation, the grand jury investigation, the Canal+ and DirecTV litigation and for five years of EchoStar's case. But no more.

It was NDS's external lawyers, Darin Snyder and Richard Stone, who told Tarnovsky he was fired. Chris later testified they told him that, based on the evidence produced in the case, 'Things couldn't be explained.' They said nothing more. But later he learned that NDS had only just been told by EchoStar's lawyers that a fingerprint from Marvin Main, Menard's employee, had been found in the packages of cash sent to Tarnovsky's Texas mailbox in August 2000. Norris later testified that Tarnovsky had been lying all the time: 'He was not candid with us regarding who sent the packages, as far as we could tell.'

This most curious of cases came to trial in May 2008. It was huge and bewildering in its complexity. Judge Carter had allocated four weeks to hear it, after weeks of closed pre-trial hearings had tightly restricted what could be covered. The Canal+ case, for example, was not to figure. Nor the polygraph tests that Tarnovsky had faced. Reference to DirecTV suing NDS was also tightly controlled, as was reference to Boris Floricic's death. NDS's lawyers wanted to use James Spertus's letter to NDS in 2004 to show that NDS had been cleared in his investigation, but Judge Carter ruled the letter inadmissible after EchoStar counsel questioned whether News had assisted Spertus in getting a job at the MPAA three months after he dropped the case (though no evidence was advanced to say that it had). Spertus was not called as a witness and therefore did not have an opportunity to give his own account. The judge made no finding against him.

The two sides of the court were a study in contrasts. NDS had twenty or so lawyers; EchoStar and NagraStar had three. The NDS back-up lawyers were working on a constant series of appeals and motions. The EchoStar lawyers spent much of their time fending off these actions, any of which might derail the case. Through legal discovery from News, EchoStar's lawyers had obtained the Headend Report that detailed the NDS hack of its Nagra card and, after lengthy pre-trial jousting, Judge Carter allowed EchoStar to subpoena Zvi Shkedy and David Mordinson to appear as witnesses in order to describe their secret trips to North America during 1998. But there was no access granted to examine Chris Tarnovsky's or Al Menard's computers—even for NDS's own independent experts. In March 2002, NDS lawyers had told all members of Operational Security to preserve any documents or emails relevant to the Canal+ case, particularly communications involving Menard and Tarnovsky. But six years later, nothing came to light.

NDS flatly denied any role in selling pirate cards and threw up many other possibilities to explain the piracy. Its witnesses testified that the EchoStar pirate software was different from the Headend software its black-hat team had developed; it was suggested that other pirate groups had created the hack, that an EchoStar employee had leaked the codes or even that Kudelski's Nagra division had sabotaged its own card.

In the course of the four weeks, the most obvious effect was on Judge Carter: 'I am now becoming increasing concerned that I made the wrong ruling' about references to the DirecTV litigation and the subsequent purchase by News Corporation,' he said. 'When this lawsuit started, I didn't fully understand apparently the potential relationship. It is an incredible oddity that DirecTV that was so hacked, [until] suddenly after the purchase by . . . Mr Murdoch representing or owning NDS, and Harper-Collins, from which money was paid to Tarnovsky. [Murdoch] buys DirecTV and hacking stops.'

He was changing his mind about restricting the Canal+ settlement as well: 'It's become relevant, and I think I was a little naive not recognizing the import of that and the timing . . . I didn't understand the timing when we got into that issue.'

He wanted to also hear about Boris (although he never did). Judge Carter had been progressively opening up the case, in an apparent realisation that what was being alleged against NDS was a whole pattern of behaviour, a seam that ran throughout its dealings. But that made it a much bigger case. And he only had four weeks. In the meantime he wanted to see the people at the top in his courtroom.

'Initially at counsel's request for NDS I had singled out Mr Rupert Murdoch at their request for some protection,' he told counsel. But no more. 'I am getting tired of hearing about different corporations who are supposedly separate entities, and, quite frankly, there are four individuals behind all these corporations—Peled, Murdoch, Ergen, and Kudelski.

EchoStar chief Charlie Ergen had been the first witness in the case. André Kudelski of Kudelski Corporation was down to testify. Abe Peled was also on the schedule. But not Rupert Murdoch. And, with Hasak in the stand, Carter was opening wide the matters that could be raised. Norris and Tarnovsky had already testified about Operation Smartcard; but, the way they told it, it had been an unqualified success. There was no reference to doing it without DirecTV's knowledge, or to losing control of the pirated cards when other pirates reversed Tarnovsky's kill command. And there was no reference to Plamen Donev developing a fix to kill off hundreds of thousands of pirate DirecTV cards in October 1998 (a month after General Motors had decided it would be selling DirecTV), only to see NDS decide not to use the fix for 'policy reasons' until fifteen months later.

It was a robust exchange over most of the day. The jury went home and because Abe Peled was scheduled as the first witness for the next morning; Chad Hagan for EchoStar took a deposition from him in the evening. Hagan launched a full-blooded interrogation, taking the NDS chief exec through such matters as the close role that Chase Carey had in overseeing NDS, Peled's relationship with Oliver Kömmerling, and the repeated attempts Kömmerling had made to tell him that Chris Tarnovsky was engaged in piracy of both Canal+ and EchoStar. The deposition lasted from 5.30 p.m. until 9 p.m. But what Hagan didn't know was that, earlier that evening, Peled had decided to leave town and not appear as a witness.

In one of the breaks in the questioning before 7 p.m., Peled booked a ticket on the 10 p.m. flight to London. After finishing the deposition he went straight to the airport. He was out of the country before the EchoStar team had an inkling that he was going, and could try to subpoena him.

When Judge Carter learned the next morning of Peled's sudden exit, he hit the roof. He made a series of increasingly unhappy addresses during the day to NDS counsel, while the jury waited outside.

'This could be construed to be an example of the very corporate irresponsibility of failing to explain the corporate entity's conduct, and it is very troubling to this Court.' For any of the people at the top of these corporate pyramids—Ergen had already testified and Kudelski was coming, which left just Peled and Murdoch in the frame—to fail to appear was 'unacceptable'.

He observed that the fact that corporate structures could be used to insulate senior executives such as Rupert Murdoch from appearing before the jury 'in a case of these kinds of allegations, satellite piracy allegations, that, if true, are monumental ... is of great concern'. He was at pains not to appear one-sided in his rulings. He said it would have been of similar gravity if

Ergen or André Kudelski had not agreed to appear to face the NDS counterclaim that EchoStar and NagraStar had improperly obtained stolen documents.

By late Friday afternoon Judge Carter had decided on dramatic steps. When the trial resumed on the following Tuesday, Peled had better be there, he said. Or he would ask EchoStar counsel to fly to London to subpoena him. If that didn't work there would be sanctions, even up to forfeiting the case.

It was a clash of wills that the jury knew nothing about. Peled duly appeared on the Tuesday. Having won the point, Judge Carter ruled, 'I don't want him embarrassed.' The questioning was far more sedate.

Then it was closing submissions, and a wait while the jury deliberated. When they filed back in with their verdict, they found NDS guilty of three penal provisions of Californian law, but awarded damages of only $45. They found NDS not guilty of two other charges. At the end of the day, whatever they thought about what NDS had been doing in earlier periods, the issue was whether Chris Tarnovsky was responsible for posting the EchoStar code on Christmas Eve 2000. On this matter, clearly the jury had not been presented with a sufficiently persuasive scenario.

John Norris in his testimony had described how one day in late 2000 Chris Tarnovsky had shown him how to reprogram an old DirecTV P2 card into an EchoStar pirate card with software he downloaded from the Net. The jury convicted NDS of pirating that one card, skipping a $45 monthly subscription. Judge Carter ruled in favour of EchoStar on a seventh matter, agreeing to impose an order on NDS not to commit further piracy.

EchoStar and NagraStar had been seeking up to $2 billion damages. The award of only $45 was devastating.

'We succeeded in showing there was piracy, but failed to convince the jury to pay damages,' André Kudelski of Kudelski Corporation said later.

Tarnovsky had been corresponding with me throughout the trial. Now he emailed me: 'We won!'

NDS had been completely vindicated, Peled crowed: 'The allegations against us have been tested to destruction.'

Judge Carter took a different view, and split the very substantial legal costs between the parties in such a way that in the end NDS contributed $5 million to EchoStar's costs. But NDS appealed the costs decision and in January 2012 the Appellate Court reversed the finding and ordered EchoStar to contribute $18 million to NDS's costs. Of the two other cases against NDS, MEASAT had dropped out a long time ago and Sogecable had dropped its case some months after that. NDS was in the clear; however, even after the costs decision, NDS's total legal costs for all the cases were estimated at more than $60 million.

It had been an expensive exercise for EchoStar as well but, just for a moment, the secret world of hackers and corporate spies had wandered into the limelight. Now it was to become hidden once more. Glimpses of our heroes thereafter became ever more fleeting.

Alan Guggenheim left NagraStar, first to run OpenTV, later as a consultant based in Texas. Markus Kuhn remained at Cambridge. Chris Tarnovsky bought himself a focused ion beam for his own home lab, and set about reverse engineering every smartcard in sight. Al Menard was packing groceries at a supermarket. Lee Gibling took up residence in Turkey, where NDS kept paying him until late 2008, when they made a final payment of £15,000 tied to a confidentiality agreement.

Yossi Tsuria with some regret stepped down as editor of NDS's publication, *Chidushei Torah*, an annual compendium of articles by NDS staff, 'which brings to expression our belief that it is possible to integrate a life of Torah creativity, with a life of technological creativity'. His last effort was a meditation on the shape of the number '8'. His wife, Anat, meanwhile was making feminist films about the difficulties facing women in Haredi communities.

Rupert and James Murdoch had toughened their stance on piracy. James, still an NDS director, told a media conference in Abu Dhabi in early 2010, 'These are property rights, these are basic property rights. There is no difference from going into a store and stealing a packet of Pringles or a handbag, and stealing something online. Right? I think it's crazy frankly. People say, "Oh, it's different, these kids, these crazy kids." No. Punish them.'

The comfortable life that Oliver Kömmerling had carved out for himself had fallen apart. 'To be frank many things happened here and the work I did for NDS [is] catching up on me now,' he emailed me in May 2011. Kudelski Corporation had bought the Canal+ smartcards' division in 2003, which meant that Oliver at CK2 indirectly worked for them. But, despite his million-dollar salary package, he refused to testify for Nagra.

Shortly after the court case, Avigail Gutman and Zvi Shkedy visited Oliver. Avigail was writing a history of NDS, Oliver said. NDS was now 51 per cent owned by a private equity firm, Permira, though News seemed to maintain management control. In March 2012 News and Permira sold NDS to technology giant, Cisco, for $5 billion. Meanwhile Oliver seemed to be back on good terms with NDS. But then he found himself the subject of a huge investigation by Viaccess, the conditional access company owned by French Telecom, whose new card was hacked in 2009. By 2011, Oliver told me he had been forced to move to Uruguay.

Gilles Kaehlin had his own problems. In 2005 one of his security officers at Canal+, Pierre Martinet, wrote a book in which it was claimed that Gilles had spied on Bruno Gaccio, the creator of the popular political satire, *Les Guignols*, a daily show using latex puppets similar to the British show *Spitting Image*, and thus a French national icon. Gilles was convicted and given a suspended sentence and a 10,000-Euro fine. Having bought a house next to Oliver's in Punta del Este in Uruguay, he wanted to return there.

But the French authorities seized his passport while they looked into his tax affairs.

Jan Saggiori continued to balance work as a security consultant with more mainstream business interests. From the start of 2001 he had been full-time with Canal+, and he is one of the three names on the patent for the SECA 2 card that replaced the first SECA card whose ROM code was posted on DR7. For a time he worked with Oliver and Kaehlin at CK2 in southern France, but he was never comfortable with Kaehlin. He came to suspect that someone at CK2 was still dealing with pirates.

Monaco, May 2011

Jan Saggiori remained one of the key figures monitoring pay TV piracy in Europe. When Oliver found himself frozen out and forced to leave Europe for South America, he believed he knew who was responsible. And so, for the first time in seven years, the old sparring partners talked to each other—a ferocious text exchange that Oliver initiated over Skype on 24 May 2011, when he returned briefly to Monaco.

'I wanted to ask you what problem you have with me? It seems that you believe that I am behind all kind of things.'

Jan replies, 'I am not thinking anything like that.' It's a conventional opening, the equivalent of pawn to king four, as the chess masters probe each other's defences. They write 80,000 words in late night chat sessions, poring over all the old history.

'Well look, I know for a fact that you also believe that I am responsible for that [Viaccess] hack,' Oliver writes. He accuses Jan of 'intoxicating' the Viaccess security team. They circle and circle. Jan denies any role, but observes that the Viaccess piracy was traced to Oliver's lab, that someone who worked for him must have done it. For days they toss that back and forth.

And then they turn to Chris Tarnovsky, now with his very own FIB.

Oliver says, 'In a way I am proud of the guy, finding his own way. I wish that he stays out of trouble, but he's not in my financial situation. Anyway I will not betray him. Not a second time. I did this idiotic mistake once.'

'Retire,' Jan urges Oliver. Pause for a while, he suggests—take a long vacation. 'Don't play having a lab in Uruguay.'

'You find this funny, don't you?' Oliver asks furiously. How could Jan possibly ask him to give up the one thing in his life he does best? 'If someone comes to you and advises you, "please stop breathing", how would you take that?' He says he knows who was really responsible for the Viaccess piracy, and can prove it.

Jan's response to Oliver's passionate raison d'être is almost dismissive ('Breathing! =HNO3? It's not the same. You are grown up') but he suggests Oliver should publish his Viaccess revelations on the Net.

'Are you nuts?' Oliver asks. 'This will completely crush me. Everybody will know that I was spying on them.' There would be one result: 'I'm dead.'

It goes on and on and on. At one point they're working together, comparing files, following the leads behind the mafia figures distributing the Viaccess pirate cards. But in the end it peters out. Whatever shared epiphanies they may achieve will be reserved for another occasion, fodder for other late-night sessions.

Elsewhere, the saga is doing a slow fade from public view. The British Home Office turned down requests by Labour parliamentarian Tom Watson for an investigation into the email references by Ray Adams and Len Withall to a 'Police Informants Fund'. In May 2012 Mark Lewis, the British lawyer who was a key figure in exposing telephone hacking by News International journalists, confirmed that he was looking into claims by a client who believed he was a victim of NDS dirty tricks. NDS lawyers immediately wrote to Lewis to point out that should any legal action arise from his investigation, the events were so distant they would be ruled out by the statute of limitations.

So here, at the finale, there is a happy ending for all parties. Everyone has been vindicated. NDS emerges untouched, without a smirch on its character. Ray Adams remains one of the most highly decorated former police officers in the history of the Met. He will tell you so himself. NDS itself was heading for new horizons after Abe Peled supervised the sale of the company to network giant Cisco in March 2012 for $5 billion. When asked whether the sale would be affected by the *Panorama* and *Australian Financial Review* reports, Peled told a Reuters reporter that Cisco had conducted its due diligence process before the deal was announced and it would not be revisited. The sale would be completed in the second half of the year. It went unsaid that selling NDS would cut all corporate ties between Rupert Murdoch and News Corporation's most precocious child.

Meanwhile, Murdoch announced that News would split off its newspapers into a separate public company. News America Marketing and News International, whose scandals together will probably end up costing shareholders more than $1.5 billion, will be quarantined off in 'Bad NewsCo'. News Corporation's entertainment arm, 'Good NewsCo', run by Chase Carey and Murdoch, will emerge from this difficult time suitably pristine and unsullied.

The flaw to this exercise in corporate dry cleaning is that cutting off or selling scandal-prone business arms does not address the governance and the management structures that allowed the scandals to develop. In the decade and a half that I have been covering NDS, I long ago concluded that its history was so outlandish and bizarre that it could not have played out in a vacuum. At the most basic level, what position did News Corporation directors and senior News management take on the controversial business practices at NDS? The two most likely options seemed to me to be either that NDS was a blind spot in Rupert Murdoch's empire that no one chose to look at too closely; or, that there was something within the News Corporation corporate culture that allowed such practices not only to be tolerated, but to prosper.

The marker for a sick management culture is that multiple scandals erupt that are not tied to a particular business or a geographical location. They break out spontaneously across a business group, driven typically by head office's demand for results, without a governance structure to question the methods used to achieve that success. As a consequence, for the last decade I have been looking for other examples of trouble within the wider News Corporation empire. These examples were present, but remained invisible until after 2007 when telephone hacking in Britain and the News America Marketing's anti-competitive behaviour began their slow public emergence.

Taken together, the controversies at NDS, News International and News America Marketing paint a pattern of failed account-ability within large segments of News Corporation. That suggests part of the problem lies with directors and senior management. But fixing a sick management culture requires more than shutting down newspapers or shedding troubled business units. This is the underlying problem presented by the split of News Corporation. Good NewsCo and Bad NewsCo will be run by executives and board members whose actions or lack of action were instrumen-tal in creating the management culture that allowed the scandals of the last decade and a half to develop. Chase Carey, who will run the dominant entertainment arm under Murdoch, was the News executive given the task of overseeing NDS. Chief finan-cial officer David DeVoe, former group counsel Arthur Siskind, and James and Lachlan Murdoch have all been directors of NDS. There is no suggestion that they were aware of any of the actions of the Operational Security team. Rather, the question is whether they should have been aware.

Not to worry. The single constant in News Corporation's corporate history is that the ship sails on. Rupert Murdoch has never been one to look back. In mid 2012, he was using his Twitter account to attack Google, whose corporate behaviour he depicted as akin to piracy. He foresaw a long and healthy future for his newspapers as well as his global television operations.

Life goes on as well for the hackers whose lives were turned upside down by the great global game that Reuven Hasak's team played.

Jan will keep chasing pirates—it's a family tradition, to root out the frauds. Oliver will keep reverse engineering cards—it's what defines him. They are creatures of the secret world. Now you see them; now you don't.

In the end, are there any answers? Is there any way really to decode what goes on in this arcane universe that operates beneath our noses? Whatever clarity, whatever picture emerges, it wavers and winks out even as we watch.

Cyber realities are not for the fainthearted. And just what will we make of this world? Who shall we call to account?

Timeline

1980

30 December   Assassination attempt on Alan Guggenheim in
                Guadeloupe

1984

27 April   Shin Beit agents led by Reuven Hasak arrest
                20 members of Jewish Underground including
                Yossi Tsuria
28 April   Zorea Commission appointed to investigate
                deaths of Arab hijackers in Bus 300 affair

1985

26 January   Kenneth Noye stabs surveillance officer, tells
                police Ray Adams will confirm he is not a killer
November   Hasak forced to resign from Shin Beit

1986

28 January   News International Wapping dispute begins
6 June   Gilles Kaehlin flown out of St Martin after riot
7 December   Rupert Murdoch bids for his father's old
                newspaper company, Herald & Weekly Times

1987

10 March	Former London policeman Daniel Morgan murdered with an axe in car park
April	Metropolitan Police open three-year corruption inquiry into Commander Ray Adams but no charges laid
July	Detective Constable Alan Holmes shoots himself after being questioned in Adams investigation

1988

February	Bruce Hundertmark for News Corp incorporates News Datacom (NDS) in Israel for $3.6 million
8 June	Murdoch announces plan to launch Sky Television
November	Hundertmark convinces Murdoch to use NDS to encrypt Sky

1989

February	Sky begins broadcasting

1990

6 November	Sky Television merges with British Satellite Broadcasting to form BSkyB as News Corp faces debt crisis
12 November	New York grand jury issues arrest warrant for NDS chief Michael Clinger who continues in his post for another year

1992

12 May	News Corp buys out minority NDS shareholders including Clinger

1993

4 May	Ray Adams takes sick leave, later resigns from Metropolitan Police

1994

March	Markus Kuhn posts screen shots of *Star Trek: The Next Generation* online
19 May	BSkyB switches to Series 09 cards
17 June	DirecTV launches in US using NDS cards
20 June	BSkyB's Series 09 code sold in auction at Dorchester Hotel London

1995

July	News counsel Arthur Siskind briefs new NDS chief Abe Peled on investigation into fraud by Michael Clinger

1996

January	Reuven Hasak sets up NDS Operational Security with Ray Adams and John Norris
26 June	Police raid 26 pirate dealers across Canada including Ron Ereiser
October	Ereiser hires Chris Tarnovsky to support DirecTV pirate cards
20 October	Tax investigators raid NDS offices in Israel, find tapes of telephone conversations in Abe Peled's safe
Late 1996	Hasak hires Oliver Kömmerling as consultant

1997

January–February	Tarnovsky becomes NDS consultant
17 April	EchoStar's Charlie Ergen uses pirated DirecTV card to show that NDS card has been pirated. Ergen sues Murdoch after he drops EchoStar merger over NDS dispute
1 July	Tarnovsky becomes fulltime NDS employee after moving to California
Late July	Plamen Donev and Vesselin Nedeltchev crack DirecTV P2 card at University of Montana after being smuggled across US border

September	NDS begins to put together black-hat team in Haifa
24 October	Oliver and Vicky Kömmerling in Toronto with 'Jellyfish' flee across US border after DirecTV and FBI put out a search and detain order
24 November	NDS reports Chris Tarnovsky in undercover role will provide pirate hack to Canadian pirates as Operation Johnny Walker

1998

April	BSkyB sues the new OnDigital pay TV business to force it to drop plans to use Canal+ SECA smartcard and use NDS instead
29 May	NDS black-hat team use focused ion beam machine at Bristol University to crack SECA and EchoStar cards
July	Zvi Shkedy and David Mordinson fly to New York but are unable to complete hack of EchoStar card
6 July	Black-hat team in Haifa creates ROM file from SECA card
August	Shkedy and Mordinson fly to Washington to work on EchoStar hack
7 September	Shkedy and Mordinson fly to Baltimore, drive to Washington to pick up EchoStar receiver, then fly to Cleveland and drive to Canada to test pirate program
4 October	Online article describes new program to hack Irdeto cards, which is about to be released by pirates in Europe
5 October	BSkyB launches digital channels
12 October	US Congress passes Digital Millenium Copyright Act

Mid-October	Rolf Deubel cracks password for Irdeto piracy program downloaded from Boris Floricic. One of Boris's files dated 14 October.
17 October	Boris Floricic disappears in Berlin Anna Murdoch resigns from News Corp board
21 October	Swiss Cheese Productions posts EchoStar logger file on Al Menard's DR7.com piracy website in Canada
22 October	Boris Floricic's body found hanging in park at Britz-Süd
23 October	Swiss Cheese Productions posts lengthy text file on DR7.com about EchoStar broadcast stream after 'months of research'
24 October	Swiss Cheese posts EEPROM for EchoStar card on DR7.com
27 October	John Luyando accuses Tarnovsky of being Swiss Cheese. In Israel, Shkedy and Mordinson complete draft of Headend Report detailing their method to pirate EchoStar cards. Final version completed 1 November.
3 November	DirecTV executives give Alan Guggenheim detailed information of how EchoStar card has been hacked
15 November	OnDigital launches using Canal+ SECA cards
30 November	Murdoch forced to sign humiliating deal selling US satellites and licenses to EchoStar

1999

8 March	Murdoch breaks off talks with Canal+ chief Pierre Lescure for merger with BSkyB
26 March	ROM code from Canal+ SECA card is posted on DR7.com site in Canada. Oliver Kömmerling downloads file in Germany and realises the date stamp on the file is a 'digital fingerprint' linking it to NDS black-hat team

27 March	Murdoch family gathers at Cavan property in Australia for wedding of Lachlan Murdoch and Sarah O'Hare
28 March	Tarnovsky sends PGP email to Jan Saggiori with part of ROM code for EchoStar card attached as a substitute for missing portion of SECA code
30 April	Avigail Gutman's Australian agent 'Joyce' obtains copy of Rolf Deubel's Irdeto software for Foxtel and Optus. Adams assigns Kömmerling to rework the software to disguise its source before it is released from Europe 'on the market'.
3 May	Rolf Deubel arrives in Melbourne
3 June	Lee Gibling on Thoic.com in Britain offers Foxtel hack for 'circa $US5,000'
August	NDS signs new four-year contract with DirecTV without disclosing that its Operation Smartcard has produced thousands of DirecTV pirate cards that NDS cannot kill
September	Roger Kinsbourg asks Jan Saggiori to write a report on European piracy for Canal+
14 September	Rolf Deubel arrested in Bangkok
Early October	New head of Canal+ security Gilles Kaehlin obtains Saggiori's report
22 October	Canal+ exec Pierre Petit emails copy of Saggiori's report to Ray Adams
	Avigail Gutman plans to distract Australian hacker from attacking StarTV by giving him a pirate system for hacking Malaysian pay TV operator Astro instead. Previously she noted, 'We don't want [the hacker] in jail until he has a hack for Irdeto'.

23 October	Plamen Donev devises solution for most of the pirate hacks of DirecTV but NDS decides not to use it because of 'politics'
Late October	Adams devises plan to blame Saggiori for SECA hack and to add him to US lawsuit in Montana for hacking DirecTV
21 November	NDS $1 billion IPO on Nasdaq stock exchange
December	Kömmerling tells Abe Peled that Tarnovsky was responsible for SECA code on DR7.com. Hasak reprimands Adams for telling Peled that Canal+ is investigating Saggiori's claim that NDS was behind the code on DR7.com.
2 February	Guggenheim flies to Edmonton for police raid on Dave Dawson's Discount Satellite

2000

5 February	Rolf Deubel arrives home in South Africa after being released from prison with the help of Thai mafia
29 February	Roger Kinsbourg phones Kömmerling while he is at Heathrow with Adams and says Kaehlin wants to meet him. When Kaehlin comes to Kömmerling's home, Adams hides in adjoining room.
1 March	Gutman arranges for Adams to supply 20 to 30 European pirate smartcards that she can supply to Australian hacker developing a new Foxtel pirate hack
29 March	Guggenheim has private detectives poised to trace shipment of cards from Discount Satellite to be reprogrammed by Al Menard. The plan fails when NDS and DirecTV appoint bailiffs to seize the store on the same day.
30 August	Narcotics officers called to investigate suspicious parcels sent to a postbox Chris Tarnovsky rents in

	San Marcos Texas find $40,100 in two packages later linked to an associate of Al Menard
24 December	Anonymous poster called 'Nipper2000' posts full codes, keys and detailed instructions on how to pirate EchoStar cards on pirate website

2001

16 January	Plamen Donev shoots DJ in leg after altercation in Kazanluk
21 January	NDS uses piracy fix devised by Donev to kill more than 200,000 DirecTV pirate cards as EchoStar piracy takes off
9 February	Customs officers knock on Tarnovsky's home to talk about the Texas packages but NDS lawyers prevent any discussion or search
6 February	News Corp in due diligence to buy DirecTV
8 March	Guggenheim meets Menard in hotel room but Menard says 'Tarnovsky would lose his job' if Menard provided information about how his EchoStar cards were hacked
4–6 May	Meeting of 'dream team' NDS hackers in Haifa ends in drunken arguments. Tarnovsky later visits Kömmerling in Germany where he tells him of Canal+ investigation.
14 August	Tarnovsky meets Kaehlin in London and tells him he is tired of working for NDS
Late September	Kömmerling has dinner in London with Abe Peled. After telling Peled in June and again in July that Tarnovsky had admitted putting SECA code on DR7.com, Kömmerling now tells Peled that Tarnovsky released the EchoStar code as well
5 October	Kaehlin meets Tarnovsky in Carlsbad, California. Kaehlin later gives evidence

	Tarnovsky confirmed using 'non-verbal communication' that NDS was responsible for posting SECA code on DR7.com.
12 December	Canal+ Technologies chief François Carayol and US lawyer James DiBoise tell Peled they have evidence linking NDS to the release of SECA codes. Peled vigorously denies the allegations.
16 December	Kaehlin meets Tarnovsky in Santa Monica. Later Kaehlin gives evidence that Tarnovsky said he would testify if called but would not be a whistleblower because he was 'too afraid for his life and for his family'

2002

January	At direction of News Corp lawyers, Tarnovsky emails Kaehlin he wishes to have no further contact. Carayol meets with Peled and senior News Corp execs through January and February.
11 March	Canal+ files California lawsuit against NDS seeking treble payout for damages of $1 billion
21 March	English schoolgirl Milly Dowler disappears. Later her voicemail is hacked by *News of the World* investigator.
27 March	OnDigital, now known as ITV Digital, goes into administration
9 April	Oliver Kömmerling signs affidavit that NDS was responsible for SECA hack
3 May	Reuven Hasak announces Adams is leaving NDS. Adams' hard drive disappears from his wife's car.
8 June	Canal+ is said to be days away from collapse when it alleviates its debt problem by agreeing to sell its Italian pay TV arm Telepiu, which has been crippled by piracy, to News Corp for an

	estimated 1 billion euros in return for dropping NDS lawsuit when the deal settles
September	San Diego Assistant district attorney empanels grand jury to consider charges against NDS
September	EchoStar and NagraStar apply to join Canal+ case against NDS. Spanish group Sogecable and Malaysian pay TV business Astro also apply to join case. DirecTV has also sued NDS separately.
Late 2002	San Diego NDS grand jury investigation transferred to Los Angeles

2003

9 April	LA district attorney's office approves NDS hiring Al Menard for $6500 a month

2004

3 February	US Attorney's office in Los Angeles closes its investigation of NDS and finds no further action is warranted
6 June	EchoStar starts its own case against NDS after Canal+ case settles

2007

31 March	NDS fires Tarnovsky for lying, three days before he was due to be deposed by EchoStar

2008

15 May	California court finds in favour of EchoStar against NDS in three of six claims but awards only $1500 damages

2012

January	US Appeals Court reverses earlier costs order by judge in 2008 trial in favour of EchoStar. Instead EchoStar must pay $17.9 million of NDS legal costs.

27 March	BBC *Panorama* program shows interviews with Lee Gibling and another moderator of NDS piracy site Thoic.com. They say NDS published pirate codes on OnDigital helping to cause its collapse in 2002. NDS strongly denies this.
29 March	*Australian Financial Review* publishes major series on worldwide acitivities of NDS Operational Security and puts thousands of Adams' emails on the internet. NDS denies allegations and forces the *AFR*'s US cloud server to take emails down. They remain available for download on the *AFR* site.

Acknowledgements

I'm deeply in debt to the many people who have helped me with this story over many years, who provided documents and leads, helped to develop and verify the material I had, who spoke to me on and off the record, who gave me serious amounts of their time, who provided encouragement, feedback and working space. Many of them cannot be named. Among those who can, I'm indebted to Jan Saggiori, Alan and Suzanne Guggenheim, Chris Tarnovsky, Lee Gibling, Roger Kinsbourg, Ron Ereiser, Rolf Deubel, Tom Watson and Oliver Kömmerling.

Also to Fiona Buffini, Richard Coleman, Ali Cromie, John Davidson, Matthew Drummond, Angus Grigg, Chris Jenkins, Stephen Scott, Chris Short, David Streitfeld, Michael Stutchbury, Vivian White and Ben Woodhead.

To my editor Richard Walsh.

And most of all to my wife, Joëlle.

Index